Let's Eat!

For workdays and special celebrations alike, reach for any of the 415 dishes inside.

PAGE 65

PAGE 236

Nothing brings families together better than a delicious home-cooked meal. And for decades, *Taste of Home* has been the place where good cooks gather to share the dishes they delight in preparing, and that their own crews love.

Inside *Taste of Home Annual Recipes,* you'll find flavorful secrets shared by some of North America's best cooks— including dozens of their crowd-pleasing appetizers, twenty-four 30-minute dinners and seven complete holiday menus.

This book includes an entire year's worth of recipes from our beloved magazine, plus hundreds of bonus dishes never before seen in *Taste of Home!* Page through and discover 415 step-by-step recipes, more than 30 variations and dozens of how-to photos sure to help you cook with confidence. Highlights include:

- **Meal Planner**
  Fill your fridge, freezer, pantry and table when you prepare recipes from this handy chapter. Grab-and-go breakfasts, lunches in a jar, no-mess foil packs and more mealtime solutions will give you the gift of time.

- **Side Dishes & Condiments**
  Dig in to creamy mashed potatoes, homemade pumpkin butter, garden-fresh summer favorites and four gorgeous pages of pickled produce, from predictable peppers to luscious fruit surprises.

- **Holiday & Seasonal Celebrations**
  Find springtime, summer picnic, autumn and winter holiday menus, plus the perfect Christmas treats, sweet giftables and the ultimate hot cocoa bar.

Icons throughout help make the most of your time and resources:

🕐 = Ready in 30 minutes or less

🍎 = Lower in calories, fat and sodium

🍲 = Pressure-cooked recipe

🍲 = Made in a slow cooker

🍳 = Made in an air fryer

5i = Uses 5 or fewer ingredients
(may call for water, salt, pepper and canola/olive oil)

❄ = Includes freezing/reheating instructions

PAGE 26

FRESH TAKES ON BELOVED STANDBYS

Sample new versions of classic favorites when you cook with *Taste of Home Annual Recipes.* In only 30 minutes, One-Pot Black Bean Enchilada Pasta (top) is a veggie-packed dinner for six with almost no cleanup. Hear oohs and ahhs when you slice into majestic Vertical Carrot Cake (center). It's easier to make than you might think—the how-to photos walk you through every step! And meet your new favorite picnic salad: Donna Gribbins's Grilled Potato & Corn Salad (bottom). It's a mashup of two of Donna's favorite summer dishes—sure to be a hit at your next barbecue!

Taste of Home

© 2023 RDA Enthusiast Brands, LLC.
1610 N. 2nd St., Suite 102,
Milwaukee WI 53212-3906
All rights reserved. Taste of Home
is a registered trademark of
RDA Enthusiast Brands, LLC

Visit us at **tasteofhome.com** for other
Taste of Home books and products.

Chief Content Officer, Home & Garden:
Jeanne Sidner
Content Director: Mark Hagen
Associate Creative Director:
Raeann Thompson
Senior Editor: Christine Rukavena
Editor: Hazel Wheaton

Senior Art Director: Courtney Lovetere
Art Director: Maggie Conners
Designer: Carrie Peterson
Deputy Editor, Copy Desk:
Dulcie Shoener
Senior Copy Editor: Ann Walter

Cover
Photographer: Mark Derse
Set Stylist: Melissa Franco
Food Stylist: Josh Rink

Pictured on cover:
Italian Cream Cheese Cake, p. 187;
Soft Garlic Breadsticks, p. 146; Creamy
Beef Lasagna, p. 90; Gorgonzola Pear
Salad, p. 25.

**International Standard
Book Number:**
D: 978-1-62145-880-7
U: 978-1-62145-881-4

International Standard Serial Number:
1094-3463
Component Number:
D 117400108H
U 117400110H

Printed in U.S.A.
10 9 8 7 6 5 4 3 2 1

**DIY RAMEN SOUP
PAGE 105**

MORE WAYS TO CONNECT:

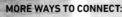

SHOP.TASTEOFHOME.COM

Contents

PORK & CHEESY
MACARONI SLIDERS
PAGE 20

Appetizers & Beverages

Whether you're looking for an irresistible dip, refreshing cocktail or fun snack-time ideas, this chapter has you covered. It's packed full of delicious options you'll be proud to share.

DISHES WE LOVE

CHIPPED BEEF CHEESE BALL

This delicious appetizer is near and dear to our family. It is a symbol of our annual Christmas and New Year's celebrations. My mom made it for more than 30 years.
—*Molly Sumner, Creve Coeur, MO*

PREP: 10 min. + chilling • **MAKES:** 2 cups

- 5 pkg. (2 oz. each) thinly sliced dried beef, divided
- 12 oz. cream cheese, softened
- ⅓ cup finely chopped sweet onion
- 4 drops Worcestershire sauce
  Ritz crackers and assorted fresh vegetables

1. Place beef in a food processor; pulse until finely chopped. In a large bowl, beat cream cheese until smooth. Stir in ⅔ cup beef, onion and Worcestershire sauce. Refrigerate the mixture, covered, at least 1 hour.

2. Place remaining beef in a small shallow bowl. Shape cheese mixture into a ball; roll in beef to coat evenly. Wrap; refrigerate at least 1 hour. Serve with crackers and vegetables.
1 TBSP.: 47 cal., 4g fat (2g sat. fat), 16mg chol., 136mg sod., 1g carb. (0 sugars, 0 fiber), 2g pro.

BROCCOLI & CHIVE-STUFFED MINI PEPPERS

Crunchy peppers perfectly balance the creamy filling in these party appetizers. Fresh chives help them stand out.
—*Jean McKenzie, Vancouver, WA*

TAKES: 30 min. • **MAKES:** 2 dozen

- 12 miniature sweet peppers
- 1 pkg. (8 oz.) cream cheese, softened
- ⅓ cup minced fresh chives
- ⅛ tsp. salt
- ⅛ tsp. pepper
- ⅔ cup finely chopped fresh broccoli
- ⅔ cup shredded cheddar cheese

1. Preheat oven to 400°. Cut peppers lengthwise in half; remove seeds. In a bowl, mix cream cheese, chives, salt and pepper; stir in broccoli. Spoon into pepper halves.

2. Place on a foil-lined baking sheet; bake until heated through, 9-11 minutes. Sprinkle with cheddar cheese. Bake until cheese is melted, 3-4 minutes longer. Cool slightly before serving.
1 STUFFED PEPPER HALF: 48 cal., 4g fat (2g sat. fat), 14mg chol., 68mg sod., 1g carb. (1g sugars, 0 fiber), 1g pro.

READER REVIEW

"Have started making these for just a daily snack at this point—still just so tasty!"
—GINA.KAPFHAMER, TASTEOFHOME.COM

CHIPPED BEEF CHEESE BALL

SLOW-COOKER
CHEESEBURGER DIP

SLOW-COOKER CHEESEBURGER DIP

This fun dip recipe uses ingredients I always have in the fridge, so it's easy to throw together on short notice.
—*Cindi DeClue, Anchorage, AK*

PREP: 25 min. • **COOK:** 1¾ hours • **MAKES:** 16 servings

1 lb. lean ground beef (90% lean)
1 medium onion, chopped
1 pkg. (8 oz.) cream cheese, cubed
2 cups shredded cheddar cheese, divided
1 Tbsp. Worcestershire sauce
2 tsp. prepared mustard
¼ tsp. salt
⅛ tsp. pepper
1 medium tomato, chopped
¼ cup chopped dill pickles
Tortilla chips or crackers

1. In a large skillet, cook beef and onion over medium-high heat until the beef is no longer pink and onion is tender, 6-8 minutes, breaking beef into crumbles; drain. Transfer to a greased 1½- or 3-qt. slow cooker. Stir in the cream cheese, 1½ cups cheddar cheese, Worcestershire, mustard, salt and pepper. Sprinkle with remaining ½ cup cheese.
2. Cook dip, covered, on low until mixture is heated through and cheese is melted, 1¾-2¼ hours. Top with chopped tomato and pickles. Serve with tortilla chips or crackers.
NOTE: Keep an eye on the dip toward the end of cooking. If it goes too long, the edges will get dark.
¼ CUP: 157 cal., 12g fat (6g sat. fat), 46mg chol., 225mg sod., 2g carb. (1g sugars, 0 fiber), 10g pro.

⑤ᵢ GINGER MINT JULEP

Mint juleps aren't just for Kentucky Derby day! Enjoy one while gathering with friends for baby shower or luncheon.
—*Ellen Riley, Murfreesboro, TN*

PREP: 15 min. + chilling • **COOK:** 5 min. + cooling
MAKES: 10 servings

2 cups sugar
2 cups water
2 cups loosely packed chopped fresh spearmint
EACH SERVING
½ to ¾ cup crushed ice
1 oz. bourbon
2 tsp. lime juice
1½ oz. ginger beer

1. For mint syrup, place sugar, water and chopped mint in a large saucepan; bring to a boil over medium heat. Cook until sugar is dissolved, stirring occasionally. Remove from heat; cool completely.
2. Strain syrup through a fine mesh strainer; discard mint. Refrigerate, covered, until cold, at least 2 hours.
3. For each serving, place ice in a mint julep cup or rocks glass. Add bourbon, lime juice and ¼ cup mint syrup; stir until mixture is cold. Top with beer.
1 SERVING: 238 cal., 0 fat (0 sat. fat), 0 chol., 4mg sod., 45g carb. (44g sugars, 0 fiber), 0 pro.

GINGER
MINT JULEP

QUICK WHITE SANGRIA

PIZZA POCKETS

These individual stuffed pizzas taste delectable with or without dipping sauce on the side. Prepare half of the calzones with ham and the other half with pepperoni to satisfy all of the diners at your event.
—*Clarice Brender, North Liberty, IA*

- -

PREP: 45 min. • **BAKE:** 20 min.
MAKES: 16 servings

- 2 cups shredded part-skim mozzarella cheese
- 1 carton (15 oz.) ricotta cheese
- ½ cup plus 3 Tbsp. grated Parmesan cheese, divided
- 6 oz. sliced pepperoni
- 2 large eggs, divided use
- 1 tsp. garlic powder
- ¾ tsp. Italian seasoning, divided
- ¼ tsp. crushed red pepper flakes, optional
- 2 loaves (1 lb. each) frozen bread dough, thawed
- ⅓ cup pizza sauce
  Additional pizza sauce, warmed, optional

1. Preheat oven to 375°. In a large bowl, combine mozzarella, ricotta, ½ cup grated Parmesan cheese, pepperoni, 1 egg, garlic powder, ½ tsp. Italian seasoning and, if desired, crushed red pepper flakes; set aside.

2. Divide bread dough into 16 pieces. On a lightly floured surface, roll each portion into a 5-in. circle. Place 1 tsp. pizza sauce and ¼ cup filling in center of each circle. Lightly brush edge of dough with water. Bring dough over filling; press firmly, then pinch or crimp seams to seal.

3. Place on greased or parchment-lined baking sheets. Lightly beat the remaining egg; brush over pockets. Sprinkle pockets with remaining 3 Tbsp. grated Parmesan cheese and ¼ tsp. Italian seasoning. Bake until deep golden brown, 20-25 minutes. Allow to cool 2-3 minutes before serving. If desired, serve with additional pizza sauce.

1 APPETIZER: 171 cal., 7g fat (3g sat. fat), 25mg chol., 392mg sod., 17g carb. (3g sugars, 1g fiber), 11g pro.

QUICK WHITE SANGRIA

I swapped in white wine for the red wine in this sunny, subtly sweet sangria. And the addition of frozen fruit lets me sip on a glass of this liquid sunshine year-round.
—*Sharon Tipton, Casselberry, FL*

- -

TAKES: 15 min. • **MAKES:** 8 servings

- ¼ cup sugar
- ¼ cup brandy
- 1 cup sliced peeled fresh or frozen peaches, thawed
- 1 cup sliced fresh or frozen sliced strawberries, thawed
- 1 medium lemon, sliced
- 1 medium lime, sliced
- 1 bottle (750 ml) dry white wine, chilled
- 1 can (12 oz.) lemon-lime soda, chilled
  Ice cubes

In a pitcher, mix the sugar and brandy until sugar is dissolved. Add the next 6 ingredients; stir gently to combine. Serve over ice.

¾ CUP: 147 cal., 0 fat (0 sat. fat), 0 chol., 9mg sod., 17g carb. (14g sugars, 1g fiber), 0 pro.

SO-EASY STICKY CHICKEN WINGS

My neighbor once shared these tangy wings with me at a potluck, and ever since they have been a family favorite. Talk about a simple game-day snack!
—*Jo Vanderwolf, Lillooet, BC*

- -

PREP: 20 min. • **COOK:** 3 hours
MAKES: 40 pieces

- 4 lbs. chicken wings
- 1 cup barbecue sauce
- 1 cup soy sauce
- 6 green onions, chopped, divided
- 1 Tbsp. sesame seeds

Using a sharp knife, cut through the 2 wing joints; discard wing tips. Place remaining wing pieces in a 4- or 5-qt. slow cooker. Stir in barbecue sauce, soy sauce and ¼ cup chopped green onions. Cook, covered, on high 3-4 hours or until tender. Sprinkle with sesame seeds and the remaining green onions.

1 PIECE: 68 cal., 4g fat (1g sat. fat), 14mg chol., 452mg sod., 3g carb. (2g sugars, 0 fiber), 6g pro.

TAKE A DIP!

Spontaneous potlucks call for simple, scrumptious snacks. Carry in these five-ingredient (or less!) dips to make a splash at your bash.

GARLIC BLUE CHEESE DIP

SMOKED SALMON DIP

MUSTARD DIP

BACON CHEDDAR DIP

YUMMY CHOCOLATE DIP

BACON CHEDDAR DIP

In a large bowl, combine 2 cups **sour cream**, 1 cup finely shredded **cheddar cheese**, 1 envelope **ranch salad dressing mix** and 2-4 cooked and crumbled strips of **bacon**. Cover and refrigerate for at least 1 hour. Serve with crackers and/or vegetables.

CUCUMBER ONION DIP

In a small bowl, beat one 8-oz. pkg. softened **cream cheese**, ½ cup finely chopped seeded peeled **cucumber**, ¼ cup finely chopped **onion**, 2 Tbsp. mayonnaise, ⅛ tsp. salt and ⅛ tsp. pepper until blended. Refrigerate until serving. Serve with rye chips or crackers.

GARLIC BLUE CHEESE DIP

In a blender, combine ½ cup **milk**, one 8-oz. pkg. cubed **cream cheese**, 1 cup crumbled **blue cheese** and 2 cloves peeled **garlic**; cover and process until blended. Serve with crackers.

HONEY PEANUT APPLE DIP

In a large bowl, beat one 8-oz. pkg. **cream cheese** until smooth. Beat in 1 cup finely chopped **peanuts**, ⅔ cup **honey** and 1 tsp. **vanilla extract** until combined. Serve with apple slices.

HORSERADISH CRAB DIP

In a large bowl, beat one 8-oz. pkg. **cream cheese**, 2-3 Tbsp. **picante sauce** and 1-2 Tbsp. prepared **horseradish** until blended. Stir in one 6-oz. can **crabmeat**. Serve with celery.

Serve with a mix of dunkers and dippers: sliced fresh fruit, crackers, pretzels, breadsticks, warm pita bread or thick potato chips.

MUSTARD DIP

In a bowl, combine one 14-oz. can **sweetened condensed milk**, ¼ cup ground or prepared **mustard**, 3 Tbsp. prepared **horseradish** and 1 Tbsp. **Worcestershire sauce** until smooth (dip will thicken as it stands). Serve with pretzels. Store in the refrigerator.

PEANUT BUTTER FRUIT DIP

In a bowl, combine 1 cup **vanilla yogurt**, ½ cup **peanut butter** and ⅛ tsp. ground **cinnamon**; mix well. Fold in ½ cup **whipped topping**. Refrigerate until serving. Serve with fruit.

RANCH JALAPENO DIP

In a blender or food processor, prepare 1 envelope **ranch salad dressing mix** according to package directions. Add 2 **pickled seeded jalapeno peppers**, 1 seeded **jalapeno pepper** and 2 Tbsp. minced **fresh cilantro**; cover and process 2-3 minutes or until combined. Cover and refrigerate at least 1 hour. Serve with tortilla chips.

SMOKED SALMON DIP

Place one 16-oz. can drained pitted ripe **olives** and 8 **green onions** cut into 2-in. pieces in a blender or food processor; cover and process for about 15 seconds. Add one 14¾-oz. can **pink salmon**, ⅔ cup **mayonnaise** and, if desired, 8 drops **liquid smoke**; process until dip reaches desired consistency. Chill. Serve with crackers.

YUMMY CHOCOLATE DIP

In a microwave, melt ¾ cup **semisweet chocolate chips**; stir until smooth. Stir in ½ cup of one 8-oz. carton **whipped topping**, ½ tsp. ground **cinnamon** and ½ tsp. **rum** or vanilla extract; cool for 5 minutes. Fold in remaining whipped topping. Serve with fruit.

STRAWBERRY RIESLING WINE SPRITZER

Nothing says spring like strawberry wine spritzers. The tarragon and black pepper in this refreshing cocktail really make it taste special! The syrup is also delicious in lemonade, iced tea, club soda and gin and tonics.
—*Zoe Ann McKinnon, St. Louis, MO*

PREP: 10 min. • **COOK:** 30 min. + chilling
MAKES: 6 servings

- 1¾ cups sliced fresh strawberries
- 1 cup sugar
- 1 cup water
- 4 to 5 tarragon sprigs
- 2 Tbsp. lime juice
- 1 tsp. whole peppercorns
- 3 cups sweet white wine, such as riesling, chilled
- 3 cups club soda, chilled

1. In a small saucepan, bring the first 6 ingredients to a boil. Reduce heat; simmer 20 minutes. Remove from heat. Cool completely. Strain mixture through a fine-mesh strainer into a small bowl (do not press berries). Refrigerate syrup until chilled.
2. For each serving, fill a tall glass with ice. Add ½ cup wine, ½ cup club soda and ¼ cup strawberry syrup. If desired, garnish with additional tarragon.
1 SERVING: 228 cal., 0 fat (0 sat. fat), 0 chol., 31mg sod., 37g carb. (35g sugars, 0 fiber), 0 pro.

GUAVA JAM BAKED BRIE EN CROUTE WITH PISTACHIOS

There's a ton of buzz around baked Brie. I decided to make it my own with guava paste and chopped pistachios. It's the same beloved app—but with a seriously tasty Cuban spin!
—*Marisel Salazar, New York, NY*

PREP: 10 min. • **BAKE:** 25 min.
MAKES: 8 servings

- 1 sheet frozen puff pastry, thawed
- 1 round Brie cheese (8 oz.)
- ⅔ cup guava paste or guava jelly, divided
- ⅔ cup chopped pistachios, divided

1. Preheat oven to 375°. Roll puff pastry into a 12-in. square. Place round of Brie in center of pastry; spread ⅓ cup guava paste over cheese; sprinkle with ⅓ cup pistachios. Fold pastry around cheese; trim excess dough. Pinch edges to seal. Place seam side down on ungreased baking sheet. Heat remaining ⅓ cup guava paste until mostly melted, pour over pastry.
2. Bake for 15 minutes. Top with remaining ⅓ cup pistachios; bake until puffed and golden brown, about 10 minutes longer. Serve warm.
1 PIECE: 370 cal., 21g fat (7g sat. fat), 28mg chol., 323mg sod., 38g carb. (17g sugars, 3g fiber), 10g pro.

CHUTNEY DEVILED EGGS

These eggs are a cinch to fill and make a popular contribution to a potluck or brunch.
—Taste of Home *Test Kitchen*

TAKES: 20 min. • **MAKES:** 1 dozen

- 6 hard-boiled large eggs
- 3 Tbsp. reduced-fat mayonnaise
- 2 Tbsp. mango chutney
- 1 Tbsp. chopped green onion
- ⅛ tsp. salt
- ⅛ tsp. pepper
  Optional: Chopped cashews and paprika

Cut eggs in half lengthwise. Remove yolks; set aside whites. In a large bowl, mash yolks. Stir in mayonnaise, chutney, green onion, salt and pepper. Stuff or pipe into egg whites. If desired, garnish with cashews and paprika. Chill until serving.
1 STUFFED EGG HALF: 49 cal., 3g fat (1g sat. fat), 70mg chol., 113mg sod., 3g carb. (2g sugars, 0 fiber), 3g pro.

BELMONT BREEZE

It may be juicy, but it's not too sweet. This flavorful refresher is the perfect drink for whiskey lovers to sip a hot day.
—Taste of Home *Test Kitchen*

TAKES: 5 min. • **MAKES:** 1 serving

- ½ to ¾ cup ice cubes
- 1½ oz. whiskey
- 1½ oz. orange juice
- 1½ oz. cranberry juice
- 1 oz. sour mix
- ¾ oz. sherry
- 1 oz. club soda
- 1 oz. lemon-lime soda
  Mint sprig and lemon wedge

1. Fill a shaker three-fourths full with ice. Place remaining ice in a cocktail glass; set aside.
2. Add the whiskey, juices, sour mix and sherry to shaker; cover and shake for 10-15 seconds or until condensation forms on outside of shaker. Strain into prepared glass. Top with sodas. Garnish with mint and lemon wedge.
1 SERVING: 223 cal., 0 fat (0 sat. fat), 0 chol., 13mg sod., 29g carb. (27g sugars, 0 fiber), 0 pro.

STRAWBERRY RIESLING WINE SPRITZER

**RHUBARB
BRUSCHETTA**

SWEET & SAVORY PINEAPPLE CHEESE BALL

When I was a kid, my mom made a cheese ball of pineapple and green peppers. Now I make it, and it's a huge hit at gatherings— the flavor combo surprises everyone!
—*Susan Harrison, Laurel, MD*

PREP: 15 min. + chilling • MAKES: 2 cheese balls (2 cups each)

- 2 pkg. (8 oz. each) reduced-fat cream cheese
- 1 can (20 oz.) crushed pineapple, well drained
- 3 cups finely chopped pecans, divided
- ¼ cup finely chopped green pepper
- 1 Tbsp. finely chopped onion
- 1 tsp. seasoned salt
  Assorted crackers

1. In a large bowl, beat cream cheese until smooth. Stir in the pineapple, 1½ cups pecans, green pepper, onion and seasoned salt. Shape into 2 balls. Wrap; refrigerate at least 30 minutes.
2. Place remaining pecans in a small shallow bowl; roll cheese balls in pecans to coat evenly. Serve with crackers.
2 TBSP.: 117 cal., 10g fat (3g sat. fat), 10mg chol., 108mg sod., 5g carb. (3g sugars, 1g fiber), 3g pro.

READER REVIEW

"This is my favorite cheese ball to make. I use 2 cans of crushed pineapple and squeeze the juice out well."
—CINCIBETTY, TASTEOFHOME.COM

RHUBARB BRUSCHETTA

Fresh rhubarb jam is spooned over cheese-topped bruschetta for a delightful spring appetizer. Be sure to spread the goat cheese on the bread slices as soon as they are removed from the broiler.
—*Margee Berry, White Salmon, WA*

TAKES: 30 min. • MAKES: 1½ dozen

- 5 tsp. olive oil, divided
- 1½ cups chopped fresh or frozen rhubarb
- ½ cup chopped red onion
- ¼ cup sugar
- 3 Tbsp. lemon juice
- 1 tsp. grated lemon zest
- ½ tsp. dried lavender flowers
- 18 slices French bread baguette (¼ in. thick)
- ½ cup crumbled goat cheese
- ¼ cup chopped pistachios

1. In a large skillet, heat 1 tsp. oil over medium-high heat. Add rhubarb, onion, sugar and lemon juice; cook and stir until tender, 5-7 minutes. Stir in zest and lavender. Remove from the heat. Mash to a chunky consistency; set aside.
2. Brush bread slices on both sides with remaining 4 tsp. oil. Place bread on ungreased baking sheets. Broil 3-4 in. from heat until golden brown, 1-2 minutes on each side. Spread with goat cheese. Top with rhubarb mixture and pistachios.
1 APPETIZER: 62 cal., 4g fat (1g sat. fat), 8mg chol., 60mg sod., 6g carb. (3g sugars, 1g fiber), 2g pro.

**SWEET & SAVORY
PINEAPPLE
CHEESE BALL**

PRESSURE-COOKER
CHERRY BOURBON
HAM BALLS

PRESSURE-COOKER CHERRY BOURBON HAM BALLS

My family loves meatballs and bourbon, so I decided to try to combine these two great flavors together. This quick and easy dish is the result. My family couldn't be happier.

—Joyce Moynihan, Lakeville, MN

- -

PREP: 45 min.
COOK: 15 min. + releasing
MAKES: 5 dozen

- 1 fully cooked boneless ham steak (1¼ lbs.)
- 1 lb. ground pork
- 1 cup soft marble rye bread crumbs
- 2 large eggs, lightly beaten
- 2 tsp. dried minced onion
- 2 tsp. ground mustard
- ½ tsp. pepper
- 1 can (14½ oz.) pitted tart cherries, undrained
- ¼ cup sugar
- ¼ cup yellow mustard
- ½ tsp. Worcestershire sauce
- 1 Tbsp. cornstarch
- ¼ cup bourbon

1. Cut ham into 2-in. pieces; place in a food processor. Process until ground; transfer to a large bowl. Add ground pork, bread crumbs, eggs, onion, ground mustard and pepper; mix lightly but thoroughly. Shape into 1½-in. balls.

2. Place trivet insert in a 6-qt. electric pressure cooker. Place meatballs on trivet, overlapping as needed. Combine the undrained cherries, sugar, mustard and Worcestershire sauce; pour over meatballs. Lock lid; close pressure-release valve. Adjust to pressure-cook on high for 15 minutes. Allow pressure to release naturally. Remove meatballs; keep warm. Remove trivet.

3. In a small bowl, mix cornstarch and bourbon until smooth; add to cooking juices in cooker. Select saute setting and adjust for low heat. Simmer, stirring constantly, until thickened, 1-2 minutes. Press cancel. Serve with meatballs.

1 MEATBALL WITH ABOUT 1 TSP. SAUCE: 39 cal., 2g fat (1g sat. fat), 16mg chol., 120mg sod., 2g carb. (1g sugars, 0 fiber), 4g pro.

OYSTERS ROCKEFELLER EGG ROLLS

OYSTERS ROCKEFELLER EGG ROLLS

Oysters Rockefeller is a classic appetizer from New Orleans that is so elegant and timeless. I love the flavor but wanted to try it in another of my favorite appetizers: egg rolls. I think the combination is a winner.

—Renee Murby, Johnston, RI

- -

PREP: 35 min. • **COOK:** 5 min./batch
MAKES: 10 servings

- 6 bacon strips, chopped
- ¼ cup all-purpose flour
- 2 cans (8 oz.) whole oysters, drained and patted dry
- ¼ tsp. salt
- ⅛ tsp. cayenne pepper
- 1 shallot, minced
- 1 Tbsp. minced garlic
- 1 tsp. dried parsley flakes
- 1 Tbsp. canola oil
- 1 pkg. (10 oz.) frozen chopped spinach, thawed and squeezed dry
- ½ tsp. grated lemon zest
- 1 large egg
- 10 egg roll wrappers
  Oil for deep-fat frying
  Optional: Seafood cocktail sauce and lemon wedges

1. In a large skillet, cook bacon over medium-high heat, stirring often, until crisp, about 5 minutes; drain, reserving drippings in skillet. Place flour in a shallow dish. Sprinkle the oysters with salt and cayenne pepper; toss oysters in flour. Cook in reserved drippings until golden brown, 3-4 minutes; drain.

2. Wipe out skillet. In same skillet, cook shallot, garlic and parsley in canola oil over medium heat until shallot is tender, 2-3 minutes. Add spinach and lemon zest; cook, stirring occasionally, until heated through, 2-3 minutes. Transfer spinach mixture to a bowl; stir in oysters and bacon.

3. In a small bowl, whisk egg and 1 tsp. water. Brush edges of an egg roll wrapper. Place ¼ cup oyster mixture in the center; fold bottom corner over filling. Fold sides over filling toward center; roll up tightly to seal. Repeat with remaining wrappers and filling.

4. In an electric skillet, heat ½ in. canola oil to 375°. Fry egg rolls until golden brown, about 2 minutes on each side. Drain on paper towels. If desired, serve egg rolls with cocktail sauce and lemon wedges.

1 EGG ROLL: 299 cal., 18g fat (3g sat. fat), 43mg chol., 427mg sod., 25g carb. (1g sugars, 2g fiber), 10g pro.

SMOKED BLUEFISH SPREAD

Growing up summers on Block Island, Rhode Island, we would surf-cast off the shores for bluefish. Its strong flavor makes it a great candidate for smoking. Use smoked fillets to make a creamy spread to serve with crackers. This is a snack that brings back memories of warm summer afternoons and cool ocean breezes.
—*Pamela Gelsomini, Wrentham, MA*

PREP: 15 min. + chilling • **MAKES:** 3 cups

- 1 lb. smoked bluefish fillets or flaked smoked trout
- 1 pkg. (8 oz.) cream cheese, softened
- ¾ cup finely chopped red onion
- ¼ cup snipped fresh dill
- ¼ cup lemon juice
- ¼ cup sour cream
- 3 Tbsp. capers, drained
- 2 Tbsp. prepared horseradish
- 2 Tbsp. grated lemon zest
  Assorted crackers, fresh vegetables and lemon wedges

1. Scrape fish from skin if needed. Place fish in a food processor; pulse until finely chopped. Combine cream cheese, red onion, dill, lemon juice, sour cream, capers, horseradish and zest; gently stir in fish. Refrigerate, covered, until serving.

2. Serve with crackers, vegetables and lemon wedges. If desired, top with additional red onion and dill.

NOTE: If you can't find smoked bluefish, this dip is also delicious with smoked mackerel, smoked salmon or smoked tuna. This dip is also delicious on a bagel for breakfast!

2 TBSP.: 64 cal., 5g fat (2g sat. fat), 14mg chol., 209mg sod., 2g carb. (1g sugars, 0 fiber), 4g pro.

WHIPPED FETA DIP

WHIPPED FETA DIP

The basis of this whipped feta dip is a great blank canvas for a variety of flavors. This version is flavored with garlic and lemon, but you might try other flavors like roasted red peppers, Greek olives or a spicy version made with crushed red pepper.
—*Dawn Parker, Surrey, BC*

TAKES: 10 min. • **MAKES:** 1⅓ cups

- 8 oz. feta cheese, crumbled
- ½ cup plain Greek yogurt
- 1 tsp. Greek seasoning
- 1 garlic clove, chopped
- ¾ tsp. grated lemon zest
- 1 Tbsp. extra virgin olive oil
  Fresh mint

Place first 5 ingredients in a food processor; process until smooth. Spoon into serving dish; drizzle with olive oil and sprinkle with mint.

2 TBSP.: 85 cal., 7g fat (4g sat. fat), 23mg chol., 311mg sod., 2g carb. (1g sugars, 0 fiber), 4g pro.

DID YOU KNOW?

Salty, crumbly Greek feta cheese is traditionally made with sheep's or goat's milk, but most American brands are made with cow's milk instead. If you're not fond of feta, you could substitute queso blanco, which is milky and mild-tasting. Consider fresh oregano instead of mint.

SMOKED BLUEFISH SPREAD

ASPARAGUS GALETTE WITH GOAT CHEESE

This galette could be an appetizer or a side dish. Cooking the vegetables beforehand gets rid of moisture so the crust becomes crispy in the oven.

—*Kellyn Kemmerer, Baltimore, MD*

- -

PREP: 1½ hours + chilling
BAKE: 30 min.
MAKES: 8 servings

- ¾ cup all-purpose flour
- ¾ cup whole wheat flour
- 1 tsp. kosher salt
- 10 Tbsp. cold unsalted butter
- 1 to 3 Tbsp. ice water

FILLING
- 2 Tbsp. unsalted butter, divided
- 2 medium leeks (white portion only), cut into ¼-in. slices
- 2 tsp. kosher salt, divided
- 1 Tbsp. olive oil
- ½ lb. sliced baby portobello mushrooms
- 1 lb. fresh asparagus, trimmed and cut into 3-in. pieces
- 1 log (4 oz.) fresh goat cheese
- 1 large egg, lightly beaten

1. Place flours and salt in a food processor; pulse until blended. Add butter; pulse until butter is the size of peas. While pulsing, add just enough ice water to form moist crumbs. Shape dough into a disk. Cover and refrigerate 1 hour or overnight.
2. In a large skillet, heat 1 Tbsp. butter over medium heat. Add leeks and 1 tsp. salt; cook and stir until softened, 5-7 minutes. Reduce heat to medium-low; cook until deep golden brown, 25-30 minutes, stirring occasionally. Remove from pan to a large bowl.
3. In the same skillet, heat oil and remaining 1 Tbsp. butter over medium heat. Add mushrooms and remaining 1 tsp. salt; cook and stir until reduced by half and crispy, about 20 minutes. Add to bowl with leeks.
4. Meanwhile, in a Dutch oven, bring 8 cups water to a boil. Add asparagus; cook, uncovered, until the stalks turn bright green, 2-3 minutes. Remove asparagus and immediately drop into ice water. Drain and pat dry; add to bowl with leeks and mushrooms.
5. Preheat oven to 400°. On a lightly floured surface, roll the dough into a 12-in. circle. Transfer crust to a parchment-lined baking sheet.
6. Crumble goat cheese over top of vegetable mixture. Spoon over crust to within 2 in. of edge. Fold crust edge over the filling, pleating as you go and leaving a 6-in. opening in the center. Brush folded crust with beaten egg. Bake until crust is golden brown and cheese is melted, 30-35 minutes. Let stand 5 minutes before cutting. Serve warm or at room temperature.
1 PIECE: 308 cal., 22g fat (12g sat. fat), 78mg chol., 797mg sod., 23g carb. (2g sugars, 3g fiber), 7g pro.

ASPARAGUS GALETTE WITH GOAT CHEESE

PEAR & CHEDDAR
Dab apple butter on a water cracker and top with aged white cheddar, a pear slice and sliced toasted almonds.

SUN-DRIED TOMATO PESTO
Layer a Ritz cracker with mascarpone cheese, sun-dried tomato pesto and a micro basil leaf.

WISE**CRACKERS**

The snappy snack base gets elevated with tasty toppers that make guests say, "Ooh...good one!"

SMOKED TROUT
Top a salt-and-pepper cracker with creme fraiche, capers, smoked trout and minced red onion.

CRAB & AVOCADO
Slather a sourdough cracker with cream cheese, then top with a peeled grapefruit slice, lump crabmeat and an avocado slice.

BUFFALO
Top a Ritz cracker with crumbled blue cheese, shredded chicken, Buffalo sauce and julienned celery.

MEDITERRANEAN
Hummus, halved green and black olives, thinly sliced garlic, crumbled feta, and a drizzle of olive oil top a hearty sourdough cracker.

SPICY PORK
Pile queso fresco, shredded pork, salsa and a jalapeno slice on a multi-seed cracker.

BISCOFF
Biscoff creamy cookie spread, sliced strawberry, shaved white chocolate and Biscoff cookie crumbles are irresistible on a water cracker.

SPAM
Load up a crispy rice cracker with hoisin sauce, seared Spam, shredded nori and spicy chili crisp.

PASTRAMI
Try honey mustard, Swiss cheese, sauerkraut, pastrami and a cornichon half on a hearty nut-and-seed cracker.

CRISPY GRILLED WINGS

My family is full of chicken-wing fiends. If there's a wing-eating contest, my husband is entering. Same goes for our 9-year-old daughter, who's very proud of her record (16 wings). Our preference is crispy wings, which can be achieved on the grill with a little cornstarch.
—*Audrey Alfaro, Rapid City, SD*

PREP: 15 min. • **GRILL:** 20 min.
MAKES: 20 pieces

- 2 lbs. chicken wings
- 1 Tbsp. olive oil
- 2 Tbsp. cornstarch
- 1½ tsp. kosher salt
- ½ tsp. garlic powder
- ½ tsp. paprika
- ½ tsp. lemon-pepper seasoning
- ½ tsp. pepper

1. Using a sharp knife, cut through the 2 wing joints; discard wing tips. Place remaining wing pieces in a large bowl. Add oil; toss to coat. Sprinkle with the remaining ingredients; toss to coat.
2. Grill wings on an oiled grill rack, covered, over medium heat or broil 4 in. from the heat until crisp and juices run clear, 20-25 minutes, turning occasionally.
1 PIECE: 60 cal., 4g fat (1g sat. fat), 14mg chol., 166mg sod., 1g carb. (0 sugars, 0 fiber), 5g pro.

HOW-TO

Cut Chicken Wings

- Place wing on a cutting board. With a sharp knife, cut through the joint at the tip end. Discard wing tip or save for making stock.
- Cut through remaining wing joint, creating a wingette and drumette. Repeat with remaining wings.

CRISPY GRILLED WINGS

SECRET INGREDIENT DEVILED EGGS

My Grandma Phyllis' secret in many of her savory dishes is the maraschino cherry. Her deviled eggs are unrivaled by any of the ones I've tried. The sweetness of the cherries balances out the heat of the jalapeno; celery and pickles give a nice crunch. It's always a party-pleaser, and the cherries will make your guests wonder what the secret is!
—*Adrienne Vradenburg, Bakersfield, CA*

TAKES: 30 min. • **MAKES:** 2 dozen

- 12 hard-boiled large eggs
- ⅓ cup mayonnaise
- 3 Tbsp. finely chopped celery
- 3 Tbsp. finely chopped sweet pickles
- 3 Tbsp. finely chopped maraschino cherries
- 2 Tbsp. Dijon mustard
- 1 Tbsp. finely chopped seeded jalapeno pepper
- ¼ tsp. salt
- ¼ tsp. pepper
- ½ tsp. smoked paprika
- ¼ tsp. ground chipotle pepper
- ¼ tsp. black sesame seeds
- 24 maraschino cherries

Cut eggs in half lengthwise. Remove yolks, reserving whites. In a small bowl, mash yolks. Stir in mayonnaise, celery, pickles, chopped cherries, mustard, jalapeno, salt and pepper. Spoon or pipe into egg whites. Sprinkle with paprika, chipotle pepper and sesame seeds. Top each with a cherry. Refrigerate, covered, until serving.

NOTE: Wear disposable gloves when cutting hot peppers; the oils can burn skin. Avoid touching your face.

1 STUFFED EGG HALF: 74 cal., 5g fat (1g sat. fat), 93mg chol., 109mg sod., 4g carb. (4g sugars, 0 fiber), 3g pro.

SECRET INGREDIENT DEVILED EGGS

OLD-FASHIONED LEMONADE

OLD-FASHIONED LEMONADE

This sweet-tart lemonade is a traditional part of my Memorial Day and Fourth of July menus. My family and friends can't get enough of the fresh-squeezed flavor.
—*Tammi Simpson, Greensburg, KY*

PREP: 10 min. • **COOK:** 5 min. + chilling • **MAKES:** 7 servings

- 1⅓ cups sugar
- 5 cups water, divided
- 1 Tbsp. grated lemon zest
- 1¾ cups lemon juice (about 10 large lemons)

In a large saucepan, combine sugar, 1 cup water and lemon zest. Cook and stir over medium heat until sugar is dissolved, about 4 minutes. Remove from heat. Stir in lemon juice and remaining water; refrigerate until cold. Serve over ice.

1 CUP: 142 cal., 0 fat (0 sat. fat), 0 chol., 1mg sod., 37g carb. (35g sugars, 0 fiber), 0 pro.

LIMEADE: Substitute lime zest for lemon zest and limes for lemons.

LAVENDER LEMONADE: Add 2 Tbsp. dried lavender to the sugar and lemon zest mixture before simmering. If desired, strain before serving.

GINGER-MINT LEMONADE: Add 1-2 Tbsp. grated fresh gingerroot and 1-2 mint sprigs to the sugar and lemon zest mixture before simmering. If desired, strain before serving.

CHEESY
PIZZA
FONDUE

PORK & CHEESY MACARONI SLIDERS

I love sliders! This sweet and savory recipe was created out of leftover ingredients I had in my fridge. It is perfect for a weeknight meal or a special-occasion potluck.
—*Rashanda Cobbins, Milwaukee, WI*

- -

PREP: 30 min. • **BAKE:** 10 min. • **MAKES:** 12 servings

- 1   cup uncooked cavatappi pasta
- 1   Tbsp. butter
- 1½ tsp. all-purpose flour
- ¼   tsp. pepper
- ½   cup 2% milk
- ¾   cup shredded sharp cheddar cheese
- 1   pkg. (18 oz.) Hawaiian sweet rolls
- 1   carton (16 oz.) refrigerated fully cooked barbecue shredded pork, warmed
- 2   Tbsp. melted butter
- 1   Tbsp. honey
- ½   tsp. ground mustard
- 1   jalapeno pepper, sliced, optional

1. Preheat oven to 375°. Cook the pasta according to package directions.
2. Meanwhile, in a small saucepan, melt butter over medium heat. Stir in flour and pepper until smooth; gradually whisk in milk. Bring to a boil, stirring constantly; cook and stir until thickened, 3-5 minutes. Stir in cheese until melted. Drain pasta; stir into cheese sauce. Set aside.
3. Place roll bottoms in a greased 13x9-in. baking dish. Layer with pork, pasta mixture and roll tops. Combine melted butter, honey and mustard. Brush over roll tops.
4. Bake 10-12 minutes or until tops are golden brown and filling is hot. If desired, top with jalapeno pepper slices.
1 SLIDER: 305 cal., 10g fat (6g sat. fat), 48mg chol., 466mg sod., 39g carb. (17g sugars, 2g fiber), 14g pro.

CHEESY PIZZA FONDUE

While I was growing up, I would sit for hours reading cookbooks from cover to cover. I've carried that love of cooking with me through the years. I found this recipe when we lived in Wisconsin.
—*Julie Barwick, Mansfield, OH*

- -

TAKES: 30 min. • **MAKES:** about 5 cups

- ½   lb. ground beef
- 1   medium onion, chopped
- 2   cans (15 oz. each) pizza sauce
- 1½ tsp. dried basil or dried oregano
- ¼   tsp. garlic powder
- 2½ cups shredded sharp cheddar cheese
- 1   cup shredded part-skim mozzarella cheese
      Breadsticks, garlic toast and green peppers

1. In a large saucepan, cook beef and onion over medium heat until meat is no longer pink, breaking meat into crumbles; drain. Stir in the pizza sauce, basil and garlic powder. Reduce heat to low. Add cheeses; stir until melted.
2. Transfer to a small fondue pot or 1½-qt. slow cooker; keep warm. Serve with breadsticks, garlic toast and green peppers.
NOTE: In addition to breadsticks, serve Cheesy Pizza Fondue with cubes of French or Italian bread.
2 TBSP.: 47 cal., 3g fat (2g sat. fat), 12mg chol., 86mg sod., 1g carb. (1g sugars, 0 fiber), 3g pro.

PORK & CHEESY
MACARONI SLIDERS

MINI BRIE EN CROUTE

Don't be fooled by the tiny size of these Brie bites—their flavor is mighty. Make sure the cheese is cold and firm before baking, which will prevent it from leaking out of the puff pastry.

—Sandy Coughlin, Bend, OR

PREP: 20 min. • **BAKE:** 20 min.
MAKES: 32 servings

- 1 pkg. (17.3 oz.) frozen puff pastry, thawed
- 1 round (8 oz.) Brie cheese
- 1 large egg
- 1 Tbsp. water

1. Preheat oven to 400°. On a lightly floured surface, unfold puff pastry. Roll out each pastry to a 10-in. square. Cut each pastry into sixteen 2½-in. squares. Cut Brie into 32 pieces; place a piece in the center of each square. Bring corners of pastry over Brie and pinch edges to seal.
2. Place 2 in. apart on a parchment-lined baking sheets. In a small bowl, whisk egg and water; brush over puffs. Bake until golden brown and puffed, 20-25 minutes. Serve warm.
1 PIECE: 100 cal., 6g fat (2g sat. fat), 11mg chol., 96mg sod., 9g carb. (0 sugars, 1g fiber), 3g pro.

BUTTERY CAJUN POPCORN

This cheesy, spicy, citrus-kissed snack is downright addictive!

—Beth Stengel, North Hollywood, CA

TAKES: 15 min. • **MAKES:** 3 qt.

- 12 cups air-popped popcorn
- ¼ cup butter, melted
- 2 Tbsp. lime juice
- 4½ tsp. Cajun seasoning
- 4 to 5 Tbsp. grated Parmesan cheese

Place popcorn in a large bowl. Combine butter and lime juice; drizzle over popcorn and toss to coat. Combine Cajun seasoning and cheese; sprinkle over popcorn and toss to coat.
1 CUP: 83 cal., 5g fat (3g sat. fat), 12mg chol., 256mg sod., 9g carb. (0 sugars, 2g fiber), 2g pro. **DIABETIC EXCHANGES:** 1 fat, ½ starch.

PARSNIP LATKES WITH LOX & HORSERADISH CREME

A horseradish-flavored creme fraiche brings zip to these crispy homemade latkes, which get a touch of sweetness from the parsnips. Add fresh dill sprigs for a garnish.

—Todd Schmeling, Gurnee, IL

PREP: 30 min. • **COOK:** 5 min./batch
MAKES: about 3 dozen

- 1 lb. potatoes, peeled
- 1 lb. parsnips, peeled
- ⅔ cup chopped green onions
- 2 large eggs, lightly beaten
- 1 tsp. salt
- ½ tsp. pepper
  Oil for deep-fat frying
- 1 cup creme fraiche or sour cream
- 1 Tbsp. snipped fresh dill
- 1 Tbsp. prepared horseradish
- ¼ tsp. salt
- ⅛ tsp. white pepper
- 1 pkg. (3 oz.) smoked salmon or lox, cut into ½-in.-wide strips
  Fresh dill sprigs
  Lemon wedges, optional

1. Coarsely grate potatoes and parsnips. Place the grated vegetables on a double thickness of cheesecloth; bring up corners and squeeze out any liquid. Transfer to a large bowl; stir in the onions, eggs, salt and pepper.
2. In an electric skillet, heat ⅛ in. oil to 375°. Drop potato mixture by heaping tablespoonfuls into hot oil. Flatten to form patties. Fry until golden brown; turn and cook the other side. Drain on paper towels.
3. Combine the creme fraiche, fresh dill, horseradish, salt and pepper. Top latkes with a dollop of creme fraiche mixture, folded strips of salmon and sprigs of dill. If desired, serve with lemon wedges.
1 APPETIZER: 71 cal., 5g fat (2g sat. fat), 17mg chol., 110mg sod., 4g carb. (1g sugars, 1g fiber), 1g pro.

PARSNIP LATKES WITH LOX & HORSERADISH CREME

**CORN & BLACK
BEAN SALAD
PAGE 35**

Salads & Dressings

Turn here for the freshest mealtime ideas. Discover new summer pasta and potato salads, delightful twists on classic Caprese, good-for-you vinaigrettes and so much more.

BEST OF THE BEST DISHES

SHRIMP, AVOCADO & GRAPEFRUIT SALAD

This colorful salad is so simple and refreshing any time of the year. You'll be surprised how well creamy avocado and tart grapefruit go together.
—*Elinor Stabile, Canmore, AB*

TAKES: 15 min. • **MAKES:** 12 servings

- ½ cup olive oil
- ¼ cup balsamic vinegar
- ¼ tsp. salt
- ⅛ tsp. pepper

SALAD
- 6 large pink grapefruit
- 6 ripe avocados, peeled, sliced and cubed
- 3 cups peeled and deveined cooked small shrimp
- 12 lettuce leaves

1. In a small bowl, whisk the oil, vinegar, salt and pepper. Cut a thin slice from the top and bottom of each grapefruit. Stand grapefruit upright on a cutting board. With a knife, cut off peel and outer membrane. Cut along the membrane of each segment to remove fruit.

2. Combine the grapefruit sections, avocados and shrimp; serve over lettuce. Drizzle with dressing; toss to coat.

1 CUP: 284 cal., 20g fat (3g sat. fat), 74mg chol., 317mg sod., 21g carb. (13g sugars, 7g fiber), 9g pro.

SHRIMP, AVOCADO & GRAPEFRUIT SALAD

GRILLED SUMMER SAUSAGE SALAD

GRILLED SUMMER SAUSAGE SALAD

It's not often that you see sausage in a salad, but I say why not? The grilled links and garden vegetables make for a garlicky, fresh-tasting, super-satisfying salad. I'll even grill the romaine on occasion!
—*Noelle Myers, Grand Forks, ND*

TAKES: 30 min. • **MAKES:** 8 servings

- 1 lb. garlic summer sausage, casing removed and quartered lengthwise
- 2 small zucchini, cut in half lengthwise
- 2 yellow summer squash, cut in half lengthwise
- 1 medium sweet red pepper, halved and seeded
- 1 medium sweet orange pepper, halved and seeded
- 2 Tbsp. olive oil
- ½ tsp. salt
- ¼ tsp. pepper
- 1 pkg. (5 oz.) spring mix salad greens
- ½ English cucumber, chopped
- 2 celery ribs with leaves, chopped
- ½ cup Italian salad dressing

1. Brush summer sausage, zucchini, yellow squash and peppers with olive oil; sprinkle with salt and pepper. Grill sausage and vegetables on an oiled rack, covered, over medium heat for 5-6 minutes on each side or until crisp-tender. Remove to a cutting board; roughly chop vegetables and sausage.

2. Place salad greens in a large bowl; add cucumber, celery, grilled vegetables and sausage. Drizzle with dressing; toss to coat. Divide among 8 bowls. If desired, sprinkle with additional black pepper.

2 CUPS: 260 cal., 21g fat (6g sat. fat), 35mg chol., 1048mg sod., 10g carb. (4g sugars, 2g fiber), 10g pro.

DIJON MUSTARD VINAIGRETTE

Here's a versatile dressing perfect for green salads or tossing with new potatoes.
—*Sarah Farmer, Waukesha, WI*

PREP: 5 min. • **MAKES:** 1 cup

- ¼ cup balsamic vinegar
- 1 Tbsp. Dijon mustard
- ½ tsp. salt
- ¼ tsp. coarsely ground pepper
- ¾ cup extra virgin olive oil

In a large bowl, whisk together the first 4 ingredients. Slowly add olive oil while whisking constantly.

2 TBSP.: 189 cal., 20g fat (3g sat. fat), 0 chol., 193mg sod., 2g carb. (2g sugars, 0 fiber), 0 pro.

CHICKEN CURRY FRUIT SALAD

Perfect for a special luncheon, this tasty combo blends chicken, apple, celery and grapes with crunchy nuts and noodles.
—*Paula Anderson, Seal Beach, CA*

PREP: 20 min. + chilling
MAKES: 6 servings

- 4 cups cubed cooked chicken breasts
- 2 celery ribs, diced
- 1 cup seedless red grapes, halved
- 1 medium apple, peeled and diced
- 1 small red onion, diced
- 1 cup fat-free mayonnaise
- 1 Tbsp. orange marmalade
- 2 tsp. lime juice
- 1 tsp. curry powder
- ½ cup lightly salted cashews
- ½ cup chow mein noodles

1. In a large bowl, combine the first 5 ingredients. In a small bowl, combine the mayonnaise, marmalade, lime juice and curry. Pour over chicken mixture and toss to coat. Cover and refrigerate for at least 1 hour.
2. Just before serving, sprinkle with cashews and chow mein noodles.

1⅓ CUPS: 305 cal., 11g fat (2g sat. fat), 76mg chol., 431mg sod., 22g carb. (12g sugars, 3g fiber), 30g pro. **DIABETIC EXCHANGES:** 4 lean meat, 1 starch, 1 fat, ½ fruit.

GORGONZOLA PEAR SALAD

This quick, easy recipe really showcases pears. When I have some leftover cooked chicken, I often add it to the recipe to make a main dish salad.
—*Candace McMenamin, Lexington, SC*

TAKES: 25 min.
MAKES: 6 servings (1¼ cups dressing)

- ⅓ cup white wine vinegar
- 1 can (15 oz.) pear halves, drained
- ½ tsp. salt
- ⅓ cup olive oil
- 6 cups torn mixed salad greens
- 2 medium pears, sliced
- 1 medium tomato, seeded and finely chopped
- ¾ cup chopped walnuts
- ¼ cup crumbled Gorgonzola cheese
  Coarsely ground pepper, optional

1. For dressing, in a blender, combine the vinegar, pear halves and salt; cover and process until smooth. While processing, gradually add oil in a steady stream.
2. In a salad bowl, combine the greens, sliced pears, tomato, walnuts and cheese. Drizzle with desired amount of dressing; toss to coat. Serve with pepper if desired. Refrigerate any leftover dressing.

1½ CUPS: 315 cal., 23g fat (4g sat. fat), 4mg chol., 301mg sod., 27g carb. (17g sugars, 5g fiber), 5g pro.

DID YOU KNOW?

Gorgonzola gets its name from the small Italian town from which it originated. Today, several American dairies also make the creamy cow's-milk cheese with blue-green veins. Tubs of crumbled Gorgonzola cheese are convenient for salads.

GORGONZOLA PEAR SALAD

TURNIP GREENS SALAD

GRILLED POTATO & CORN SALAD

Corn salad and potato salad are summer classics. I smashed 'em together for a pleasing dish that we love with burgers.
—*Donna Gribbins, Shelbyville, KY*

PREP: 45 min. • **GRILL:** 25 min. + chilling
MAKES: 10 servings

- 2 lbs. medium Yukon Gold potatoes, cut into ¼-in. thick slices
- 2 Tbsp. olive oil, divided
- 2 poblano peppers
- 4 medium ears sweet corn, husked
- 6 green onions
- ⅔ cup sour cream
- ¼ cup mayonnaise
- 2 Tbsp. lime juice
- 1 cup crumbled Cotija cheese
- ¼ cup chopped fresh cilantro
- 1½ tsp. grated lime zest
- ½ tsp. salt
- ¼ tsp. pepper
  Optional: Lime wedges, fresh cilantro leaves and additional crumbled Cotija cheese

1. Place potatoes in a large saucepan; add water to cover. Bring to a boil. Reduce heat; cook, uncovered, 5 minutes. Drain potatoes and toss with 1 Tbsp. oil.
2. Grill poblanos, covered, over high heat 8-10 minutes or until skins are blistered and blackened on all sides, turning occasionally. Immediately place the peppers in a small bowl; let stand, covered, 20 minutes. Reduce the grill temperature to medium heat.
3. Brush corn with remaining 1 Tbsp. oil. Place potatoes in a grill basket. Grill corn and potatoes, covered, over medium heat 12-15 minutes or until tender and lightly browned, turning occasionally. Cool slightly. Grill green onions until blackened, 5-6 minutes. Cut into 1-in. pieces and place in a large bowl. Peel off and discard charred skin from poblanos; remove stems and seeds. Cut peppers into ½-in. pieces and add to onions. Cut corn from cobs; add corn and potatoes to peppers.
4. Whisk sour cream, mayonnaise and lime juice; stir in cheese, cilantro, zest, salt and pepper. Add to veggies; stir to coat. Chill at least 1 hour. If desired, serve with lime, cilantro and additional cheese.
¾ CUP: 260 cal., 14g fat (5g sat. fat), 25mg chol., 347mg sod., 28g carb. (5g sugars, 3g fiber), 7g pro.

TURNIP GREENS SALAD

I created this recipe using items from my garden. Because most people cook turnip greens, I wanted to present those same greens in a way that would retain their nutrient content.
—*James McCarroll, Murfreesboro, TN*

TAKES: 30 min. • **MAKES:** 8 servings

- 1 bunch fresh turnip greens (about 10 oz.)
- 5 oz. fresh baby spinach (about 8 cups)
- 1 medium cucumber, halved and thinly sliced
- 1 cup cherry tomatoes, halved
- ¾ cup dried cranberries
- ½ medium red onion, thinly sliced
- ⅓ cup crumbled feta cheese
- 1 garlic clove
- ½ tsp. kosher salt
- ⅓ cup extra virgin olive oil
- 2 Tbsp. sherry vinegar
- 1 tsp. Dijon mustard
- ¼ tsp. pepper
- ⅛ tsp. cayenne pepper

1. Trim and discard root end of turnip greens. Coarsely chop leaves. Place in a large bowl. Add spinach, cucumber, tomatoes, cranberries, red onion and feta.
2. Place garlic on a cutting board; sprinkle with salt. Using the flat side of a knife, mash garlic. Continue to mash until it reaches a paste consistency. Transfer to a small bowl. Whisk in oil, vinegar, mustard, pepper and cayenne until blended. Drizzle over salad; toss to coat. Serve immediately.
1¼ CUPS: 161 cal., 10g fat (2g sat. fat), 3mg chol., 203mg sod., 17g carb. (12g sugars, 3g fiber), 3g pro. **DIABETIC EXCHANGES:** 2 vegetable, 2 fat, ½ starch.

HOW-TO

Massage Tough Cooking Greens

To make tough kale or turnip greens more tender and palatable, place washed greens in a large bowl. Sprinkle with a little salt or olive oil if desired, then rub greens vigorously between your hands. After a few minutes, you'll have perfectly tender greens for your salad.

GRILLED POTATO
& CORN SALAD

PARSNIP, PEAR & PECAN SALAD

I didn't try parsnips until I was well into my 40s, but now I can't get enough of them. This salad is so delicious, I defy your kids to turn their noses up at it. Just don't tell them it's healthy.

—*Jodi Taffel, Altadena, CA*

PREP: 20 min. • **BAKE:** 15 min.
MAKES: 8 servings

- 1 cup shredded Parmesan cheese
- 2 cups peeled parsnips, julienned
- 1 cup chopped D'Anjou pears (½-in. cubes)
- ½ cup chopped pecans
- ½ cup fresh shelled or frozen peas, thawed
- ½ cup pomegranate seeds
- ½ cup pine nuts
- 1 tsp. kosher salt
- ½ tsp. pepper
- ⅓ cup mayonnaise
- 3 Tbsp. water

1. Preheat oven to 400°. Drop Parmesan cheese, 2 tablespoonfuls at a time, ½ in. apart onto a lightly greased or parchment-lined baking sheet. There should be 8 circles. Bake until the cheese is melted and golden brown, 12-15 minutes. Cool cheese crisps completely.

2. Combine next 8 ingredients. Mix thoroughly. Stir together mayonnaise and water. Add to salad; toss to coat. Serve with Parmesan crisps.

1 CUP: 254 cal., 20g fat (4g sat. fat), 8mg chol., 461mg sod., 14g carb. (6g sugars, 4g fiber), 7g pro.

STRAWBERRY-PINEAPPLE COLESLAW

STRAWBERRY-PINEAPPLE COLESLAW

Sweet fruit, tangy coleslaw dressing and colorful, crisp cabbage make a wonderful combination to share with others. I like to include the nuts because they add a healthy crunch.

—*Victoria Pederson, Ham Lake, MN*

PREP: 15 min. + chilling
MAKES: about 14 servings

- 2 pkg. (14 oz. each) coleslaw mix
- 1 jar (13 oz.) coleslaw salad dressing
- 1 cup salted cashews or macadamia nuts
- 1 cup dried cranberries
- 1 cup chopped fresh or canned pineapple
- 1 cup chopped fresh sugar snap peas
- 1 cup chopped fresh strawberries
- ½ cup sweetened shredded coconut
- ½ cup chopped green onions

Combine all ingredients in a large bowl; toss to coat. Cover and refrigerate slaw until serving.

¾ CUP: 244 cal., 15g fat (3g sat. fat), 3mg chol., 272mg sod., 26g carb. (19g sugars, 3g fiber), 3g pro.

TROPICAL FRUIT COMPOTE

My mother used to make this recipe when I was a child. My four kids always ate more fruit when I dressed it up this way.

—*Maxine Otis, Hobson, MT*

PREP: 20 min. + chilling
MAKES: 2 servings

- 1 cup apricot nectar, divided
  Dash to ⅛ tsp. ground cloves
  Dash to ⅛ tsp. ground cinnamon
- 1 Tbsp. cornstarch
- 2 Tbsp. lemon juice
- 1 firm banana, cut into ½-in. slices
- 4 fresh strawberries, sliced
- 1 kiwifruit, halved and thinly sliced

1. In a small saucepan, bring ¾ cup apricot nectar, cloves and cinnamon to a boil. Combine cornstarch and remaining ¼ cup apricot nectar until smooth; gradually whisk into nectar mixture. Return to a boil; cook and stir until thickened and bubbly, 1-2 minutes. Remove from the heat; stir in lemon juice. Cool.

2. Stir in banana, strawberries and kiwi. Chill at least 1 hour before serving.

1 CUP: 174 cal., 1g fat (0 sat. fat), 0 chol., 7mg sod., 44g carb. (29g sugars, 4g fiber), 2g pro.

PARSNIP, PEAR & PECAN SALAD

GRILLED NECTARINES WITH BURRATA & HONEY

The classic Caprese gets a sweet makeover with this inspired summer starter. Burrata, mint and honey are served over nectarine halves—or any stone fruit you like—in this creamy, dreamy dish.
—*Anthony Gans, Hawthorne, CA*

TAKES: 15 min. • **MAKES:** 6 servings

- 3 medium ripe nectarines, halved and pitted
  Cooking spray
- 8 oz. burrata cheese
- 2 Tbsp. honey
- 12 fresh mint leaves
  Flaky sea salt, such as Maldon

1. Heat a grill pan over medium-high heat. Spritz cut sides of nectarines with cooking spray. Place cut sides down on pan. Grill until just tender, 4-5 minutes. Meanwhile, drain burrata; cut into 6 slices.
2. Arrange nectarine halves, cut side up, on a serving platter. Top with burrata, honey and mint; sprinkle with salt.
1 SERVING: 160 cal., 8g fat (5g sat. fat), 27mg chol., 60mg sod., 15g carb. (13g sugars, 1g fiber), 7g pro.

PEACH CAPRESE SALAD

During summer, I like to use the fresh ingredients I receive weekly from my local food share, and that's how this salad was created. I use large balls of mozzarella torn into pieces, but you could use smaller mozzarella pearls.
—*Mounir Echariti, Mendham, NJ*

TAKES: 15 min. • **MAKES:** 2 servings

- 4 oz. fresh buffalo mozzarella cheese
- 2 cups torn leaf lettuce
- 1 medium peach, cut into wedges
- 1 large heirloom tomato, cut into wedges
- ½ cup loosely packed basil leaves
- 2 Tbsp. extra virgin olive oil
- 1 Tbsp. balsamic vinegar
- ¼ tsp. flaky sea salt
- ⅛ tsp. coarsely ground pepper

Tear mozzarella into large pieces. On 2 large plates, arrange lettuce, peach wedges, tomato wedges, mozzarella and basil. Drizzle with olive oil and vinegar; sprinkle with salt and pepper.
1 SERVING: 343 cal., 26g fat (10g sat. fat), 45mg chol., 336mg sod., 15g carb. (12g sugars, 3g fiber), 12g pro.

CHILI VERDE ESQUITES (MEXICAN CORN SALAD)

The sausages add a wallop of flavor in this kicked-up corn salad! We leave half the kernels raw for crunch, and quickly pickle shallots and chilis in some lime juice for brightness. Half the Cotija cheese gets added for creaminess while the mixture is hot, and the other half is added as a topping once it's cooled.
—*Cara Nicoletti, Wellesley, MA*

PREP: 20 min. • **COOK:** 10 min. + cooling
MAKES: 8 servings

- 5 Tbsp. lime juice
- 3 Tbsp. olive oil
- 6 medium ears sweet corn, husked
- 2 shallots, sliced into rings
- 1 serrano pepper, sliced into rings, optional
- 1 pkg. (12 oz.) Seemore Fully Cooked Chicken Chili Verde Sausages
- 1 Tbsp. canola oil
- ½ cup Cotija cheese, crumbled and divided
- 1 cup roughly chopped fresh cilantro leaves, divided

1. In a large serving bowl, whisk together lime juice and olive oil. Cut kernels off corn cobs. Add half to the serving bowl; stir in shallots and, if desired, serrano. Set aside.
2. Crumble sausages into small pieces. In a large cast-iron or stainless steel skillet over medium-high heat, cook and stir sausage in canola oil until golden brown, about 5 minutes. With a slotted spoon, transfer sausage to paper towel.
3. In same pan, add remaining corn to drippings; cook over high heat, not stirring, until lightly charred on 1 side, 2-3 minutes. Transfer corn to shallot mixture; add sausage and ¼ cup Cotija cheese. Toss to combine; let stand for 15-20 minutes or until cooled to room temperature. Stir in ½ cup cilantro. Top with remaining ½ cup cilantro and ¼ cup Cotija cheese.
¾ CUP: 229 cal., 14g fat (3g sat. fat), 40mg chol., 364mg sod., 18g carb. (6g sugars, 2g fiber), 12g pro. **DIABETIC EXCHANGES:** 2 lean meat, 2 fat, 1 starch.

GRILLED NECTARINES WITH BURRATA & HONEY

LEMON ARTICHOKE ROMAINE SALAD

BERRY NECTARINE SALAD

In my circle, no summer celebration is complete without this most-requested vibrant fruit medley. The creamy topping is the perfect accent, so don't skimp!
—*Mindee Myers, Lincoln, NE*

PREP: 15 min. + chilling
MAKES: 8 servings

 4 medium nectarines, sliced
 ¼ cup sugar
 1 tsp. lemon juice
 ½ tsp. ground ginger
 3 oz. reduced-fat cream cheese
 2 cups fresh raspberries
 1 cup fresh blueberries

1. In a large bowl, toss nectarines with sugar, lemon juice and ginger. Refrigerate, covered, 1 hour, stirring once.
2. Drain nectarines, reserving juices. Gradually beat reserved juices into cream cheese. Gently combine nectarines and berries; serve with cream cheese mixture.
1 SERVING: 109 cal., 3g fat (2g sat. fat), 8mg chol., 46mg sod., 21g carb. (15g sugars, 4g fiber), 2g pro. **DIABETIC EXCHANGES:** 1 fruit, ½ starch, ½ fat.

LEMON ARTICHOKE ROMAINE SALAD

I created this dish when I was trying to duplicate a very lemony Caesar salad. This version is not only delicious but more healthful, too.
—*Kathy Armstrong, Post Falls, ID*

TAKES: 15 min. • **MAKES:** 8 servings

 10 cups torn romaine
 4 plum tomatoes, chopped
 1 can (14 oz.) water-packed quartered artichoke hearts, rinsed and drained
 1 can (2¼ oz.) sliced ripe olives, drained
 3 Tbsp. water
 3 Tbsp. lemon juice
 3 Tbsp. olive oil
 2 garlic cloves, minced
 1 tsp. salt
 1 tsp. coarsely ground pepper
 ⅓ cup shredded Parmesan cheese

1. Place first 4 ingredients in a large bowl. Place all remaining ingredients except cheese in a jar with a tight-fitting lid; shake well. Pour over salad; toss to coat.
2. Sprinkle salad with Parmesan cheese. Serve immediately.
1½ CUPS: 105 cal., 7g fat (1g sat. fat), 2mg chol., 541mg sod., 8g carb. (2g sugars, 2g fiber), 4g pro. **DIABETIC EXCHANGES:** 2 vegetable, 1½ fat.

TOASTED PECAN VINAIGRETTE

Besides salad greens, put this nutty vinaigrette over grilled chicken breast.
—*Sarah Farmer, Waukesha, WI*

PREP: 5 min. • **MAKES:** 1 cup

 ¼ cup red wine vinegar
 1 shallot, finely chopped
 1 tsp. Dijon mustard
 ½ tsp. salt
 ¼ tsp. coarsely ground pepper
 ¾ cup extra virgin olive oil
 ⅓ cup finely chopped pecans, toasted

In a large bowl, whisk together first 5 ingredients. Slowly add olive oil while whisking constantly. Stir in pecans just before serving.
2 TBSP.: 215 cal., 24g fat (3g sat. fat), 0 chol., 164mg sod., 2g carb. (0 sugars, 0 fiber), 1g pro.

TEST KITCHEN TIP

For the best results, start with all the ingredients at room temperature. If the oil is cool or cold, it is much more difficult to form the emulsion. To get the most flavor out of these simple ingredients, mix up the vinaigrette and let it sit at room temperature for 1 to 3 hours before serving.

CITRUS AVOCADO SPINACH SALAD

Tossing this salad together with creamy avocado and tangy citrus is so simple, and you don't even need to peel the oranges.
—*Karole Friemann, Kimberling City, MO*

TAKES: 15 min. • **MAKES:** 8 servings

 8 cups fresh baby spinach (about 6 oz.)
 3 cups refrigerated citrus salad, drained
 2 medium ripe avocados, peeled and sliced
 1 cup crumbled blue cheese
    Toasted sliced almonds, optional
    Salad dressing of your choice, optional

Divide spinach among 8 plates; top with citrus salad and avocados. Sprinkle with cheese and, if desired, dressing and almonds. Serve immediately.
1 SERVING: 168 cal., 10g fat (4g sat. fat), 13mg chol., 231mg sod., 16g carb. (10g sugars, 3g fiber), 5g pro.

BERRY
NECTARINE
SALAD

GYRO SALAD WITH
TZATZIKI DRESSING

GYRO SALAD WITH TZATZIKI DRESSING

If you're fond of gyros, you will love this garden-fresh salad showcasing ground lamb, crumbled feta cheese, Greek olives, tomatoes and creamy cucumber dressing.
—Taste of Home *Test Kitchen*

TAKES: 30 min. • **MAKES:** 6 servings

DRESSING

- 1 cucumber, peeled and coarsely shredded
- ½ tsp. salt
- ½ cup sour cream
- ¾ cup plain yogurt
- 2 Tbsp. white vinegar
- 1 garlic clove, minced
- ½ tsp. dill weed
- ¼ tsp. cracked black pepper

SALAD

- ½ lb. ground lamb or ground beef
- 1 small onion, chopped
- 1 tsp. Greek seasoning or oregano leaves
- 1 pkg. (10 oz.) hearts of romaine salad mix
- 2 tomatoes, chopped
- 1 pkg. (4 oz.) crumbled feta cheese
- ½ cup pitted Greek olives, drained
  Toasted pita bread wedges

1. In a large bowl, sprinkle cucumber with salt; mix well. Let stand 5 minutes. Drain. Stir in remaining dressing ingredients. Cover and refrigerate.

2. In a large skillet over medium-high heat, cook lamb, onion and Greek seasoning until lamb is no longer pink, stirring to break the meat into crumbles; drain.

3. Arrange salad mix on a large serving platter; top with tomatoes, cheese, olives and lamb. Spoon dressing over salad. Serve immediately with pita wedges.

1 SERVING: 236 cal., 16g fat (7g sat. fat), 43mg chol., 807mg sod., 10g carb. (4g sugars, 3g fiber), 14g pro.

RASPBERRY VINAIGRETTE

RASPBERRY VINAIGRETTE

Who knew you could add fruits to dressings? This raspberry vinaigrette is sweet and tart, making it the perfect summer dressing for any salad.
—*Debbie Jones, Hollywood, MD*

TAKES: 10 min. • **MAKES:** about ¾ cup

- ½ cup vegetable oil
- ¼ cup Raspberry Vinegar (recipe at right)
- 4 tsp. sugar
- 2 tsp. Dijon mustard

Combine all ingredients in a jar with a tight-fitting lid; shake well. Store in the refrigerator. Just before serving, shake dressing again.

2 TBSP.: 176 cal., 18g fat (2g sat. fat), 0 chol., 40mg sod., 3g carb. (3g sugars, 0 fiber), 0 pro. **DIABETIC EXCHANGES:** 3 fat.

TEST KITCHEN TIPS

- It's easy to make **Raspberry Vinegar** from scratch! Bring 2 cups of fresh or frozen unsweetened raspberries, ¾ cup of cider vinegar, ⅓ cup of honey and 1 cinnamon stick to a boil. Reduce the heat, cover and simmer for 20 minutes. Allow the mixture to cool before straining through a cheesecloth. Pour into a container, cover and refrigerate until you're ready to use.

- Store **Raspberry Vinaigrette** in an airtight container in the refrigerator. We recommend using it within the first few days while it's freshest. Try using it in a raspberry slaw or a strawberry garden salad.

- Switch things up by adding balsamic vinegar or finely chopped shallot to this vinaigrette recipe.

LEMONY
CHICKEN SALAD

LEMONY CHICKEN SALAD

Every busy cook will appreciate the convenience of being able to prepare this refreshing salad ahead of time. And your family will enjoy a marvelous meal.
—*Joan Gatling, Bernalillo, NM*

- -

PREP: 25 min. + chilling • **MAKES:** 8 servings

- ⅔ cup Miracle Whip or mayonnaise
- ⅔ cup sour cream
- 1 Tbsp. lemon juice
- 1½ tsp. grated lemon zest
- 1 tsp. salt
- ½ tsp. dried tarragon
- ¼ tsp. pepper
- 4 cups diced cooked chicken
- 1 cup thinly sliced celery
- 1 cup chopped green pepper
- 2 large red apples, cut into ½-in. pieces, optional
- ½ cup chopped onion
- ¼ cup minced fresh parsley
- 1 cup chopped walnuts

In a large bowl, combine the first 7 ingredients. Stir in chicken, celery, green pepper, apples if desired, onion and parsley. Cover and refrigerate for several hours. Stir in walnuts just before serving.
1 CUP: 333 cal., 23g fat (5g sat. fat), 83mg chol., 508mg sod., 8g carb. (4g sugars, 2g fiber), 24g pro.

GRILLED PEACH COUSCOUS SALAD

You'll feel inspired at the farmers market with the recipe for this couscous salad in tow. Grilled peaches and limes plus a subtly sweet dressing bring pizazz.
—*Emily King, Fayetteville, AR*

- -

PREP: 20 min. + cooling • **GRILL:** 10 min. • **MAKES:** 8 servings

- ½ cup uncooked couscous
- 1 medium lime
- 2 medium firm ripe peaches, halved and pitted
- 1 tsp. plus ¼ cup canola oil, divided
- 1 English cucumber, halved and sliced
- 1 cup cherry tomatoes, halved
- ¼ medium red onion, thinly sliced
- 1 Tbsp. agave nectar
- 2 tsp. white wine vinegar
- ½ tsp. salt
- ¼ tsp. pepper

1. Prepare couscous according to package directions; fluff. Transfer to a large bowl; let cool. Meanwhile, finely grate enough zest from lime to measure 1½ tsp.; set aside for dressing. Slice lime in half. Brush peach and lime halves with 1 tsp. oil. Grill peaches, covered, over medium heat until tender, 3-4 minutes on each side. Remove to a cutting board. Grill lime halves just until tender, about 1 minute.
2. When cool enough to handle, chop the peaches and add to couscous. Stir in cucumber, tomatoes and red onion. Squeeze juice from lime into a small bowl. Add agave, vinegar, salt, pepper, reserved lime zest and remaining ¼ cup oil. Whisk until blended. Pour over salad; toss to coat.
¾ CUP: 144 cal., 8g fat (1g sat. fat), 0 chol., 150mg sod., 18g carb. (7g sugars, 2g fiber), 2g pro. **DIABETIC EXCHANGES:** 1½ fat, 1 starch.

GRILLED PEACH
COUSCOUS SALAD

CAPRESE PASTA SALAD

CORN & BLACK BEAN SALAD

This colorful, crunchy salad is chock-full of great tastes that all ages will love. Try it with a variety of summer entrees or as a snack with tortilla chips!
—*Krista Frank, Rhododendron, OR*

- -

PREP: 15 min. + chilling
MAKES: 8 servings

- 1 can (15¼ oz.) whole kernel corn, drained
- 1 can (15 oz.) black beans, rinsed and drained
- 2 large tomatoes, finely chopped
- 1 large red onion, finely chopped
- ¼ cup minced fresh cilantro
- 2 garlic cloves, minced

DRESSING
- 2 Tbsp. sugar
- 2 Tbsp. white vinegar
- 2 Tbsp. canola oil
- 1½ tsp. lime juice
- ¼ tsp. salt
- ¼ tsp. ground cumin
- ¼ tsp. pepper

In a large bowl, combine the first 6 ingredients. In a small bowl, whisk dressing ingredients; pour over corn mixture and toss to coat. Cover and refrigerate at least 1 hour. Stir before serving. Serve with a slotted spoon.
⅔ CUP: 142 cal., 4g fat (0 sat. fat), 0 chol., 326mg sod., 21g carb. (8g sugars, 4g fiber), 4g pro. **DIABETIC EXCHANGES:** 1 starch, 1 fat.

CAPRESE PASTA SALAD

This easy pasta salad is always a favorite, especially when summer tomatoes are at their peak. It comes together quickly, but if you can make it ahead of time, the flavors seem to get better after it's chilled for a few hours.
—*Debby Harden, Lansing, MI*

- -

PREP: 35 min. • **MAKES:** 17 servings

- 1 pkg. (16 oz.) penne pasta
- 3 large heirloom tomatoes (about 2 lbs.), seeded and chopped
- ¾ lb. fresh mozzarella cheese, cut into ½-in. pieces
- ½ cup loosely packed basil leaves, chopped
- ⅓ cup olive oil
- ¼ cup lemon juice
- 1 shallot, finely chopped
- 1 garlic clove, minced
- 1 tsp. sugar
- ¾ tsp. salt
- ½ tsp. grated lemon zest
- ¼ tsp. pepper

1. Cook pasta according to the package directions. Drain and rinse in cold water. Transfer to a large bowl. Gently stir in the tomatoes, cheese and basil.
2. In a small bowl, whisk the remaining ingredients. Drizzle over salad and toss to coat. Refrigerate until serving.
TO MAKE AHEAD: Caprese pasta salad can be made ahead of time and stored covered in the fridge. For best results, use it within 3 to 4 days. For best results, wait to add the basil until you're ready to serve so it doesn't wilt.
¾ CUP: 204 cal., 9g fat (4g sat. fat), 16mg chol., 137mg sod., 23g carb. (3g sugars, 2g fiber), 8g pro.

TEST KITCHEN TIP

There are many ways you can make this pasta salad your own! Try swapping a different pasta shape— such as farfalle, cavatappi or rotini—for the penne pasta. Or throw in a few additional ingredients. We recommend grilled chicken or some homemade pesto.

CORN & BLACK BEAN SALAD

GRANDMOTHER'S
CHICKEN & DUMPLINGS
PAGE 39

Soups & Sandwiches

Served separately or paired in a classic one-two combo, soups and sandwiches are a flexible option for busy meal planners. For lunch or a light dinner, these recipes can be prepared in under an hour or simmer all day to be ready when you are.

ALL-TIME FAVORITES

CHORIZO BURGERS

CHORIZO BURGERS

A chorizo burger? You bet! Pickled veggie toppers complement the spicy patties especially well.
—Robert J. Johnson, Chino Valley, AZ

- -

PREP: 20 min. + standing
GRILL: 15 min. • **MAKES:** 2 servings

- ⅓ cup sugar
- ⅓ cup water
- ⅓ cup cider vinegar
- ½ large red onion, halved and thinly sliced
- 1 jalapeno pepper, seeded and sliced
- 6 oz. ground beef or bison
- ¼ lb. fresh chorizo or bulk spicy pork sausage
- ¼ tsp. salt
- ¼ tsp. pepper
- 2 sesame seed hamburger buns, split
- ½ cup fresh baby spinach
- 2 Tbsp. peeled and grated horseradish

1. In a large bowl, whisk sugar, water and vinegar together until sugar is dissolved. Add red onion and jalapeno; let stand at least 1 hour.
2. Combine beef and chorizo; shape mixture into two ¾-in.-thick patties. Sprinkle with salt and pepper.
3. Grill burgers, covered, over medium heat until a thermometer reads 160°, 6-8 minutes on each side. Grill buns over medium heat, cut side down, until toasted, 30-60 seconds.
4. Drain pickled vegetables. Serve burgers on buns with spinach, pickled vegetables and horseradish.
1 BURGER: 555 cal., 30g fat (11g sat. fat), 103mg chol., 1264mg sod., 36g carb. (10g sugars, 5g fiber), 34g pro.

AIR-FRYER PECAN CHICKEN SLIDERS

I love coating chicken in pecans instead of breadcrumbs because it gives such a wonderful crunch and flavor. If you don't have an air fryer you can bake the chicken in the oven for the same great taste.
—Amy Freeze, Avon Park, FL

- -

PREP: 30 min. • **COOK:** 10 min./batch
MAKES: 2 dozen

- 12 small boneless skinless chicken thighs (about 2 lbs.)
- 4 cups finely chopped pecans
- 1 large egg, beaten
- ¼ cup 2% milk
- 1 tsp. salt
- 1 tsp. pepper
- 2 to 3 dashes hot pepper sauce, such as Tabasco
  Cooking spray

BOURBON BERRY JAM
- 1 pkg. (16 oz.) frozen unsweetened mixed berries
- 1 cup sugar
- ⅓ cup bourbon
- ¼ cup cornstarch

SLAW
- 1 pkg. (16 oz.) tri-color coleslaw mix
- ½ cup mayonnaise
- 3 Tbsp. sugar
- 3 Tbsp. lime juice
- 2 pkg. (12 oz. each) Hawaiian sweet rolls, split

1. Preheat air fryer to 375°. Flatten the chicken to ½-in. thickness; cut each thigh in half. Place pecans in a shallow dish. In another shallow dish, whisk together egg, milk, salt, pepper and pepper sauce. Dip each chicken piece in the egg mixture, then coat with pecans.
2. In batches, arrange chicken in a single layer on greased tray in air-fryer basket; spritz with cooking spray. Cook until golden brown, 8-10 minutes, turning once.
3. Meanwhile, combine jam ingredients in a saucepan over medium-high heat. Bring to a boil, reduce heat and simmer until thick, 1-2 minutes. Remove from heat; crush berries to desired consistency.
4. For slaw, in a large bowl, combine coleslaw mix, mayonnaise, sugar and lime juice. To assemble, spoon 1 heaping Tbsp. jam onto bottom of each roll. Layer with hot chicken and slaw; replace tops.
1 SLIDER: 335 cal., 18g fat (4g sat. fat), 42mg chol., 228mg sod., 33g carb. (19g sugars, 3g fiber), 11g pro.

AIR-FRYER PECAN CHICKEN SLIDERS

GRANDMOTHER'S
CHICKEN & DUMPLINGS

Make Dumplings

Rather than a filled dough, Amish-style dumplings are a broad, flat egg noodle with a tender texture.

Mix. The broth is essential. Using broth instead of water ensures your dumplings will be packed with flavor.

Knead. Work the dough until it just comes together and is slightly springy. Be patient and let the dough rest for a bit before rolling.

Roll and slice. Roll your dumplings thin and cut into squares with a pastry wheel or pizza cutter.

Boil. Add the dumplings to boiling (not just hot!) broth to cook fully.

GRANDMOTHER'S CHICKEN & DUMPLINGS

When I was a child, my grandmother could feed our entire large family with a single chicken—and lots of dumplings.
—Cathy Carroll, Bossier City, LA

PREP: 45 min. + standing • **COOK:** 30 min.
MAKES: 10 servings

- 1 large chicken (6 lbs.)
- 2 medium carrots, chopped
- 2 celery ribs, sliced
- 1 large onion, sliced
- 4 qt. water
- 2 Tbsp. white vinegar
- 2 tsp. salt

DUMPLINGS
- 2 cups all-purpose flour
- 1½ tsp. salt
- 1 large egg
- ½ cup reserved chicken broth
- ½ tsp. pepper

1. Place the chicken, carrots, celery and onion in a large Dutch oven or stockpot. Add water, vinegar and salt (adding more water, if necessary, to cover chicken). Bring to a boil. Reduce heat; cover and simmer until meat nearly falls from the bones. Remove chicken from broth; allow to cool. Strain broth, discarding vegetables and seasonings.

2. Remove meat from bones; discard skin and bones. Cut meat into bite-sized pieces; set aside and keep warm. Set aside 1 cup broth; cool to lukewarm.

3. To make dumplings, combine flour and salt. Make a well in flour mixture; add egg. Gradually stir ¼ cup of the reserved broth into the egg, picking up flour as you go. Continue until flour is used up, adding additional broth as needed until dough is consistency of pie dough. Pour any remaining reserved broth back into stockpot.

4. Turn dough onto a floured surface; knead in additional flour to make a stiff dough. Let dough rest for 15 minutes.

5. On a floured surface, roll out dough into a 17-in. square. Cut into 1-in. square pieces. Dust with additional flour; let dry for 30-60 minutes.

6. Bring broth to a boil (you should have about 4 qt.). Drop dumplings into boiling broth. Reduce heat; cover and simmer until a toothpick inserted into the center of a dumpling comes out clean (do not lift the cover while simmering), about 10 minutes. Uncover; add reserved chicken. Stir in pepper.

1 CUP: 310 cal., 9g fat (2g sat. fat), 114mg chol., 981mg sod., 22g carb. (2g sugars, 1g fiber), 34g pro.

GRILLED VEGETABLE PESTO SANDWICHES

Sandwiches are always a hit, and great during the hot summer months. Most of my family is vegetarian, so I created a delicious, healthy sandwich they could enjoy without sacrificing flavor. Adapt the ingredients to availability or personal tastes—different cheeses or vegetables, or Italian bread instead of ciabatta.

—*Tanya Mehta, Philadelphia, PA*

PREP: 25 min. • **GRILL:** 10 min. • **MAKES:** 2 servings

- 1 medium zucchini
- 1 yellow summer squash
- 1 medium sweet red pepper, quartered
- 1 medium onion, cut into ½-in. slices
- 1 Tbsp. olive oil
- 2 tsp. paprika
- 1 tsp. garlic powder
- 1 tsp. balsamic vinegar
- ½ tsp. salt
- ½ tsp. pepper
- 2 Tbsp. butter, softened
- 2 ciabatta rolls, split
- 2 Tbsp. prepared pesto
- 4 slices Asiago cheese
- ½ cup spring mix salad greens
- 6 large fresh basil leaves

1. Slice zucchini and summer squash lengthwise into ¼-in.-thick slices. Place in a large bowl with red pepper, onion, oil, paprika, garlic powder, vinegar, salt and pepper; toss to coat.
2. Grill vegetables on an oiled rack, covered, over medium heat, until crisp-tender, 3-4 minutes on each side. Remove and keep warm. Spread softened butter over cut sides of rolls. Grill rolls, cut side down, over medium heat until toasted, 30-60 seconds.
3. To assemble, spread pesto over roll bottoms. Layer with zucchini, squash, red pepper and onion. Top with cheese. Grill, covered, until cheese is melted, 1-2 minutes. Remove from heat; top with salad mix and basil. Replace roll top. Serve immediately.
1 SANDWICH: 748 cal., 37g fat (15g sat. fat), 58mg chol., 1476mg sod., 91g carb. (15g sugars, 9g fiber), 23g pro.

CHICKEN PARMESAN STROMBOLI

CHICKEN PARMESAN STROMBOLI

I love chicken Parmesan and my family loves stromboli, so one day I combined the two using a few convenience products. It turned out better than I could have hoped for. It's now a staple in our house.

—*Cyndy Gerken, Naples, FL*

PREP: 20 min. • **BAKE:** 20 min. • **MAKES:** 6 servings

- 4 frozen breaded chicken tenders (about 1½ oz. each)
- 1 tube (13.8 oz.) refrigerated pizza crust
- 8 slices part-skim mozzarella cheese
- ⅓ cup shredded Parmesan cheese
- 1 Tbsp. olive oil
- ½ tsp. garlic powder
- ¼ tsp. dried oregano
- ¼ tsp. pepper
  Marinara sauce, warmed

1. Prepare chicken tenders according to package directions. Preheat oven to 400°. Unroll pizza crust onto a parchment-lined baking sheet. Layer with the mozzarella, chicken tenders and Parmesan to within ½ in. of edges. Roll up jelly-roll style, starting with a short side; pinch seam to seal and tuck ends under. Combine olive oil, garlic powder, oregano and pepper; brush over top.
2. Bake until crust is dark golden brown, 18-22 minutes. Let stand 5 minutes before slicing. Serve with marinara sauce for dipping.
1 PIECE: 408 cal., 18g fat (7g sat. fat), 34mg chol., 859mg sod., 42g carb. (5g sugars, 2g fiber), 21g pro.

READER REVIEW

"This recipe is beyond delicious. It is the best stromboli I've ever made. This is one of those recipes that you're going to want to sneak into the fridge at midnight just to have more of. If I could give it higher than five stars I would!"

—SHELBY, TASTEOFHOME.COM

GRILLED VEGETABLE PESTO SANDWICHES

ASPARAGUS & EGG SALAD WITH WALNUTS & MINT

I found this recipe while I was hiding from a pot of brisket, which is the kind of thing that happens three days after Passover. That brisket was instantly relegated to a side dish.

—*Deb Perelman, New York, NY*

TAKES: 30 min. • **MAKES:** 4 servings

- 4 large eggs, cold
- ½ cup grated Parmesan cheese
- ½ cup finely chopped walnuts, toasted
- 1 tsp. grated lemon zest
- 1 tsp. kosher salt
- ½ tsp. coarsely ground pepper
- ½ tsp. crushed red pepper flakes
- 1 lb. fresh asparagus, trimmed
- ¼ cup fresh lemon juice
- ¼ cup lightly packed fresh mint leaves, chopped
- ¼ cup olive oil, preferably extra virgin

1. In a saucepan, bring to a boil enough water to cover eggs by an inch. Gently lower in the eggs and reduce heat to a simmer. Boil for 8½ minutes, then quickly transfer eggs to an ice-cold water bath. Leave them there while you prepare the other ingredients, but ideally for at least 10 minutes.

2. Place Parmesan, walnuts, and lemon zest in the bottom of a large bowl, along with 1 tsp. salt, ½ tsp. coarsely ground pepper, and ½ tsp. red pepper flakes. Stir to combine.

3. Cut the asparagus on a sharp angle into very thin slices and add to the Parmesan mixture. Add ¼ cup lemon juice and toss some more. Taste and adjust the flavors to your preference by adding more salt, pepper, red pepper flakes, or lemon juice. Add mint and olive oil; toss, adjusting seasoning again.

4. Peel eggs. Cut each in half, then cut each half into 6 to 8 chunks. Add to bowl with the asparagus and gently stir just to combine.

5. Eat as is, or scoop mixture onto 6 to 8 toasts or 3 large matzo sheets, halved into 6 more manageable toasts.

1 SERVING: 349 cal., 31g fat (6g sat. fat), 195mg chol., 740mg sod., 8g carb. (2g sugars, 2g fiber), 13g pro.

PRESSURE-COOKER SONORAN CLAM CHOWDER

Being from New England originally, I always appreciated a good rich clam chowder. But living in the Southwest the past 35 years, I have learned to appreciate Sonoran flavors. This recipe blends a comfort-food memory with my current home flavor profiles.

—*James Scott, Phoenix, AZ*

PREP: 35 min. • **COOK:** 5 min.
MAKES: 10 servings (2½ qt.)

- 6 thick-sliced peppered bacon strips, chopped
- 3 Tbsp. butter
- 1 medium onion, chopped
- 1 medium sweet red pepper, chopped
- 2 cans (4 oz. each) chopped green chiles
- 4 garlic cloves, minced
- 3 cans (6½ oz. each) chopped clams, undrained
- 4 cups diced Yukon Gold potatoes (about 1½ lbs.)
- ½ cup chicken stock
- 2 cups half-and-half cream
- 1 envelope taco seasoning
- 2 Tbsp. chopped fresh cilantro, divided

1. Select saute setting on a 6-qt. electric pressure cooker. Adjust for medium heat; add bacon. Cook until crisp, stirring occasionally. Remove with a slotted spoon; drain on paper towels. Discard drippings, reserving 2 Tbsp. in pot. Add butter to drippings in pressure cooker. Add onion, red pepper and chiles; cook and stir until tender, 7-9 minutes. Add garlic; cook 1 minute longer. Press cancel.

2. Drain clams, reserving juice. Pour juice into pressure cooker; set clams aside. Stir potatoes and stock into pressure cooker. Lock lid; close pressure-release valve. Adjust to pressure-cook on high for 4 minutes. Allow pressure to release naturally for 4 minutes; quick-release any remaining pressure.

3. Select saute setting and adjust for low heat. Add clams, cream, taco seasoning and 1 Tbsp. cilantro; simmer, uncovered, 4-5 minutes or until the mixture is heated through, stirring occasionally. Press cancel. Serve with reserved bacon and remaining 1 Tbsp. cilantro.

NOTE: This can also be served with a dollop of sour cream on top to add richness, and with tortilla chips as a twist on traditional oyster crackers.

1 CUP: 271 cal., 15g fat (7g sat. fat), 61mg chol., 935mg sod., 23g carb. (4g sugars, 2g fiber), 11g pro.

PRESSURE-COOKER SONORAN CLAM CHOWDER

CREAMY SWEET POTATO, APPLE & LEEK SOUP

❄ CREAMY SWEET POTATO, APPLE & LEEK SOUP

This soup is a total breeze to make—it's very doable for a weeknight dinner. Serve it up with a big green salad and you've got the perfect low-fuss meal. The leftovers are even better—the flavors become more pronounced over time—so I often enjoy it for lunch the next day, too.
—Liz Harris, Newburyport, MA

- -

PREP: 20 min. • **COOK:** 40 min.
MAKES: 4 servings

 2 Tbsp. extra virgin olive oil
 4 cups cubed peeled sweet potatoes
 1 cup thinly sliced leek
   (white portion only)
 1 medium apple, peeled and chopped
 2 garlic cloves, minced
 1 Tbsp. minced fresh gingerroot
 1 Tbsp. tomato paste
 ¾ tsp. salt
 ¼ tsp. paprika
 ¼ tsp. pepper
 4 cups vegetable stock
 ½ cup heavy whipping cream
CROUTONS
 2 cups cubed bread (rustic Italian or
   French)
 2 Tbsp. grated Parmesan cheese
 4½ tsp. extra virgin olive oil
 ⅛ tsp. pepper
TOPPING
 2 Tbsp. minced fresh parsley
 2 Tbsp. heavy whipping cream

1. In a Dutch oven, heat oil over medium-high heat. Add potatoes, leeks and apple; cook, stirring occasionally, until leeks are just tender, 7-8 minutes.
2. Stir in the garlic, ginger, tomato paste, salt, paprika and pepper; cook until very fragrant, 2-3 minutes. Stir in the stock, scraping any browned bits from bottom of pot. Bring mixture to a boil; reduce heat and simmer, covered with the lid slightly ajar, until the potatoes are very soft, 25-30 minutes. Remove from heat; cool slightly. Process in a blender or food processor until smooth; return to pan. Stir in cream; heat through.
3. Meanwhile, for croutons, preheat oven to 350°. In a large bowl, toss bread cubes with Parmesan cheese, oil and pepper. Spread in a single layer on a 15x10x1-in. baking pan. Bake until golden brown and crispy, 10-15 minutes, stirring once. Serve hot soup with croutons, parsley and cream.

FREEZE OPTION: Freeze cooled soup in freezer containers. To use, partially thaw in refrigerator overnight. Heat through in a saucepan, stirring occasionally; add broth or cream if necessary.
1½ CUPS: 451 cal., 27g fat (11g sat. fat), 45mg chol., 1235mg sod., 48g carb. (12g sugars, 6g fiber), 6g pro.

⏱ BURGER SLIDERS WITH SECRET SAUCE

These sliders are super easy to put together and are always a hit! I love that they are fast food without having to go to a restaurant. Take them to a party, make them for dinner or serve them on game day. The meat can also be made ahead of time in preparation for your gathering.
—April Lee Wiencek, Chicago, IL

- -

TAKES: 30 min. • **MAKES:** 12 sliders

 2 large eggs, beaten
 ¾ cup minced onion, divided
 2 tsp. garlic powder
 1 tsp. salt
 1 tsp. pepper
 2 lbs. ground beef
 1 pkg. (17 oz.) dinner rolls
 ½ cup Thousand Island salad dressing,
   divided
 10 slices American cheese
 12 sliced dill pickles
 1½ cups shredded iceberg lettuce
 1 Tbsp. butter, melted
 1 Tbsp. sesame seeds, toasted

1. Preheat oven to 350°. In a large bowl, combine eggs, ½ cup minced onion, garlic powder, salt and pepper. Add ground beef; mix lightly but thoroughly. Place meat mixture on a large parchment-lined baking sheet; shape meat into two 6x8-in. rectangles, each about ½ in. thick. Bake until a thermometer reads 160°, 15-20 minutes.
2. Meanwhile, without separating rolls, cut bread in half horizontally. Spread ¼ cup of dressing evenly over bottom halves of rolls.
3. Blot meat with paper towels to remove excess fat; top meat with cheese and return to oven. Bake until cheese has just melted, 2-3 minutes.
4. Place meat on bottom halves of rolls; spread with remaining ¼ cup dressing. Layer with pickles, remaining ¼ cup minced onion and shredded lettuce; replace with top halves of rolls. Brush butter on top of rolls and sprinkle with sesame seeds; cut into sandwiches. Serve immediately.
1 SLIDER: 397 cal., 21g fat (8g sat. fat), 105mg chol., 785mg sod., 26g carb. (6g sugars, 2g fiber), 22g pro.

BURGER SLIDERS
WITH SECRET SAUCE

CHIPOTLE
BEEF CHILI

FLAVORFUL WHITE
CHICKEN CHILI

SWEET POTATO &
BLACK BEAN CHILI

Just Chillin'

Before the big game kicks off, hold a competition of your own. Invite each member of your crew to bring their twist on chili, then pile on the toppings and tally up the scorecards. Hello, bragging rights!

SWEET POTATO & BLACK BEAN CHILI

My whole family enjoys this chili, but my daughter especially loves it. I like to make it because it's so easy and very flavorful.
—Joy Pendley, Ortonville, MI

- -

PREP: 25 min. • **COOK:** 30 min.
MAKES: 8 servings (2 qt.)

- 1 Tbsp. olive oil
- 3 large sweet potatoes, peeled and cut into ½-in. cubes
- 1 large onion, chopped
- 2 Tbsp. chili powder
- 3 garlic cloves, minced
- 1 tsp. ground cumin
- ¼ tsp. cayenne pepper
- 2 cans (15 oz. each) black beans, rinsed and drained
- 1 can (28 oz.) diced tomatoes, undrained
- ¼ cup brewed coffee
- 2 Tbsp. honey
- ½ tsp. salt
- ¼ tsp. pepper
  Optional: Shredded Monterey Jack cheese, shredded Mexican cheese blend, pickled red onions and thinly sliced green onions

1. In a nonstick Dutch oven, heat oil over medium heat. Add sweet potatoes and onions. Cook and stir until crisp-tender, 8-10 minutes. Add chili powder, garlic, cumin and cayenne; cook and stir 1 minute longer. Stir in beans, tomatoes, coffee, honey, salt and pepper.
2. Bring to a boil. Reduce heat; cover and simmer until the sweet potatoes are tender, 30-35 minutes. Serve with toppings as desired.
1 CUP: 283 cal., 2g fat (0 sat. fat), 0 chol., 579mg sod., 59g carb. (22g sugars, 11g fiber), 9g pro.

FLAVORFUL WHITE CHICKEN CHILI

 Lime, cumin and cilantro add a nice punch to this chicken chili. It's a healthier twist on classic chili that you're sure to love.
—Donna Lindecamp, Morganton, NC

- -

PREP: 25 min. • **COOK:** 1 hour
MAKES: 7 servings

- 2 cans (14½ oz. each) chicken broth
- 3 bone-in chicken breast halves (8 oz. each), skin removed
- 1 large onion, chopped
- 2 garlic cloves, minced
- 1 tsp. ground cumin
- 1 tsp. dried oregano
- ¼ tsp. salt
- ¼ tsp. cayenne pepper
- 2 cans (15½ oz. each) great northern beans, rinsed and drained
- 1½ cups frozen corn or frozen white corn
- ⅓ cup lime juice
  Optional: Shredded cheddar cheese, sour cream, minced fresh cilantro and tortilla strips

1. In a Dutch oven, combine the first 8 ingredients. Bring to a boil. Reduce the heat; cover and simmer until a thermometer inserted in the chicken reads 170°, 35-40 minutes. Remove chicken from broth; allow to cool.
2. Remove meat from bones; discard bones. Shred chicken and return to pan. Mash half the beans. Add all the beans, corn and lime juice to chicken mixture. Return to a boil. Reduce heat; cover and simmer 15-20 minutes or until flavors are blended. Serve with toppings as desired.
1 CUP: 224 cal., 3g fat (1g sat. fat), 41mg chol., 803mg sod., 28g carb. (2g sugars, 7g fiber), 22g pro. **DIABETIC EXCHANGES:** 3 lean meat, 2 starch.

CHIPOTLE BEEF CHILI

I love spicy food, so this chili really hits the spot. If you are sensitive to chile peppers, start out with fewer chipotles.
—Steven Schend, Grand Rapids, MI

- -

PREP: 15 min. • **COOK:** 6 hours
MAKES: 10 servings (about 3 qt.)

- 4 lbs. beef flank steak, cut into 1-in. pieces
- 2 to 4 chipotle peppers in adobo sauce, chopped
- ¼ cup chopped onion
- 1 Tbsp. chili powder
- 2 garlic cloves, minced
- 1 tsp. salt
- ½ tsp. ground cumin
- 3 cans (15 oz. each) tomato puree
- 1 can (14½ oz.) beef broth
- ¼ cup minced fresh cilantro
  Optional: Cotija cheese, sliced jalapeno peppers and sliced radishes

In a 4- or 5-qt. slow cooker, combine the first 9 ingredients. Cook, covered, on low until meat is tender, 6-8 hours. Stir in cilantro. Serve with toppings as desired.
FREEZE OPTION: Freeze cooled chili in freezer containers. To use, partially thaw in refrigerator overnight. Heat through in a saucepan, stirring occasionally; add broth or water if necessary.
1¼ CUPS: 230 cal., 9g fat (4g sat. fat), 54mg chol., 668mg sod., 12g carb. (3g sugars, 2g fiber), 25g pro. **DIABETIC EXCHANGES:** 3 lean meat, 2 vegetable.

READER REVIEW

"This was very easy and very tasty! For our liking, I added 1 Tbsp. more of the chili powder. Will use this again!"
—KARENKEEFE, TASTEOFHOME.COM

CAJUN POPCORN SHRIMP SANDWICHES

You can adjust the heat level in these seafood sandwiches by tweaking the amount of seasoning and hot sauce. I use even more hot sauce for dipping!

—Kent Whitaker, Rossville, GA

TAKES: 30 min. • **MAKES:** 4 servings

- 2 Tbsp. butter, melted
- 1 tsp. garlic powder
- ¼ to ½ tsp. Cajun seasoning
- 3½ cups frozen breaded popcorn shrimp
- ½ cup mayonnaise
- 1 Tbsp. hot pepper sauce
- 1 tsp. sweet pickle relish
- ½ tsp. prepared mustard
- 8 pita pocket halves, warmed
- 1 cup shredded lettuce
- 8 thin slices tomato

1. In a bowl, combine butter, garlic powder and Cajun seasoning. Toss with shrimp. Prepare shrimp according to package directions for baking.
2. Combine the mayonnaise, pepper sauce, relish and mustard. Spread into warmed pitas. Fill pitas with shrimp, lettuce and tomato slices.

2 FILLED PITA HALVES: 668 cal., 40g fat (8g sat. fat), 96mg chol., 1139mg sod., 58g carb. (5g sugars, 3g fiber), 18g pro.

SHORTCUT MEATBALL & TORTELLINI MINESTRONE SOUP

This hearty soup is quick to prepare with shortcut ingredients and ready in less than an hour. Add a salad and a warm, crusty loaf of bread or breadsticks to round out the meal.

—Joan Hallford, North Richland Hills, TX

TAKES: 30 min.
MAKES: 8 servings (2¾ qt.)

- 2 cans (14½ oz. each) beef broth
- 1 jar (24 oz.) marinara sauce
- 3 cups frozen mixed vegetables, thawed
- 1 can (15½ oz.) navy beans, rinsed and drained
- 24 frozen fully cooked Italian meatballs, thawed
- 5 oz. frozen chopped spinach, thawed and squeezed dry (about ½ cup)
- 1 pkg. (9 oz.) refrigerated cheese tortellini
   Shredded Parmesan cheese

In a Dutch oven, combine broth, marinara sauce and mixed vegetables. Bring to a boil; add beans, meatballs and spinach. Simmer, uncovered, for 5 minutes. Stir in tortellini; cook 7 minutes longer. Serve with Parmesan cheese.

1⅓ CUPS: 384 cal., 15g fat (6g sat. fat), 36mg chol., 1467mg sod., 44g carb. (7g sugars, 9g fiber), 21g pro.

SUPREME PIZZA SOUP

SUPREME PIZZA SOUP

A local restaurant serves a delicious baked tomato soup that tastes like a cheese pizza; I took it a step further and added all the fixings of a supreme pizza. Add your favorite pizza toppings to make it your own. If you can't find tomato and sweet basil bisque try using canned tomato bisque and add Italian seasoning.

—Susan Bickta, Kutztown, PA

TAKES: 30 min. • **MAKES:** 6 servings (2 qt.)

- 6 slices frozen garlic Texas toast
- 2 oz. bulk Italian sausage
- ¼ cup chopped onion
- ¼ cup chopped green pepper
- ⅓ cup sliced pepperoni, chopped
- 3 containers (15½ oz. each) ready-to-serve tomato-basil soup
- 1 cup whole milk
- 2 plum tomatoes, peeled and chopped
- 12 slices provolone cheese
- 18 slices pepperoni
- 6 Tbsp. grated Parmesan cheese

1. Prepare Texas toast according to package directions. Meanwhile, in a large saucepan, cook sausage, onion and green pepper over medium-high heat until sausage is no longer pink and vegetables are tender, about 5 minutes, breaking sausage into crumbles. Add chopped pepperoni; cook 3 minutes longer. Stir in soup, milk and tomatoes; heat through.
2. Place six 10-oz. broiler-safe bowls or ramekins on a baking sheet. Ladle soup into bowls; top each with 1 toast, 2 slices cheese and 3 pepperoni slices; sprinkle with Parmesan. Broil 4 in. from heat until cheese is melted.

1⅓ CUPS: 576 cal., 32g fat (14g sat. fat), 60mg chol., 1548mg sod., 51g carb. (18g sugars, 3g fiber), 24g pro.

CAJUN POPCORN SHRIMP SANDWICHES

COPYCAT FRIED CHICKEN SANDWICH

After trying all the major fast-food chains' chicken sandwiches, I decided to come up with my own version. I know everyone says theirs is better than the original, but mine really is.
—Ralph Jones, San Diego, CA

- -

PREP: 15 min. + marinating
COOK: 20 min./batch • **MAKES:** 6 servings

- 3 boneless skinless chicken breast halves (6 oz. each)
- ¾ cup buttermilk
- 2 tsp. hot pepper sauce
- 2 large eggs, beaten
- 2 cups all-purpose flour
- 1 Tbsp. plus 1 tsp. garlic powder
- 1 Tbsp. each onion powder and paprika
- 2 tsp. pepper
- 1 tsp. salt
- ⅓ cup canola oil
- 6 brioche hamburger buns, split
  Optional: Shredded lettuce, sliced tomatoes, pickle slices, onion slices and mayonnaise

1. Cut each chicken breast horizontally in half; place in a large bowl. Add buttermilk and hot sauce; toss to coat. Refrigerate, covered, 8 hours or overnight.
2. Preheat air fryer to 400°. Stir the eggs into chicken mixture (temporarily remove chicken if necessary). In a shallow dish, whisk flour, garlic powder, onion powder, paprika, pepper and salt. Remove chicken from buttermilk mixture. Dredge chicken in the flour mixture, firmly patting to help coating adhere. Repeat, dipping chicken again in the buttermilk mixture and then dredging in the flour mixture.
3. Place chicken on a wire rack over a baking sheet. Refrigerate, uncovered, for 30 minutes. Using a pastry brush, lightly dab both sides of chicken with oil until no dry breading remains.
4. In batches, arrange chicken in a single layer on greased tray in air-fryer basket. Cook 7-8 minutes on each side or until a thermometer reads 165° and coating is golden brown and crispy. Remove chicken; keep warm.
5. Toast buns in air fryer until golden brown, 2-3 minutes. Top bun bottoms with the chicken. If desired, serve with optional toppings.

1 SANDWICH: 384 cal., 17g fat (3g sat. fat), 136mg chol., 777mg sod., 31g carb. (8g sugars, 3g fiber), 26g pro.

TEST KITCHEN TIP

Deep-frying isn't as healthy as air-frying, but it works well as an alternative. To deep-fry the chicken, follow the same steps to prepare and bread the chicken, then fry it in batches in 375° oil until it's golden brown and no longer pink, 5-7 minutes.

COPYCAT FRIED
CHICKEN SANDWICH

SEAFOOD CHOWDER WITH SEASONED OYSTER CRACKERS

SEAFOOD CHOWDER WITH SEASONED OYSTER CRACKERS

Full of fish, shrimp and scallops, this comforting chowder has been pleasing my family for many years. The seasoned oyster crackers add a bit of spice.
—*Virginia Anthony, Jacksonville, FL*

PREP: 45 min. • **COOK:** 25 min.
MAKES: 12 servings (4½ qt.)

- 1 Tbsp. unsalted butter, melted
- 1 Tbsp. marinade for chicken
- 1 tsp. hot pepper sauce
- ¼ tsp. curry powder
- ¼ tsp. paprika
- 1¼ cups oyster crackers
CHOWDER
- 8 bacon strips, chopped
- 1½ lbs. red potatoes, cut into ½-in. cubes
- 2 cups thinly sliced leeks (white portion only)
- ¼ cup all-purpose flour
- ¾ tsp. dried thyme
- 1 carton (32 oz.) reduced-sodium chicken broth
- 4 cups clam juice
- 1 pkg. (12 oz.) frozen corn
- 1½ cups diced zucchini
- 1 lb. grouper or tilapia fillets, cut into 1-in. cubes
- ¾ lb. uncooked medium shrimp, peeled and deveined
- ½ lb. bay scallops
- 1 cup half-and-half cream
- 1 tsp. salt
- ¼ tsp. white pepper

1. Preheat oven to 350°. In a small bowl, combine the butter, marinade, pepper sauce, curry and paprika. Add crackers; toss to coat.

2. Transfer to a greased 15x10x1-in. baking pan. Bake 8-10 minutes or until golden brown, stirring twice. Set aside.

3. In a stockpot, cook bacon over medium heat until crisp. Using a slotted spoon, remove to paper towels to drain.

4. Saute potatoes and leeks in bacon drippings; stir in flour and thyme until blended. Gradually whisk in broth and clam juice. Bring to a boil, stirring constantly. Cook and stir 1-2 minutes longer. Reduce heat; cover and simmer for 10 minutes or until potatoes are tender.

5. Add the corn, zucchini, grouper, shrimp and scallops; cook until fish flakes easily with a fork, 2-4 minutes. Stir in the cream, salt and pepper; heat through. Serve with crackers and bacon.

1½ CUPS: 295 cal., 12g fat (5g sat. fat), 80mg chol., 885mg sod., 25g carb. (3g sugars, 2g fiber), 22g pro.

TURKEY, BACON & CORN CHOWDER

This recipe uses lots of Thanksgiving leftovers to create a thick turkey chowder. My grandmother always made her own stock with the turkey carcass, but prepared chicken stock makes preparation easier. Every so often, my grandmother would even add chopped hard-boiled eggs to this chowder, which gave it a nice richness.
—*Susan Bickta, Kutztown, PA*

PREP: 25 min. • **COOK:** 50 min.
MAKES: 16 servings (4 qt.)

- 1 lb. thick-sliced bacon strips, chopped
- 3 celery ribs, sliced
- 1 medium onion, chopped
- 1 medium carrot, chopped
- ½ cup chopped red onion
- 1 bay leaf
- ¼ cup all-purpose flour
- 1 carton (32 oz.) chicken stock
- 1 can (10½ oz.) condensed cream of chicken soup, undiluted
- 1 pkg. (8 oz.) cream cheese, softened
- ¾ cup whole milk
- ¾ cup heavy whipping cream
- 3½ cups frozen corn (about 17.5 oz.)
- 2½ cups cubed cooked turkey
- 2 cups refrigerated shredded hash brown potatoes (about 10 oz.)
- ¾ cup turkey gravy
- 1 Tbsp. dried parsley flakes
  Thinly sliced green onions, optional

1. In a Dutch oven, cook bacon over medium heat until crisp, stirring occasionally. Remove with a slotted spoon; drain on paper towels. Discard drippings, reserving ¼ cup in pot.

2. Add celery, onion, carrot, red onion and bay leaf; cook and stir over medium-high heat until vegetables are tender, 8-10 minutes.

3. Stir in flour until blended; gradually whisk in stock. Bring to a boil, stirring constantly; cook and stir 2 minutes. Add soup, cream cheese, milk and cream; mix well. Stir in corn, turkey, hash browns, gravy, parsley and ¾ cup reserved bacon; reduce heat. Cook, covered, 20 minutes, stirring occasionally.

4. Discard bay leaf. Serve with remaining bacon and, if desired, green onions.

1 CUP: 289 cal., 19g fat (9g sat. fat), 63mg chol., 603mg sod., 17g carb. (4g sugars, 2g fiber), 14g pro.

ROCK & RYE PORK ROAST SANDWICHES

Detroit's Faygo Rock & Rye soda (or pop, as we call it in Michigan) gives these pork roast sandwiches such distinctive flavor with notes of vanilla and cherry. These sandwiches are a hit at summer picnics and Faygo pop brings back fond memories of growing up in Michigan.
—*Jennifer Gilbert, Brighton, MI*

PREP: 20 min. • **COOK:** 2 hours 5 min. • **MAKES:** 8 servings

- ½ tsp. garlic salt
- ½ tsp. paprika
- ½ tsp. pepper
- 1 boneless pork shoulder butt roast (1 to 2 lbs.)
- 4 cups Faygo Rock & Rye soda or cherry vanilla cream soda
- 1 cup ketchup
- 3 Tbsp. steak sauce
- 2 Tbsp. liquid smoke
- 1 Tbsp. light brown sugar
- 1 Tbsp. cider vinegar
- 8 hamburger buns, split

1. Preheat oven to 300°. Combine garlic salt, paprika and pepper; rub over roast. Place in an ovenproof Dutch oven; add soda. Bake, covered, until pork is tender, 2-2¼ hours.

2. Remove roast; shred with 2 forks. Skim fat from cooking juices. Return 1 cup juices to the pot. Add ketchup, steak sauce, liquid smoke, brown sugar and vinegar. Bring to a boil; cook for 5 minutes. Return meat to pot; heat through. Adjust with additional cooking juices as desired. Serve on hamburger buns.

FREEZE OPTION: Freeze cooled meat mixture and juices in freezer containers. To use, partially thaw in refrigerator overnight. Heat through in a saucepan, stirring occasionally; add water if necessary.

1 SANDWICH: 273 cal., 7g fat (2g sat. fat), 34mg chol., 864mg sod., 37g carb. (17g sugars, 1g fiber), 14g pro.

ROCK & RYE PORK ROAST SANDWICHES

CAPRESE SANDWICH

CAPRESE SANDWICH

This is a staple sandwich in my family that we make several times a month when things are hectic and we need a fast, fresh and healthy meal. It's always a hit! The sandwiches are excellent for a warm-weather dinner when you don't want to turn on your oven, or for a picnic lunch. Pair with a crisp, fruity white wine and a pasta salad or fancy potato chips.
—*Stacey Johnson, Tacoma, WA*

TAKES: 15 min. • **MAKES:** 4 servings

- 6 Tbsp. wasabi mayonnaise or plain mayonnaise
- 8 slices sourdough bread (½-in. thick), toasted
- 2 large heirloom tomatoes, sliced
- ½ tsp. sea salt
- ½ tsp. coarsely ground pepper
- ½ large sweet onion, thinly sliced
- 8 oz. fresh mozzarella cheese, sliced
- ½ cup fresh basil leaves

Spread mayonnaise on 1 side of each slice of toast. Top half the toast slices with tomatoes, salt and pepper. Add onion, mozzarella and basil; top with remaining bread slices.

1 SANDWICH: 463 cal., 29g fat (11g sat. fat), 52mg chol., 753mg sod., 34g carb. (6g sugars, 2g fiber), 17g pro.

TEST KITCHEN TIP

If you want to add protein to this sandwich, go with grilled chicken, salami or prosciutto. Otherwise, grilled or roasted eggplant would make the sandwich a bit more hearty.

Make Veggie Burgers

Raising a veggie burger to the status of "best ever" involves just a couple of extra steps to improve the texture and elevate the flavors.

Bake the beans. Don't skip this step! Baking the beans gives the burger more texture and that pleasant, firmer bite.

Toast and saute. Enhance the flavor of your spices and nuts with a quick toast. Then pop the shallots and carrots into the same pan.

Shape up. Give the ingredients a quick spin in a food processor and then shape the patties. No need to chill these—head right to the pan!

Fry 'em. A few minutes on each side is all they need. Finish with a bit of barbecue sauce

BEST EVER VEGGIE BURGER

It was so hard finding a veggie burger that tasted good, didn't fall apart on the grill and was easy to make—so I decided to create my own.
—Sarah Tramonte, Milwaukee, WI

- -

PREP: 30 min. • **COOK:** 10 min.
MAKES: 4 servings

- 1 cup canned black beans, rinsed and drained
- 1 cup chopped walnuts
- 1½ tsp. ground cumin
- ½ tsp. ground fennel seed
- ¼ tsp. smoked paprika
- 1 Tbsp. oil from sun-dried tomatoes
- ¼ cup shredded carrot
- 1 large shallot, minced
- 2 Tbsp. oil-packed sun-dried tomatoes, chopped
- 1 garlic clove, minced
- ¼ cup old-fashioned oats
- 1 Tbsp. chia seeds
- 2 tsp. reduced-sodium soy sauce
- ½ tsp. garlic salt
- 1 Tbsp. olive oil
   Optional: Barbecue sauce, toasted hamburger buns, Sriracha mayo, lettuce, red onion and tomato

1. Preheat oven to 325°. Spread beans evenly on a parchment-lined rimmed baking pan. Bake until beans start to split open, 6-8 minutes.

2. Meanwhile, in a large dry nonstick skillet over medium heat, cook and stir walnuts, cumin, fennel and smoked paprika until fragrant, 2-3 minutes. Remove from pan and cool.

3. In the same skillet, heat the oil from the sun-dried tomatoes over medium heat. Add carrot, shallot and sun-dried tomatoes; cook and stir until tender, about 5 minutes. Add the garlic; cook 1 minute longer. Remove from the heat; cool slightly.

4. Transfer carrot mixture to a food processor. Add beans, walnut mixture, oats, chia seeds, soy sauce and garlic salt. Pulse until combined. Shape into four 4-in. patties.

5. In the same skillet over medium heat, cook patties in olive oil until browned, 3-4 minutes on each side. If desired, baste with barbecue sauce and serve on buns with toppings of your choice.

1 BURGER: 357 cal., 28g fat (3g sat. fat), 0 chol., 479mg sod., 22g carb. (2g sugars, 7g fiber), 9g pro.

READER REVIEW

"I have made these 3 times. People love these burgers. You do have to be a little careful when cooking them, but it is worth it."
—SHELEIGH144, TASTEOFHOME.COM

BEST EVER VEGGIE BURGER

SLOW-COOKED BARBECUED BEEF SANDWICHES

❄️ CHIPOTLE CARROT SOUP

This vegetarian soup packs big flavor, and I love that it is made in just one pot. The cilantro and Cotija balance the heat from the chipotles in adobo sauce, but if you prefer mild seasoning, use as little as one teaspoon of the adobo sauce.
—*Rebecca Jennex, Madison Heights, MI*

PREP: 15 min. • **COOK:** 40 min. • **MAKES:** 10 servings (2½ qt.)

- 1   Tbsp. olive oil
- 1   medium onion, chopped
- 2   garlic cloves, minced
- 2   tsp. adobo sauce from canned chipotle peppers
- 1½ tsp. salt
- ½   tsp. adobo seasoning
- ¾   tsp. ground cumin
- ½   tsp. pepper
- 2   lbs. carrots, chopped
- 6   cups vegetable stock
- ½   cup roasted sweet red peppers, chopped
- 1   Tbsp. lime juice
- ½   cup Cotija cheese
- ¼   cup minced fresh cilantro
     Lime wedges, optional

1. In a Dutch oven heat oil over medium-high heat. Add onion; cook and stir until tender, 3-4 minutes. Add garlic; cook 1 minute longer. Stir in adobo sauce, salt, adobo seasoning, cumin and pepper. Add carrots and stock; bring to a boil. Reduce heat. Simmer, covered, until carrots are tender, about 20 minutes.
2. Add roasted peppers; remove soup from heat. Cool slightly. Process in batches in blender or food processor until smooth. Return to pan; stir in lime juice. Heat through. Serve with Cotija cheese, cilantro and, if desired, lime wedges.
FREEZE OPTION: Before adding toppings, cool soup. Freeze soup in freezer containers. To use, partially thaw in refrigerator overnight. Heat through in a saucepan, stirring occasionally; add broth if necessary. Sprinkle with toppings.
1 CUP: 88 cal., 3g fat (1g sat. fat), 6mg chol., 967mg sod., 12g carb. (5g sugars, 3g fiber), 2g pro.

🍲 ❄️ SLOW-COOKED BARBECUED BEEF SANDWICHES

Chuck roast makes delicious shredded beef sandwiches after simmering in a rich homemade sauce all day. The meat really is tender and juicy, and it only takes minutes to prepare.
—*Tatina Smith, San Angelo, TX*

PREP: 20 min. • **COOK:** 8¼ hours • **MAKES:** 12 servings

- 1   boneless beef chuck roast (3 lbs.)
- 1½ cups ketchup
- ¼   cup packed brown sugar
- ¼   cup barbecue sauce
- 2   Tbsp. Worcestershire sauce
- 2   Tbsp. Dijon mustard
- 1   tsp. liquid smoke, optional
- ½   tsp. salt
- ¼   tsp. garlic powder
- ¼   tsp. pepper
- 12 sandwich buns, split
     Optional: Sliced onions, dill pickles and pickled jalapenos

1. Cut roast in half and place in a 3- or 4-qt. slow cooker. In a small bowl, combine ketchup, brown sugar, barbecue sauce, Worcestershire sauce, mustard, liquid smoke if desired, and seasonings. Pour over beef.
2. Cook, covered, on low for 8-10 hours or until meat is tender. Remove meat; cool slightly. Skim fat from cooking liquid.
3. Shred beef with 2 forks; return to the slow cooker. Cover and cook for 15 minutes or until heated through. Using a slotted spoon, place ½ cup beef on each bun. Serve with onions, pickles and jalapenos if desired.
FREEZE OPTION: Place individual portions of the cooled meat mixture in freezer containers. To use, partially thaw in the refrigerator overnight. Microwave, covered, on high in a microwave-safe dish until heated through, gently stirring; add broth or water if necessary.
1 SANDWICH: 458 cal., 15g fat (5g sat. fat), 74mg chol., 1052mg sod., 49g carb. (18g sugars, 1g fiber), 30g pro.

CHIPOTLE CARROT SOUP

**SMOKED KIELBASA
WITH RICE**
PAGE 66

Quick Fixes

You can still sit down to a hearty homemade dinner, no matter what the day has thrown at you. Turn here for go-to meals perfect for when you're pressed for time—each clocks in at 30 minutes or less.

CHECK OUT THESE SPECIALTIES

HAMBURGER STEAKS WITH MUSHROOM GRAVY

Here's a meat-and-potatoes meal that no one will want to miss. It makes for a hearty dish the whole family will cozy up to in no time!
—*Denise Wheeler, Newaygo, MI*

TAKES: 25 min. • **MAKES:** 4 servings

- 1 large egg
- ½ cup dry bread crumbs
- 1 envelope onion soup mix, divided
  Dash pepper
- 1 lb. ground beef
- 3 Tbsp. all-purpose flour
- 1¾ cups cold water
- 1 tsp. Worcestershire sauce
- 1 jar (4½ oz.) whole mushrooms, drained
  Hot cooked mashed potatoes

1. In a large bowl, combine the egg, bread crumbs, 2 Tbsp. soup mix and pepper. Crumble beef over mixture and mix lightly but thoroughly. Shape into 4 patties.

2. In a large cast-iron or other heavy skillet, cook patties over medium heat until a thermometer reads 160°, and juices run clear, 4-5 minutes on each side. Set aside and keep warm.

3. Combine the flour, water, Worcestershire sauce and remaining soup mix until blended; stir into skillet. Add mushrooms. Bring to a boil; cook and stir until thickened, about 5 minutes. Serve sauce with patties and mashed potatoes.

1 PATTY WITH ½ CUP GRAVY: 325 cal., 15g fat (6g sat. fat), 123mg chol., 920mg sod., 20g carb. (2g sugars, 2g fiber), 25g pro.

ONE-POT SAUSAGE & BASIL PASTA

ONE-POT SAUSAGE & BASIL PASTA

There's nothing better than coming home and putting dinner on the table in 30 minutes. It's easy to add different kinds of sausage or seasonings to make this your own.
—*Erin Raatjes, New Lenox, IL*

TAKES: 30 min. • **MAKES:** 8 servings

- 1 pkg. (16 oz.) spaghetti
- 1 pkg. (13 to 14 oz.) smoked turkey sausage, thinly sliced
- 3 cups grape tomatoes, halved
- 2 cups fresh basil leaves, loosely packed
- 1 large onion, thinly sliced
- 4 garlic cloves, thinly sliced
- 4½ cups water
- 1 cup grated Parmesan cheese
- ¾ tsp. salt
- ½ tsp. pepper
- ¾ tsp. crushed red pepper flakes, optional

In a Dutch oven, combine the first 7 ingredients. Bring to a boil; reduce heat and simmer, uncovered, 8-10 minutes or until pasta is al dente, stirring occasionally. Stir in cheese, salt and pepper. If desired, mix in pepper flakes and top with additional Parmesan.

1 CUP: 332 cal., 6g fat (3g sat. fat), 37mg chol., 862mg sod., 49g carb. (5g sugars, 3g fiber), 19g pro.

READER REVIEW

"I was a little skeptical about putting everything in the pot at once but was quite pleasantly surprised with the results. Creamy, delicious sauce, nice bite with the onions, tasty sausage. Only thing I might do differently is add the basil at the end by tearing off pieces into the pot."
—RENEEMURBY994, TASTEOFHOME.COM

HAMBURGER STEAKS WITH MUSHROOM GRAVY

AIR-FRYER CHICKEN CORDON BLEU

My son loves chicken cordon bleu, but I'm not a fan of store-bought versions. My recipe has all the yummy flavors in a 30-minute meal. Leftovers freeze well.
—*Ronda Eagle, Goose Creek, SC*

TAKES: 30 min. • MAKES: 4 servings

4   boneless skinless chicken breast halves (4 oz. each)
¼   tsp. salt
¼   tsp. pepper
4   slices deli ham
2   slices aged Swiss cheese, halved
1   cup panko bread crumbs
    Cooking spray

SAUCE
1   Tbsp. all-purpose flour
½   cup 2% milk
¼   cup dry white wine
3   Tbsp. finely shredded Swiss cheese
⅛   tsp. salt
    Dash pepper

1. Preheat air fryer to 365°. Sprinkle chicken breasts with salt and pepper. Place on greased tray in air-fryer basket. Cook for 10 minutes. Top each chicken breast with 1 slice ham and ½ slice cheese, folding ham in half and covering chicken as much as possible. Sprinkle with bread crumbs. Carefully spritz crumbs with cooking spray. Cook until a thermometer inserted in chicken reads 165°, 5-7 minutes longer.
2. For sauce, in a small saucepan, whisk flour and milk until smooth. Bring to a boil, stirring constantly; cook and stir until thickened, 1-2 minutes.
3. Reduce to medium heat. Add wine and cheese; cook and stir 2-3 minutes or until cheese is melted and sauce is thickened and bubbly. Stir in salt and pepper. Keep warm over low heat until ready to serve. Serve with chicken.

1 CHICKEN BREAST HALF WITH 3 TBSP. SAUCE: 272 cal., 8g fat (3g sat. fat), 83mg chol., 519mg sod., 14g carb. (2g sugars, 1g fiber), 32g pro. **DIABETIC EXCHANGES:** 4 lean meat, 1 starch, 1 fat.

AIR-FRYER
CHICKEN
CORDON BLEU

CHEESEBURGER
QUESADILLAS

CHEESEBURGER QUESADILLAS

I created these fun cheeseburger quesadilla mashups in honor of my family's two favorite foods. They are so yummy and easy to make!
—*Jennifer Stowell, Deep River, IA*

TAKES: 25 min. • MAKES: 4 servings

1   lb. ground beef
1   cup ketchup
⅓   cup prepared mustard
4   bacon strips, cooked and crumbled
2   Tbsp. Worcestershire sauce
⅔   cup mayonnaise
2   Tbsp. 2% milk
2   Tbsp. dill pickle relish
¼   tsp. pepper
8   flour tortillas (8 in.)
1   cup shredded cheddar cheese
    Optional: Shredded lettuce and chopped tomatoes

1. In a large skillet, cook beef over medium heat, until no longer pink, 6-8 minutes, crumbling beef; drain. Stir in the ketchup, mustard, bacon and Worcestershire sauce; bring to a boil. Reduce heat; simmer, uncovered, 5-7 minutes or until slightly thickened, stirring occasionally.
2. Meanwhile, in a small bowl, combine mayonnaise, milk, relish and pepper.
3. Preheat griddle over medium heat. Sprinkle 4 tortillas with cheese; top with beef mixture and remaining tortillas. Place on griddle; cook until tortillas are golden brown and cheese is melted, 1-2 minutes on each side. Serve with sauce and, if desired, lettuce and tomatoes.

1 QUESADILLA WITH ABOUT ¼ CUP SAUCE: 1002 cal., 60g fat (17g sat. fat), 110mg chol., 2115mg sod., 75g carb. (18g sugars, 4g fiber), 39g pro.

30-MINUTE COQ AU VIN

I love being able to fix a fancy gourmet dish in such a short amount of time and still have it turn out so delicious. To reduce fat, use chicken tenderloin pieces or skinless chicken breasts. This recipe is really fabulous served with rice.

—Judy VanCoetsem, Cortland, NY

- -

TAKES: 30 min. • **MAKES:** 6 servings

¼ cup all-purpose flour
1 tsp. dried thyme
1 tsp. salt, divided
6 boneless skinless chicken thighs (4 oz. each)
1 Tbsp. olive oil
6 cups quartered baby portobello mushrooms
2 cups sliced fresh carrots
3 pieces Canadian bacon, chopped
1 Tbsp. tomato paste
1 cup chicken broth
1 cup dry red wine
Chopped fresh thyme, optional

1. In a shallow dish, combine flour, thyme and ½ tsp. salt. Dip the chicken in flour mixture to coat both sides; shake off excess.
2. In a Dutch oven or high-sided skillet, heat oil over medium-high heat. Cook chicken until golden brown, 3-4 minutes per side. Remove from pan; keep warm.
3. In same pan, cook mushrooms, carrots, bacon, tomato paste and remaining ½ tsp. salt for 2 minutes. Add broth and wine; bring to a boil. Return chicken to pan; reduce heat. Cook 8-10 minutes or until chicken reaches 170° and carrots are just tender. If desired, top with fresh thyme.
1 SERVING: 255 cal., 11g fat (3g sat. fat), 80mg chol., 648mg sod., 9g carb. (4g sugars, 2g fiber), 26g pro. **DIABETIC EXCHANGES:** 3 lean meat, ½ starch, ½ fat.

TEST KITCHEN TIPS

- Any dry red wine will work in this recipe. Think merlot, cabernet sauvignon and pinot noir.
- Coq au vin is traditionally served with a starchy side such as mashed potatoes, French bread or noodles.

30-MINUTE
COQ AU VIN

SENSATIONAL SPICED SALMON

A sweet and spicy rub gives this quick salmon entree fantastic flavor. Paired with a green veggie and rice, it's a delightful weeknight dinner that's special enough for company.
—*Michele Doucette, Stephenville, NL*

TAKES: 25 min. • **MAKES:** 4 servings

- 2 Tbsp. brown sugar
- 4 tsp. chili powder
- 2 tsp. grated lemon zest
- ¾ tsp. ground cumin
- ½ tsp. salt
- ¼ tsp. ground cinnamon
- 4 salmon fillets (4 oz. each)

Preheat oven to 350°. Combine the first 6 ingredients; rub over salmon. Place in an 11x7-in. baking dish coated with cooking spray. Bake, uncovered, until fish flakes easily with a fork, 15-20 minutes.

1 FILLET: 244 cal., 13g fat (3g sat. fat), 67mg chol., 392mg sod., 9g carb. (7g sugars, 1g fiber), 23g pro. **DIABETIC EXCHANGES:** 3 lean meat, ½ starch.

MEAT LOAF IN A MUG

Here's a quick, delicious single serving of meat loaf. This smart take on a classic gives you traditional meat loaf flavor with hardly any cleanup and no leftovers!
—*Ruby Matt, Garnavillo, IA*

TAKES: 15 min. • **MAKES:** 1 serving

- 2 Tbsp. 2% milk
- 1 Tbsp. ketchup
- 2 Tbsp. quick-cooking oats
- 1 tsp. onion soup mix
- ¼ lb. lean ground beef

1. In a small bowl, combine milk, ketchup, oats and soup mix. Crumble beef over mixture and mix lightly but thoroughly. Pat into a microwave-safe mug or custard cup coated with cooking spray.
2. Cover and microwave on high for 3 minutes or until meat is no longer pink and a thermometer reads 160°; drain. Let stand for 3 minutes. If desired, serve with additional ketchup.

1 SERVING: 316 cal., 14g fat (5g sat. fat), 100mg chol., 471mg sod., 14g carb. (6g sugars, 1g fiber), 33g pro.

PIZZA CAPRESE

One of my favorite pizzas is so simple to make and comes together so quickly. Pizza Caprese is simply heirloom tomatoes, fresh mozzarella and really good extra virgin olive oil. I could have this every day!
—*Beth Berlin, Oak Creek, WI*

TAKES: 30 min. • **MAKES:** 6 servings

- 1 pkg. (6½ oz.) pizza crust mix
- 2 Tbsp. extra virgin olive oil, divided
- 2 garlic cloves, thinly sliced
- 1 large tomato, thinly sliced
- 4 oz. fresh mozzarella cheese, sliced
- ⅓ cup loosely packed basil leaves

1. Preheat oven to 425°. Prepare pizza dough according to package directions. With floured hands, press dough onto a greased 12-in. pizza pan.
2. Drizzle 1 Tbsp. olive oil over dough and sprinkle with sliced garlic. Bake until crust is lightly browned, 10-12 minutes. Top with tomato and fresh mozzarella; bake until cheese is melted, 5-7 minutes longer. Drizzle with remaining 1 Tbsp. olive oil and top with basil. Serve immediately.

1 PIECE: 208 cal., 9g fat (3g sat. fat), 15mg chol., 196mg sod., 23g carb. (3g sugars, 1g fiber), 7g pro.

PEANUT TURKEY SATAY

I found this tasty recipe years ago and immediately served it to dinner guests. It's easy and fun and takes only minutes to cook, but it makes a fancy entree for special occasions. The peanut butter and soy sauce lend a nice Asian flavor.
—*Lisa Mahon Fluegeman, Cincinnati, OH*

TAKES: 15 min. • **MAKES:** 2 servings

- 4½ tsp. red wine vinegar
- 4½ tsp. reduced-sodium soy sauce
- 1 Tbsp. sugar
- 1 Tbsp. creamy peanut butter
- ¼ tsp. ground ginger
- ½ lb. turkey breast tenderloins

1. In a small bowl, whisk the first 5 ingredients; set aside 1 Tbsp. for basting. Cut turkey into long strips (about 1½ in. wide by ¼ in. thick). Add to soy sauce mixture in bowl; toss to coat.
2. Weave turkey strips accordion-style onto 2 metal or soaked wooden skewers. Broil 3-4 in. from the heat until turkey is no longer pink, 2-3 minutes on each side, basting with reserved soy sauce mixture.

1 SKEWER: 202 cal., 6g fat (1g sat. fat), 56mg chol., 552mg sod., 9g carb. (7g sugars, 1g fiber), 29g pro. **DIABETIC EXCHANGES:** 3 lean meat, ½ starch.

PIZZA CAPRESE

EASY GROUND BEEF STROGANOFF

BLACK BEAN & SWEET POTATO RICE BOWLS

I have three hungry boys in my house, so dinners need to be quick and filling, and it helps to get in some veggies, too. This one is a favorite because it's hearty and fun to tweak with different ingredients.
—Kim Van Dunk, Caldwell, NJ

TAKES: 30 min. • **MAKES:** 4 servings

- ¾ cup uncooked long grain rice
- ¼ tsp. garlic salt
- 1½ cups water
- 3 Tbsp. olive oil, divided
- 1 large sweet potato, peeled and diced
- 1 medium red onion, finely chopped
- 4 cups chopped fresh kale (tough stems removed)
- 1 can (15 oz.) black beans, rinsed and drained
- 2 Tbsp. sweet chili sauce
  Optional: Lime wedges and additional sweet chili sauce

1. Place rice, garlic salt and water in a large saucepan; bring to a boil. Reduce heat; simmer, covered, 15-20 minutes or until water is absorbed and rice is tender. Remove from heat; let stand 5 minutes.
2. Meanwhile, in a large skillet, heat 2 Tbsp. oil over medium-high heat; saute sweet potato 8 minutes. Add onion; cook and stir until potato is tender, 4-6 minutes. Add fresh kale; cook and stir until tender, 3-5 minutes. Stir in beans; heat through.
3. Gently stir 2 Tbsp. chili sauce and remaining oil into rice; add to potato mixture. If desired, serve with lime wedges and additional chili sauce.
2 CUPS: 435 cal., 11g fat (2g sat. fat), 0 chol., 405mg sod., 74g carb. (15g sugars, 8g fiber), 10g pro.

EASY GROUND BEEF STROGANOFF

This ground beef Stroganoff is one of the dishes my family requests most often whenever I ask what they'd like for dinner. It takes only minutes and it tastes great, so I always honor the request.
—Julie Curfman, Chehalis, WA

TAKES: 25 min. • **MAKES:** 3 servings

- ½ lb. ground beef
- 1 cup sliced fresh mushrooms
- 1 medium onion, chopped
- 1 garlic clove, minced
- 1 can (10¾ oz.) condensed cream of mushroom or cream of chicken soup, undiluted
- ¼ tsp. pepper
- 1 cup sour cream
- 3 cups cooked egg noodles
  Chopped fresh parsley, optional

In a large skillet, cook beef, mushrooms, onion and garlic over medium heat until meat is no longer pink; drain. Stir in soup and pepper. Cook until heated through, 2-3 minutes. Reduce heat. Stir in sour cream; cook until heated through. Serve with noodles. If desired, top with chopped fresh parsley.
1 SERVING: 554 cal., 28g fat (14g sat. fat), 141mg chol., 797mg sod., 44g carb. (7g sugars, 3g fiber), 26g pro.

READER REVIEW

*"Love the sour cream and cream of mushroom soup together. A good go-to recipe when you have very little time and want to whip together an inexpensive comfort food dish.
So simple!"*

—TLEE_INHAWAII, TASTEOFHOME.COM

BLACK BEAN & SWEET POTATO RICE BOWLS

PINEAPPLE PORK STIR-FRY

There's no need for takeout when you've got this pineapple pork recipe in your collection. Omit the cayenne pepper if serving young kids.
—Taste of Home *Test Kitchen*

- -

TAKES: 30 min. • **MAKES:** 6 servings

- 1 can (8 oz.) unsweetened pineapple chunks, undrained
- 3 Tbsp. cornstarch, divided
- 1 Tbsp. plus ½ cup cold water, divided
- ¾ tsp. garlic powder
- 1 pork tenderloin (1 lb.), cut into thin strips
- ½ cup soy sauce
- 3 Tbsp. brown sugar
- ½ tsp. ground ginger
- ¼ tsp. cayenne pepper
- 2 Tbsp. canola oil, divided
- 4 cups fresh broccoli florets
- 1 cup fresh baby carrots, cut in half lengthwise
- 1 small onion, cut into wedges
  Hot cooked rice
  Chopped green onion, optional

1. Drain pineapple, reserving ¼ cup juice; set aside. In a small bowl, combine 2 Tbsp. cornstarch, 1 Tbsp. water, garlic powder and 1 Tbsp. reserved pineapple juice. Pour into shallow dish; add pork and turn to coat.
2. In a small bowl, combine the soy sauce, brown sugar, ginger, cayenne and remaining water, cornstarch and reserved pineapple juice until smooth; set aside.
3. In a large skillet or wok over medium-high heat, stir-fry pork in 1 Tbsp. oil until no longer pink; remove and keep warm.
4. Stir-fry broccoli, carrots and onion in remaining oil until tender. Stir cornstarch mixture and add to the pan. Bring to a boil; cook and stir for 2 minutes or until thickened. Add pork and pineapple; heat through. Serve with rice, and, if desired, green onion.
1 CUP: 230 cal., 7g fat (1g sat. fat), 42mg chol., 1295mg sod., 21g carb. (13g sugars, 2g fiber), 19g pro.

APPLESAUCE BARBECUE CHICKEN

PINEAPPLE PORK STIR-FRY

APPLESAUCE BARBECUE CHICKEN

You only need a few ingredients to create this sweet and peppery chicken. The subtle flavor of apple makes this tender barbecue dish stand out from the rest.
—Darla Andrews, Boerne, TX

- -

TAKES: 20 min. • **MAKES:** 4 servings

- 4 boneless skinless chicken breast halves (6 oz. each)
- ½ tsp. pepper
- 1 Tbsp. olive oil
- ⅔ cup chunky applesauce
- ⅔ cup spicy barbecue sauce
- 2 Tbsp. brown sugar
- 1 tsp. chili powder

Sprinkle chicken with pepper. In a large skillet, brown the chicken in olive oil on both sides. In a small bowl, combine the remaining ingredients; pour over the chicken. Cover and cook until a thermometer reads 165°, 7-10 minutes.
FREEZE OPTION: Cool chicken; transfer to a freezer container and freeze for up to 3 months. Thaw in the refrigerator overnight. Cover and microwave on high until heated through, 8-10 minutes, stirring once.
1 CHICKEN BREAST HALF: 308 cal., 8g fat (2g sat. fat), 94mg chol., 473mg sod., 22g carb. (19g sugars, 1g fiber), 35g pro.

TURKEY ENCHILADAS

I enjoy entering recipe contests almost as much as I enjoy cooking. This dish is my favorite nontraditional way to use leftover turkey. It's become one of my family's favorite dinners, too!
—*Jo Groth, Plainfield, IA*

TAKES: 30 min. • **MAKES:** 10 servings

- ½ cup chopped onion
- 1 can (4 oz.) chopped green chiles, drained, divided
- 3 Tbsp. butter, divided
- ⅓ cup taco sauce
- 1 cup sour cream, divided
- ⅛ tsp. chili powder
- 2½ cups cooked cubed turkey
- 2 cups shredded cheddar cheese, divided
- 10 flour tortillas (8 in.)
- 2 Tbsp. all-purpose flour
- 1 cup chicken broth
- ½ cup chopped fresh tomatoes

1. In a skillet, saute onion and 2 Tbsp. green chilies in 1 Tbsp. butter until onion is tender. Remove from the heat. Add the taco sauce, ¼ cup sour cream and chili powder. Stir in turkey and ½ cup cheese.
2. Divide the mixture evenly among tortillas. Roll up and place seam side down in greased 13x9-in. baking dish.
3. In a small saucepan, melt remaining butter. Stir in flour until blended; gradually stir in broth. Bring to a boil; cook and stir 2 minutes or until thickened. Remove from heat; cool slightly. Stir in the remaining sour cream and remaining peppers.
4. Pour sauce over enchiladas. Bake, uncovered, at 325° for 40 minutes. Sprinkle remaining cheese, then tomatoes over top. Bake 5-10 minutes longer or until cheese is melted.
1 ENCHILADA: 404 cal., 21g fat (11g sat. fat), 84mg chol., 617mg sod., 32g carb. (2g sugars, 2g fiber), 21g pro.

TEST KITCHEN TIP

To quickly seed a tomato, cut it into wedges. Swipe your finger over each wedge to remove the gel pocket and seeds. This is nice for when you don't need perfectly seeded tomatoes.

TZATZIKI CHICKEN

I like to make classic chicken recipes for my family but the real fun is trying a fresh new twist.
—*Kristen Heigl, Staten Island, NY*

TAKES: 30 min. • **MAKES:** 4 servings

- 1½ cups finely chopped peeled English cucumber
- 1 cup plain Greek yogurt
- 2 garlic cloves, minced
- 1½ tsp. chopped fresh dill
- 1½ tsp. olive oil
- ⅛ tsp. salt

CHICKEN
- ⅔ cup all-purpose flour
- 1 tsp. salt
- 1 tsp. pepper
- ¼ tsp. baking powder
- 1 large egg
- ⅓ cup 2% milk
- 4 boneless skinless chicken breast halves (6 oz. each)
- ¼ cup canola oil
- ¼ cup crumbled feta cheese
  Lemon wedges, optional

1. For sauce, mix the first 6 ingredients; refrigerate until serving.
2. In a shallow bowl, whisk together flour, salt, pepper and baking powder. In another bowl, whisk together egg and milk. Pound chicken breasts with a meat mallet to ½-in. thickness. Dip in flour mixture to coat both sides; shake off excess. Dip in egg mixture, then again in flour mixture.
3. In a large skillet, heat oil over medium heat. Cook chicken until golden brown and juices run clear, 5-7 minutes per side. Top with cheese. Serve with sauce and, if desired, lemon wedges.
1 CHICKEN BREAST HALF WITH ⅓ CUP SAUCE: 482 cal., 27g fat (7g sat. fat), 133mg chol., 737mg sod., 17g carb. (4g sugars, 1g fiber), 41g pro.

TZATZIKI CHICKEN

VEGGIE FAJITAS

LEMON-BATTER FISH

Fishing is a popular recreational activity where we live, so folks are always looking for ways to prepare their catches. My husband ranks this as one of his favorites.
—*Jackie Hannahs, Cedar Springs, MI*

- -

TAKES: 25 min. • **MAKES:** 6 servings

- 1½ cups all-purpose flour, divided
- 1 tsp. baking powder
- ¾ tsp. salt
- ½ tsp. sugar
- 1 large egg, lightly beaten
- ⅔ cup water
- ⅔ cup lemon juice, divided
- 2 lbs. perch or walleye fillets, cut into serving-sized pieces
  Oil for frying
  Lemon wedges, optional

1. Combine 1 cup flour, baking powder, salt and sugar. In another bowl, combine egg, water and ⅓ cup lemon juice; stir into dry ingredients until smooth.
2. Place remaining ⅓ cup lemon juice and remaining ½ cup flour in separate shallow bowls. Dip fillets in lemon juice, then flour, then coat with egg mixture.
3. In a large skillet, heat 1 in. oil over medium-high heat. Fry fillets until golden brown and fish flakes easily with a fork, 2-3 minutes on each side. Drain on paper towels. If desired, serve with lemon.

5 OZ. COOKED FISH: 384 cal., 17g fat (2g sat. fat), 167mg chol., 481mg sod., 22g carb. (1g sugars, 1g fiber), 33g pro.

HOW-TO

Keep Fish Fresh

Fish stays freshest when stored on ice. To keep it ice cold without making a mess or damaging the fish's texture, place frozen gel packs or blue ice blocks in a container, then top with the wrapped fish. Place in the meat drawer and use within a few days. Wash the ice packs with hot soapy water before re-use.

VEGGIE FAJITAS

For scrumptious and super healthy party fare, these colorful, hearty fajitas packed with crisp-tender veggies are perfect.
—*Sarah Mercer, Wichita, KS*

- -

TAKES: 25 min. • **MAKES:** 8 fajitas

- 1 small zucchini, thinly sliced
- 1 medium yellow summer squash, thinly sliced
- ½ lb. sliced fresh mushrooms
- 1 small onion, halved and sliced
- 1 medium carrot, julienned
- 1 tsp. salt
- ½ tsp. pepper
- 1 Tbsp. canola oil
- 8 flour tortillas (8 in.), warmed
- 2 cups shredded cheddar cheese
- 1 cup sour cream
- 1 cup salsa

In a large cast-iron or other heavy skillet, saute vegetables with salt and pepper in oil until crisp-tender, 5-7 minutes. Using a slotted spoon, place about ½ cup vegetable mixture down the center of each tortilla. Sprinkle each with ¼ cup cheese; top with sour cream and salsa. Fold in sides.

1 FAJITA: 375 cal., 21g fat (10g sat. fat), 35mg chol., 853mg sod., 35g carb. (4g sugars, 3g fiber), 13g pro.

PINEAPPLE CHICKEN CASSEROLE

I'm always looking for one-dish dinners like this casserole that save time and cleanup. I love to cook, but with teaching school, playing handbells at church and juggling my husband's and teen twins' schedules, I have little time in the kitchen.
—*Susan Warren, North Manchester, IN*

- -

TAKES: 30 min. • **MAKES:** 4 servings

- 2 cups cubed cooked chicken
- 1 can (10½ oz.) condensed cream of mushroom soup, undiluted
- 1 cup pineapple tidbits
- 2 celery ribs, chopped
- 1 Tbsp. chopped green onion
- 1 Tbsp. reduced-sodium soy sauce
- 1 can (3 oz.) chow mein noodles, divided

1. Preheat oven to 350°. In a large bowl, combine the first 6 ingredients. Fold in 1 cup chow mein noodles.
2. Transfer to a greased shallow 2-qt. baking dish. Sprinkle with remaining noodles. Bake, uncovered, until heated through, 20-25 minutes. If desired, top with additional green onions.

1½ CUPS: 335 cal., 12g fat (3g sat. fat), 65mg chol., 1010mg sod., 30g carb. (10g sugars, 3g fiber), 23g pro.

LEMON-BATTER FISH

ONE-POT
BLACK BEAN
ENCHILADA PASTA

ONE-POT BLACK BEAN ENCHILADA PASTA

I love this cozy pasta dish because it is ready in less than 30 minutes and is full of healthy ingredients—just what a busy weeknight meal calls for.
—*Nora Rushev, Reitnau, Switzerland*

TAKES: 30 min. • **MAKES:** 6 servings

- 4 cups uncooked mini penne or other small pasta
- 4 cups vegetable broth or water
- 1 can (15 oz.) black beans, rinsed and drained
- 1 can (14½ oz.) diced tomatoes, undrained
- 1 medium sweet yellow pepper, chopped
- 1 medium sweet red pepper, chopped
- 1 cup fresh or frozen corn, thawed
- 1 can (10 oz.) enchilada sauce
- 2 Tbsp. taco seasoning
- ½ cup shredded cheddar cheese
  Optional: Fresh cilantro leaves, cherry tomatoes and lime wedges

In a Dutch oven or large skillet, combine the first 9 ingredients. Bring to a boil; reduce heat. Simmer, uncovered, until pasta is al dente and sauce has thickened slightly, 12-15 minutes. Add cheese; stir until melted. Serve with desired toppings.
1¾ CUPS: 444 cal., 5g fat (2g sat. fat), 9mg chol., 1289mg sod., 84g carb. (8g sugars, 8g fiber), 18g pro.

TEST KITCHEN TIPS

- Top this enchilada pasta with sliced avocado, sour cream, olives and green onions.
- Try adding a protein to the pasta, like shredded cooked chicken or leftover taco meat.
- Switch to no-salt-added tomatoes and black beans to cut the sodium by about 300mg per serving.

QUICK & EASY SKILLET LASAGNA

QUICK & EASY SKILLET LASAGNA

No

This is a relatively new recipe to our family. We enjoy it and have made it quite a few times over the past few months. It's the perfect solution when you feel like lasagna but don't have time to bake it in the oven! You can also vary the taste depending on the type of pasta sauce or Italian dressing you use. Serve with salad or garlic bread.
—*Wendy Masters, East Garafraxa, ON*

TAKES: 30 min. • **MAKES:** 6 servings

- 1 lb. lean ground beef (90% lean)
- 1 jar (24 oz.) pasta sauce
- 2 cups water
- 1 large sweet red pepper, chopped
- ¼ cup Italian salad dressing
- 1 tsp. garlic powder
- 10 uncooked lasagna noodles, broken into 2-in. pieces
- 1½ cups 2% cottage cheese
- 1 cup shredded part-skim mozzarella cheese

1. In a large skillet, cook beef over medium heat until no longer pink; drain. Stir in pasta sauce, water, red pepper, dressing and garlic powder. Bring to a boil; stir in noodles. Reduce heat to medium-low. Cook, covered, until noodles are tender, 10-15 minutes, stirring occasionally.
2. Stir in cottage cheese; heat through. Remove from heat; top with mozzarella cheese. Cover and let stand until cheese is melted, about 5 minutes.
1 SERVING: 462 cal., 15g fat (6g sat. fat), 62mg chol., 857mg sod., 49g carb. (15g sugars, 5g fiber), 32g pro.

SMOKED KIELBASA WITH RICE

SMOKED KIELBASA WITH RICE

With a little bit of zip and just the right amount of smokiness, this sausage-and-rice medley will please a crowd. For an appetizer, omit the rice and serve the sausage pieces with toothpicks.
—*Nicole Jackson, El Paso, TX*

TAKES: 25 min. • **MAKES:** 6 servings

  2   lbs. smoked kielbasa or Polish sausage, halved lengthwise and cut into ¼-in. slices
  ¼   cup finely chopped onion
  3   bacon strips, finely chopped
  ¾   cup honey barbecue sauce
  ¼   cup packed brown sugar
  1   Tbsp. prepared horseradish
  2   tsp. water
  2   tsp. minced garlic
  ½   tsp. crushed red pepper flakes
      Hot cooked rice

In a Dutch oven, saute the kielbasa, onion and bacon until onion is tender; drain. Add the barbecue sauce, brown sugar, horseradish, water, garlic and pepper flakes. Bring to a boil; cook and stir for 2-3 minutes or until sauce is thickened. Serve with rice.
FREEZE OPTION: Place cooled individual portions in freezer containers without rice. Freeze up to 3 months. To use, thaw in refrigerator overnight. Place in a saucepan. Heat through, gently stirring; add water if necessary. Serve with rice.
¾ CUP: 586 cal., 42g fat (15g sat. fat), 105mg chol., 2052mg sod., 27g carb. (20g sugars, 0 fiber), 21g pro.

ITALIAN SAUSAGE VEGGIE SKILLET

We love Italian sausage sandwiches, but because the bread isn't diet friendly for me, I created this recipe to satisfy my craving. If you like some heat, use hot peppers in place of the sweet peppers.
—*Tina M. Howells, Salem, OH*

TAKES: 30 min. • **MAKES:** 6 servings

  4   cups uncooked whole wheat spiral pasta
  1   lb. Italian turkey sausage, casings removed
  1   medium onion, chopped
  1   garlic clove, minced
  2   medium zucchini, chopped
  1   large sweet red pepper, chopped
  1   large sweet yellow pepper, chopped
  1   can (28 oz.) diced tomatoes, drained
  ¼   tsp. salt
  ¼   tsp. pepper

1. Cook pasta according to package directions; drain.
2. Meanwhile, in large skillet, cook sausage and onion over medium-high heat until sausage is no longer pink, 5-7 minutes. Add garlic and cook 1 minute longer. Add zucchini and peppers; cook until crisp-tender, 3-5 minutes. Add tomatoes, salt and pepper. Cook and stir until vegetables are tender and begin to release their juices, 5-7 minutes. Serve with pasta.
1⅓ CUPS: 251 cal., 6g fat (1g sat. fat), 28mg chol., 417mg sod., 35g carb. (4g sugars, 6g fiber), 16g pro. **DIABETIC EXCHANGES:** 2 vegetable, 2 lean meat, 1½ starch.

ITALIAN SAUSAGE VEGGIE SKILLET

**MUSHROOM &
BROWN RICE HASH
WITH POACHED EGGS**

MUSHROOM &
BROWN RICE HASH
WITH POACHED EGGS

I made my mother's famous roast beef hash healthier by using cremini mushrooms instead of beef, and brown rice instead of potatoes. It's ideal for a light main dish.
—*Lily Julow, Lawrenceville, GA*

- -

TAKES: 30 min. • **MAKES:** 4 servings

- 2 **Tbsp. olive oil**
- 1 **lb. sliced baby portobello mushrooms**
- ½ **cup chopped sweet onion**
- 1 **pkg. (8.8 oz.) ready-to-serve brown rice**
- 1 **large carrot, grated**
- 2 **green onions, thinly sliced**
- ½ **tsp. salt**
- ¼ **tsp. pepper**
- ¼ **tsp. caraway seeds**
- 4 **large eggs, cold**

1. In a large skillet, heat oil over medium-high heat; saute mushrooms until lightly browned, 5-7 minutes. Add sweet onion; cook 1 minute. Add rice and carrot; cook and stir until the vegetables are tender, 4-5 minutes. Stir in green onions, salt, pepper and caraway seeds; heat through.
2. Meanwhile, place 2-3 in. water in a large saucepan or skillet with high sides. Bring to a boil; adjust heat to maintain a gentle simmer. Break the cold eggs, 1 at a time, into a small bowl; holding bowl close to surface of water, slip each egg into water.
3. Cook, uncovered, until whites are completely set and yolks begin to thicken but are not hard, 3-5 minutes. Using a slotted spoon, lift eggs out of water. Serve over rice mixture.
1 SERVING: 282 cal., 13g fat (3g sat. fat), 186mg chol., 393mg sod., 26g carb. (4g sugars, 3g fiber), 13g pro. **DIABETIC EXCHANGES:** 1½ starch, 1½ fat, 1 medium-fat meat.

TEST KITCHEN TIPS

- This is a great weeknight dinner or brunch option for anyone following a gluten-free diet.
- White button mushrooms can be used in place of baby portobellos, but baby portobellos add a richer, more earthy flavor to the dish.

BRUSCHETTA STEAK

My husband and I love bruschetta, especially in the summertime with fresh tomatoes and herbs from our garden.
—*Kristy Still, Broken Arrow, OK*

- -

TAKES: 25 min. • **MAKES:** 4 servings

- 3 **medium tomatoes, chopped**
- 3 **Tbsp. minced fresh basil**
- 3 **Tbsp. chopped fresh parsley**
- 2 **Tbsp. olive oil**
- 1 **tsp. minced fresh oregano or ½ tsp. dried oregano**
- 1 **garlic clove, minced**
- ¾ **tsp. salt, divided**
- 1 **lb. beef flat iron or top sirloin steak, cut into four portions**
- ¼ **tsp. pepper**
  Grated Parmesan cheese, optional

1. Combine first 6 ingredients; stir in ¼ tsp. salt.
2. Sprinkle the beef with pepper and remaining salt. Grill, covered, over medium heat or broil 4 in. from heat until meat reaches desired doneness (for medium-rare, a thermometer should read 135°; medium, 140°), 4-6 minutes per side. Top with tomato mixture. If desired, sprinkle with cheese.
1 STEAK WITH ½ CUP TOMATO MIXTURE: 280 cal., 19g fat (6g sat. fat), 73mg chol., 519mg sod., 4g carb. (2g sugars, 1g fiber), 23g pro. **DIABETIC EXCHANGES:** 3 lean meat, 1½ fat, 1 vegetable.

BRUSCHETTA STEAK

**HERB GARDEN
GRILLED CHICKEN
PAGE 82**

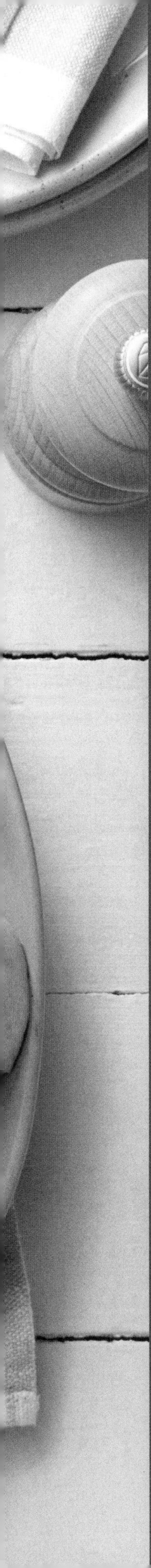

Main Dishes

Whether you're looking for a cozy casserole, awesome grilled dish, one-pot supper or pressure-cooked meal, you'll discover luscious new entrees for your repertoire here.

MOST-REQUESTED RECIPES

**PRESSURE-COOKER
TEX-MEX RISOTTO**

MAPLE SAGE GRILLED CHICKEN

Maple and sage are reserved for the fall no more! My family devours these sweet and savory chicken fillets in the summer—or any time.
—*Sue Gronholz, Beaver Dam, WI*

PREP: 15 min. + marinating • **GRILL:** 15 min. • **MAKES:** 6 servings

- ¾ cup unsweetened apple juice, divided
- ½ cup packed brown sugar
- 6 Tbsp. olive oil
- ¼ cup cider vinegar
- ¼ cup maple syrup, divided
- 3 Tbsp. Dijon mustard
- 1 Tbsp. minced fresh sage or 1 tsp. dried sage leaves
- 3 garlic cloves, minced
- 1½ tsp. salt
- 6 boneless skinless chicken breast halves (6 oz. each)

1. In a large bowl, whisk 4 Tbsp. apple juice, brown sugar, olive oil, vinegar, 2 Tbsp. maple syrup, mustard, sage, garlic and salt until blended. Pour 1 cup marinade into a shallow dish. Add chicken; turn to coat. Refrigerate 8 hours or overnight. Cover and refrigerate remaining marinade.

2. Drain chicken, discarding marinade in dish. Place chicken on oiled grill rack. Grill, covered, over medium heat until a thermometer reads 165°, 7-8 minutes on each side.

3. Meanwhile, in a small saucepan, combine reserved marinade, remaining ½ cup apple juice and remaining 2 Tbsp. maple syrup. Bring to a boil; cook until liquid is reduced by half, 5-7 minutes. Serve with chicken.

1 CHICKEN BREAST WITH 1 TBSP. SAUCE: 419 cal., 12g fat (3g sat. fat), 167mg chol., 410mg sod., 13g carb. (12g sugars, 0 fiber), 61g pro.

PRESSURE-COOKER TEX-MEX RISOTTO

I love food with lots of flavor and a Mexican twist, but am too lazy to stand over a pot of risotto. My pressure cooker gave me the opportunity to marry my love of Mexican food and creamy risotto with no muss, no fuss.
—*Sharon Marx, Grand Blanc, MI*

PREP: 20 min. • **COOK:** 15 min. • **MAKES:** 6 servings

- 1 Tbsp. olive oil
- ½ large sweet orange pepper, chopped
- 1 jalapeno pepper, seeded and minced, optional
- 1½ cups uncooked arborio rice
- 2½ cups reduced-sodium chicken broth
- ½ lb. boneless skinless chicken breasts, cut into 1½-in. cubes
- 1 can (10 oz.) diced tomatoes and green chiles, undrained
- 1 can (15 oz.) black beans, rinsed and drained
- 1½ cups shredded Manchego cheese
- 1 cup frozen corn, thawed
- ½ cup chopped fresh cilantro

1. Select saute setting on a 6-qt. electric pressure cooker. Adjust for medium heat; add oil. When oil is hot, cook and stir orange pepper and, if desired, jalapeno, until crisp-tender, 2-3 minutes. Add rice, cook and stir 1 minute longer. Press cancel. Add broth, chicken and diced tomatoes.

2. Lock lid; close pressure-release valve. Adjust to pressure-cook on high for 6 minutes. Allow pressure to release naturally for 5 minutes; quick-release any remaining pressure. Stir in beans, cheese, corn and cilantro; heat through. Garnish with additional cilantro if desired.

1⅓ CUPS: 446 cal., 13g fat (7g sat. fat), 49mg chol., 742mg sod., 57g carb. (2g sugars, 5g fiber), 23g pro.

**MAPLE SAGE
GRILLED CHICKEN**

SHRIMP DE JONGHE TRIANGLES

Shrimp de Jonghe was invented in Chicago. It is usually baked and served in a casserole dish, but my version is a handheld. The shrimp filling is perfect with the crunchy pastry dough.

—*Arlene Erlbach, Morton Grove, IL*

PREP: 30 min. • **BAKE:** 20 min.
MAKES: 4 servings

- 5 Tbsp. butter, divided
- ½ cup panko bread crumbs
- 1 tsp. garlic powder, divided
- 1 lb. uncooked shrimp (31-40 per lb.), peeled and deveined, tails removed
- ⅔ cup spreadable garlic and herb cream cheese, divided
- ½ cup sherry or chicken broth
- ¼ cup minced fresh parsley
- ½ tsp. dried tarragon
- ⅛ tsp. ground nutmeg
- 1 sheet frozen puff pastry, thawed
- 1 large egg, room temperature, beaten
  Lemon wedges, optional

1. Preheat oven to 400°. In a large skillet, melt 2 Tbsp. butter over medium heat. Add bread crumbs and ¼ tsp. garlic powder. Cook and stir until toasted, 3-4 minutes. Transfer to a small bowl; wipe pan clean.

2. In the same skillet, melt remaining 3 Tbsp. butter over medium heat. Add shrimp and remaining ¾ tsp. garlic powder; cook and stir until shrimp turn pink, 6-8 minutes. Reduce heat to low; stir in ⅓ cup cream cheese, sherry, parsley, tarragon and nutmeg until combined. Remove from heat.

3. On a lightly floured surface, unfold puff pastry. Roll into a 12-in. square. Cut into four 6-in. squares. Spread remaining ⅓ cup cream cheese over squares to within ½ in. of edges. Using a slotted spoon, place about ½ cup shrimp mixture on 1 side of each square. Fold dough over filling. Press edges with a fork to seal. Brush beaten egg over tops. Prick tops with a fork. Sprinkle with reserved crumb mixture, pressing lightly to adhere. Place on a parchment-lined baking sheet. Bake until golden brown, 20-25 minutes. If desired, serve with lemon wedges.

1 TRIANGLE: 616 cal., 37g fat (15g sat. fat), 208mg chol., 586mg sod., 43g carb. (2g sugars, 5g fiber), 26g pro.

TEST KITCHEN TIPS

- For this recipe, we suggest using uncooked shrimp in order to keep them tender as they bake inside the pastry. Cooked shrimp may become tough and overcooked as the pastries bake, so we don't recommend using it.

- These shrimp pastries can be hand-held or served with a knife and fork—the choice is completely yours! There is no need for an accompanying sauce, as the filling is nice and creamy.

ONE-POT CREAMY TOMATO PASTA

Here's a creamy vegan recipe with tons of fresh sauteed vegetables. The spicy tomato sauce with sweet sun-dried tomatoes is the highlight of this dish. It's the perfect one-pot meal for when you want something easy.
—*Michelle Miller, Bend, OR*

PREP: 20 min. • **COOK:** 30 min.
MAKES: 4 servings

- ⅓ cup unsalted cashews, soaked overnight
- 1 can (14½ oz.) diced tomatoes, undrained
- 2 Tbsp. tomato paste
- 1½ tsp. dried oregano
- 1 tsp. garlic powder
- 1 tsp. onion powder
- 1 tsp. sea salt
- ½ tsp. ground cumin
- ¼ tsp. crushed red pepper flakes, optional
- ¼ cup olive oil
- 1 medium red onion, thinly sliced
- 2 garlic cloves, minced
- ½ lb. fresh asparagus, trimmed and cut into 2-in. pieces
- ½ lb. Broccolini or broccoli spears, cut into 3-in. pieces
- 1 cup sliced fresh carrots
- 2½ to 3 cups water
- ½ cup julienned soft sun-dried tomatoes (not packed in oil)
- 8 oz. uncooked gluten-free spiral pasta

1. In a blender, puree drained cashews and next 7 ingredients until smooth; mix in crushed red pepper flakes if desired. Set aside.
2. In a Dutch oven or large skillet, heat oil over medium heat. Add onion; cook and stir until browned, 4-5 minutes. Stir in garlic; cook 1 minute longer. Add the asparagus, Broccolini and carrots; cook until tender, 10-12 minutes. Remove from pan; set aside.
3. In same pan, add tomato mixture and cook for 2 minutes. Add water, sun-dried tomatoes and pasta. Bring to a boil; reduce heat and simmer until pasta is al dente, 10-12 minutes, adding more water as necessary and stirring occasionally. Stir in cooked vegetables and toss to coat. Serve immediately.
1¾ CUPS: 500 cal., 21g fat (3g sat. fat), 0 chol., 712mg sod., 72g carb. (13g sugars, 10g fiber), 10g pro.

❄ CHICKEN CORDON BLEU BAKE

A friend shared this awesome hot dish recipe with me. I freeze several pans to share with neighbors or for days when I'm scrambling at mealtime.
—*Rea Newell, Decatur, IL*

PREP: 20 min. • **BAKE:** 40 min.
MAKES: 2 casseroles (6 servings each)

- 2 pkg. (6 oz. each) reduced-sodium stuffing mix
- 1 can (10¾ oz.) condensed cream of chicken soup, undiluted
- 1 cup 2% milk
- 8 cups cubed cooked chicken
- ½ tsp. pepper
- ¾ lb. sliced deli ham, cut into 1-in. strips
- 1 cup shredded Swiss cheese
- 3 cups shredded cheddar cheese

1. Preheat oven to 350°. Prepare stuffing mixes according to package directions. Meanwhile, whisk together soup and milk.
2. Toss the chicken with pepper; divide between 2 greased 13x9-in. baking dishes. Layer with ham, Swiss cheese, 1 cup cheddar cheese, soup mixture and stuffing. Sprinkle with the remaining cheddar cheese.
3. Bake, covered, 30 minutes. Uncover casseroles; bake until cheese is melted, 10-15 minutes.
FREEZE OPTION: Cover and freeze the unbaked casseroles. To use, partially thaw in refrigerator overnight. Remove from refrigerator 30 minutes before baking. Preheat oven to 350°. Bake, covered, until heated through and a thermometer inserted in center reads 165°, about 45 minutes. Uncover; bake until cheese is melted, 10-15 minutes.
1 CUP: 555 cal., 29g fat (15g sat. fat), 158mg chol., 1055mg sod., 26g carb. (5g sugars, 1g fiber), 46g pro.

ONE-POT CREAMY TOMATO PASTA

SAUSAGE & APPLE QUINOA CASSEROLE

GRILLED LAMB WITH MINT-PEPPER JELLY

I used zippy jalapeno pepper jelly to make the predictable duo of lamb and mint a little more exciting, and it paid off big time. This is my surefire way of getting people who aren't typically fans of lamb to enjoy it.
—*Lori Stefanishion, Drumheller, AB*

PREP: 15 min. + marinating • GRILL: 30 min. + standing
MAKES: 4 servings

- 2 racks of lamb (1½ lbs. each), trimmed
- 3 Tbsp. Greek seasoning
- ¼ cup balsamic vinegar
- ¼ cup olive oil
- 2 Tbsp. lemon juice
- 2 Tbsp. soy sauce
- 3 garlic cloves, minced
- ½ cup fresh mint leaves, minced
- ½ cup mild jalapeno pepper jelly
- 1 Tbsp. hot water
  Chopped fresh oregano

1. Rub lamb with Greek seasoning. Refrigerate, covered, 2 hours. In a shallow bowl, whisk vinegar, oil, lemon juice, soy sauce and garlic until combined. Add lamb and turn to coat. Refrigerate, covered, 4-6 hours or overnight, turning once or twice.
2. In a small bowl, mix mint, jelly, and hot water until combined. Refrigerate, covered, until serving.
3. Drain the lamb, discarding marinade in dish. Cover rib ends of lamb with foil. Grill, covered, on an oiled rack, over direct medium-high heat 2 minutes on each side. Turn; move to indirect heat. Cook, covered, until meat reaches desired doneness (for medium-rare, a thermometer should read 135°; medium, 140°; medium-well, 145°), 25-30 minutes longer. Let stand 10 minutes before serving with sauce; sprinkle with fresh oregano and additional fresh mint.
½ RACK WITH 4 TBSP. SAUCE: 471 cal., 24g fat (7g sat. fat), 99mg chol., 1841mg sod., 33g carb. (24g sugars, 1g fiber), 31g pro.

SAUSAGE & APPLE QUINOA CASSEROLE

Our family loves the variety this dish offers. It's not like anything else I've made before and the pressure cooker does a really great job with it.
—*Brenna Norby, Grand Forks, ND*

PREP: 25 min. • COOK: 10 min. • MAKES: 6 servings

- 1 Tbsp. olive oil
- 1 pkg. (14 oz.) smoked kielbasa or Polish sausage, cut into ½-in. slices
- 1 small onion, chopped
- 1 cup chicken broth
- 1 cup apple cider or juice
- ¼ tsp. salt
- 1 pkg. (16 oz.) frozen cut kale or frozen chopped spinach
- 1 cup quinoa, rinsed
- 1 medium apple, chopped
- ¼ cup chopped pecans
- ¼ cup dried cranberries
- 1 tsp. dried sage leaves

1. Select saute setting on a 6-qt. electric pressure cooker. Adjust for medium heat; add oil. When oil is hot, cook and stir sausage, adding onion after 5 minutes, until sausage is browned and onion crisp-tender, about 5 more minutes. Remove and keep warm. Add broth, cider and salt to pressure cooker. Cook 1 minute, stirring to loosen browned bits from pan. Press cancel.
2. Stir in kale, quinoa and reserved sausage mixture. Lock lid; close pressure-release valve. Adjust to pressure-cook on high for 7 minutes. Quick-release pressure. Stir in remaining ingredients; cover and let stand 5 minutes.
1¼ CUPS: 443 cal., 29g fat (7g sat. fat), 44mg chol., 701mg sod., 40g carb. (15g sugars, 5g fiber), 15g pro.

GRILLED LAMB WITH MINT-PEPPER JELLY

BLOCK ISLAND
LITTLENECKS
WITH CHORIZO

BLOCK ISLAND LITTLENECKS WITH CHORIZO

Every summer my family digs clams on the shores of Block Island, Rhode Island. This dish highlights the fresh, sweet and salty flavor of clams, and the chorizo adds a little kick. The best is dipping crusty bread into the delicious broth! Quick and easy to put together, this is the perfect dinner on a hot summer night!
—Pamela Gelsomini, Wrentham, MA

PREP: 20 min. • COOK: 25 min.
MAKES: 8 servings (4 qt.)

- 3 lbs. fresh littleneck clams
- 1 bunch Swiss chard, stems removed and chopped (about 4 cups)
- ½ lb. fully cooked Spanish chorizo links, chopped
- 1 can (15 oz.) cannellini beans, rinsed and drained
- 1 medium onion, chopped
- 1 cup fresh or frozen corn
- 4 garlic cloves, minced
- 1 tsp. salt
- 1 tsp. pepper
- 1 bottle (12 oz.) beer
- ⅓ cup olive oil
  Grilled French bread baguette slices

1. Place clams in a stockpot; top with the next 8 ingredients. Add beer and oil; bring to a boil. Reduce heat; simmer, covered, for 10 minutes.
2. Stir; cook, covered, until clams open, 5-7 minutes longer. Discard any unopened clams. Ladle mixture into bowls; serve with grilled bread.
2 CUPS: 265 cal., 17g fat (4g sat. fat), 28mg chol., 729mg sod., 16g carb. (3g sugars, 4g fiber), 12g pro.

HOW-TO

Clean Clams

Clean your clams as soon as you bring them home from the market. First, check for any clams that are broken, chipped or open, and discard them. Fill a bowl with cold water and submerge clams for 20 minutes to 1 hour to allow the sand to filter out of the shells. Lift each clam individually out of the water and scrub it to rid the shell of any excess grit. Refrigerate, uncovered, until ready to use.

PRESSURE-COOKER
BLOODY MARY POT ROAST

PRESSURE-COOKER BLOODY MARY POT ROAST

When I picked up a bottle of Bloody Mary mix, the clerk said she sometimes used it to marinate a roast. I gave that a try and then decided to add many of the flavors that others love in a Bloody Mary.
—Renee Page, Rochelle, IL

PREP: 25 min. + marinating
COOK: 45 min. + releasing
MAKES: 6 servings

- 1 cup Bloody Mary mix, divided
- 2 Tbsp. Worcestershire sauce, divided
- 1 Tbsp. juice from pepperoncini
- 1 tsp. celery salt, divided
- 1 boneless beef chuck roast (2 to 3 lbs.)
- 1 Tbsp. canola oil
- 1 small onion, chopped
- ¾ cup beef stock
- 1 Tbsp. tomato paste
- 1 celery rib, chopped
- 5 pepperoncini
- 2 garlic cloves, minced
- ½ tsp. pepper

1. In a large bowl or shallow dish, combine ¾ cup of the Bloody Mary mix, 1 Tbsp. Worcestershire sauce, pepperoncini juice and ½ tsp. celery salt. Add beef; turn to coat. Cover and refrigerate 4-5 hours, turning occasionally.

2. Drain beef, discarding marinade. Select saute setting on a 6-qt. electric pressure cooker. Adjust for medium heat; add oil. When oil is hot, brown roast on all sides; remove from cooker. Add onions; cook and stir until lightly browned, 4-5 minutes. Remove from cooker. Add beef stock to pressure cooker. Cook 1 minute, stirring to loosen browned bits from pan. Stir in tomato paste, remaining ¼ cup Bloody Mary mix and 1 Tbsp. Worcestershire. Press cancel.

3. Return roast and onions to cooker. Add celery, pepperoncini, garlic, pepper and remaining ½ tsp. celery salt. Lock lid; close pressure-release valve. Adjust to pressure-cook on high for 45 minutes. Allow pressure to release naturally for 10 minutes; quick-release any remaining pressure. Remove roast to a serving platter; tent with foil. Let stand 10 minutes before serving. If desired, thicken cooking juices to serve with roast.

FREEZE OPTION: Freeze cooled meat mixture and juice in freezer containers. To use, partially thaw in refrigerator overnight. Heat through in a saucepan, stirring occasionally; add broth if necessary.

4 OZ. COOKED BEEF: 299 cal., 17g fat (6g sat. fat), 98mg chol., 429mg sod., 4g carb. (2g sugars, 0 fiber), 31g pro.

PARMESAN PORK TENDERLOIN

❄ MEXICAN MEAT LOAF

Being a working mother with a small budget and little time, I often rely on ground beef. When our son was getting bored with meat loaf, I made this taco-seasoned version. Everyone loves it with sour cream and extra salsa.

—*Alice McCauley, Beaumont, TX*

PREP: 10 min. • **BAKE:** 65 min. + standing • **MAKES:** 8 servings

- 4 cups cooked shredded hash brown potatoes
- ¼ cup salsa
- 1 large egg, lightly beaten
- 2 Tbsp. vegetable soup mix
- 2 Tbsp. taco seasoning
- 2 cups shredded cheddar cheese, divided
- 2 lbs. ground beef

1. Preheat oven to 350°. In a large bowl, combine the hash browns, salsa, egg, soup mix, taco seasoning and 1 cup cheese. Crumble beef over mixture and mix lightly but thoroughly. Shape into a 12-in. loaf. Place in a 13x9-in. baking dish.

2. Bake, uncovered, for 1 hour or until a thermometer reads 160°. Sprinkle with remaining cheese; bake 5 minutes longer or until cheese is melted. Let stand for 10 minutes before slicing. If desired, serve with additional salsa.

FREEZE OPTION: Cover and freeze unbaked meat loaf in an airtight container. Cover and freeze remaining 1 cup cheese. To use, thaw in the refrigerator overnight. Bake, uncovered, at 350° until a thermometer reads 160°, about 1 hour. Sprinkle with remaining 1 cup cheese; bake until the cheese is melted, about 5 minutes longer. Let stand 10 minutes before slicing. If desired, serve with additional salsa.

1 PIECE: 376 cal., 23g fat (11g sat. fat), 121mg chol., 699mg sod., 12g carb. (1g sugars, 1g fiber), 28g pro.

MEXICAN MEAT LOAF

PARMESAN PORK TENDERLOIN

I am of Danish descent and love all things pork, both old recipes and new. Here's a dish I came up with myself.

—*John Hansen, Marstons Mills, MA*

PREP: 25 min. • **COOK:** 25 min. • **MAKES:** 2 servings

- 1 pork tenderloin (¾ lb.)
- 6 Tbsp. grated Parmesan cheese
- 1 small sweet onion, sliced and separated into rings
- 1½ cups sliced fresh mushrooms
- 1 garlic clove, minced
- 2 tsp. butter, divided
- 2 tsp. olive oil, divided
- ¼ cup reduced-sodium beef broth
- 2 Tbsp. port wine or additional beef broth
- ⅛ tsp. salt, optional
- ⅛ tsp. each dried basil, thyme and rosemary, crushed
  Dash pepper
- ½ tsp. cornstarch
- 3 Tbsp. water

1. Cut pork into ½-in. slices; flatten to ⅛-in. thickness. Coat with Parmesan cheese; set aside.

2. In a large skillet, saute the onion, mushrooms and garlic in 1 tsp. butter and 1 tsp. oil until tender; remove and keep warm. In the same skillet, cook pork in the remaining 1 tsp. butter and 1 tsp. oil in batches over medium heat until juices run clear, about 2 minutes on each side. Remove and keep warm.

3. Add broth to pan, scraping to loosen browned bits. Stir in wine or additional broth; add seasonings. Bring to a boil. Reduce heat; simmer, uncovered, for 5 minutes. Combine the cornstarch and water until smooth; stir into pan juices. Bring to a boil; cook and stir until thickened, about 2 minutes. Serve with pork and the onion mixture.

1 SERVING: 388 cal., 19g fat (8g sat. fat), 118mg chol., 472mg sod., 11g carb. (6g sugars, 2g fiber), 43g pro.

COPYCAT CHICKEN NUGGETS

I developed this recipe specifically to mimic our favorite restaurant's chicken nuggets. The first time I made them I knew I had a winner: The whole family fought over who got the last one! And the Dijon sauce with barbecue and honey is a tangy bonus.

—Jeni Pittard, Statham, GA

- -

PREP: 20 min. + marinating
COOK: 5 min./batch • **MAKES:** 8 servings

- 2 lbs. boneless skinless chicken breasts, cut into bite-sized pieces
- 1 Tbsp. dill pickle juice
- ½ cup cornstarch
- 1 Tbsp. soy sauce
- 1 large egg white
- ⅛ tsp. salt
- ⅛ tsp. pepper
- ¼ tsp. garlic powder
- ¼ tsp. paprika
- 1 Tbsp. Dijon mustard

DIPPING SAUCE
- ¼ cup Dijon mustard
- 3 Tbsp. barbecue sauce
- 2 Tbsp. honey
- Oil for frying

1. In a bowl, add chicken and dill pickle juice; toss to coat. Marinate at room temperature for 30 minutes. Meanwhile, combine the next 8 ingredients to form a thick batter. Add batter to the chicken mixture and toss to coat.

2. For dipping sauce, combine mustard, barbecue sauce and honey; set aside.

3. In a deep skillet or electric skillet, heat 1 in. oil to 375°. Fry chicken pieces, a few at a time, until browned and juices run clear, 1-2 minutes on each side. Drain on paper towels. Serve with sauce.

1 SERVING: 307 cal., 16g fat (2g sat. fat), 63mg chol., 514mg sod., 14g carb. (6g sugars, 0 fiber), 24g pro.

READER REVIEW

"These chicken nuggets were SO delicious and taste just like Chick-fil-A. Don't let the thick batter worry you like it did me. I thought I had my measurements wrong. Once it goes onto the chicken, it thins out. So good. I'm keeping this in rotation."

—JUDY3990, TASTEOFHOME.COM

COPYCAT CHICKEN NUGGETS

PRESSURE-COOKER PAPRIKA SHRIMP & RICE

My family loves seafood, as well as rice dishes, so this was a clear winner with them! You can set your oven at its lowest temperature and use it to keep the cooked vegetables and shrimp warm, without overcooking them, as your pressure cooker cooks the rice. If serving on individual plates instead of a big platter or bowl, accompany each serving with a small sprig of basil and a lemon wedge or two for squeezing.

—Joyce Conway, Westerville, OH

- -

PREP: 30 min. • **COOK:** 10 min. + releasing
MAKES: 4 servings

- 5 Tbsp. canola oil, divided
- 1 large sweet onion, chopped
- 1 cup chopped sweet pepper, such as yellow, orange or red
- ¾ lb. uncooked shrimp (16-20 per lb.), peeled and deveined
- 1 tsp. granulated garlic
- 1 tsp. paprika
- ½ tsp. crushed red pepper flakes
- 1½ cups chicken broth
- 1 pkg. (10 oz.) uncooked saffron rice
- 1 cup cannedpetite diced tomatoes
- 2 Tbsp. chopped fresh basil
- Lemon wedges

1. Select saute setting on a 6-qt. electric pressure cooker. Adjust for medium heat; add 2 Tbsp. oil. When oil is hot, cook and stir onion and pepper until crisp-tender, 4-5 minutes. Remove and keep warm.

2. Toss shrimp with granulated garlic, paprika and pepper flakes. Add remaining 3 Tbsp. oil to pan. When oil is hot, add shrimp. Cook and stir until shrimp turn pink, 5-6 minutes. Remove and keep warm. Add broth to pressure cooker. Cook 30 seconds, stirring to loosen browned bits from pan. Press cancel. Stir in rice.

3. Lock lid; close pressure-release valve. Adjust to pressure-cook on high for 8 minutes. Allow pressure to release naturally for 10 minutes, then quick-release any remaining pressure. Stir in tomatoes, shrimp and reserved pepper mixture; heat through. Top with basil; serve with lemon wedges.

1½ CUPS: 525 cal., 19g fat (2g sat. fat), 103mg chol., 1455mg sod., 68g carb. (9g sugars, 3g fiber), 22g pro.

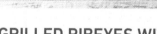
GRILLED RIBEYES WITH HATCH CHILE BUTTER

EASY ITALIAN SAUSAGE & PEPPERS

My sister was hosting a birthday party and asked me to bring sausage and peppers. I'd never made them before, so I altered a braised pepper recipe. Now family members request this dish often.
—Jeanne Corsi, Arnold, PA

- -

PREP: 15 min. • **COOK:** 20 min.
MAKES: 12 servings

- 3 lbs. Italian sausage links, cut into ¾-in. slices
- 4 medium green peppers, cut into thin strips
- 1 medium onion, thinly sliced and quartered
- 1 Tbsp. butter
- 1 Tbsp. olive oil
- 3 Tbsp. chicken broth
- 1 Tbsp. minced fresh parsley
- ½ tsp. salt
- ¼ tsp. pepper
- ½ tsp. lemon juice
- 6 plum tomatoes, coarsely chopped
  Hot cooked polenta, optional

1. In a Dutch oven or large skillet, cook the sausage over medium heat until no longer pink; drain. Add the next 9 ingredients.
2. Cover and cook until vegetables are crisp-tender, 10-12 minutes, stirring occasionally. Add tomatoes and heat through. If desired, serve with polenta.
1 SERVING: 224 cal., 17g fat (6g sat. fat), 48mg chol., 657mg sod., 5g carb. (3g sugars, 1g fiber), 12g pro.

ON THE SIDE: SOFT POLENTA

Bring **6 cups chicken broth** or water to a boil in a large saucepan over high heat. While whisking constantly, slowly add **2 cups cornmeal**. Continue whisking until mixture thickens, 2-3 minutes. Reduce heat to low; cook 45 minutes, stirring occasionally, until polenta is smooth and is the consistency of soft scrambled eggs. If desired, stir in **¼ cup butter** or olive oil, and **salt and pepper to taste**. Serve immediately. **Makes 12 servings.**

GRILLED RIBEYES WITH HATCH CHILE BUTTER

In summer, succulent ribeye steaks call for my flavor-packed compound butter, swirled with Hatch chiles, cilantro, lime juice and garlic.
—David Ross, Spokane Valley, WA

- -

PREP: 45 min. • **GRILL:** 10 min.
MAKES: 6 servings

- 2 whole green chiles, such as Hatch or poblano pepper
- 1 cup minced fresh cilantro
- ½ cup butter, softened
- 2 garlic cloves, minced
- 2 tsp. minced fresh oregano
- 1 Tbsp. lime juice
- ½ tsp. salt, divided
- ½ tsp. pepper, divided
- 3 lbs. beef ribeye steaks
- 1 Tbsp. olive oil
- 1 tsp. coarse sea salt
  Pickled jalapeno slices, optional

1. Cut peppers lengthwise in half. Remove stems and seeds; flatten slightly. Grill chiles, skin side down, until skins blister, about 3 minutes. Immediately place peppers in a small bowl; let stand, covered, 20 minutes.
2. Peel off and discard charred skin. Place grilled peppers, cilantro, butter, garlic, oregano, lime juice, ¼ tsp. salt and ¼ tsp. pepper in a food processor; pulse until just combined. Refrigerate until firm.
3. Brush steaks with oil and sprinkle with remaining ¼ tsp. salt and ¼ tsp. pepper. Grill steaks, covered, over medium-high heat or broil 4 in. from heat until meat reaches desired doneness (for medium-rare, a thermometer should read 135°; medium, 140°; medium-well, 145°), about 4 minutes on each side. Let stand for 5 minutes. Cut into thin slices.
4. Meanwhile, in a small saucepan, melt half the chile butter. Drizzle over steaks. Serve remaining butter with steaks. Sprinkle with coarse sea salt. If desired, garnish steaks with jalapeno slices and additional oregano.
5 OZ. COOKED BEEF WITH 5 TSP. BUTTER: 657 cal., 53g fat (25g sat. fat), 174mg chol., 815mg sod., 2g carb. (0 sugars, 0 fiber), 40g pro.

EASY ITALIAN
SAUSAGE &
PEPPERS

BAKED CHICKEN FAJITAS

I can't remember when or where I found this oven-baked fajitas recipe, but I've used it nearly every week since. We like it with hot sauce for added spice.
—*Amy Trinkle, Milwaukee, WI*

PREP: 15 min. • **BAKE:** 20 min. • **MAKES:** 6 servings

- 1 lb. boneless skinless chicken breasts, cut into thin strips
- 1 can (14½ oz.) diced tomatoes and green chiles, drained
- 1 medium onion, cut into thin strips
- 1 medium green pepper, cut into thin strips
- 1 medium sweet red pepper, cut into thin strips
- 2 Tbsp. canola oil
- 2 tsp. chili powder
- 2 tsp. ground cumin
- ¼ tsp. salt
- 12 flour tortillas (6 in.), warmed
  Optional toppings: Sliced avocado, tomato wedges and lime wedges

1. In a 13x9-in. baking dish coated with cooking spray, combine the chicken strips, tomatoes, onion and peppers. Combine the oil, chili powder, cumin and salt. Drizzle over chicken mixture; toss to coat.
2. Bake, uncovered, at 400° for 20-25 minutes or until chicken is no longer pink and vegetables are tender. Spoon onto tortillas; fold or roll tortillas to serve. Serve with toppings as desired.
2 FAJITAS: 375 cal., 14g fat (3g sat. fat), 42mg chol., 838mg sod., 40g carb. (3g sugars, 5g fiber), 22g pro.

MARINATED PORK KABOBS

MARINATED PORK KABOBS

When the grill comes out for the summer, so does this recipe. This entree was originally intended to be made with lamb, but crowd-favorite pork, layered with seasonal veggies, works so well in these kabobs.
—*Bobbie Jo Miller, Fallon, NV*

PREP: 15 min. + marinating • **GRILL:** 30 min. • **MAKES:** 8 servings

- 2 cups plain yogurt
- 2 Tbsp. lemon juice
- 4 garlic cloves, minced
- ½ tsp. ground cumin
- ¼ tsp. ground coriander
- 2 lbs. pork tenderloin, cut into 1½-in. cubes
- 8 small white onions, halved
- 8 cherry tomatoes
- 1 medium sweet red pepper, cut into 1½-in. pieces
- 1 medium green pepper, cut into 1½-in. pieces
  Salt & pepper to taste

1. In a shallow dish, combine yogurt, lemon juice, garlic, cumin and coriander. Add pork and turn to coat; cover and refrigerate 6 hours or overnight.
2. Alternate pork, onions, tomatoes and peppers on 8 metal or soaked wooden skewers. Season to taste with salt and pepper. Grill, covered, over medium heat until the meat juices run clear, 15-20 minutes, turning occasionally.
1 KABOB: 190 cal., 5g fat (2g sat. fat), 67mg chol., 63mg sod., 11g carb. (7g sugars, 2g fiber), 25g pro. **DIABETIC EXCHANGES:** 3 lean meat, 1 vegetable, ½ fat.

BAKED CHICKEN FAJITAS

SPINACH & SQUASH PIEROGI CASSEROLE

This casserole can be spiced to your liking. Once you've mastered the recipe, try using other savory pierogi in place of the potato and cheese version. Serve a salad or yummy bread as a side with this recipe for added punch.
—*Susan Skrtich, Hamilton, ON*

PREP: 35 min. • **BAKE:** 55 min. + standing
MAKES: 6 servings

- 1 tsp. olive oil
- 1 medium onion, chopped
- 1 Tbsp. minced garlic
- 1 Tbsp. minced fresh basil
- ½ tsp. salt
- ½ tsp. pepper
- 1 cup meatless pasta sauce
- 1 pkg. (14 oz.) frozen potato and cheese pierogi, thawed
- 1½ cups frozen chopped spinach, thawed and squeezed dry
- 1 large egg, room temperature, lightly beaten
- 1 cup frozen cubed butternut squash (about 5 oz.)
- 1½ cups shredded part-skim mozzarella cheese
- ½ cup sour cream, optional

1. Preheat oven to 350°. Line a 9x5-in. loaf pan with foil, letting ends extend up sides; grease foil.
2. In a small skillet, heat oil over medium-high heat. Add onion; cook and stir until tender, 6-8 minutes. Add garlic, basil, salt and pepper; cook 1 minute longer. Remove from the heat.
3. Spread ½ cup pasta sauce into prepared pan. Top with pierogi; press firmly. Top with the onion mixture. Mix spinach and egg; spoon over onion mixture. Spread squash evenly over spinach; spoon remaining ½ cup pasta sauce over top. Sprinkle with cheese. Bake until bubbly and cheese is golden brown, 55-65 minutes.
4. Let stand 10 minutes. Lifting with foil, remove from pan. Cut into slices. Serve with sour cream if desired.
1 SERVING: 269 cal., 9g fat (4g sat. fat), 54mg chol., 855mg sod., 33g carb. (10g sugars, 4g fiber), 14g pro.

SLOW-COOKED BARBECUED BEEF BRISKET

SLOW-COOKED BARBECUED BEEF BRISKET

I enjoy fixing a sit-down meal for my husband and myself every evening, so this entree is often on the menu. It is fairly inexpensive and takes very little effort to prepare. The tender beef tastes wonderful.
—*Anita Keppinger, Philomath, OR*

PREP: 10 min. • **COOK:** 4 hours
MAKES: 8 servings

- 1 tsp. salt
- 1 tsp. chili powder
- ½ tsp. garlic powder
- ¼ tsp. onion powder
- ¼ tsp. celery seed
- ¼ tsp. pepper
- 1 fresh beef brisket (2½ lbs.), trimmed

SAUCE
- ½ cup ketchup
- ½ cup chili sauce
- ¼ cup packed brown sugar
- 2 Tbsp. cider vinegar
- 2 Tbsp. Worcestershire sauce
- 1 to 1½ tsp. liquid smoke, optional
- ½ tsp. ground mustard

1. In a small bowl, combine the first 6 ingredients; rub over brisket. Place in a 3-qt. slow cooker.
2. In a large bowl, combine the sauce ingredients. Pour half over the brisket; set the remaining sauce aside.
3. Cover and cook on high for 4-5 hours or until meat is tender. Serve with the reserved sauce.
1 SERVING: 242 cal., 6g fat (2g sat. fat), 60mg chol., 810mg sod., 16g carb. (14g sugars, 0 fiber), 29g pro.

SPINACH & SQUASH PIEROGI CASSEROLE

**HERB GARDEN
GRILLED CHICKEN**

AIR-FRYER SAUSAGE PIZZA

I've always loved personal-size pizzas, and when I figured out how to make them in my air fryer, I was in pizza heaven! It's so easy, and now that my boys can customize their own pies, everyone in the family is happy.
—*Margo Zoerner, Pleasant Prairie, WI*

PREP: 30 min. • **BAKE:** 10 min./batch • **MAKES:** 4 pizzas

  1 loaf (1 lb.) frozen bread dough, thawed
  1 cup pizza sauce
  ½ lb. bulk Italian sausage, cooked and drained
1⅓ cups shredded part-skim mozzarella cheese
  1 small green pepper, sliced into rings
  1 tsp. dried oregano
     Crushed red pepper flakes, optional

1. On a lightly floured surface, roll and stretch dough into four 4-in. circles. Cover; let rest for 10 minutes.
2. Preheat air fryer to 400°. Roll and stretch each dough into a 6-in. circle. Place 1 crust on greased tray in air-fryer basket. Carefully spread with ¼ cup pizza sauce, ⅓ cup sausage, ⅓ cup cheese, a fourth of the green pepper rings and a pinch of oregano. Cook until crust is golden brown, 6-8 minutes. If desired, sprinkle with pepper flakes. Repeat with remaining ingredients.
1 PIZZA: 615 cal., 26g fat (9g sat. fat), 58mg chol., 1513mg sod., 64g carb. (9g sugars, 6g fiber), 29g pro.

HERB GARDEN GRILLED CHICKEN

One of my favorite things about spring is picking fresh herbs from my garden. It makes for an easy, flavorful chicken dinner. You can substitute any variety of herbs in this recipe, or roast it in the oven instead of grilling.
—*Jenn Tidwell, Fair Oaks, CA*

PREP: 20 min. • **GRILL:** 1¼ hours + standing • **MAKES:** 6 servings

  3 Tbsp. olive oil
  2 Tbsp. minced fresh oregano or 2 tsp. dried oregano
  2 Tbsp. minced fresh thyme or 2 tsp. dried thyme
  2 Tbsp. lemon juice
  2 Tbsp. red wine vinegar
  1 shallot, minced
  1 Tbsp. minced fresh lemon balm or 1 tsp. grated lemon zest
  1 Tbsp. minced fresh rosemary or 1 tsp. dried rosemary, crushed
  2 garlic cloves, minced
1½ tsp. salt
  ½ tsp. crushed red pepper flakes
  1 broiler/fryer chicken (3 to 4 lbs.)

1. Prepare grill for indirect heat using a drip pan. In a small bowl, mix the first 11 ingredients. With fingers, carefully loosen skin from chicken; rub seasoning mixture under and over skin. Tuck wings under chicken and tie legs.
2. Place chicken over drip pan and grill, covered, over indirect medium heat 1¼-1½ hours or until a thermometer inserted in thickest part of thigh reads 170°-175°, rotating occasionally. Remove chicken from grill; tent with foil. Let stand 15 minutes before carving.
5 OZ. COOKED CHICKEN: 364 cal., 24g fat (6g sat. fat), 104mg chol., 681mg sod., 3g carb. (0 sugars, 0 fiber), 33g pro.

**AIR-FRYER
SAUSAGE PIZZA**

ZUCCHINI LASAGNA

I plant zucchini every year, and we always seem to have more than we can use! This recipe is a particularly delicious way to use our abundant crop.

—*Charlotte McDaniel, Williamsville, IL*

- -

PREP: 20 min. • **BAKE:** 40 min. + standing • **MAKES:** 6 servings

- 1 lb. lean ground beef (90% lean)
- ¼ cup chopped onion
- ½ tsp. dried oregano
- ½ tsp. dried basil
- ¼ tsp. salt
- ¼ tsp. pepper
- 1 can (15 oz.) tomato sauce
- 1 large egg, lightly beaten
- 1 cup 2% cottage cheese
- 4 medium zucchini (about 1¾ lbs.)
- 3 Tbsp. all-purpose flour
- 1 cup shredded part-skim mozzarella cheese
   Additional shredded mozzarella cheese, optional

1. Preheat oven to 375°. In large skillet, cook and crumble beef with onion over medium-high heat 5-7 minutes or until beef is no longer pink. Stir in seasonings and tomato sauce. Bring to a boil; simmer, uncovered, 5 minutes. In a bowl, mix egg and cottage cheese.

2. Trim ends of zucchini; cut lengthwise into ¼-in.-thick slices. Toss zucchini with the flour. Layer half the slices in a greased 13x9-in. baking dish. Top with cottage cheese mixture and half the meat sauce. Add the remaining zucchini; sprinkle with any remaining flour. Spread with remaining meat sauce; sprinkle with 1 cup mozzarella cheese.

3. Bake, uncovered, until heated through, about 40 minutes. If desired, sprinkle with additional cheese. Let stand 10 minutes before serving.

FREEZE OPTION: Line a metal 13x9-in. pan with parchment. Assemble lasagna as directed, reserving final addition of 1 cup shredded cheese. Cover and freeze lasagna and remaining cheese separately. To use, preheat oven to 375°. Bake frozen lasagna, covered, for 50 minutes. Sprinkle with remaining 1 cup shredded mozzarella cheese. Bake, uncovered, until a thermometer inserted in center reads 165°, 50-55 minutes longer. If desired, sprinkle with additional cheese. Let stand 10 minutes before serving.

1 SERVING: 273 cal., 13g fat (5g sat. fat), 92mg chol., 725mg sod., 14g carb. (6g sugars, 3g fiber), 27g pro. **DIABETIC EXCHANGES:** 3 lean meat, 1 starch, 1 fat.

TEST KITCHEN TIPS

Follow these tips to ensure your lasagna is the perfect texture and not too watery:

- Be sure to slice your zucchini no thicker than ¼ in. thick.
- You can also sprinkle the slices with salt and let them sit for 15 minutes to draw out moisture.
- Once baked, let your lasagna sit for 10-15 minutes before cutting to let the dish reabsorb the moisture so that it doesn't run out of the bottom in a soupy mess.

ZUCCHINI
LASAGNA

EASY CHICKEN CREOLE

While I was growing up, my family spent time in Haiti, where we enjoyed eating many authentic dishes just like this. It's now a meal my family requests often.
—*Maxine Weaver, Petersburg, WV*

PREP: 15 min. • **COOK:** 20 min.
MAKES: 10 servings

- 1 cup sliced celery
- 1 cup chopped green pepper
- 1 cup chopped onion
- ¼ cup canola oil
- 2 garlic cloves, minced
- ¼ cup all-purpose flour
- 5 cups chicken broth
- 6 cups shredded or cubed cooked chicken
- 2 cans (6 oz. each) tomato paste
- ¼ cup chopped fresh parsley
- 4 tsp. Worcestershire sauce
- 2 tsp. lemon juice
- 1 tsp. salt
- ½ tsp. each pepper, sugar and dried thyme
- 12 to 16 drops hot pepper sauce
  Hot cooked rice

1. In a large skillet over medium heat, saute the celery, green pepper and onion in oil until tender; Add minced garlic; cook 1 minute longer. Add flour; cook and stir for 5 minutes or until browned.

2. Stir in broth. Bring to a boil; cook and stir for 2 minutes. Add the remaining ingredients except rice. Return to a boil. Reduce the heat; cover and simmer for 10 minutes or until heated through. Serve with rice. If desired, top with additional chopped parsley.

1 CUP: 259 cal., 12g fat (2g sat. fat), 75mg chol., 821mg sod., 10g carb. (5g sugars, 2g fiber), 27g pro.

DID YOU KNOW?

Celery, onion and green pepper is a classic Creole combination called holy trinity or Cajun mirepoix. Standard mirepoix uses carrots instead of green pepper.

COPYCAT PASTA DA VINCI

I fell in love with this dish at the Cheesecake Factory and experimented until I duplicated it. I think mine is just as good if not better! The sauce can be made ahead and then refrigerated or frozen. Thaw if frozen and warm gently in a large skillet. Just cook the pasta and you have a delicious dinner on a weeknight.
—*Trisha Kruse, Eagle, ID*

PREP: 25 min. • **COOK:** 35 min.
MAKES: 8 servings

- 1 pkg. (16 oz.) penne pasta
- 1 large red onion, diced
- 2 Tbsp. olive oil
- 3 garlic cloves, minced
- 1½ lbs. boneless skinless chicken breasts, cubed
- ½ lb. sliced fresh mushrooms
- 2 cups dry white wine
- 1 can (14½ oz.) beef broth
- 1 pkg. (8 oz.) cream cheese, softened
- ½ cup butter, softened
- ½ cup half-and-half cream, room temperature
- ½ tsp. salt
- ¼ tsp. pepper
- ½ cup grated Parmesan cheese, divided
  Minced fresh parsley, optional

1. Cook pasta according to package directions for al dente. Meanwhile, in a large skillet, cook onion in oil over medium heat until softened, 4-5 minutes. Add the garlic, cook 1 minute longer. Stir in the chicken and mushrooms. Cook, stirring frequently, until chicken is no longer pink, 5-7 minutes. With a slotted spoon, remove mixture; set aside.

2. To the same skillet, add wine and broth; bring mixture to a simmer. Cook until liquid is reduced by half, 15-20 minutes. Reduce heat to low; add cream cheese and butter, whisking until melted. Whisk in cream, salt and pepper. Add chicken mixture to pan; heat through on low. Toss with pasta and ¼ cup Parmesan cheese. Top with remaining ¼ cup Parmesan cheese and, if desired, parsley.

1½ CUPS: 634 cal., 31g fat (16g sat. fat), 118mg chol., 706mg sod., 49g carb. (5g sugars, 3g fiber), 30g pro.

EASY CHICKEN CREOLE

CUBE STEAKS
WITH GRAVY

Here's a hearty home-style dinner your family will love after a busy day. The slow-cooked beef is wonderful served over mashed potatoes or noodles.
—*Judy Long, Limestone, TN*

PREP: 15 min. • **COOK:** 8½ hours
MAKES: 6 servings

⅓ cup all-purpose flour
6 beef cube steaks (4 oz. each)
1 Tbsp. canola oil
1 large onion, sliced and separated into rings
3 cups water, divided
1 envelope brown gravy mix
1 envelope mushroom gravy mix
1 envelope onion gravy mix
Hot mashed potatoes or cooked noodles

1. Place flour in shallow dish. Add the steaks, 1 or 2 at a time, and turn to coat completely.
2. In a skillet, cook steaks in oil until lightly browned on each side. Transfer to a 3-qt. slow cooker. Add the onion and 2 cups water. Cover and cook on low for 8 hours or until meat is tender.
3. In a bowl, whisk together gravy mixes with remaining water. Add to slow cooker; cook 30 minutes longer. Serve over mashed potatoes or noodles.
1 SERVING: 245 cal., 7g fat (2g sat. fat), 64mg chol., 850mg sod., 16g carb. (4g sugars, 1g fiber), 29g pro.

PRESSURE-COOKER THAI SWEET CHILI PORK BOWLS

My family loves pork tenderloin as well as Thai food, so I decided to combine the two in this easy pressure-cooker dish. It's very simple to put together and is perfect for a weeknight. Don't forget the cilantro, lime and Sriracha sauce—they really make the dish stand out.
—*Debbie Glasscock, Conway, AR*

PREP: 20 min. • **COOK:** 20 min. + releasing
MAKES: 6 servings

2 pork tenderloins (1 lb. each)
½ lb. sliced fresh mushrooms
1 large sweet onion, cut into 1-in. pieces
1 large sweet red pepper, cut into 1-in. pieces
1 cup hoisin sauce
¾ cup sweet chili sauce
¼ cup reduced-sodium soy sauce
2 Tbsp. lime juice
2 garlic cloves, minced
1½ tsp. minced fresh gingerroot
1 tsp. rice vinegar
Torn fresh cilantro leaves
Hot cooked rice, julienned green onions, lime wedges and Sriracha chili sauce

1. Place pork in a 6-qt. electric pressure cooker. Top with mushrooms, onion and red pepper. Whisk together hoisin sauce, chili sauce, soy sauce, lime juice, garlic, ginger and rice vinegar; pour over vegetables. Lock lid; close pressure-release valve. Adjust to pressure-cook on high for 20 minutes. Allow pressure to release naturally.
2. Remove pork; shred with 2 forks. Return pork to pressure cooker; heat through. Sprinkle with cilantro and green onions; serve with rice, lime wedges and Sriracha.
1 SERVING: 384 cal., 7g fat (2g sat. fat), 86mg chol., 1664mg sod., 44g carb. (33g sugars, 3g fiber), 34g pro.

PRESSURE-COOKER
THAI SWEET CHILI
PORK BOWLS

CUBE STEAKS
WITH GRAVY

AIR-FRYER PORK TENDERLOIN

PRESSURE-COOKER CUBAN CHICKEN

I love the flavors of Cuban food. Lots of citrus, garlic, cilantro and spices; I could eat it every day. I found I could create that slow-cooked flavor using my Instant Pot and my family is now eating Cuban food a lot more.
—*Courtney Stultz, Weir, KS*

PREP: 15 min. • **COOK:** 10 min. • **MAKES:** 4 servings

- 1 lb. boneless skinless chicken breasts
- 1 cup chicken broth
- ½ cup fresh cilantro leaves, chopped
- ½ cup orange juice
- 2 Tbsp. lime juice
- 1 Tbsp. olive oil
- 3 garlic cloves, minced
- 1 tsp. smoked paprika
- 1 tsp. dried oregano
- ½ tsp. salt
- ½ tsp. ground cumin
- ¼ tsp. pepper

1. Place chicken and broth in a 6-qt. electric pressure cooker. Lock lid; close pressure-release valve. Adjust to pressure-cook on high for 6 minutes. Quick-release pressure. A thermometer inserted in chicken should read at least 165°.

2. Remove chicken; shred with 2 forks. Drain cooking juices. Return chicken to pressure cooker. Add remaining ingredients. Select saute setting and adjust for low heat; simmer uncovered, until heated through, 3-4 minutes, stirring occasionally. Press cancel.

FREEZE OPTION: Freeze the cooled meat mixture and juices in freezer containers. To use, partially thaw in refrigerator overnight. Heat through in a saucepan, stirring occasionally; add broth if necessary.

⅔ CUP: 175 cal., 6g fat (1g sat. fat), 63mg chol., 373mg sod., 5g carb. (3g sugars, 1g fiber), 24g pro. **DIABETIC EXCHANGES:** 3 lean meat, 1 fat.

AIR-FRYER PORK TENDERLOIN

I originally developed this recipe to brown on the stove and finish in the oven, but you can make it even quicker in an air fryer—and it's just as tasty.
—*Lynn Faria, Southington, CT*

PREP: 10 min. • **COOK:** 20 min. + standing • **MAKES:** 2 servings

- 1 pork tenderloin (¾ lb.)
- 1 Tbsp. spicy brown mustard
- 2 tsp. canola oil
- 1 tsp. garlic powder
- 1 tsp. onion powder
- ½ tsp. pepper

Preheat air fryer to 375°. Trim silver skin from tenderloin if desired; pat dry. In a small bowl, stir together remaining ingredients; spread over tenderloin. Place in greased tray in air-fryer basket. Cook 18 to 20 minutes or until a thermometer reads 145°. Let stand 10 minutes before slicing.

5 OZ. COOKED PORK: 257 cal., 11g fat (2g sat. fat), 95mg chol., 145mg sod., 2g carb. (0 sugars, 0 fiber), 34g pro. **DIABETIC EXCHANGES:** 5 lean meat, 1 fat

READER REVIEW

"We love doing pork tenderloins in the air fryer. I like doing them on the rotisserie attachment, but they are just as good made on the tray. I used granulated garlic instead of the garlic powder. Will definitely make again."

—GRANDMASCOOKING22, TASTEOFHOME.COM

PRESSURE-COOKER CUBAN CHICKEN

**BANH MI
BABY BACK RIBS**

BANH MI BABY BACK RIBS

We love both banh mi and ribs. This creative entree has all the flavors of the beloved Vietnamese sandwich—sans bread. Sprinkle the pork with roasted peanuts and sesame seeds, in addition to the other garnishes, for a fun crunch.
—*Bonnie Geavaras-Bootz, Chandler, AZ*

- -

PREP: 3 hours • **GRILL:** 15 min.
MAKES: 4 servings

- 4 **lbs. pork baby back ribs**
- 2 **whole garlic bulbs**
- 1 **large navel orange, quartered**
- 1 **cup Korean barbecue sauce, divided**
- ¾ **cup rice vinegar**
- ½ **cup sugar**
- ⅓ **cup water**
- ½ **cup shredded carrots**
- ½ **cup shredded daikon radish**
- ½ **cup thinly sliced green onions**

Toppings: Thinly sliced cucumber, sliced fresh jalapeno pepper, cilantro leaves and lime wedges

1. Preheat oven to 325°. Place ribs in a large roasting pan. Remove papery outer skin from garlic bulbs, but do not peel or separate the cloves. Cut off top of garlic bulbs, exposing individual cloves; add to roasting pan. Add orange; cover pan with heavy-duty foil and seal tightly. Bake until tender, 2-2½ hours, brushing with ½ cup barbecue sauce halfway through cooking.
2. Meanwhile, in a small saucepan, combine vinegar, sugar and water. Bring mixture to a boil over high heat; cook until sugar is dissolved, about 2 minutes. Let cool completely. Place carrots, radish and green onions in a bowl; add brine. Refrigerate until serving.

3. Prepare grill for medium direct heat. Carefully remove ribs from roasting pan; discard garlic and orange. Place ribs on the grill rack; brush with some of the remaining ½ cup barbecue sauce. Grill, covered, over medium heat until browned, 15-20 minutes, turning and brushing occasionally with sauce. Cut ribs into serving-sized portions. Serve with pickled vegetables, toppings and remaining sauce.
1 SERVING: 718 cal., 50g fat (16g sat. fat), 163mg chol., 1499mg sod., 23g carb. (17g sugars, 1g fiber), 45g pro.

SLOW-COOKER
ARIZONA POBLANO PORK

SLOW-COOKER ARIZONA POBLANO PORK

We love seasonal poblano peppers, so this easy dish with many southwestern seasonings is a family favorite. It can be served in a variety of ways, too. It's great with rice and beans, or in a taco with hot sauce.
—*Johnna Johnson, Scottsdale, AZ*

PREP: 20 min. • **COOK:** 3 hours
MAKES: 8 servings

- 1   boneless pork loin roast (3 to 4 lbs.)
- 3   Tbsp. fajita seasoning mix, divided
- 1   Tbsp. olive oil
- 1   can (14½ oz.) fire-roasted diced tomatoes, undrained
- 1   large red onion, chopped
- 1½ cups chopped seeded fresh poblano peppers
- ¼   cup beef broth
- 1   tsp. chili powder
- ¾   tsp. ground cumin
- ½   tsp. garlic powder
- ½   tsp. cayenne pepper
       Optional: Hot cooked rice and a chipotle hot sauce, such as Cholula

1. Sprinkle pork roast with 2 Tbsp. fajita seasoning. In a large skillet, heat oil over medium heat; brown meat. Transfer meat to a 5- or 6-qt. slow cooker. In a large bowl, combine the next 8 ingredients and remaining 1 Tbsp. fajita seasoning; pour over meat. Cook, covered, on low until a thermometer inserted in pork reads at least 145°, about 3 hours.
2. Remove roast; cool slightly. Cut pork into bite-sized pieces; return to slow cooker. Heat through. If desired, serve pork with rice and hot sauce.
FREEZE OPTION: Place cubed roast in freezer containers; top with cooking juices. Cool and freeze. To use, partially thaw in refrigerator overnight. Heat through in a saucepan, stirring occasionally.
1¼ CUPS: 274 cal., 10g fat (3g sat. fat), 85mg chol., 588mg sod., 10g carb. (4g sugars, 1g fiber), 34g pro.

SOUTHERN-STYLE MEAT LOAF

When my husband and I moved to the South, we discovered our love for pimiento cheese! Its addition lends a southern flare to this tried-and-true American favorite.
—*Patricia Getson, Wilmington, NC*

PREP: 30 min. • **BAKE:** 1 hour + standing
MAKES: 6 servings

- 2   tsp. olive oil
- ½   cup chopped sweet onion
- ⅓   cup chopped celery
- ½   cup shredded carrots
- 3   garlic cloves, minced
- 2   large eggs, lightly beaten
- ⅓   cup crushed saltines (about 10 crackers)
- ⅓   cup crushed Ritz crackers (about 10 crackers)
- 2   Tbsp. Italian seasoning
- 1   Tbsp. dried parsley flakes
- 1   tsp. salt
- 1   tsp. pepper
- 1½ lbs. lean ground beef (90% lean)
- 1   carton (12 oz.) refrigerated pimiento cheese
       Hot mashed red potatoes
       Optional: Shredded sharp cheddar cheese and sliced jalapeno pepper

1. Preheat oven to 350°. In a large skillet, heat oil over medium-high heat. Add the onion and celery; cook and stir until crisp-tender, 4-5 minutes. Add carrots and garlic; cook and stir until tender, 1-2 minutes longer. Transfer vegetable mixture to a large bowl. Add the eggs, crackers and seasonings. Add beef; mix lightly but thoroughly
2. Shape into an 8x4-in. loaf in a greased 11x7-in. baking dish. Bake, covered, for 45 minutes. Uncover and bake until a thermometer reads 160°, 15-20 minutes longer. Let stand 10 minutes. Cut into slices; spread with pimiento cheese. Serve with potatoes and, if desired, shredded cheese and jalapeno.
1 SERVING: 436 cal., 27g fat (10g sat. fat), 160mg chol., 1226mg sod., 17g carb. (3g sugars, 1g fiber), 31g pro.

SOUTHERN-STYLE MEAT LOAF

BAKED FETA PASTA

CREAMY BEEF LASAGNA

The creamy Stroganoff-like filling in this distinctive lasagna makes it a stick-to-your-ribs entree. My family loves the delicious taste, and I appreciate that it's inexpensive to fix.
—*Jane Frawley, Charles Town, WV*

PREP: 20 min. • **BAKE:** 45 min. + standing • **MAKES:** 12 servings

> 1½ lbs. ground beef
> 2 cans (15 oz. each) tomato sauce
> ¼ cup chopped onion
> 2 tsp. sugar
> 2 tsp. salt
> 2 tsp. Worcestershire sauce
> ½ tsp. garlic salt
> 2 pkg. (8 oz. each) cream cheese, softened
> 1 cup sour cream
> ¼ cup 2% milk
> 12 lasagna noodles, cooked and drained
> 1 cup shredded cheddar cheese
> Optional: Minced fresh parsley and crushed red pepper flakes

1. In a skillet, cook beef over medium heat until no longer pink; drain. Stir in tomato sauce, onion, sugar, salt, Worcestershire sauce and garlic salt. In a bowl, beat cream cheese, sour cream and milk until smooth.

2. In a greased 13x9-in. baking dish, layer a third of the meat sauce, 4 noodles and a third of cream cheese mixture. Repeat layers twice.

3. Cover and bake at 350° for 40 minutes. Uncover; sprinkle with cheddar cheese. Bake 5 minutes longer or until cheese is melted. Let stand 15 minutes before cutting. If desired, sprinkle with minced parsley and red pepper flakes.

1 PIECE: 429 cal., 28g fat (14g sat. fat), 88mg chol., 1031mg sod., 27g carb. (6g sugars, 2g fiber), 20g pro.

TEST KITCHEN TIPS

- No-bake or oven-ready noodles will work in this recipe. For best results, don't rinse or soak oven-ready noodles prior to assembly. Make sure the entire surface of each noodle is covered with sauce and/or the cream cheese mixture so the noodles soften properly. Cover the pan with foil so the noodles steam while baking and the edges don't dry out.
- To make this dish ahead, simply assemble, cover and store in the refrigerator for 1-2 days before baking. However, we don't recommend freezing this lasagna for later use because the cream cheese mixture will not freeze well.

BAKED FETA PASTA

There's a reason this recipe went viral on TikTok! Baked Feta Pasta is about to become a new household favorite. It's simple to throw together and incredibly creamy and delicious.
—*Sarah Tramonte, Milwaukee, WI*

PREP: 15 min. • **BAKE:** 30 min. • **MAKES:** 8 servings

> 2 pints cherry tomatoes
> 3 garlic cloves, halved
> ½ cup olive oil
> 1 pkg. (8 oz.) block feta cheese
> 1 tsp. sea salt
> ¼ tsp. coarsely ground pepper
> 1 pkg. (16 oz.) rigatoni or other short pasta
> Fresh basil leaves, coarsely chopped

1. Preheat oven to 400°. In a 13x9-in. baking dish, combine the tomatoes, garlic and ¼ cup olive oil. Place the block of feta in the center, moving tomatoes so cheese is sitting on the pan bottom. Drizzle feta with remaining oil and sprinkle with salt and pepper. Bake until tomato skins start to split and the garlic has softened, 30-40 minutes.

2. Meanwhile, cook pasta according to package directions for al dente. Drain, reserving 1 cup pasta water.

3. Stir feta mixture, lightly pressing tomatoes, until combined. Add pasta and toss to combine. Stir in enough reserved pasta water to achieve desired consistency. Sprinkle with basil.

1 SERVING: 373 cal., 16g fat (6g sat. fat), 25mg chol., 507mg sod., 46g carb. (5g sugars, 3g fiber), 12g pro.

CREAMY BEEF
LASAGNA

PRESSURE-COOKER PUERTO RICAN PERNIL

PRESSURE-COOKER PUERTO RICAN PERNIL

Picture this—you're sitting on the beach, sun shining, waves crashing and a mojito in your hand when the most wonderful aroma wafts over to you. It's a citrusy, spicy, and mouthwatering pork roast more flavorful than anything you've ever tasted. Cooking and eating this should remind you of the best parts of island life. It's OK to use fresh-squeezed orange juice or lime juice, or a combination of both instead of the grapefruit juice, but please, don't ever make this with bottled juice.

—*Cristina Carrera, Kenosha, WI*

PREP: 25 min. • **COOK:** 1 hour + releasing
MAKES: 8 servings

- 1 whole garlic bulb, peeled and separated, divided
- 1 medium onion, quartered
- ½ large grapefruit, juiced
- 3 Tbsp. fresh oregano leaves
- 3 Tbsp. olive oil, divided
- 1 serrano pepper, seeded and chopped, optional
- 2 tsp. ground cumin
- 1 tsp. salt
- 1 boneless pork shoulder roast (4 to 5 lbs.)
- ½ cup chicken broth
  Hot cooked rice, corn tortillas and lime wedges

1. Place half the garlic cloves, onion, grapefruit juice, oregano, 1 Tbsp. oil, serrano pepper if desired, cumin and salt in a food processor; process until mostly smooth. Reserve 6 Tbsp. marinade for serving.

2. Pour remaining marinade into a shallow dish. Cut slits into roast; insert remaining garlic cloves. Place pork in dish; turn to coat. Cover and refrigerate at least 1 hour and up to 12 hours. Cover and refrigerate remaining marinade.

3. Drain pork, reserving marinade in dish. Select saute or browning setting on a 6-qt. electric pressure cooker. Adjust for medium heat; add remaining 2 Tbsp. oil. When oil is hot, brown roast on all sides; remove roast. Add broth to pressure cooker. Cook 1 minute, stirring to loosen browned bits from pan. Press cancel.

4. Add marinade from marinade dish and return roast to pan. Lock lid; close pressure-release valve. Adjust to pressure-cook on high for 60 minutes. Allow pressure to release naturally for 10 minutes; quick-release any remaining pressure.

5. Pull pork apart in large chunks. Serve with rice, tortillas, lime wedges and reserved marinade.

5 OZ. COOKED PORK: 434 cal., 28g fat (9g sat. fat), 135mg chol., 491mg sod., 4g carb. (1g sugars, 0 fiber), 39g pro.

GREEK OUZO PORK KABOBS

Do dinner like the Mediterraneans with these delightfully different kabobs. The ouzo, an anise-flavored liqueur, and the tzatziki dipping sauce give you a real taste of the Greek islands.
—*Francine Lizotte, Surrey, BC*

PREP: 25 min. + marinating • GRILL: 15 min. • MAKES: 6 servings

- ½ cup olive oil
- ¼ cup lemon juice
- ¼ cup honey
- 2 Tbsp. balsamic vinegar
- 1 Tbsp. minced garlic
- 1 Tbsp. minced fresh oregano or 1 tsp. dried oregano
- 1 Tbsp. minced fresh thyme or 1 tsp. dried thyme
- 1½ tsp. minced fresh rosemary or ¾ tsp. dried rosemary, crushed
- ½ tsp. salt
- ¼ tsp. pepper
- ¼ cup ouzo or anise liqueur
- 2 lbs. pork tenderloin, cut into 1½-in. cubes
- 2 large green peppers, cut into 1½-in. pieces
- 24 cherry tomatoes
- 1 large sweet onion, cut into 1½-in. pieces
  Refrigerated tzatziki sauce, optional

1. In a small bowl, whisk the first 10 ingredients until blended. Pour ½ cup marinade into a shallow dish; stir in ouzo. Add the pork; turn to coat. Refrigerate 8 hours or overnight. Cover and refrigerate remaining marinade.

2. Drain pork, discarding marinade in dish. On 12 metal or soaked wooden skewers, alternately thread pork and vegetables. Grill kabobs, uncovered, over medium heat or broil 4 in. from heat until until the pork is tender and vegetables are crisp-tender, 12-15 minutes, turning occasionally and basting frequently with reserved marinade during the last 5 minutes. If desired, top with additional fresh thyme and rosemary and serve with tzatziki.

2 KABOBS: 336 cal., 15g fat (3g sat. fat), 85mg chol., 178mg sod., 17g carb. (13g sugars, 2g fiber), 32g pro. **DIABETIC EXCHANGES:** 4 lean meat, 2 fat, 1 vegetable, ½ starch.

GREEK OUZO
PORK KABOBS

LIGHT-BUT-
HEARTY TUNA
CASSEROLE

LIGHT-BUT-HEARTY TUNA CASSEROLE

My boyfriend grew up loving his mother's tuna casserole and says he can't even tell that this one is light! We have it at least once a month. I usually serve it with a salad, but it has enough veggies to stand on its own.
—*Heidi Carofano, Brooklyn, NY*

PREP: 20 min. • BAKE: 25 min. • MAKES: 4 servings

- 3 cups uncooked yolk-free noodles
- 1 can (10¾ oz.) reduced-fat reduced-sodium condensed cream of mushroom soup, undiluted
- ½ cup fat-free milk
- 2 Tbsp. reduced-fat mayonnaise
- ½ tsp. ground mustard
- 1 jar (6 oz.) sliced mushrooms, drained
- 1 can (5 oz.) albacore white tuna in water
- ¼ cup chopped roasted sweet red pepper

TOPPING
- ¼ cup dry bread crumbs
- 1 Tbsp. butter, melted
- ½ tsp. paprika
- ¼ tsp. Italian seasoning
- ¼ tsp. pepper

1. Preheat the oven to 400°. Cook noodles according to the package directions.In a large bowl, combine soup, milk, mayonnaise and mustard. Stir in the mushrooms, tuna and red pepper. Drain noodles; add to soup mixture and stir until blended. Transfer to a greased 8-in. square baking dish.

2. Combine topping ingredients; sprinkle over casserole. Bake until bubbly, 25-30 minutes.

1½ CUPS: 322 cal., 9g fat (3g sat. fat), 32mg chol., 843mg sod., 39g carb. (7g sugars, 4g fiber), 18g pro.

SESAME-SOY
STRING BEANS
PAGE 110

HOMEMADE
PORK DUMPLINGS
PAGE 111

GINGER SCALLION &
SOY STEAMED FISH
PAGE 109

Meal Planner

Smart cooks save time and money by planning ahead. Find grab-and-go homemade breakfasts, lunches in a jar, and simple foil-pack dinners here. Plus: Mix and match our favorite Asian dishes for a feast that rivals any takeout.

DISHES WE LOVE

Speedy At Sunrise

When you're feeling behind on the rise-and-shine, turn to these breezy breakfasts. Make-ahead recipes mean no morning mayhem!

HOW-TO

Freeze Breakfast Biscuit Cups

Freeze cooled biscuit cups in a freezer container, separating layers with waxed paper. To use, microwave 1 frozen biscuit cup on high until heated through, 50-60 seconds.

BREAKFAST BISCUIT CUPS

BREAKFAST BISCUIT CUPS

The first time I made these, my husband and his assistant coach came into the kitchen as I pulled the pan from the oven. They devoured the biscuit cups!
—*Debra Carlson, Columbus Junction, IA*

PREP: 30 min. • **BAKE:** 20 min.
MAKES: 8 servings

- ⅓ lb. bulk pork sausage
- 1 Tbsp. all-purpose flour
- ⅛ tsp. salt
- ½ tsp. pepper, divided
- ¾ cup plus 1 Tbsp. 2% milk, divided
- ½ cup frozen cubed hash brown potatoes, thawed
- 1 Tbsp. butter
- 2 large eggs
- ⅛ tsp. garlic salt
- 1 can (16.3 oz.) large refrigerated flaky biscuits
- ½ cup shredded Colby-Monterey Jack cheese

1. In a large skillet, cook sausage over medium heat until no longer pink; drain. Stir in the flour, salt and ¼ tsp. pepper until blended; gradually add ¾ cup milk. Bring to a boil; cook and stir until thickened, about 2 minutes. Remove from heat and set aside.
2. In another large skillet over medium heat, cook potatoes in butter until tender. Whisk the eggs, garlic salt and remaining milk and pepper; add to skillet. Cook and stir until almost set.
3. One at a time, press biscuits onto the bottom and up the sides of 8 ungreased muffin cups. Spoon the egg mixture, half the cheese, and the sausage into cups; sprinkle with remaining cheese.
4. Bake at 375° until golden brown, 18-22 minutes. Cool 5 minutes before removing from pan.
1 BISCUIT CUP: 303 cal., 18g fat (6g sat. fat), 72mg chol., 774mg sod., 26g carb. (7g sugars, 1g fiber), 9g pro.

GOLDEN OAT PANCAKES

My husband's just face lights up when I make these country-style flapjacks. Serve them for a weekend breakfast or brunch, or freeze and reheat them later.
—*Raymonde Bourgeois, Swastika, ON*

TAKES: 25 min. • **MAKES:** 5 servings

- 1 cup old-fashioned oats
- 1⅓ cups 2% milk
- ¾ cup all-purpose flour
- 4 tsp. baking powder
- 4 tsp. brown sugar
- ¼ tsp. salt
- 2 large eggs, room temperature, lightly beaten
- 3 Tbsp. canola oil

1. In a small bowl, mix oats and milk; let stand 5 minutes. In a large bowl, whisk flour, baking powder, brown sugar and salt.
2. Stir eggs and oil into oat mixture. Add to flour mixture; stir just until moistened.
3. Lightly grease a griddle; heat over medium heat. Pour batter by ¼ cupfuls onto griddle. Cook until bubbles on top begin to pop and bottoms are golden brown. Turn; cook until second side is golden brown.
2 PANCAKES: 270 cal., 13g fat (2g sat. fat), 80mg chol., 498mg sod., 30g carb. (7g sugars, 2g fiber), 8g pro.

HOW-TO

Freeze Golden Oat Pancakes

Freeze cooled pancakes between layers of waxed paper in a freezer container. To use, place pancakes on an ungreased baking sheet, cover with foil and reheat in a preheated 375° oven 5-10 minutes. Or place 2 pancakes on a microwave-safe plate and microwave 1-1¼ minutes or until heated through.

GOLDEN OAT PANCAKES

SCRAMBLED EGG MUFFINS

After enjoying scrambled egg muffins at a local restaurant, I came up with this savory version that my husband likes even better. Freeze the extras to reheat on busy mornings.
—Cathy Larkins, Marshfield, MO

- -

TAKES: 30 min. • **MAKES:** 1 dozen

- ½ lb. bulk pork sausage
- 12 large eggs, room temperature
- ½ cup chopped onion
- ¼ cup chopped green pepper
- ½ tsp. salt
- ¼ tsp. garlic powder
- ¼ tsp. pepper
- ½ cup shredded cheddar cheese

1. Preheat oven to 350°. In a large skillet, cook sausage over medium heat until no longer pink, breaking it into crumbles; drain.
2. In a large bowl, beat eggs. Add onion, green pepper, salt, garlic powder and pepper. Stir in sausage and cheese.
3. Spoon by ⅓ cupfuls into greased muffin cups. Bake until a knife inserted in the center comes out clean, 20-25 minutes.
FREEZE OPTION: Cool baked egg muffins. Place on waxed paper-lined baking sheets, cover and freeze until firm. Transfer to freezer container; return to freezer. To use, place in greased muffin pan, cover loosely with foil and reheat in a preheated 350° oven until heated through. Or microwave each muffin on high 30-60 seconds or until heated through..
1 MUFFIN: 133 cal., 10g fat (4g sat. fat), 224mg chol., 268mg sod., 2g carb. (1g sugars, 0 fiber), 9g pro.

READER REVIEW

"Added some mushrooms and diced potatoes. Kids love them on the way out the door. Good job!"

—BOB555E, TASTEOFHOME.COM

FLUFFY BANANA PANCAKES

FLUFFY BANANA PANCAKES

I love to make pancakes for my family on Saturday mornings. Since we often have ripe bananas, I decided to add them to a batch of pancake batter. The results were delicious!
—Lori Stevens, Riverton, UT

- -

TAKES: 30 min. • **MAKES:** 7 servings

- 1 cup all-purpose flour
- 1 cup whole wheat flour
- 3 Tbsp. brown sugar
- 1 tsp. baking powder
- 1 tsp. baking soda
- 1 tsp. ground cinnamon
- ½ tsp. salt
- 2 large eggs, room temperature
- 2 cups buttermilk
- 2 Tbsp. canola oil
- 1 tsp. vanilla extract
- 1 ripe medium banana, finely chopped
- ⅓ cup finely chopped walnuts

1. In a large bowl, combine the first 7 ingredients. In another bowl, whisk eggs, buttermilk, oil and vanilla until blended. Add to dry ingredients, stirring just until moistened. Fold in banana and walnuts.

2. Pour batter by ¼ cupfuls onto a lightly greased hot griddle. Cook until bubbles begin to form on top and bottoms are golden brown. Turn; cook until second side is golden brown.
FREEZE OPTION: Freeze cooled pancakes between layers of waxed paper in a freezer container. To use, place pancakes on an ungreased baking sheet, cover with foil and reheat in a preheated 375° oven 5-10 minutes. Or place 2 pancakes on a microwave-safe plate and microwave on high for 40-50 seconds or until heated through.
2 PANCAKES: 283 cal., 10g fat (2g sat. fat), 63mg chol., 503mg sod., 40g carb. (12g sugars, 4g fiber), 9g pro. **DIABETIC EXCHANGES:** 2½ starch, 1½ fat.
FLUFFY STRAWBERRY PANCAKES: Replace chopped banana with ¾ cup chopped fresh strawberries; proceed as directed.
FLUFFY PEACH PANCAKES: Replace chopped banana with ¾ cup chopped fresh or frozen peaches; proceed as directed.
FLUFFY BLUEBERRY PANCAKES: Replace chopped banana with ¾ cup chopped fresh or frozen blueberries; proceed as directed.

BREAKFAST WRAPS

We like quick and simple morning meals during the week, and these wraps can be prepped ahead of time. With just a minute in the microwave, breakfast is ready to go.
—*Betty Kleberger, Florissant, MO*

TAKES: 15 min. • **MAKES:** 4 servings

- 6 large eggs
- 2 Tbsp. 2% milk
- ¼ tsp. pepper
- 1 Tbsp. canola oil
- 1 cup shredded cheddar cheese
- ¾ cup diced fully cooked ham
- 4 flour tortillas (8 in.), warmed

1. In a small bowl, whisk the eggs, milk and pepper. In a large skillet, heat oil. Add egg mixture; cook and stir over medium heat until eggs are completely set. Stir in cheese and ham.

2. Spoon egg mixture down the center of each tortilla; roll up.

1 SERVING: 436 cal., 24g fat (10g sat. fat), 364mg chol., 853mg sod., 28g carb. (1g sugars, 0 fiber), 25g pro.

PIZZA BREAKFAST WRAPS: Prepare recipe as directed, replacing cheddar cheese and ham with mozzarella cheese and cooked sausage. Serve with warm marinara sauce on the side.

PULLED PORK BREAKFAST WRAPS: Prepare recipe as directed, replacing cheddar cheese and ham with smoked Gouda cheese and precooked pulled pork. Serve with warm barbecue sauce on the side.

HOW-TO

Freeze Breakfast Wraps

Wrap cooled egg wrap in foil or parchment and freeze in a freezer container. To use, thaw in refrigerator overnight. Remove foil or parchment; wrap tortilla in a moist paper towel. Microwave on high until heated through, 30-60 seconds. Serve immediately.

BREAKFAST WRAPS

Freezer Flapjacks

When there's no time for freshly griddled pancakes in the morning, grab your frozen stash for homemade breakfast in a flash.

BLUEBERRY OATMEAL PANCAKES

✳ BLUEBERRY OATMEAL PANCAKES

Wonderful blueberry flavor abounds in these thick and moist pancakes. My kids adore them, and I love that they're easy to make or reheat on busy mornings.
—*Amy Spainhoward, Bowling Green, KY*

PREP: 20 min. • COOK: 5 min./batch
MAKES: 7 servings (1¼ cups syrup)

- 2 cups all-purpose flour
- 2 packets (1.51 oz. each) instant maple and brown sugar oatmeal mix
- 2 Tbsp. sugar
- 2 tsp. baking powder
- ⅛ tsp. salt
- 2 large egg whites
- 1 large egg
- 1½ cups fat-free milk
- ½ cup reduced-fat sour cream
- 2 cups fresh or frozen blueberries

BLUEBERRY SYRUP
- 1½ cups fresh or frozen blueberries
- ½ cup sugar

1. In a large bowl, combine the first 5 ingredients. In another bowl, whisk the egg whites, egg, milk and sour cream. Stir into dry ingredients just until moistened. Fold in blueberries.
2. Spoon batter by ¼ cupfuls onto a hot griddle coated with cooking spray. Turn when bubbles form on top of pancake; cook until second side is golden brown.
3. In a microwave-safe bowl, combine the syrup ingredients. Microwave, uncovered, on high for 1 minute; stir. Microwave until hot and bubbly, 1-2 minutes longer. Serve warm with pancakes.

2 PANCAKES WITH ABOUT 2 TBSP.
SYRUP: 336 cal., 3g fat (1g sat. fat), 29mg chol., 302mg sod., 68g carb. (32g sugars, 4g fiber), 10g pro.

HOW-TO

Freeze Those Flapjacks

For each of these recipes, place cooked and cooled pancakes in a single layer on a parchment-lined baking sheet. Freeze until solid, about 30 minutes. Stack frozen pancakes, separating layers with parchment. Store in an airtight container. To reheat, microwave until hot, 20-30 seconds.

BUTTERMILK PANCAKES

✳ BUTTERMILK PANCAKES

You just can't beat a basic buttermilk pancake for a down-home hearty breakfast. Pair it with sausage and fresh fruit for a mouthwatering morning meal.
—*Betty Abrey, Imperial, SK*

PREP: 10 min. • COOK: 5 min./batch
MAKES: 2½ dozen

- 4 cups all-purpose flour
- ¼ cup sugar
- 2 tsp. baking soda
- 2 tsp. salt
- 1½ tsp. baking powder
- 4 large eggs, room temperature
- 4 cups buttermilk

1. In a large bowl, combine the flour, sugar, baking soda, salt and baking powder. In another bowl, whisk the eggs and buttermilk until blended; stir into dry ingredients just until moistened.
2. Pour batter by ¼ cupfuls onto a lightly greased hot griddle; turn when bubbles form on top. Cook until second side is golden brown.

3 PANCAKES: 270 cal., 3g fat (1g sat. fat), 89mg chol., 913mg sod., 48g carb. (11g sugars, 1g fiber), 11g pro.

PECAN APPLE PANCAKES: To flour mixture, stir in 1¾ tsp. ground cinnamon, ¾ tsp. ground ginger, ¾ tsp. ground mace and ¾ tsp. ground cloves. To batter, fold in 2½ cups shredded peeled apples and ¾ cup chopped pecans.

BLUEBERRY PANCAKES: Fold in 1 cup fresh or frozen blueberries.

BANANA WALNUT PANCAKES: Fold in 2 finely chopped ripe bananas and ⅔ cups finely chopped walnuts.

BANANA NUT PANCAKES

PUMPKIN-FLAVORED PANCAKES

I created these light pumpkin-flavored pancakes with two kinds of flour and a blend of spices for a delightful taste. Serve them for brunch as a hearty eye-opener or for a fun meat-free dinner.
—Vicki Floden, Story City, IA

TAKES: 20 min. • **MAKES:** 6 servings

1½ cups all-purpose flour
½ cup whole wheat flour
2 Tbsp. brown sugar
2 tsp. baking powder
1 tsp. ground cinnamon
½ tsp. salt
½ tsp. ground ginger
½ tsp. ground nutmeg
2 cups fat-free milk
½ cup canned pumpkin
1 large egg white, lightly beaten
2 Tbsp. canola oil

1. In a large bowl, combine the first 8 ingredients. In a small bowl, combine the milk, pumpkin, egg white and oil; stir into dry ingredients just until moistened.
2. Pour batter by ¼ cupfuls onto a lightly greased hot griddle; turn pancakes when bubbles form on top. Cook until second side is golden brown.
2 PANCAKES: 240 cal., 5g fat (1g sat. fat), 1mg chol., 375mg sod., 41g carb. (9g sugars, 3g fiber), 8g pro. **DIABETIC EXCHANGES:** 2½ starch, 1 fat.

BANANA NUT PANCAKES

I enjoy these versatile pancakes since they are a satisfying breakfast and can be a deliciously different dessert.
—Diane Hixon, Niceville, FL

TAKES: 20 min. • **MAKES:** 9 pancakes

3 oz. cream cheese, softened
½ cup whipped topping
1 cup pancake mix
1 Tbsp. sugar
1 large egg
¾ cup 2% milk
2 tsp. canola oil
1 medium ripe banana, mashed
½ cup chopped pecans
  Optional: Sliced ripe banana and chopped pecans

1. In a small bowl, beat cream cheese until smooth. Mix in whipped topping (mixture will be stiff); set aside.
2. In a large bowl, combine pancake mix and sugar. Beat the egg, milk and oil; add to pancake mix and mix well. Fold in banana and pecans.
3. Pour batter by ¼ cupfuls onto a lightly greased hot griddle; turn when bubbles form on top of pancakes. Cook until second side is golden brown. Serve with cream cheese topping and, if desired, bananas and pecans.
3 PANCAKES: 543 cal., 34g fat (12g sat. fat), 110mg chol., 624mg sod., 50g carb. (23g sugars, 5g fiber), 12g pro.

PUMPKIN-FLAVORED PANCAKES

COCOA PANCAKES

These chocolaty whole wheat pancakes feel like a special morning treat. The vanilla yogurt and raspberries are fresh additions. Use one whole egg if you don't have egg substitute on hand.
—Lisa DeMarsh, Mount Solon, VA

TAKES: 25 min. • **MAKES:** 8 pancakes

- ¾ cup whole wheat flour
- ¼ cup sugar
- 2 Tbsp. baking cocoa
- 1 tsp. baking powder
- ⅛ tsp. salt
- ⅛ tsp. ground nutmeg
- ¾ cup fat-free milk
- ¼ cup egg substitute
- 1 Tbsp. reduced-fat butter, melted
- 1 cup fresh raspberries
- ½ cup fat-free vanilla yogurt
  Grated chocolate, optional

1. In a small bowl, combine the first 6 ingredients. Combine the milk, egg substitute and butter; add to dry ingredients just until moistened.

2. Pour batter by scant ¼ cupfuls onto a lightly greased hot griddle; turn when bubbles form on top. Cook until second side is lightly browned. Serve with fresh raspberries, yogurt and, if desired, grated chocolate.

NOTE: This recipe was tested with Land O'Lakes light stick butter.

2 PANCAKES WITH ¼ CUP RASPBERRIES AND 2 TBSP. YOGURT: 201 cal., 2g fat (1g sat. fat), 6mg chol., 249mg sod., 40g carb. (19g sugars, 5g fiber), 8g pro. **DIABETIC EXCHANGES:** 2½ starch.

TEST KITCHEN TIPS

- Consider adding chopped nuts, chia seeds, sunflower kernels or even a few tablespoons of rolled oats for some crunchy texture as well as a little protein boost.
- For sweetness, add quartered banana slices, fresh berries or mini chocolate chips.
- Make 'em mocha by dissolving 2 Tbsp. instant espresso powder into the milk before stirring it into the batter.

COCOA PANCAKES

Jar Excellence

Ditch the PB&J and tuna salad! These creative meals-in-one are just what you need to pack for your 9-to-5.

DIY RAMEN SOUP

DIY RAMEN SOUP

This favorite is a healthier alternative to most commercial varieties. Feel free to customize the veggies.
—*Michelle Clair, Seattle, WA*

- -

TAKES: 25 min. • **MAKES:** 2 servings

- 1 pkg. (3 oz.) ramen noodles
- 1 Tbsp. reduced-sodium chicken base
- 1 to 2 tsp. Sriracha chili sauce
- 1 tsp. minced fresh gingerroot
- ½ cup shredded carrots
- ½ cup shredded cabbage
- 2 radishes, halved and sliced
- ½ cup sliced fresh shiitake mushrooms
- 1 cup shredded cooked chicken breast
- ¼ cup fresh cilantro leaves
- 2 lime wedges
- 1 hard-boiled large egg, halved
- 4 cups boiling water

1. Cook ramen noodles according to the package directions (do not use seasoning packet); cool.

2. In each of two 1-qt. wide-mouth canning jars, layer half of each ingredient in the following order: ramen noodles, chicken base, chili sauce, ginger, carrots, cabbage, radishes, mushrooms, chicken breast and cilantro. Place lime wedges and egg halves in two 4-oz. glass jars or other airtight containers. Cover all 4 containers and refrigerate until ready to serve.

3. To serve, pour 2 cups boiling water into each 1-qt. glass jar; let stand until warmed through or until the chicken base has dissolved. Stir to combine seasonings. Squeeze lime juice over soup; place an egg half on top.

1 SERVING: 380 cal., 6g fat (1g sat. fat), 147mg chol., 1386mg sod., 47g carb. (4g sugars, 3g fiber), 32g pro.

TEST KITCHEN TIPS

- Easily dress up cooked ramen by stirring in some peanut butter, chopped green onion or sliced hard-boiled egg.
- Add some snow peas, julienned peppers, sliced mushrooms or other salad-bar fixings to ramen during the last minute of cooking.
- Ramen eggs traditionally have a jammy yolk. Reduce boil time to 6-7 minutes for golden results.

PRESSURE-COOKER FLAN IN A JAR

Spoil yourself or the people you love with these simply delightful portable custards—a cute and fun take on the Mexican dessert classic. Tuck a jar into your lunchbox for a sweet treat.
—*Megumi Garcia, Milwaukee, WI*

- -

PREP: 25 min. • **COOK:** 10 min. + chilling
MAKES: 6 servings

- ½ cup sugar
- 1 Tbsp. hot water
- 1 cup coconut milk or whole milk
- ⅓ cup whole milk
- ⅓ cup sweetened condensed milk
- 2 large eggs plus 1 large egg yolk, lightly beaten
  Dash salt
- 1 tsp. vanilla extract
- 1 tsp. dark rum, optional

1. In a small heavy saucepan, spread sugar; cook, without stirring, over medium-low heat until it begins to melt. Gently drag melted sugar to center of pan so sugar melts evenly. Cook, stirring constantly, until melted sugar turns a deep amber color, about 2 minutes. Immediately remove from heat and carefully stir in hot water. Quickly pour into 6 hot 4-oz. jars.

2. In a small saucepan, heat coconut milk and whole milk until bubbles form around side of pan; remove from heat. In a large bowl, whisk condensed milk, eggs, egg yolk and salt until blended but not foamy. Slowly stir in hot milk; stir in vanilla and, if desired, rum. Strain through a fine sieve. Pour egg mixture into prepared jars. Center lids on jars; screw on bands until fingertip tight.

3. Place trivet insert and 1 cup water in a 6-qt. electric pressure cooker. Place jars on trivet, offset-stacking as needed. Lock lid; close pressure-release valve. Adjust to pressure-cook on high for 6 minutes.

4. Let pressure release naturally for 10 minutes; quick-release any remaining pressure. Cool jars 30 minutes at room temperature. Refrigerate until cold, about 1 hour. Run a knife around sides of jars; invert flans onto dessert plates.

NOTE: You can use rum extract in place of the dark rum.

⅓ CUP: 223 cal., 10g fat (8g sat. fat), 100mg chol., 306mg sod., 28g carb. (27g sugars, 0 fiber), 5g pro.

PRESSURE-COOKER FLAN IN A JAR

BACON ALFREDO PASTA IN A JAR

Frankly, this is just...yum. I captured my favorite summery pasta in a jarred meal. So delicious. So simple. Tip it all into a bowl and enjoy!

—Keri Whitney, Castro Valley, CA

TAKES: 20 min. • **MAKES:** 4 servings

- 6 cups cooked penne pasta
- 1 cup refrigerated Alfredo sauce
- 1 jar (8 oz.) roasted sweet red peppers, drained and coarsely chopped
- ¾ cup frozen peas
- 6 ready-to-serve fully cooked bacon strips, chopped
- ¼ cup fresh basil leaves, coarsely chopped
- ¼ cup grated Parmesan cheese

1. In each of four 1-pint wide-mouth canning jars, divide and layer ingredients in the following order: pasta, Alfredo sauce, red pepper, peas, bacon, basil and Parmesan cheese. Cover and refrigerate until serving.

2. Pour each jar into a microwave-safe bowl; toss to combine. Microwave until heated through.

1 SERVING: 488 cal., 18g fat (9g sat. fat), 34mg chol., 787mg sod., 60g carb. (6g sugars, 4g fiber), 19g pro.

TACO SALAD IN A JAR

TACO SALAD IN A JAR

We created a make-and-take version of a reader's delightful taco salad so it can be enjoyed for lunch on the go.

—Taste of Home Test Kitchen

TAKES: 30 min. • **MAKES:** 4 servings

- 1 lb. lean ground beef (90% lean)
- ⅔ cup water
- 1 envelope reduced-sodium taco seasoning
- 1 medium ripe avocado, peeled and cubed
- 1 Tbsp. finely chopped red onion
- 1 garlic clove, minced
- ½ tsp. lemon juice
- ¾ cup reduced-fat sour cream
- ¾ cup salsa
- 2 medium tomatoes, chopped
- 1 can (2¼ oz.) sliced ripe olives, drained
- 1 small cucumber, peeled and chopped
- 5 green onions, chopped
- 1 cup shredded cheddar cheese
- 4 cups shredded lettuce
  Tortilla chips, optional

1. In a small skillet, cook beef over medium heat until no longer pink; crumble beef; drain. Stir in water and taco seasoning. Bring to a boil; cook and stir for 2 minutes. Cool.

2. In a small bowl, mash avocado with onion, garlic and lemon juice. In each of four 1-qt. wide-mouth canning jars, divide and layer ingredients in the following order: Sour cream, salsa, beef, tomatoes, olives, cucumber, green onions, avocado mixture, cheese and lettuce. Cover and refrigerate until serving. To serve, transfer salads into bowls; toss to combine. If desired, serve with tortilla chips.

1 SERVING: 483 cal., 29g fat (12g sat. fat), 103mg chol., 1087mg sod., 24g carb. (11g sugars, 5g fiber), 34g pro.

BACON ALFREDO PASTA IN A JAR

HAM & SWISS SALAD IN A JAR

Home cook Stacy Huggins from Valley Center, California, sent us a great recipe for a ham and Swiss salad, and we turned it into this ultra portable version.
—Taste of Home *Test Kitchen*

- -

TAKES: 25 min. • **MAKES:** 4 servings

¾	cup mayonnaise
⅓	cup reduced-fat sour cream
2	Tbsp. water
1½	tsp. white wine vinegar
¼	tsp. sugar
⅛	tsp. salt
⅛	tsp. pepper
⅓	lb. cubed fully cooked ham
2	cups frozen peas, thawed
1	small red onion, halved and thinly sliced
6	hard-boiled large eggs, chopped
¼	lb. bacon strips, cooked and crumbled
1	cup shredded Swiss cheese
4	cups torn iceberg lettuce (about ½ head)
6	cups fresh baby spinach

In a small bowl, whisk the first 7 ingredients. In each of four 1-qt. wide-mouth canning jars, divide and layer ingredients in the following order: mayonnaise mixture, ham, peas, onion, eggs, bacon, cheese, lettuce and spinach. Cover and refrigerate until serving. Transfer each salad into a bowl; toss to combine.
1 SERVING: 691 cal., 54g fat (14g sat. fat), 344mg chol., 1110mg sod., 18g carb. (8g sugars, 5g fiber), 36g pro.

HAM & SWISS SALAD IN A JAR

CHOPPED GREEK SALAD IN A JAR

CHOPPED GREEK SALAD IN A JAR

Here's a lunchbox-friendly salad with lots of zesty flair. Prepare the jars on Sunday, and you'll have four grab-and-go lunches ready for the workweek.
—Taste of Home *Test Kitchen*

- -

TAKES: 20 min. • **MAKES:** 4 servings

¼	cup pepperoncini juice
¼	cup extra virgin olive oil
¼	cup minced fresh basil
2	Tbsp. lemon juice
½	tsp. pepper
¼	tsp. salt
¼	cup finely chopped pepperoncini
1	can (15 oz.) garbanzo beans or chickpeas, rinsed and drained
2	celery ribs, sliced
½	cup Greek olives
1	medium tomato, chopped
½	cup crumbled feta cheese
8	cups chopped romaine

In a small bowl, whisk the first 6 ingredients. In each of four 1-qt. wide-mouth canning jars, divide and layer ingredients in the following order: olive oil mixture, pepperoncini, garbanzo beans, celery, Greek olives, tomato, feta and romaine. Cover and refrigerate until serving. Transfer salads into bowls; toss to combine.
1 SERVING: 332 cal., 23g fat (4g sat. fat), 8mg chol., 795mg sod., 25g carb. (5g sugars, 8g fiber), 9g pro.

Celebrate Lunar New Year

Choose one or more of these Asian recipes to serve up good luck in the coming year.

GINGER SCALLION &
SOY STEAMED FISH

GINGER SCALLION & SOY STEAMED FISH

Eating steamed fish is a Lunar New Year tradition, as fish is meant to represent prosperity to come. My version is light and fresh with a zing of ginger.
—*Emma Lovewell, New York, NY*

PREP: 15 min. • **COOK:** 20 min.
MAKES: 4 servings

- 2 green onions, thinly sliced
- 2 Tbsp. julienned fresh gingerroot
- 4 fresh cilantro sprigs
- ¼ cup reduced-sodium soy sauce
- 2 Tbsp. hot water
- 1 Tbsp. mirin (sweet rice wine)
- ⅛ tsp. sugar
- 1 whitefish fillet (1½ lbs.), such as sea bass, cod or branzino
- 3 Tbsp. canola oil, divided

1. In a small bowl, combine green onions, ginger and cilantro. In another small bowl, stir together soy sauce, hot water, mirin and sugar until dissolved. Set both bowls aside.
2. Prepare a wok for steaming or place a steamer basket in a large saucepan over 1 in. water; bring to a simmer. Place the fish on a heat-proof plate that will fit in steamer; place plate in steamer. Adjust heat to maintain a gentle simmer. Cover and steam until fish just begins to flake easily with a butter knife, 10-15 minutes.
3. Meanwhile, in a small saucepan, heat 2 Tbsp. oil until hot. Add two-thirds of the ginger mixture; stir-fry 1 minute or until very aromatic. Add the soy sauce mixture; simmer until green onions and cilantro are wilted, about 30 seconds.
4. Drain any liquid from fish plate. Pour soy mixture over fish. Top with remaining ginger mixture. In a small skillet, heat remaining 1 Tbsp. oil until hot. Gently pour over the ginger mixture. Serve immediately.

5 OZ. COOKED FISH: 350 cal., 20g fat (3g sat. fat), 105mg chol., 665mg sod., 3g carb. (2g sugars, 0 fiber), 35g pro.

DID YOU KNOW?

In Mandarin, the word for fish (yu) sounds just like the word for abundance. Often on Lunar New Year, fish is served whole, but this filleted version will be just as lucky.

SLOW-COOKED THAI DRUNKEN NOODLES

I really love pad kee mao and was inspired to try my recipe in the slow cooker on a really busy day. It came out tasting great! I was so happy to have it ready to go when we got home. You can easily substitute chicken, turkey or beef for pork.
—*Lori McLain, Denton, TX*

PREP: 25 min. • **COOK:** 5 hours + standing
MAKES: 6 servings

- 1 lb. boneless pork ribeye chops, chopped
- 1 medium onion, halved and sliced
- 1 can (8¾ oz.) whole baby corn, drained, optional
- 1 small sweet red pepper, sliced
- 1 small green pepper, sliced
- 1¾ cups sliced fresh mushrooms
- ½ cup chicken broth
- ½ cup soy sauce
- ¼ cup honey
- 2 garlic cloves, minced
- 2 tsp. Sriracha chili sauce
- ¼ tsp. ground ginger
- 8 oz. thick rice noodles or linguine
- 1 cup fresh snow peas
  Thinly sliced fresh basil

1. Place pork, onion, corn, if desired, peppers and mushrooms in a 6- or 7-qt. slow cooker. Whisk broth, soy sauce, honey, garlic, Sriracha chili sauce and ginger until blended; pour over top. Cook, covered, on low 5-6 hours or until pork is cooked through and the vegetables are tender.
2. Meanwhile, cook pasta according to package directions; do not overcook. Drain noodles and rinse under cold water. Stir noodles and peas into slow cooker; let stand 15 minutes. Garnish with basil.

1½ CUPS: 360 cal., 9g fat (3g sat. fat), 44mg chol., 1467mg sod., 47g carb. (14g sugars, 2g fiber), 21g pro.

SLOW-COOKED THAI DRUNKEN NOODLES

SESAME-SOY STRING BEANS

CHINESE PORK FRIED RICE

Here's an all-time classic scaled down for two. The peas and carrots add color and crunch to this savory dinner.
—*Peggy Vaught, Glasgow, WV*

TAKES: 25 min. • **MAKES:** 2 servings

1   boneless pork loin chop (6 oz.), cut into ½-in. pieces
¼   cup finely chopped carrot
¼   cup chopped fresh broccoli
¼   cup frozen peas
1   green onion, chopped
1   Tbsp. butter
1   large egg, lightly beaten
1   cup cold cooked long grain rice
4½ tsp. reduced-sodium soy sauce
⅛   tsp. garlic powder
⅛   tsp. ground ginger

1. In a large skillet, saute the pork, carrot, broccoli, peas and onion in butter until pork is no longer pink, 3-5 minutes. Remove from skillet and set aside.
2. In same skillet, cook and stir egg over medium heat until completely set. Stir in the rice, soy sauce, garlic powder, ginger and pork mixture; heat through. If desired, garnish with additional green onions.
1 CUP: 338 cal., 13g fat (6g sat. fat), 163mg chol., 597mg sod., 29g carb. (3g sugars, 2g fiber), 24g pro. **DIABETIC EXCHANGES:** 3 lean meat, 2 starch.

SESAME-SOY STRING BEANS

These crisp green beans make a quick, delicious side dish for your celebration—or any dinner, really! They get their wonderful umami flavor from a simple dressing using sesame oil and soy sauce.
—*Emma Lovewell, New York, NY*

TAKES: 20 min. • **MAKES:** 4 servings

2   Tbsp. canola oil
1   lb. fresh green beans, trimmed
3   Tbsp. reduced-sodium soy sauce
1   Tbsp. sesame oil
¼   cup water
2   garlic cloves, minced
1   tsp. minced fresh gingerroot

In a large skillet or wok, heat oil over medium-high heat. Add beans and cook 2 minutes. Gradually add soy sauce and sesame oil, stirring constantly. Add water; cook, covered 5 minutes. Stir in garlic and ginger; cook, uncovered until beans are crisp-tender and water has cooked off, 3-5 minutes.
1 SERVING: 137 cal., 11g fat (1g sat. fat), 0 chol., 438mg sod., 9g carb. (3g sugars, 4g fiber), 3g pro. **DIABETIC EXCHANGES:** 2 fat, 1 vegetable.

TEST KITCHEN TIP

Instead of snapping off the ends of each green bean like Grandma did, trim a bunch in seconds. Gather beans in a small pile, lining up the tips on 1 side. Cut off tips with a single slice using a chef's knife. Flip the pile over and do the same on the other side.

CHINESE PORK FRIED RICE

Make Dumplings

Homemade pot stickers are as easy as fill, fold, pleat, repeat. They're fun to make with a helper, too.

Fill. Spoon filling into center of dumpling wrapper.

Fold. Wet half the wrapper edge with water, then pinch at the center to adhere.

Pleat. Beginning at the center, pleat the front side of the wrapper to each edge. The back side should be flat.

HOMEMADE PORK DUMPLINGS

HOMEMADE PORK DUMPLINGS

I grew up eating dumplings. My mom used to make them, and my brother and I would sit in the kitchen to help her make around 100 dumplings in one sitting! We used to freeze them and eat them throughout the month.
—*Emma Lovewell, New York, NY*

- -

PREP: 1 hour • **COOK:** 25 min.
MAKES: about 3 dozen

- 12 oz. lean ground pork
- 2   green onions, minced
- 2   Tbsp. minced fresh gingerroot
- 2   garlic cloves, minced
- 3   Tbsp. soy sauce
- 1   Tbsp. sesame oil
- 1   pkg. (10 oz.) round pot sticker or gyoza wrappers
- 1   Tbsp. canola oil
- ½   cup water

DIPPING SAUCE
- ¼   cup soy sauce
- 2   Tbsp. rice vinegar
- 1   Tbsp. minced fresh gingerroot

1. In a large bowl, combine the first 6 ingredients; mix lightly but thoroughly.

2. Place 1 level Tbsp. filling in the center of each wrapper. (Cover remaining wrappers with a slightly damp paper towel until ready to use.) Moisten half of the wrapper edge with water. Fold wrapper over filling; pinch center to adhere. On each side of the pinched area, pleat the front wrapper edge 3 times, leaving the back side unpleated. Pinch edge to seal. Place on a baking sheet, gently flattening the bottom.

3. In a large skillet, heat oil over medium heat. Add dumplings, flat side down, and cook until bottoms are golden brown, 3-5 minutes. Add ½ cup water; cook, covered, until most of the water has evaporated, about 5 minutes. Remove lid; cook until water has evaporated and filling is no longer pink, 1-2 minutes.

4. Meanwhile, in a small bowl, stir together dipping sauce ingredients. Serve hot dumplings with dipping sauce.

1 DUMPLING WITH ABOUT ½ TSP. SAUCE: 49 cal., 2g fat (0 sat. fat), 6mg chol., 222mg sod., 5g carb. (0 sugars, 0 fiber), 3g pro.
VEGGIE DUMPLINGS: Omit pork filling. In a large bowl, stir together 2 cups finely diced mushrooms, 1 cup finely shredded cabbage, 6 oz. finely diced extra-firm tofu, 2 minced green onions, 2 Tbsp. minced gingerroot, 2 Tbsp. soy sauce and 1 Tbsp. sesame oil. Proceed with recipe as directed.

Do the Salsa

Whether you begin with this versatile home-canned salsa or another recipe, here are 14 fun ways to use it to spark up your meals.

TOMATO BOUNTY SALSA

TOMATO BOUNTY SALSA

I like to make this mild-tasting salsa with yellow tomatoes, but feel free to try other varieties. Use the salsa as a dip for chips or as a condiment for meats.
—Joanne Surfus, Sturgeon Bay, WI

PREP: 1½ hours • **PROCESS:** 20 min.
MAKES: 8 pints

- 9 lbs. yellow tomatoes (25 to 30 medium)
- 4 medium onions, finely chopped
- 2 cans (6 oz. each) tomato paste
- 1 large sweet red pepper, finely chopped
- ¾ cup white vinegar
- 4 jalapeno peppers, seeded and chopped
- 4 garlic cloves, minced
- 3 tsp. salt
- ½ tsp. pepper

1. In a large saucepan, bring 8 cups water to a boil. Add tomatoes, a few at a time; boil for 30 seconds. Drain and immediately place tomatoes in ice water. Drain and pat dry; peel and finely chop.
2. In a stockpot, combine the remaining ingredients. Stir in tomatoes. Bring to a boil over medium-high heat. Reduce the heat; simmer, uncovered, until desired thickness, about 20 minutes. Carefully ladle hot mixture into hot 1-pint jars, leaving ½-in. headspace. Remove air bubbles; wipe rims and adjust lids. Process the jars for 20 minutes in a boiling-water canner.
NOTE: When cutting hot peppers, disposable gloves are recommended. Avoid touching your face.
¼ CUP: 20 cal., 0 fat (0 sat. fat), 0 chol., 117mg sod., 4g carb. (3g sugars, 1g fiber), 1g pro. **DIABETIC EXCHANGES:** 1 free food.

READER REVIEW

"I've made this three times now. I put some of it up in cans and keep the rest in the fridge to eat now. It's really delicious. Sometimes I add the seeds and ribs of one of the jalapenos for a little more heat."

—RUBYSHOE, TASTEOFHOME.COM

FIESTA RAVIOLI

I adapted this recipe to suit our taste for spicy food. The ravioli taste like mini enchiladas. I serve them with a Mexican-inspired salad and pineapple sherbet for dessert.
—Debbie Purdue, Westland, MI

TAKES: 20 min. • **MAKES:** 6 servings

- 1 pkg. (25 oz.) frozen beef ravioli
- 1 can (10 oz.) enchilada sauce
- 1 cup salsa
- 2 cups shredded Monterey Jack cheese
- 1 can (2¼ oz.) sliced ripe olives, drained

1. Cook ravioli according to package directions. Meanwhile, in a large skillet, combine enchilada sauce and salsa. Cook and stir over medium heat until heated through.
2. Drain ravioli; add to sauce and gently stir to coat. Top with cheese and olives. Cover and cook over low heat until cheese is melted, 3-4 minutes.
1 SERVING: 470 cal., 20g fat (9g sat. fat), 74mg chol., 1342mg sod., 48g carb. (4g sugars, 6g fiber), 23g pro.

PEPPER & SALSA COD

After tasting a similar dish at the grocery store, my husband figured out how to make this awesome, healthy cod topped with salsa and peppers.
—Robyn Gallagher, Yorktown, VA

TAKES: 30 min. • **MAKES:** 2 servings

- 2 cod or haddock fillets (6 oz. each)
- 1 tsp. olive oil
- ¼ tsp. salt
  Dash pepper
- ⅓ cup orange juice
- ¼ cup salsa
- ⅓ cup julienned green pepper
- ⅓ cup julienned sweet red pepper
  Hot cooked rice

1. Preheat oven to 350°. Brush both sides of the fillets with oil; place in a greased 11x7-in. baking dish. Sprinkle with salt and pepper. Pour orange juice over fish; top with salsa and peppers.
2. Bake, covered, until fish just begins to flake easily with a fork, 17-20 minutes. Serve with rice.
1 SERVING: 183 cal., 3g fat (1g sat. fat), 65mg chol., 512mg sod., 9g carb. (6g sugars, 1g fiber), 27g pro. **DIABETIC EXCHANGES:** 4 lean meat, 1 vegetable, ½ fat.

FIESTA RAVIOLI

**AIR-FRYER
QUESADILLAS**

🕐 🍴 5️⃣

AIR-FRYER QUESADILLAS

I like to make these for party appetizers. Just cut them into thinner triangles. You can also switch up the cheese and the salsa to suit your taste.
—*Terri Keeney, Greeley, CO*

TAKES: 10 min. • **MAKES:** 6 servings

1½ cups shredded Mexican cheese blend
½ cup salsa
4 flour tortillas (8 in.), warmed
   Cooking spray

Preheat air fryer to 375°. Combine cheese and salsa; spread over half of each tortilla. Fold tortilla over. In batches, place tortillas in a single layer on a greased tray in air-fryer basket; spritz with cooking spray. Cook until golden brown and the cheese has melted, 5-7 minutes. Cut into wedges.
1 SERVING: 223 cal., 11g fat (5g sat. fat), 25mg chol., 406mg sod., 21g carb. (1g sugars, 1g fiber), 9g pro.

HOW-TO

Clean the Air-Fryer Coil

If you detect smoking or an off odor when using an air fryer, there may be oil or residue on the heating coil. To clean, simply unplug the machine, let cool, then wipe the coil with a damp cloth—just as you'd clean the heating element on an electric stove.

🕐

CHICKEN TACO POCKETS

We love these easy taco-flavored bundles made with crescent dough. They make a quick and easy lunch or supper with a bowl of soup or a crisp green salad. I also like to cut them into smaller servings for parties.
—*Donna Gribbins, Shelbyville, KY*

TAKES: 25 min. • **MAKES:** 8 servings

2 tubes (8 oz. each) refrigerated crescent rolls
½ cup salsa, plus more for serving
½ cup sour cream
2 Tbsp. taco seasoning
1 cup shredded rotisserie chicken
1 cup shredded cheddar cheese
   Optional: Shredded lettuce, guacamole and additional sour cream

1. Preheat oven to 375°. Unroll 1 tube crescent dough and separate into 2 rectangles; press perforations to seal. Repeat with second tube. In a bowl, combine salsa, sour cream and taco seasoning. Spoon chicken onto the left side of each rectangle; top with salsa mixture. Sprinkle with cheese. Fold dough over filling; pinch edges to seal.
2. Place on an ungreased baking sheet. Bake pockets until golden brown, 13-15 minutes. Cut in half. Serve with salsa and toppings as desired.
NOTE: Take extra care when pressing the crescent dough to seal the perforations. Patch any thin spots to prevent the filling from leaking while the pockets bake.
½ POCKET: 393 cal., 24g fat (7g sat. fat), 47mg chol., 896mg sod., 29g carb. (7g sugars, 0 fiber), 16g pro.

**CHICKEN TACO
POCKETS**

THE TEX-MEX TREATMENT

CHICKEN ENCHILADA STUFFED POTATO SKINS

CAULIFLOWER SALAD

MEXICAN DEVILED EGGS

EGG & SAUSAGE TACOS

TACO SALAD WAFFLES

Start with your favorite salsa...and end with serious deliciousness. Community Cooks spice up breakfast, lunch and dinner with a jar of the piquant sauce.

BLACK BEAN CHICKEN

Mix 3 tsp. **chili powder**, 1 tsp. **cumin**, 1 tsp. **pepper** and ¼ tsp. **salt**; sprinkle over both sides of 4 **boneless skinless chicken breasts**. In a nonstick skillet, brown chicken in 2 tsp. **canola oil** over medium heat. Add 1 can rinsed **black beans**, 1 cup **corn** and 1 cup **salsa**; cook, covered, until a thermometer inserted reads 165°, 10-15 minutes. Cut chicken into slices.
CC *Molly Andersen*

CAULIFLOWER SALAD

Cut 1 medium head **cauliflower** into florets. Steam until tender, 6-8 minutes. Drop into ice water. Drain and pat dry. Toss with 16 oz. **salsa**, 1 Tbsp. **garlic oil** and ¼ tsp. **pepper**; top with 1 cup **parsley leaves**. Refrigerate 30 minutes before serving.
CC *Ann Sheehy*

CHICKEN ENCHILADA STUFFED POTATO SKINS

Bake 3 large baking **potatoes** at 350° until tender, about 1 hour. Cool slightly; cut in half lengthwise. Scoop out pulp, leaving thin shells. Place shells on an ungreased baking sheet. In a skillet, cook 1 chopped small **onion** in 1 Tbsp. **olive oil** over medium-high heat until tender, 4-5 minutes. Add 1 Tbsp. minced **garlic**; cook 1 minute longer. Add 1¼ cups **salsa**, 6 oz. **cream cheese**, ½ tsp. **salt**, ½ tsp. **chili powder** and ¼ tsp. **ground cumin**. Cook until cream cheese is melted, 1-2 minutes. Stir in 3 cups cubed **cooked chicken**. Divide filling among potato skins; top with 1 cup **shredded Mexican cheese**. Place on baking sheet. Bake, uncovered, until heated through and cheese is melted, 15-20 minutes. If desired, top with **sour cream** and **pickled jalapenos**.
CC *Debbie Glasscock*

EASY SOUTHWEST PIZZA

Place 2 **naan flatbreads** on a baking sheet; spread with ½ cup **salsa**. Sprinkle with 2 tsp. **dried Mexican oregano**; top with 2 cups **shredded Mexican cheese**. Bake at 350° until cheese is melted and crust is golden, 8-10 minutes. Serve with desired toppings.
CC *Jolene Martinelli*

EGG & SAUSAGE TACOS

In a skillet, cook and crumble 8 oz. **breakfast sausage** over medium heat until no longer pink, 5-7 minutes. Drain on paper towels. Whisk 8 **large eggs**; pour eggs into skillet. Cook and stir until eggs are scrambled. Stir in ¾ cup **salsa** and cooked sausage. Serve in twelve **5-in. flour tortillas** with desired toppings.
CC *Shawna Welsh-Garrison*

MAYAN POTATO QUESADILLAS

Combine 1 cup **mashed potatoes**, ½ cup **tomatillo salsa** and ¼ cup thinly sliced **green onions**. Top half of 2 **large flour tortillas** with potato mixture; sprinkle each with ½ cup **shredded cheddar cheese**. Fold tortillas to close. Lightly **butter** tops and bottoms of quesadillas. Cook in a skillet over medium heat until golden brown and heated through, 2-3 minutes on each side. Cut into wedges.
CC *Marina Castle-Kelley*

MEXICAN DEVILED EGGS

Slice 8 **hard-boiled large eggs** in half lengthwise; remove yolks and set whites aside. Mash yolks with ½ cup **shredded cheddar cheese**, ¼ cup **mayonnaise**, ¼ cup **salsa**, 2 Tbsp. sliced **green onions**, 1 Tbsp. **sour cream** and **salt**. Stuff into egg whites.
CC *Susan Klemm*

RICOTTA TART

Beat 2 **large eggs**. Stir in 1 cup **ricotta**, 1 cup **shredded sharp cheddar cheese**, 2 Tbsp. **salsa**, ½ tsp. **salt** and ½ tsp. **pepper**. Roll out 1 **sheet pie crust** onto a foil-lined baking sheet. Spread cheese mixture to within 1 in. of edge. Fold crust over edge of filling. Bake at 400° until golden brown, 22-26 minutes. Let stand for 5 minutes before cutting.
CC *Teri Rasey*

SOUTHWESTERN PINEAPPLE PORK CHOPS

Sprinkle 4 **boneless pork chops** with ½ tsp. **garlic pepper**. In a large skillet, brown chops in 1 Tbsp. **canola oil**; remove. In same skillet, combine one 8-oz. can undrained **unsweetened crushed pineapple** and 1 cup **medium salsa**. Bring to a boil. Return chops to the pan. Cover and simmer until a thermometer inserted in pork reads 145°, 10-15 minutes. Let stand for 5 minutes before serving. Sprinkle with minced **fresh cilantro**.
CC *Lisa Varner*

TACO SALAD WAFFLES

In a skillet, cook and crumble 1 lb. **ground beef** over medium heat until no longer pink; drain. Stir in 1 cup **salsa**, one 4-oz. can chopped **green chiles** and an envelope **taco seasoning**. Bring to a boil. Reduce heat; simmer 5 minutes. Toast 8 **frozen waffles** according to package directions. Serve with beef mixture and desired toppings.
CC *Trisha Kruse*

Foiled Again!

When fun-filled days have you pressed for time, prep a packet loaded with fresh and hearty ingredients, then let 'em sizzle together for a sensational supper with super simple cleanup.

CHICKEN &
ZUCCHINI
FOIL PACKS

CHICKEN & ZUCCHINI FOIL PACKS

I enjoy foil-wrapped dinners cooked on the grill because there are no pots or pans to wash. You can try this with most fresh vegetables you have on hand.
—Dianna Smith, Newport, TN

PREP: 45 min. • **GRILL:** 15 min.
MAKES: 2 servings

- 1 large sweet onion, thinly sliced
- 1 tsp. olive oil
- 4 large fresh button mushrooms, thinly sliced
- 2 Tbsp. tomato paste
- 2 Tbsp. chopped fresh basil
- 1 tsp. chopped fresh oregano
- 1 cup chicken broth or stock
- 2 boneless skinless chicken breasts (6 oz. each)
- ¼ tsp. salt
- ¼ tsp. pepper
- 1 medium zucchini, thinly sliced

1. Prepare grill for medium heat or preheat oven to 450°. In a large skillet, cook the onion in oil over medium-high heat until crisp-tender, 4-5 minutes. Add the mushrooms; cook until tender, 4-5 minutes. Stir in tomato paste, basil and oregano; cook until tomato paste starts to caramelize, 6-8 minutes. Stir in broth, stirring to loosen browned bits from pan. Bring to a boil; cook until sauce has thickened, 8-10 minutes. Remove from heat; cool slightly.

2. Cut each chicken breast into 3 long strips. Divide chicken strips between two 18x12-in. pieces of heavy-duty nonstick foil, placing food on the dull side of foil; sprinkle with salt and pepper and top with zucchini. Spoon tomato mixture over zucchini. Fold foil around mixture, sealing tightly.

3. Place packets on grill or in oven; cook 15-20 minutes or until chicken is no longer pink, turning once. Open packets carefully to allow steam to escape. If desired, top with additional basil.

1 PACKET: 302 cal., 7g fat (2g sat. fat), 94mg chol., 838mg sod., 21g carb. (12g sugars, 3g fiber), 39g pro. **DIABETIC EXCHANGES:** 5 lean meat, 1½ starch, ½ fat.

CHEESE-TOPPED POTATOES IN FOIL

CHEESE-TOPPED POTATOES IN FOIL

Whenever we go camping, cheesy potato packets are a must. They just may remind you of scalloped potatoes. In the winter, I bake them in the oven.
—Denise Wheeler, Newaygo, MI

PREP: 15 min. • **COOK:** 35 min.
MAKES: 8 servings

- 2½ lbs. potatoes (about 3 large), peeled and cut into ¼-in. slices
- 1 medium onion, finely chopped
- 5 bacon strips, cooked and crumbled
- ¼ cup butter, melted
- ½ tsp. salt
- ¼ tsp. pepper
- 6 slices process American cheese
  Sour cream, optional

1. Prepare campfire or grill for medium heat. In a large bowl, toss potatoes with onion, bacon, butter, salt and pepper. Place on a large piece of greased heavy-duty foil (about 36x12-in. rectangle). Fold foil around potatoes, sealing tightly.

2. Cook on campfire or in covered grill until the potatoes are tender, about 15 minutes per side. Open foil carefully to allow steam to escape; place cheese over potatoes. Cook until cheese is melted, 1-2 minutes. If desired, serve with sour cream.

¾ CUP: 217 cal., 11g fat (7g sat. fat), 24mg chol., 454mg sod., 21g carb. (3g sugars, 2g fiber), 7g pro

HOW-TO

Fold a Foil Packet

For each foil packet, tear off a. piece of aluminum foil as recipe directs. Place foil dull side up and add ingredients to the center. To seal, meet long sides of foil together over the center. Crease the sides together and tightly fold downward to create a 1-in. fold. Continue to fold downward until the foil lies flat against the packet's top. Then use the same folding method to bring the short sides inward.

TILAPIA FLORENTINE FOIL PACKETS

As a park ranger, I've cooked a lot of meals outdoors. I often assemble foil packs and toss them into my backpack with some ice. Then when I set up camp, it's easy to cook them over a campfire. If I'm at home, I use my grill, and the food is just as good.
—*Ralph Jones, San Diego, CA*

- -

PREP: 20 min. • **GRILL:** 20 min.
MAKES: 8 servings

- 2 beef top sirloin steaks (1½ lbs. each)
- 3 lbs. red potatoes, cut into ½-in. cubes
- 1 medium onion, chopped
- 4 tsp. minced fresh rosemary
- 1 Tbsp. minced garlic
- 2 tsp. salt
- 1 tsp. pepper

1. Prepare the grill for medium heat or preheat oven to 450°. Cut each steak into 4 pieces, for a total of 8 pieces. In a large bowl, combine steak, potatoes, onion, rosemary, garlic, salt and pepper.
2. Divide mixture among eight 18x12-in. pieces of heavy-duty foil, placing food on dull side of foil. Fold the foil around potato mixture, sealing tightly.
3. Place packets on grill or in oven; cook until potatoes are tender, 8-10 minutes on each side. Open packets carefully to allow steam to escape. If desired, sprinkle with additional rosemary.
1 PACKET: 348 cal., 7g fat (3g sat. fat), 69mg chol., 677mg sod., 29g carb. (2g sugars, 3g fiber), 40g pro. **DIABETIC EXCHANGES:** 5 lean meat, 2 starch.

TEST KITCHEN TIPS

- If it's a rainy day, or you simply don't want to fire up the grill, you can opt for the oven. Bake the steak and potato foil packs in a 400° oven for about 20-25 minutes.
- You can assemble the packs up to 8 hours ahead of time. Keep them in the fridge until you're ready to cook.

🍎

TILAPIA FLORENTINE FOIL PACKETS

I just love fish and serving healthy food to my family. This is a winner in my house!
—*Shanna Belz, Prineville, OR*

- -

PREP: 30 min. • **GRILL:** 15 min.
MAKES: 4 servings

- 12 cups fresh baby spinach
- 1 Tbsp. butter
- 1 Tbsp. extra virgin olive oil, divided
- 4 tilapia fillets (6 oz. each)
- ½ tsp. salt
- ¼ tsp. pepper
- ½ large sweet or red onion, thinly sliced
- 2 Tbsp. fresh lemon juice
- 2 garlic cloves, minced
  Lemon wedges, optional

1. Prepare grill for medium-high heat or preheat oven to 475°. In a large skillet, cook spinach in butter and 1 tsp. oil over medium-high heat until wilted, 8-10 minutes.
2. Divide spinach among four 18x12-in. pieces of heavy-duty nonstick foil, placing food on dull side of foil. Place tilapia on top of spinach; sprinkle with salt and pepper. Top with onion, lemon juice, garlic and remaining 2 tsp. olive oil. Fold foil around mixture, sealing tightly.
3. Place packets on grill or on a baking pan in oven. Cook until fish just begins to flake easily with a fork, 12-15 minutes. Open packets carefully to allow steam to escape. Serve with lemon wedges if desired.
1 PACKET: 233 cal., 8g fat (3g sat. fat), 90mg chol., 453mg sod., 8g carb. (3g sugars, 2g fiber), 35g pro. **DIABETIC EXCHANGES:** 5 lean meat, 1 vegetable, 1 fat.

**STEAK & POTATO
FOIL PACKS**

SWEET POTATO
KALE PILAF
PAGE 124

Side Dishes & Condiments

Find the perfect accent to your meals among the more than three dozen choices here. With everything from creamy comfort-food classics and crisp veggie sides to surprising pickles, relishes and pumpkin butter, we've got you covered.

BEST OF THE BEST DISHES

CHEESY SAUSAGE POTATOES

For a satisfying brunch, try these tender potato slices with lots of sausage and cheese. Everyone loves them and afterward the pan is always empty.
—*Linda Hill, Marseilles, IL*

- -

TAKES: 25 min. • **MAKES:** 10 servings

- 3 lbs. potatoes, peeled and cut into ¼-in. slices
- 1 lb. bulk pork sausage
- 1 medium onion, chopped
- ¼ cup butter, melted
- 2 cups shredded cheddar cheese

1. Place potatoes in a large saucepan and cover with water. Bring to a boil. Reduce the heat; simmer, uncovered, until tender, 8-10 minutes. Meanwhile, crumble the sausage into a large skillet; add onion. Cook over medium heat until meat is no longer pink; drain if necessary.
2. Drain the potatoes; arrange in an ungreased 13x9-in. baking dish. Drizzle with butter. Add sausage mixture and stir gently. Sprinkle with cheese.
3. Bake, uncovered, at 350° until cheese is melted, 5-7 minutes.
¾ CUP: 252 cal., 13g fat (8g sat. fat), 37mg chol., 220mg sod., 26g carb. (2g sugars, 3g fiber), 9g pro.

READER REVIEW

"Just made it for a second time. So easy and delicious. I added ½ tsp. of sweet basil to the butter before adding it to the potatoes, and I use red potatoes so I don't have to peel them."

—NICOLEMG, TASTEOFHOME.COM

CHEESY SAUSAGE POTATOES

PUMPKIN CRANBERRY CHUTNEY

PUMPKIN CRANBERRY CHUTNEY

I decided to make a chutney with leftover fall pumpkins. This has become a family favorite with turkey, chicken, ham and roast pork.
—*Maryalice Wood, Langley, BC*

- -

PREP: 1¼ hours • **PROCESS:** 10 min. • **MAKES:** 5 half-pints

  3½ cups cubed fresh pumpkin
  2 cups white vinegar
  1 cup chopped onion
  1 cup chopped peeled ripe pears or apples
  1 cup packed brown sugar
  1 cup fresh or frozen cranberries
  ½ cup cider vinegar
  ¼ cup dried cranberries
  2 Tbsp. canning salt
  2 tsp. each ground ginger, cinnamon, allspice and pepper
    Dash ground turmeric

1. In a Dutch oven, bring all ingredients to a boil. Reduce heat; simmer, uncovered, until slightly thickened and pumpkin is tender, 1-1¼ hours.

2. Carefully ladle hot mixture into 5 hot half-pint jars, leaving ½-in. headspace. Remove air bubbles and adjust headspace, if necessary, by adding hot mixture. Wipe rims. Center lids on jars; screw on bands until fingertip tight.

3. Place jars into canner with simmering water, ensuring that they are completely covered with water. Bring to a boil; process for 10 minutes. Remove jars and cool.

¼ CUP: 67 cal., 0 fat (0 sat. fat), 0 chol., 712mg sod., 17g carb. (14g sugars, 1g fiber), 0 pro.

RIB SHACK LOADED MASHED POTATOES

Idaho is well known for being the potato state—even our license plates say "Famous Potatoes"! This is my version of the scrumptious smashers that are served at a local barbecue joint. Everyone who tries them there begs for the recipe, which the place won't give out, so I made my own copycat version. These can be made ahead and kept warm in the slow cooker.
—*Trisha Kruse, Eagle, ID*

- -

TAKES: 30 min. • **MAKES:** 12 servings

  2½ lbs. potatoes, peeled and cubed
  1 cup 2% milk, warmed
  ½ cup spreadable garlic and herb cream cheese
  3 Tbsp. butter, softened
  1 lb. bacon strips, cooked and crumbled
  1 cup shredded cheddar cheese
  ½ cup shredded Parmesan cheese
  3 green onions, chopped
  2 Tbsp. minced fresh parsley or 2 tsp. dried parsley flakes
  ¼ tsp. salt
  ¼ tsp. pepper

Place potatoes in a Dutch oven; add water to cover. Bring to a boil. Reduce heat; cook, uncovered, until tender, 15-20 minutes. Drain and return to pan; gently mash potatoes while gradually adding milk, cream cheese spread and butter to reach desired consistency. Stir in remaining ingredients.

⅔ CUP: 238 cal., 15g fat (8g sat. fat), 41mg chol., 477mg sod., 15g carb. (2g sugars, 1g fiber), 10g pro.

RIB SHACK LOADED MASHED POTATOES

TERRIFIC TOMATO TART

Signature Mediterranean ingredients—including basil, tomatoes, feta and phyllo—meld beautifully in this fresh and airy flatbread-like dish, ideal for your next summer get-together.
—*Diane Halferty, Corpus Christi, TX*

PREP: 15 min. • **BAKE:** 20 min. • **MAKES:** 8 servings

- 12 sheets phyllo dough (14x9 in.)
- 2 Tbsp. olive oil
- 2 Tbsp. dry bread crumbs
- 2 Tbsp. prepared pesto
- ¾ cup crumbled feta cheese, divided
- 1 medium tomato, cut into ¼-in. slices
- 1 large yellow tomato, cut into ¼-in. slices
- ¼ tsp. pepper
- 5 to 6 fresh basil leaves, thinly sliced

1. Preheat oven to 400°. Place 1 sheet of phyllo dough on a baking sheet lined with parchment; brush with ½ tsp. oil and sprinkle with ½ tsp. bread crumbs. (Keep remaining phyllo covered with a damp towel to prevent it from drying out.) Repeat layers, being careful to brush oil all the way to edges.
2. Fold each side ¾ in. toward center to form a rim. Spread with pesto and sprinkle with half the feta cheese. Alternately arrange the red and yellow tomato slices over cheese. Sprinkle with pepper and remaining feta.
3. Bake until crust is golden brown and crispy, 20-25 minutes. Cool on a wire rack for 5 minutes. Remove parchment before cutting. Garnish with basil.
1 PIECE: 135 cal., 7g fat (2g sat. fat), 7mg chol., 221mg sod., 13g carb. (1g sugars, 1g fiber), 5g pro.

TERRIFIC TOMATO TART

SWEET POTATO KALE PILAF

SWEET POTATO KALE PILAF

The combination of sweet potatoes, bacon, asparagus and kale makes this simple wild rice dish taste amazing! To save time and dishes, you can easily cook the rice in a pressure cooker and also use it to saute the other ingredients.
—*Courtney Stultz, Weir, KS*

PREP: 15 min. • **COOK:** 1 hour • **MAKES:** 8 cups

- 1 cup uncooked wild rice
- 2¼ cups vegetable broth or water
- 1 tsp. olive oil
- 4 bacon strips, chopped
- 1 lb. fresh asparagus, trimmed and cut into 2-in. pieces
- 1 large sweet potato, peeled and chopped
- ½ cup chopped red onion
- 1 cup chopped fresh kale
- 1 garlic clove, minced
- ½ tsp. salt
- ½ tsp. pepper
-    Chopped fresh parsley

1. Rinse wild rice thoroughly; drain. In a large saucepan, combine broth, rice and oil; bring to a boil. Reduce heat; simmer, covered, until rice is fluffy and tender, 50-55 minutes. Drain if necessary.
2. Meanwhile, in a large skillet, cook bacon over medium heat until crisp. Remove to paper towels to drain. Add asparagus, sweet potato and onion to drippings; cook and stir over medium-high heat until potatoes are crisp-tender, 8-10 minutes.
3. Stir in kale, garlic, salt and pepper. Cook and stir until vegetables are tender, 8-10 minutes. Stir in rice and reserved bacon. Sprinkle with parsley.
¾ CUP: 156 cal., 5g fat (2g sat. fat), 7mg chol., 350mg sod., 23g carb. (5g sugars, 3g fiber), 5g pro. **DIABETIC EXCHANGES:** 1½ starch, 1 fat.

DAD'S CREAMED PEAS & PEARL ONIONS

When I was growing up, it was a family tradition to make creamed peas with pearl onions for every Thanksgiving and Christmas dinner. My dad would not be a happy camper if he didn't see this dish on the table. It was his favorite! I made it for my own family while our kids were growing up; my daughter now makes this dish for her family.
—Nancy Heishman, Las Vegas, NV

TAKES: 25 min. • **MAKES:** 6 servings

- 5 cups frozen peas (about 20 oz.), thawed and drained
- 2 cups frozen pearl onions (about 9 oz.), thawed and drained
- 2 celery ribs, finely chopped
- ¾ cup chicken broth
- ½ tsp. salt
- ½ tsp. pepper
- ½ tsp. dried thyme
- ½ cup sour cream
- 10 bacon strips, cooked and crumbled
- ¾ cup salted cashews

In a large skillet, combine the first 7 ingredients; bring to a boil. Reduce heat to medium; cook, uncovered, until the onions are tender and most of liquid is evaporated, 8-10 minutes, stirring occasionally. Remove from heat; stir in sour cream. Top with bacon and cashews.
¾ CUP: 322 cal., 18g fat (6g sat. fat), 19mg chol., 783mg sod., 26g carb. (10g sugars, 7g fiber), 14g pro.

DAD'S CREAMED PEAS & PEARL ONIONS

SWEET POTATO WEDGES WITH CHILI MAYO

Cajun spices bring the zing to roasted sweet potatoes—a side dish my family eats frequently. We dunk them in chili-spiced mayo.
—Raymonde Bourgeois, Swastika, ON

PREP: 15 min. • **BAKE:** 30 min. • **MAKES:** 8 servings (1 cup dip)

- 6 small sweet potatoes
- 2 Tbsp. olive oil
- 2 to 3 Tbsp. Cajun seasoning

DIP
- 1 cup mayonnaise
- 4 tsp. lemon juice
- 2 tsp. chili powder or chili garlic sauce
- 2 tsp. Dijon mustard

1. Preheat oven to 400°. Peel and cut each potato lengthwise into 8 wedges. Toss with oil and Cajun seasoning; divide between 2 greased 15x10x1-in. pans.
2. Roast potatoes until tender, 30-45 minutes, turning once. Meanwhile, mix dip ingredients; serve with potatoes.
1 SERVING: 322 cal., 26g fat (4g sat. fat), 10mg chol., 600mg sod., 22g carb. (9g sugars, 3g fiber), 2g pro.

CAPE COD CORN PUDDING

A family member passed along this recipe for corn baked with cheddar and ricotta. Don't skip the fresh basil—it adds a hint of sweet flavor reminiscent of mint and anise.
—Melinda Messer, Benson, NC

PREP: 20 min. • **BAKE:** 30 min. + standing • **MAKES:** 8 servings

- ¼ cup butter, cubed
- 5 cups frozen corn (about 24 oz.)
- 1 medium onion, finely chopped
- 4 large eggs, lightly beaten
- 2 cups whole milk
- 1 cup whole-milk ricotta cheese
- ½ cup cornmeal
- 1 Tbsp. sugar
- 1 tsp. salt
- ¾ tsp. pepper
- 1½ cups shredded cheddar cheese, divided
- 2 Tbsp. chopped fresh basil, optional

1. Preheat oven to 375°. In a 6-qt. stockpot, heat butter over medium-high heat. Add corn and onion; cook and stir until onion is crisp-tender, 6-8 minutes. Remove from heat.
2. In a large bowl, whisk eggs, milk, ricotta cheese, cornmeal, sugar, salt and pepper. Stir in ¾ cup cheddar cheese, corn mixture and, if desired, basil.
3. Transfer to a greased 11x7-in. baking dish. Sprinkle with the remaining cheddar cheese. Bake, uncovered, until set, 30-35 minutes. Let stand 10 minutes before serving.
1 SERVING: 378 cal., 21g fat (12g sat. fat), 148mg chol., 582mg sod., 34g carb. (9g sugars, 2g fiber), 17g pro.

GINGER ORANGE SQUASH

GINGER ORANGE SQUASH

Bursting with citrus flavor, this tender side dish complements autumn dinner parties and weeknight suppers alike. Our Test Kitchen developed the five-ingredient recipe—which is low in fat and sodium—so you can spend less time in the kitchen and more time with family.
—Taste of Home *Test Kitchen*

PREP: 15 min. • **BAKE:** 50 min.
MAKES: 10 servings

- 2 butternut squash (2 lbs. each), peeled and cut into 1½-in. cubes
- 1 cup thawed orange juice concentrate
- 3 Tbsp. coarsely chopped fresh gingerroot
- ½ tsp. pepper
- 4 tsp. butter, melted

1. Line a 15x10x1-in. baking pan with foil and coat with cooking spray; set aside. In a large bowl, toss the squash, orange juice concentrate, ginger and pepper. Arrange in a single layer in prepared pan.
2. Bake at 375° until squash is tender, 50-55 minutes, stirring twice. Stir in butter before serving.
½ CUP: 129 cal., 2g fat (1g sat. fat), 4mg chol., 23mg sod., 29g carb. (15g sugars, 5g fiber), 2g pro. **DIABETIC EXCHANGES:** 1 starch, 1 fruit, ½ fat.

BACON-ALMOND GREEN BEANS

I adapted this from a magazine recipe that required a lot of work. My beans are quicker and easier to prepare but still taste great.
—*Jackie Matthews, Yucca Valley, CA*

TAKES: 30 min. • **MAKES:** 6 servings

- 1½ lbs. fresh green beans, trimmed and cut into 1½-in. pieces
- 3 Tbsp. butter
- 3 Tbsp. brown sugar
- 2¼ tsp. soy sauce
- 2¼ tsp. Worcestershire sauce
- 4 to 5 Tbsp. real bacon bits
- 4 to 5 Tbsp. sliced almonds, toasted

1. Place beans in a large saucepan and cover with water. Bring to a boil; cook, uncovered, for 8-10 minutes or until crisp-tender.
2. Meanwhile, melt butter in a large skillet over medium heat. Stir in the brown sugar, soy sauce and Worcestershire sauce. Cook 1 minute or until sugar is dissolved.
3. Drain beans; add to the skillet. Cook and stir for 2 minutes or until heated through. Sprinkle with bacon and almonds; toss to coat. Serve with a slotted spoon.
¾ CUP: 149 cal., 9g fat (4g sat. fat), 19mg chol., 352mg sod., 15g carb. (10g sugars, 4g fiber), 5g pro.

SPECIAL CAULIFLOWER SIDE DISH

Dijon mustard adds a little zip to my dish. All the flavors blend so nicely that it's become a a top choice when I want to make cauliflower.
—*Rita Reinke, Wauwatosa, WI*

TAKES: 30 min. • **MAKES:** 6 servings

- 4 cups fresh cauliflowerets
- 2 Tbsp. plain yogurt
- 2 Tbsp. mayonnaise
- 1 tsp. Dijon mustard
- ¼ tsp. dill weed
- ¼ tsp. salt
- ¼ tsp. garlic powder
- ½ cup shredded cheddar cheese

1. Preheat oven to 350°. Place cauliflower in a steamer basket; place in a large saucepan over 1 in. of water. Bring to a boil; cover and steam until crisp-tender, 6-8 minutes.
2. Meanwhile, in a small bowl, combine yogurt, mayonnaise, mustard, dill, salt and garlic powder.
3. Transfer cauliflower to an ungreased 3-cup baking dish; top with yogurt mixture and cheese. Bake, uncovered, until the cauliflower is heated through and cheese is melted, 8-10 minutes.
⅔ CUP: 88 cal., 7g fat (3g sat. fat), 12mg chol., 222mg sod., 4g carb. (2g sugars, 2g fiber), 4g pro.

TEST KITCHEN TIP

You can use any of your favorite shredded cheeses in this recipe. Shredded Parmesan is a tasty option, though you may want to back off on the salt in the recipe.

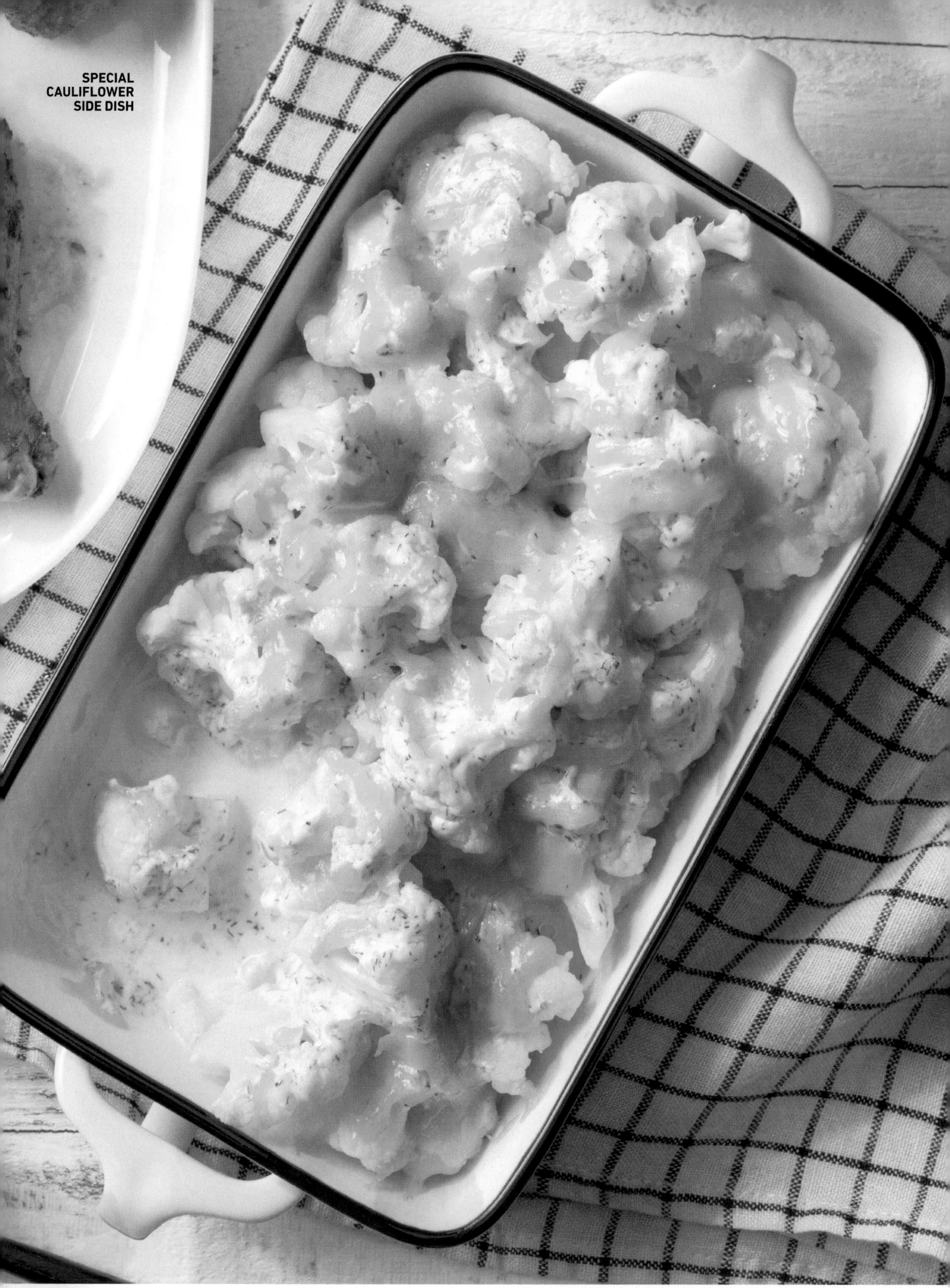
SPECIAL
CAULIFLOWER
SIDE DISH

RISOTTO WITH LEMON
& SPRING VEGETABLES

RISOTTO WITH LEMON & SPRING VEGETABLES

This dish has the fresh flavors of spring and looks so colorful. It can be made vegetarian by using vegetable broth and leaving out the ham. Because it's so versatile, you can use whatever vegetables are in season or what your family prefers.
—Mary Lou Timpson, Centennial Park, AZ

PREP: 20 min. • **COOK:** 50 min.
MAKES: 8 servings

- ½ lb. fresh asparagus, trimmed
- 5 cups chicken stock
- 6 Tbsp. butter, divided
- 1 lb. fresh baby spinach, thinly sliced
- 1 tsp. salt
- 1 medium leek (white portion only), finely sliced
- 1½ cups uncooked arborio rice
- 2 garlic cloves, minced
- ½ cup dry white wine or chicken stock
- 2 Tbsp. lemon juice
- ¾ cup cubed fully cooked ham
- 1 Tbsp. grated lemon zest
- 1 cup grated Parmesan cheese

1. Preheat oven to 425°. Place asparagus on a rimmed baking sheet. Roast until crisp-tender, 10-12 minutes. When cool enough to handle, cut into 1-in. pieces; set aside.

2. In a large saucepan, bring stock to a simmer; keep hot. In a Dutch oven, heat 2 Tbsp. butter over medium-high heat. Add spinach and salt; cook and stir until tender. Remove spinach and keep warm. In the same pan, heat 2 Tbsp. butter. Add the leek; cook and stir 2-3 minutes or until tender. Add rice, garlic and remaining 2 Tbsp. butter; cook and stir until rice is coated, 1-2 minutes.

3. Stir in wine and lemon juice. Reduce heat to maintain a simmer; cook and stir until wine is absorbed. Add the hot stock, ½ cup at a time, cooking and stirring until the stock has been absorbed after each addition, until rice is tender but firm to the bite, and risotto is creamy. Stir in ham, zest, asparagus and spinach; heat through. Remove from heat; stir in cheese. Serve immediately, with additional cheese if desired.

1 CUP: 308 cal., 13g fat (8g sat. fat), 39mg chol., 1082mg sod., 37g carb. (2g sugars, 2g fiber), 13g pro.

CHIVE SMASHED POTATOES

No need to peel the potatoes—in fact, this is the only way we make mashed potatoes anymore. Mixing in the flavored cream cheese is a delightful twist.
—Beverly A. Norris, Evanston, WY

TAKES: 30 min. • **MAKES:** 12 servings

- 4 lbs. red potatoes, quartered
- 2 tsp. chicken bouillon granules
- 1 carton (8 oz.) spreadable chive and onion cream cheese
- ½ cup half-and-half cream
- ¼ cup butter, cubed
- 1 tsp. salt
- ¼ tsp. pepper
  Chopped chives, optional

1. Place potatoes and bouillon in a Dutch oven and cover with 8 cups water. Bring to a boil. Reduce heat; cover and cook until tender, 15-20 minutes.

2. Drain and return to pan. Mash potatoes with cream cheese, cream, butter, salt and pepper. If desired, garnish with chives.

⅔ CUP: 219 cal., 11g fat (7g sat. fat), 31mg chol., 428mg sod., 26g carb. (3g sugars, 3g fiber), 5g pro.

KALE WITH BACON

The hearty bacon and garlic flavor makes this a great way to enjoy vitamin-rich kale.
—Margaret Allen, Abingdon, VA

PREP: 15 min. • **COOK:** 25 min.
MAKES: 6 servings

- 2 bunches kale, trimmed and torn
- 8 bacon strips, diced
- 2 large onions, chopped
- 4 garlic cloves, minced
- 1 tsp. salt
- ½ tsp. pepper

1. In a large saucepan, bring 1 in. of water to a boil. Add kale; cook 10-15 minutes or until tender.

2. Meanwhile, in a large nonstick skillet, cook bacon over medium heat until crisp. Using a slotted spoon, remove to paper towels; drain, reserving 1 tsp. drippings. In the drippings, cook and stir onions and garlic until onion is tender.

3. Drain the kale; stir into onion mixture. Add the salt, pepper and reserved bacon; heat through.

½ CUP: 161 cal., 7g fat (2g sat. fat), 9mg chol., 604mg sod., 20g carb. (7g sugars, 4g fiber), 8g pro. **DIABETIC EXCHANGES:** 1½ starch, 1 fat.

CHIVE SMASHED POTATOES

Yeah, You Can Pickle That!

Sweet corn? Of course! Strawberries? Sure! Grapes? Go for it! Think beyond cucumbers and graze your garden for unpredictable produce that's ripe for the pickling.

Pickled Jalapeno Rings: Top your nachos, fold into tuna salad, mix into a pimiento cheese spread.

Pickled Daikon & Carrots: Add to a banh mi sandwich, serve with grilled or roasted meats, pile onto a cheeseburger.

Pickled Corn: Swirl into ramen soup, add to your favorite salsa, layer in a quesadilla.

Pickled Bell Peppers: Serve with grilled steak or pork, toss in a salad, garnish a Bloody Mary.

Pickled Jalapeno Rings

I used to can Hungarian hot and mild peppers with my dad every year, but those are hard to find in California, so I started pickling jalapenos instead. These are better than any store-bought version.
—*Lou Kostura, Belmont, CA*

- -

PREP: 15 min. + chilling • **MAKES:** 32 servings

- 1   lb. jalapeno peppers, sliced into rings
- 1   cup fresh dill sprigs
- 5   garlic cloves
- 1½ cups water
- ⅔   cup white vinegar
- 5   tsp. kosher salt
- 4   tsp. mixed pickling spices

In a clean 1-qt. glass jar, layer a quarter each of the jalapenos, dill and garlic; repeat, filling the jar. In a saucepan, bring water, vinegar, salt and pickling spices to a simmer until salt dissolves. Pour into jar to cover peppers; seal. Let stand until cool. Refrigerate at least 7 days; store up to 1 month.
NOTE: Wear disposable gloves when cutting hot peppers; the oils can burn skin. Avoid touching your face.
2 TBSP.: 5 cal., 0 fat (0 sat. fat), 0 chol., 180mg sod., 1g carb. (0 sugars, 0 fiber), 0 pro.

Pickled Corn

When fresh corn is in season and you're overeating it straight off the cob, try pickling it instead!
—*Amanda Phillips, Portland, OR*

- -

PREP: 15 min. + chilling • **MAKES:** 16 servings

- 4   medium ears sweet corn, husked
- 1   cup white vinegar
- ½   cup water
- ¼   cup sugar
- 2   garlic cloves, thinly sliced
- 1   tsp. salt
- ½   tsp. coarsely ground pepper
- 1   pinch crushed red pepper flakes

Cut corn from cobs; place in a large bowl. In a saucepan, combine vinegar, water, sugar, garlic, salt, pepper and pepper flakes. Bring to a boil; reduce heat and simmer until sugar dissolves, 1-2 minutes. Pour mixture over corn; cool. Transfer to jars, if desired; seal tightly. Refrigerate at least 2 hours before serving. Store in the refrigerator for up to 2 months.
½ CUP: 24 cal., 0 fat (0 sat. fat), 0 chol., 19mg sod., 5g carb. (2g sugars, 1g fiber), 1g pro.

Sweet & Spicy Pickled Red Seedless Grapes:
Use for bruschetta over ricotta, toss in a salad, serve with cheddar cheese.

Spicy Pickled Strawberries:
Add to a charcuterie board, tuck into a grilled cheese sandwich, fold into salsa.

SWEET & SPICY PICKLED RED SEEDLESS GRAPES

PICKLED DAIKON & CARROTS

Pickled Daikon & Carrots

This recipe is inspired by a pickle my family and I enjoyed at a local Asian restaurant. It is a delicious side to serve with roasted meats as well as a tasty condiment on a burger or sandwich. You won't miss the high-fat dressing or mayonnaise.
—*Lisa Keys, Kennet Square, PA*

PREP: 20 min. + chilling
MAKES: 16 servings

- 1 medium daikon radish, peeled and julienned
- 1 cup julienned carrots
- 2 jalapeno peppers, seeded and thinly sliced
- ¾ cup water
- ¾ cup white vinegar
- ⅓ cup sugar
- 1 tsp. kosher salt
- 2 drops liquid smoke, optional

In a large bowl, combine daikon, carrots and jalapenos. In a saucepan, bring water, vinegar, sugar, salt and, if desired, liquid smoke to a boil. Simmer until sugar dissolves. Pour mixture over vegetables, ensuring vegetables are submerged; cool. Transfer to jars, if desired; cover tightly. Refrigerate, covered, at least 1 hour before serving. Store in the refrigerator for up to 2 weeks, stirring occasionally.
NOTE: Wear disposable gloves when cutting hot peppers; the oils can burn skin. Avoid touching your face.
¼ CUP: 9 cal., 0 fat (0 sat. fat), 0 chol., 22mg sod., 2g carb. (1g sugars, 1g fiber), 0 pro. **DIABETIC EXCHANGES:** 1 Free food.

Pickled Bell Peppers

Well received at potlucks, these colorful sliced peppers add zest to the menu—and they're a smart way to use peppers from the garden. I also like to make them as a zippy side for lunch or dinner at home.
—*Heather Prendergast, Sundre, AB*

PREP: 20 min. + chilling
MAKES: 16 servings

- 2 each medium green, sweet red and yellow peppers, julienned
- 1 large red onion, halved and thinly sliced
- 2 tsp. mixed pickling spices
- ½ tsp. celery seed
- 1 cup sugar
- 1 cup cider vinegar
- ⅓ cup water

1. In a large glass bowl, combine peppers and onion. Place pickling spices and celery seed on a double thickness of cheesecloth. Gather corners of the cloth to enclose seasonings; tie securely with string.
2. In a small saucepan, combine sugar, vinegar, water and spice bag. Bring to a boil; boil 1 minute. Transfer spice bag to pepper mixture. Pour vinegar mixture over top; cool. Refrigerate, covered, 24 hours, stirring occasionally.
3. Discard spice bag. Transfer mixture to jars, if desired; cover tightly. Refrigerate pickled peppers up to 1 month.
¼ CUP: 67 cal., 0 fat (0 sat. fat), 0 chol., 2mg sod., 17g carb. (15g sugars, 1g fiber), 1g pro.

PICKLED JALAPENO RINGS

PICKLED CORN

PICKLED BELL PEPPERS

SPICY PICKLED STRAWBERRIES

Spicy Pickled Strawberries

I developed a unique healthy recipe to feature my most-loved spring and summer fruit. My favorite way to serve these strawberries is as an appetizer with cheese.
—*Roxanne Chan, Albany, CA*

PREP: 10 min. + chilling
MAKES: 6 servings

- ½ cup rice vinegar
- 1 tsp. chili garlic sauce
- 1 tsp. toasted sesame oil
- ½ tsp. grated orange zest
- ½ tsp. black sesame seeds
- 1 green onion, minced
- 2 lbs. fresh strawberries, hulled

In a large bowl, combine the first 6 ingredients. Add strawberries and stir to coat. Refrigerate at least 1 hour. Transfer to jars, if desired; cover tightly. Store in refrigerator up to 2 days.

¾ CUP: 85 cal., 1g fat (0 sat. fat), 0 chol., 347mg sod., 19g carb. (14g sugars, 3g fiber), 1g pro.

Sweet & Spicy Pickled Red Seedless Grapes

These flavor-packed grapes are unique and delicious on a fab antipasto, pickle or cheese tray.
—*Cheryl Perry, Hertford, NC*

PREP: 35 min. • **PROCESS:** 10 min.
MAKES: 4 pints

- 5 cups seedless red grapes
- 4 jalapeno peppers, seeded and sliced
- 2 Tbsp. minced fresh gingerroot
- 2 cinnamon sticks (3 in.), halved
- 4 whole star anise
- 2 tsp. coriander seeds
- 2 tsp. mustard seed
- 2 cups packed brown sugar
- 2 cups white wine vinegar
- 1 cup water
- 1 cup dry red wine
- 1½ tsp. canning salt

1. Pack grapes into 4 hot 1-pint jars to within 1½ in. of the tops. Divide jalapenos, ginger, cinnamon, star anise, coriander seeds and mustard seed among jars.

2. In a large saucepan, combine brown sugar, vinegar, water, wine and canning salt. Bring to a boil; cook until liquid is reduced to 3 cups, 15-18 minutes.

3. Carefully ladle hot liquid over grape mixture in each jar, leaving ½-in. headspace. Remove air bubbles and adjust headspace, if necessary, by adding hot liquid. Wipe rims. Center lids on jars; screw on bands until fingertip tight.

4. Place jars into canner, ensuring that they are completely covered with water. Bring to a boil; process for 10 minutes. Remove jars and cool.

NOTES: Wear disposable gloves when cutting hot peppers; the oils can burn skin. Avoid touching your face. The processing time listed is for altitudes of 1,000 feet or less. For altitudes up to 3,000 feet, add 5 minutes; 6,000 feet, add 10 minutes; 8,000 feet, add 15 minutes; 10,000 feet, add 20 minutes.

¼ CUP: 32 cal., 0 fat (0 sat. fat), 0 chol., 7mg sod., 8g carb. (7g sugars, 0 fiber), 0 pro.

STRAWBERRY LIMONCELLO JAM

BUTTERNUT SQUASH JUMBLE

I took this to a Thanksgiving potluck one year when I couldn't go home for the holiday, and it was a huge hit. It's different without being too nontraditional. It's also delicious at room temperature, so it's one less thing to worry about when you're trying to figure out serving times. I like Gorgonzola for this, but any blue cheese would work. If you can find the pre-crumbled cheese, even better.
—*Kara Brocious, Indianapolis, IN*

PREP: 20 min. • **BAKE:** 40 min. • **MAKES:** 10 servings

- 1 medium butternut squash (2 to 2½ lbs.), peeled and cut into 1-in. cubes
- 2 to 2½ lbs. large sweet potatoes, peeled and cut into 1-in. cubes
- 2 Tbsp. olive oil
- 1 tsp. salt
- ¾ tsp. dried thyme
- ½ tsp. pepper
- 1 cup crumbled Gorgonzola cheese
- 1 cup chopped pecans, toasted
- ¾ cup dried cranberries
- ¼ cup chopped fresh parsley

Preheat oven to 425°. In a large bowl, combine squash, sweet potatoes, olive oil, salt, thyme and pepper; transfer to a greased 15x10x1-in. baking pan. Roast until tender, 40-45 minutes, stirring occasionally. To serve, place mixture in a serving dish. Sprinkle with cheese, pecans, cranberries and parsley.
1 CUP: 311 cal., 14g fat (4g sat. fat), 10mg chol., 402mg sod., 45g carb. (21g sugars, 8g fiber), 6g pro.

STRAWBERRY LIMONCELLO JAM

This is one of my top-selling jams at the farmers market during the spring. It's amazing over a scoop of fresh vanilla ice cream, on a toasted waffle, or served with fresh goat cheese and crackers.
—*Krystal Wertman, Humble, TX*

PREP: 30 min. • **PROCESS:** 10 min. • **MAKES:** about 10 half-pints

- 5 cups crushed strawberries (about 3 lbs.)
- ½ cup water
- ¼ cup lemon juice
- 6 Tbsp. powdered fruit pectin
- 7 cups sugar
- ½ cup limoncello
- 1 tsp. grated lemon zest
- 10 half-pint jars

1. In a Dutch oven, combine strawberries, water and lemon juice. Stir in pectin. Bring to a full rolling boil over high heat, stirring constantly. Stir in sugar; return to a full rolling boil. Boil and stir 1 minute. Immediately stir in limoncello and zest.
2. Remove from heat; skim off foam. Ladle hot mixture into 10 hot half-pint jars, leaving ¼-in. headspace. Remove air bubbles and adjust headspace, if necessary, by adding hot mixture. Wipe rims. Center lids on jars; screw on bands until fingertip tight.
3. Place jars in a canner with simmering water, ensuring that they are completely covered with water. Bring to a boil; process for 10 minutes. Remove jars and cool.
2 TBSP.: 75 cal., 0 fat (0 sat. fat), 0 chol., 0 sod., 19g carb. (19g sugars, 0 fiber), 0 pro.

THYME GRILLED VEGETABLES

I love these little garden potatoes. It's easy to put these in a foil pan and grill them. Your kitchen won't get hot, and cleanup is a breeze.
—*Christine Wall, Bartlett, IL*

PREP: 20 min. • **GRILL:** 50 min. • **MAKES:** 9 servings

- 16 small red potatoes (about 2 lbs.), halved
- ½ cup chicken broth
- ¼ cup olive oil
- 2 Tbsp. minced fresh thyme or 2 tsp. dried thyme
- ½ tsp. salt
- 1 each large green, sweet red and yellow peppers, julienned
- 1 jar (15 oz.) pearl onions, drained

1. In an ungreased 13x9-in. disposable foil pan, combine the potatoes, broth, oil, thyme and salt. Grill, covered, over medium heat for 25 minutes.
2. Stir in peppers and onions. Grill 25-30 minutes longer or until vegetables are tender.
¾ CUP: 163 cal., 6g fat (1g sat. fat), 0 chol., 191mg sod., 25g carb. (4g sugars, 3g fiber), 3g pro. **DIABETIC EXCHANGES:** 1 starch, 1 vegetable, 1 fat.

**BUTTERNUT
SQUASH JUMBLE**

CREAMY CELERY ROOT
& PEARL ONIONS

CREAMY CELERY ROOT & PEARL ONIONS

I have made creamed onions for several recent Thanksgivings and wanted to change the recipe, so I decided to add celery root. It's perfect with the onions, and the creamy sauce is addicting!
—*Tina Mirilovich, Johnstown, PA*

PREP: 15 min. • **COOK:** 20 min. • **MAKES:** 8 servings

- 1 large celery root (about 1½ lbs.), peeled and cubed
- 3 Tbsp. butter
- 1 pkg. (14.4 oz.) pearl onions, thawed
- ¾ cup chicken broth
- 1 tsp. sugar
- ½ tsp. salt
- 1½ cups heavy whipping cream
- 2 Tbsp. minced fresh parsley
- ½ tsp. pepper

1. Place celery root in a 6-qt. stockpot; add water to cover. Bring to a boil. Reduce heat; simmer, uncovered, until tender, 4-6 minutes. Drain; set aside.
2. In a large skillet or Dutch oven, heat butter over medium heat. Add pearl onions, broth, sugar and salt. Cook onions, stirring often, until onions begin to brown, 12-15 minutes. Add celery root and cream; simmer until slightly thickened, 3-5 minutes. Stir in parsley and pepper.

⅔ CUP: 250 cal., 21g fat (13g sat. fat), 63mg chol., 379mg sod., 14g carb. (6g sugars, 3g fiber), 3g pro.

A CREOLE'S PEACH JAM

Making jam is my, well, jam! I've even turned it into a career! This peachy spread gets its pep from cayenne and was inspired by family in The Big Easy.
—*Ashlie Thomas, Graham, NC*

PREP: 45 min. • **PROCESS:** 10 min. + cooling • **MAKES:** 6 half-pints

- 2 pkg. (1¾ oz. each) pectin for lower sugar recipes
- 3 cups sugar, divided
- 4 lbs. peeled, pitted peaches, finely chopped
- 2 Tbsp. lemon juice
- 1½ Tbsp. minced fresh rosemary
- 1 fresh cayenne pepper, minced

1. In a Dutch oven or stockpot off the heat, stir together pectin and ¼ cup sugar. Add peaches, lemon juice, rosemary and cayenne pepper; bring to a full rolling boil over high heat, stirring constantly. Stir in the remaining 2¾ cups sugar; return to a full rolling boil. Boil and stir 1 minute.
2. Remove from heat, skim off foam. Ladle hot mixture into 6 hot half-pint jars, leaving ¼-in. headspace. Remove air bubbles and adjust headspace, if necessary, by adding hot mixture. Wipe rims. Center lids on jars; screw on bands until fingertip tight.
3. Place jars into canner with simmering water, ensuring they are completely covered with water. Bring to a boil; process for 10 minutes. Remove jars and cool.

2 TBSP.: 64 cal., 0 fat (0 sat. fat), 0 chol., 21mg sod., 16g carb. (16g sugars, 1g fiber), 0g pro.

AIR-FRYER CUMIN CARROTS

Carrots make a super side—big on flavor and a breeze to cook. Plus, I can actually get my husband to eat these fragrant, deeply spiced veggies.
—*Taylor Kiser, Brandon, FL*

PREP: 20 min. • **COOK:** 15 min. • **MAKES:** 4 servings

- 2 tsp. coriander seeds
- 2 tsp. cumin seeds
- 1 lb. carrots, peeled and cut into 4½-in. sticks
- 1 Tbsp. melted coconut oil or butter
- 2 garlic cloves, minced
- ¼ tsp. salt
- ⅛ tsp. pepper
  Minced fresh cilantro, optional

1. Preheat air fryer to 325°. In a dry small skillet, toast coriander and cumin seeds over medium heat 45-60 seconds or until aromatic, stirring frequently. Cool slightly. Grind in a spice grinder, or with a mortar and pestle, until finely crushed.
2. Place carrots in a large bowl. Add melted coconut oil, garlic, salt, pepper and crushed spices; toss to coat. Place on greased tray in air-fryer basket.
3. Cook until crisp-tender and lightly browned, 12-15 minutes, stirring occasionally. If desired, sprinkle with cilantro.

1 SERVING: 86 cal., 4g fat (3g sat. fat), 0 chol., 228mg sod., 12g carb. (5g sugars, 4g fiber), 1g pro. **DIABETIC EXCHANGES:** 1 vegetable, 1 fat.

AIR-FRYER CUMIN CARROTS

HARVEST
PUMPKIN
BUTTER

BASIL CHEESE BUTTERFLY PASTA

Kids love pasta, especially when it is shaped like fun butterflies. The lemon and basil pairs with Parmesan cheese to transform plain pasta into something totally different and kid-approved!
—*Lauren Reiff, East Earl, PA*

TAKES: 20 min. • **MAKES:** 4 servings

    3   cups uncooked bow tie pasta
    1   garlic clove, minced
    1   Tbsp. olive oil
    1   Tbsp. lemon juice
    1   tsp. dried basil
    ½   tsp. salt
    ¼   tsp. pepper
    ½   cup grated Parmesan cheese

1. In a large saucepan, cook the pasta according to package directions. Drain pasta and set aside.
2. In the same saucepan, saute garlic in oil for 1 minute. Stir in the lemon juice, basil, salt and pepper. Return pasta to the pan. Add cheese and toss to coat.
1 CUP: 275 cal., 7g fat 2g sat. fat), 9mg chol., 479mg sod., 43g carb. (2g sugars, 2g fiber), 10g pro.

CREOLE RICE

I've found a fast and fantastic way to turn leftover rice into a spectacular side dish. I spice it up with Creole seasoning and pepper to give it a boost of flavor. No one will figure out the zippy combination is a second-day dish.
—*Sundra Hauck, Bogalusa, LA*

TAKES: 10 min. • **MAKES:** 4 servings

    ¼   cup butter, cubed
    1   tsp. Creole seasoning
    ⅛   tsp. pepper
    2   cups cooked long grain rice
        Ground paprika, optional

In a small saucepan, melt butter; add Creole seasoning and pepper. Cook over medium heat for 3 minutes. Stir in rice. Cover and heat through.
¾ CUP: 203 cal., 12g fat (7g sat. fat), 31mg chol., 282mg sod., 22g carb. (0 sugars, 0 fiber), 2g pro.

HARVEST PUMPKIN BUTTER

Stir up a fresh alternative to traditional apple butter by making this scrumptious spread. It's yummy on English muffins or any kind of toasted bread.
—*Marlene Muckenhirn, Delano, MN*

PREP: 10 min. + chilling • **COOK:** 15 min.
MAKES: 1¼ cups

    1   cup canned pumpkin
    ½   cup honey
    ¼   cup molasses
    1   Tbsp. lemon juice
    ¾   tsp. ground cinnamon
        English muffins, split and toasted

1. In a small saucepan, combine the first 5 ingredients. Bring to a boil, stirring frequently. Reduce heat; simmer, uncovered, until thickened, about 15 minutes.
2. Cool, then refrigerate for at least 1 hour. Serve on English muffins.
2 TBSP.: 79 cal., 0 fat (0 sat. fat), 0 chol., 4mg sod., 21g carb. (19g sugars, 0 fiber), 0 pro.

QUICK BARBECUED BEANS

This may be a simple, classic recipe, but cooking it on the grill introduces a subtle flavor. The dish features a nice blend of beans, and preparation time is minimal.
—*Millie Vickery, Lena, IL*

TAKES: 25 min. • **MAKES:** 5 servings

    1   can (16 oz.) kidney beans, rinsed and drained
    1   can (15½ oz.) great northern beans, rinsed and drained
    1   can (15 oz.) pork and beans
    ½   cup barbecue sauce
    2   Tbsp. brown sugar
    2   tsp. prepared mustard

1. In an ungreased 8-in. square disposable foil pan, combine all ingredients.
2. Grill beans, covered, over medium heat until heated through, 15-20 minutes, stirring occasionally.
¾ CUP: 264 cal., 2g fat (0 sat. fat), 0 chol., 877mg sod., 51g carb. (15g sugars, 13g fiber), 14g pro.

MAPLE MISO SWEET POTATO CASSEROLE

This recipe takes a beloved holiday side dish and gives it a savory twist to complement its traditionally sweet flavors.
—*Sara Schwabe, Bloomington, IN*

PREP: 35 min. • **BAKE:** 30 min. • **MAKES:** 6 servings

2 Tbsp. tahini
2 lbs. sweet potatoes (about 2 large), peeled and cubed

TOPPING
¼ cup all-purpose flour
¼ cup packed brown sugar
2 Tbsp. cold butter
2 Tbsp. sesame seeds

FILLING
3 Tbsp. butter
3 Tbsp. maple syrup
2 Tbsp. white miso paste
1 Tbsp. rice vinegar
½ tsp. ground cinnamon
½ tsp. ground ginger

1. Preheat oven to 375°. Place tahini in freezer for 20 minutes. Place sweet potatoes in a 6-qt. stockpot; add water to cover. Bring to a boil. Reduce heat; cook, uncovered, until tender, 10-12 minutes. Meanwhile, make topping by combining flour and sugar; cut in butter and chilled tahini until crumbly. Stir in sesame seeds.
2. Drain potatoes; return to pan. Beat until mashed. Add butter, maple syrup, miso paste, rice vinegar, cinnamon and ginger. Transfer to a greased 13x9-in. baking dish. Sprinkle topping over mixture.
3. Bake, covered, 15 minutes. Uncover; bake until topping is golden brown, 15- 20 minutes.
⅔ CUP: 386 cal., 15g fat (7g sat. fat), 25mg chol., 383mg sod., 60g carb. (32g sugars, 6g fiber), 5g pro.

BACON-WRAPPED ASPARAGUS

MAPLE MISO SWEET POTATO CASSEROLE

BACON-WRAPPED ASPARAGUS

My husband and I grill dinner almost every night, and I love grilling asparagus for a side dish. I serve these bacon-wrapped spears with grilled meat and sliced fresh tomatoes for a wonderful meal.
—*Trisha Kitts, Dickinson, TX*

TAKES: 30 min. • **MAKES:** 2 servings

10 fresh asparagus spears, trimmed
Cooking spray
⅛ tsp. pepper
5 bacon strips, halved lengthwise

1. Place asparagus on a sheet of waxed paper; coat with cooking spray. Sprinkle with pepper; turn to coat. Wrap a bacon piece around each spear; secure ends with toothpicks.
2. Grill, uncovered, over medium heat until bacon is crisp, 4-6 minutes on each side. Discard toothpicks.
5 PIECES : 120 cal., 8g fat (3g sat. fat), 21mg chol., 372mg sod., 4g carb. (1g sugars, 1g fiber), 9g pro.

TEST KITCHEN TIP

You can also cook bacon-wrapped asparagus in the oven. Place the spears on a foil-lined baking sheet; bake at 400° until the bacon is crisp, 15-20 minutes, turning if needed.

SWEET ZUCCHINI RELISH

Classic relish is made with cucumbers, but this tangy and sweet zucchini relish is packed with zucchini, peppers and onions. I use it on burgers, on sandwiches and in any recipes that normally call for pickle relish.

—Jyl Basinger, Cave City, AR

PREP: 1 hour + chilling • **PROCESS:** 15 min. • **MAKES:** 5 pints

- 10 cups shredded zucchini (about 3½ lbs.)
- 4 large onions, chopped
- 2 medium green peppers, chopped
- 2 medium sweet red peppers, chopped
- ⅓ cup canning salt
- 2½ cups sugar
- 2½ cups cider vinegar
- 4 tsp. cornstarch
- 1 tsp. ground turmeric
- 1 tsp. curry powder
- 1 tsp. celery seed
- ½ tsp. pepper

1. In a large container, combine the zucchini, onions, peppers and salt. Cover and refrigerate overnight. Drain; rinse and drain again.

2. In a stockpot, combine the sugar, vinegar, cornstarch and seasonings; bring to a boil. Add zucchini mixture; return to a boil. Reduce heat; simmer, uncovered, until slightly thickened, 12-15 minutes. Remove from the heat.

3. Carefully ladle hot mixture into hot 1-pint jars, leaving ½-in. headspace. Remove air bubbles; wipe rims and adjust lids. Process for 15 minutes in a boiling-water canner. Relish may be kept in refrigerator for up to 1 week.

¼ CUP: 68 cal., 0 fat (0 sat. fat), 0 chol., 288mg sod., 16g carb. (14g sugars, 1g fiber), 1g pro.

SAUTEED BROCCOLI

SAUTEED BROCCOLI

When I needed a new recipe for cooking broccoli, I came up with my own. It makes a nice side dish for most entrees.

—Jim MacNeal, Waterloo, NY

TAKES: 20 min. • **MAKES:** 10 servings

- 1 cup chopped onion
- 1 cup julienned sweet red pepper
- ¼ cup olive oil
- 12 cups fresh broccoli florets
- 1⅓ cups water
- 3 tsp. minced garlic
- ½ tsp. salt
- ½ tsp. pepper

In a Dutch oven, saute onion and red pepper in oil for 2-3 minutes or until crisp-tender. Stir in the broccoli, water, garlic, salt and pepper. Cover and cook over medium heat for 5-6 minutes or until broccoli is crisp-tender.

¾ CUP: 82 cal., 6g fat (1g sat. fat), 0 chol., 142mg sod., 7g carb. (2g sugars, 2g fiber), 3g pro. **DIABETIC EXCHANGES:** 1 vegetable, 1 fat.

READER REVIEW

"This is a delicious and easy-to-prepare recipe. I reduced the recipe to make two large main-dish servings to go with baked chicken. I added a dash of red pepper flakes and a sprinkling of Romano cheese to each serving."

—ANNR, TASTEOFHOME.COM

SWEET ZUCCHINI RELISH

MASHED POTATOES

Mashed potatoes go with just about any meal, so keep this recipe handy. We like to use good ol' russets or Yukon Golds.
—Taste of Home *Test Kitchen*

TAKES: 30 min.
MAKES: 6 servings (about 4½ cups)

- 6 medium russet potatoes (about 2 lbs.), peeled and cubed
- ½ cup warm whole milk or heavy whipping cream
- ¼ cup butter, cubed
- ¾ tsp. salt
  Dash pepper

Place potatoes in a large saucepan; add water to cover. Bring to a boil. Reduce heat to medium; cook, uncovered, until easily pierced with a fork, 20-25 minutes. Drain. Add remaining ingredients; mash until light and fluffy.

¾ CUP: 168 cal., 8g fat (5g sat. fat), 22mg chol., 367mg sod., 22g carb. (3g sugars, 1g fiber), 3g pro.

LEMON PARMESAN ORZO

A splash of lemon and a shower of chopped parsley make this orzo one of my family's most requested springtime sides. It's fantastic with chicken, pork and fish, or you can eat it on its own as a light lunch.
—Leslie Palmer, Swampscott, MA

TAKES: 20 min. • **MAKES:** 4 servings

- 1 cup uncooked whole wheat orzo pasta
- 1 Tbsp. olive oil
- ¼ cup grated Parmesan cheese
- 2 Tbsp. minced fresh parsley
- ½ tsp. grated lemon zest
- ¼ tsp. salt
- ¼ tsp. pepper

Cook the orzo according to the package directions; drain. Transfer to a small bowl; drizzle with oil. Stir in the remaining ingredients.

½ CUP: 191 cal., 6g fat (1g sat. fat), 4mg chol., 225mg sod., 28g carb. (0 sugars, 7g fiber), 7g pro. **DIABETIC EXCHANGES:** 2 starch, ½ fat.

MONTEREY CORN BAKE

This 50-year-old recipe came from my mother-in-law, who taught me how to cook. It is one of my family's favorite dishes. It yields enough for a group, or you can cut it in half to serve a few.
—Irene Redick, Trenton, ON

PREP: 15 min. • **BAKE:** 25 min.
MAKES: 6 servings

- 1 medium onion, chopped
- 5 Tbsp. butter, divided
- 2 cups sliced fresh mushrooms
- 1 medium sweet red pepper, chopped
- ½ tsp. salt
- ¼ tsp. pepper
- 1 garlic clove, minced
- 1 pkg. (16 oz.) frozen corn, thawed
- 2 cups shredded Colby-Monterey Jack cheese
- 2 tsp. brown sugar
- ½ cup dry bread crumbs
- 2 Tbsp. minced fresh parsley

1. Preheat oven to 375°. In a large skillet, saute onion in 2 Tbsp. butter until tender. Add the mushrooms, red pepper, salt and pepper; cook and stir until vegetables are tender, about 5 minutes. Add garlic; cook 1 minute longer.

2. In a greased 2-qt. baking dish, layer half of the corn, mushroom mixture, cheese and brown sugar; repeat layers.

3. Melt the remaining butter; toss with bread crumbs and parsley. Sprinkle over the casserole.

4. Bake, uncovered, until golden brown, 25-30 minutes.

1 SERVING: 359 cal., 22g fat (15g sat. fat), 62mg chol., 624mg sod., 30g carb. (5g sugars, 3g fiber), 13g pro.

MONTEREY CORN BAKE

ORANGE CRANBERRY BREAD
PAGE 155

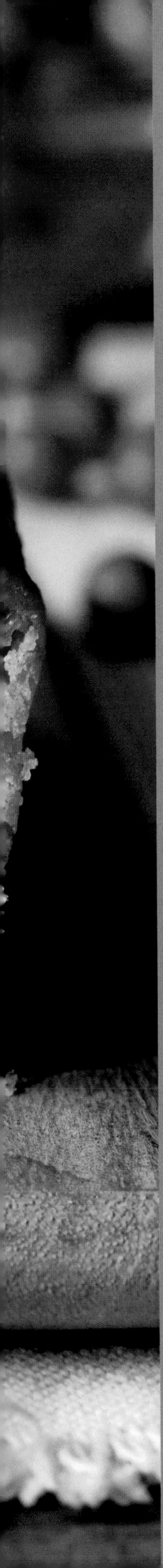

Breads, Rolls & Muffins

Put on the coffee...and grab the jam, honey and butter. Perfect sweet rolls, doughnuts and quick breads await your special mornings. Plus, savory dinner options will make the meal grand.

ALL-TIME FAVORITES

CHERRY-TARRAGON DINNER ROLLS

My grandmother made these for every big holiday, and we were all clamoring at the table to get our hands on one. Use any remaining rolls as bread for a slider sandwich.
—Jeanne Holt, St. Paul, MN

PREP: 30 min. + rising • **BAKE:** 15 min.
MAKES: 1 dozen

- 1 pkg. (¼ oz.) active dry yeast
- ¾ cup warm 2% milk (110° to 115°)
- 2 large eggs, room temperature, divided use
- 2 Tbsp. butter, melted
- 4½ tsp. sugar
- 1 Tbsp. minced fresh chives
- 2½ tsp. grated orange zest
- 1¼ tsp. salt
- 1¼ tsp. dried tarragon
- 2½ to 3 cups all-purpose flour
- ½ cup chopped dried cherries
- ⅓ cup chopped pistachios

1. In a small bowl, dissolve yeast in warm milk. In a large bowl, combine 1 egg, butter, sugar, chives, zest, salt, tarragon, yeast mixture and 1½ cups flour; beat on medium speed until smooth. Stir in enough remaining flour to form a stiff dough (dough will be sticky).

2. Turn dough onto a floured surface; knead 6-8 minutes or until smooth and elastic. Knead in cherries and pistachios. Place in a greased bowl, turning once to grease the top. Cover and let rise in a warm place until doubled, about 1 hour.

3. Punch down dough. Turn onto a lightly floured surface; divide and shape into 12 balls. Roll each into a 10-in. rope. Fold in half; twist together. Shape into a ring and pinch ends together. Repeat with remaining ropes. Place 2 in. apart on greased baking sheets. Cover with kitchen towels; let rise in a warm place until almost doubled, about 30 minutes.

4. Preheat oven to 375°. In a small bowl, whisk the remaining egg; brush over rolls. Bake 11-13 minutes or until golden brown. Remove from pans to wire racks; serve warm.

1 ROLL: 179 cal., 5g fat (2g sat. fat), 30mg chol., 293mg sod., 29g carb. (7g sugars, 1g fiber), 5g pro.

LAVENDER POPPY SEED MUFFINS

LAVENDER POPPY SEED MUFFINS

These muffins are so easy to put together. The lavender flavor really works well with lemon. If you've never baked with lavender before, start with just 1 or 2 teaspoons for a more subtle flavor.
—Elisabeth Larsen, Pleasant Grove, UT

PREP: 15 min. • **BAKE:** 20 min.
MAKES: 1 dozen

- 2 cups all-purpose flour
- ½ cup sugar
- 4 tsp. poppy seeds
- 1 Tbsp. dried lavender flowers
- 3 tsp. baking powder
- 2 tsp. grated lemon zest
- ½ tsp. salt
- ¾ cup 2% milk
- ½ cup butter, melted
- 1 large egg, room temperature
- 2 Tbsp. coarse sugar

1. Preheat oven to 400°. In a large bowl, whisk the first 7 ingredients. In another bowl, whisk milk, melted butter and egg until blended. Add to flour mixture; stir just until moistened.

2. Fill 12 paper-lined muffin cups three-fourths full; sprinkle with coarse sugar. Bake until a toothpick inserted in center comes out clean, 20-25 minutes. Cool 5 minutes before removing from pan to a wire rack. Serve warm.

1 MUFFIN: 203 cal., 9g fat (5g sat. fat), 37mg chol., 293mg sod., 27g carb. (11g sugars, 1g fiber), 3g pro.

CHERRY-TARRAGON DINNER ROLLS

APPLE DUMPLING PULL-APART BREAD

I converted a basic sweet dough into this incredible apple-filled, pull-apart loaf. The results are anything but basic. It takes time, but I guarantee it's worth it. Using both sauces is twice as tasty.
—*Gina Nistico, Denver, CO*

PREP: 45 min. + rising • **BAKE:** 1¼ hours
MAKES: 12 servings

- ¼ cup butter, softened
- 3 lbs. medium Honeycrisp apples, peeled and sliced ¼ in. thick
- ¼ cup sugar
- ¼ cup packed brown sugar
- ½ tsp. salt
- ½ tsp. ground cinnamon
- ¼ tsp. ground allspice
- ¼ cup apple cider
- 1 tsp. vanilla extract

DOUGH
- 1 pkg. (¼ oz.) active dry yeast
- ¾ cup warm water (110° to 115°)
- ¾ cup warm 2% milk (110° to 115°)
- ¼ cup sugar
- 3 Tbsp. canola oil
- 2 tsp. salt
- 3¾ to 4¼ cups all-purpose flour

CIDER SAUCE & GLAZE
- 4 cups apple cider, divided
- ½ cup packed brown sugar
- 1 cup confectioners' sugar
- 4 oz. cream cheese, softened
- ½ cup butter, divided
- 1½ tsp. vanilla extract, divided

1. In a Dutch oven over medium heat, melt butter. Add next 6 ingredients; stir to combine. Cook, covered, stirring occasionally, until apples have softened and released their juices, 10-12 minutes. With a slotted spoon, transfer apples to a 15x10x1-in. rimmed baking pan; spread into a single layer. Add cider to Dutch oven and bring to a boil; cook, stirring, until juices thicken and reduce to ½ cup, 10-12 minutes. Remove from heat; add vanilla extract. Pour over apple slices; cool completely. (Filling can be made 24 hours in advance and refrigerated.)
2. For dough, dissolve yeast in warm water. Add milk, sugar, oil, salt and 1¼ cups flour. Beat on medium speed until smooth, 2-3 minutes. Stir in enough remaining flour to form a soft dough.

3. Turn onto a floured surface; knead until smooth and elastic, 6-8 minutes. Place in a greased bowl, turning once to grease top. Cover and let rise in a warm place until doubled, about 1 hour.
4. Punch down dough. Turn onto a lightly floured surface. Roll into an 18x12-in. rectangle; spread apple mixture to within ½ in. of edges. Cut into twenty-four 3x3-in. squares. Make 4 stacks of 6 squares each; place stacks on their edges in a greased 9x5-in. loaf pan. Cover and let rise until doubled, about 45 minutes. Meanwhile, preheat oven to 350°.

5. Bake for 1¼-1½ hours or until well browned. For cider sauce, bring 3½ cups cider and brown sugar to a boil. Cook, stirring, until sauce is reduced to 1 cup, about 25 minutes. For the glaze, beat confectioners' sugar, cream cheese, ¼ cup butter, 1 tsp. vanilla and enough remaining apple cider to reach desired consistency.
6. Add remaining butter and vanilla to cider sauce. Cook and stir until sauce is thickened. Cool slightly. Drizzle sauce and glaze over bread.

1 SERVING: 544 cal., 20g fat (10g sat. fat), 42mg chol., 633mg sod., 88g carb. (54g sugars, 3g fiber), 6g pro.

APPLE DUMPLING PULL-APART BREAD

RHUBARB ROSEMARY FLATBREAD

SOFT GARLIC BREADSTICKS

I love the convenience of my bread machine to mix the dough for these buttery golden breadsticks that are mildly seasoned with garlic and basil. I like to use this dough when making pizza, too. It yields two 12-inch crusts.
—*Charles Smith, Baltic, CT*

- -

PREP: 30 min. + rising • **BAKE:** 20 min.
MAKES: 20 breadsticks

  1 cup plus 2 Tbsp. water (70° to 80°)
  2 Tbsp. olive oil
  3 Tbsp. grated parmesan cheese
  2 Tbsp. sugar
  3 tsp. garlic powder
1½ tsp. salt
 ¾ tsp. minced fresh basil or
     ¼ tsp. dried basil
  3 cups bread flour
  2 tsp. active dry yeast
  1 Tbsp. butter, melted

1. In bread machine pan, place the first 9 ingredients in order suggested by manufacturer. Select the dough setting (check dough after 5 minutes of mixing; add 1 to 2 Tbsp. water or flour if needed).
2. When cycle is completed, turn dough onto a lightly floured surface. Divide into 20 portions. Shape each into a ball; roll each into a 9-in. rope. Place on greased baking sheets. Cover and let rise in a warm place for 40 minutes or until doubled.
3. Bake at 350° for 18-22 minutes or until golden brown. Remove to wire racks to cool. Brush warm breadsticks with butter. If desired, sprinkle with additional grated Parmesan cheese.

1 BREADSTICK: 88 cal., 2g fat (1g sat. fat), 2mg chol., 196mg sod., 15g carb., 1g fiber), 3g pro.

RHUBARB ROSEMARY FLATBREAD

I love the simple ingredients of this recipe and the exceptional combination of flavors! The kitchen smells awesome whenever I bake these flatbreads. Using rhubarb in a savory bread is new to many people, but it never fails to delight!
—*Maryalice Wood, Langley, BC*

- -

PREP: 35 min. + rising • **BAKE:** 15 min.
MAKES: 8 servings

  1 Tbsp. quick-rise yeast
  1 tsp. sugar
  1 cup warm water (110° to 115°)
  3 to 4 rhubarb ribs, trimmed
  3 to 3½ cups all-purpose flour
  4 Tbsp. olive oil, divided
1½ tsp. sea salt, divided
  3 fresh rosemary sprigs, divided
  1 large egg, room temperature
 ⅛ tsp. freshly ground pepper
     Honey, optional

1. In a small bowl, dissolve the yeast and sugar in warm water. Meanwhile, finely chop enough rhubarb to measure ½ cup. Slice each remaining rhubarb rib lengthwise into 4 thin strips; cut strips into 4-in. pieces; reserve for topping.

2. In a large bowl, combine 2 cups flour, 2 Tbsp. oil, 1 tsp. salt, chopped rhubarb and the yeast mixture. Remove and finely chop rosemary leaves from 2 sprigs (discard stems); add to flour mixture. Beat on medium speed until smooth. Stir in enough remaining flour to form a soft dough (dough will be sticky).
3. Turn dough onto a floured surface; knead 6-8 minutes or until smooth and elastic. Place in a greased bowl, turning once to grease the top. Cover dough and let rise in a warm place until doubled, about 25 minutes.
4. Preheat the oven to 450°. Punch down dough. Turn onto a lightly floured surface; divide into 4 portions. Roll each portion to a 7x5-in. rectangle. Place on a parchment-lined baking sheet. In a small bowl, whisk egg with remaining 2 Tbsp. oil; roll the reserved rhubarb strips in egg wash. Gently press 3-5 strips into top of each piece of dough. Brush remaining egg wash over tops. Remove leaves from remaining rosemary sprig; sprinkle leaves over tops (discard stem). Sprinkle with remaining ½ tsp. salt and the pepper.
5. Bake until golden brown and rhubarb is tender, 13-15 minutes. If desired, drizzle with honey before serving.

½ FLATBREAD: 251 cal., 8g fat (1g sat. fat), 23mg chol., 372mg sod., 38g carb. (1g sugars, 2g fiber), 6g pro.

READER REVIEW

"These breadsticks are simply the best! After they're done, I brush them with butter and then sprinkle garlic salt over the top. Everyone loves them!"

—NORTHVIEW5, TASTEOFHOME.COM

HONEY CHALLAH

I use these shiny beautiful loaves as the centerpiece of my holiday spread. I love the taste of honey, but you can also add chocolate chips, cinnamon, orange zest or almonds. Leftover slices work well in bread pudding or for French toast.
—*Jennifer Newfield, Los Angeles, CA*

- -

PREP: 45 min. + rising • **BAKE:** 30 min.
MAKES: 2 loaves (24 servings each)

  2 pkg. (¼ oz. each) active dry yeast
  ½ tsp. sugar
1½ cups warm water (110° to 115°), divided
  5 large eggs, room temperature
⅔ cup plus 1 tsp. honey, divided
  ½ cup canola oil
  2 tsp. salt
  6 to 7 cups bread flour
  1 cup boiling water
  2 cups golden raisins
  1 Tbsp. water
  1 Tbsp. sesame seeds

1. In a small bowl, dissolve yeast and sugar in 1 cup warm water. Separate 2 eggs; refrigerate the whites. Place egg yolks and eggs in a large bowl. Add ⅔ cup honey, oil, salt, yeast mixture, 3 cups flour and remaining warm water; beat on medium speed for 3 minutes. Stir in enough remaining flour to form a soft dough (dough will be sticky).

2. Pour boiling water over raisins in a small bowl; let stand for 5 minutes. Drain and pat dry. Turn dough onto a floured surface; knead until smooth and elastic, 6-8 minutes. Knead in raisins. Place in a greased bowl, turning once to grease the top. Cover dough and let rise in a warm place until almost doubled, about 1½ hours.

3. Punch down dough. Turn onto a lightly floured surface. Divide dough in half. Divide 1 portion into 6 pieces. Roll each into a 16-in. rope. Place ropes parallel on a greased baking sheet; pinch ropes together at the top.

4. To braid, take the rope on the left and carry it over the 2 ropes beside it, then slip it under the middle rope and carry it over the last 2 ropes. Lay the rope down parallel to the other ropes; it is now on the far right side. Repeat these steps until you reach the end. As the braid moves to the right, you can pick up the loaf and recenter it on your work surface as needed. Pinch ends to seal and tuck under. For a fuller loaf, using your hands, push the ends of the loaf closer together. Repeat process with remaining dough. Cover with kitchen towels; let rise in a warm place until almost doubled, about 30 minutes.

5. Preheat oven to 350°. In a small bowl, whisk the 2 chilled egg whites and honey with water; brush over loaves. Sprinkle with sesame seeds. Bake 30-35 minutes or until bread is golden brown and sounds hollow when tapped. Remove from pans to a wire rack to cool.

1 PIECE: 125 cal., 3g fat (0 sat. fat), 19mg chol., 107mg sod., 21g carb. (8g sugars, 1g fiber), 3g pro.

HONEY
CHALLAH

SCALLION & CHEDDAR CATHEAD BISCUITS

Southerners are known for giving their recipes colorful names. This one got its name because each extra-large drop biscuit is as big as a cat's head. The treats are crisp and golden outside, soft and pillowy inside, and filled with scallions, cheddar cheese and just the right amount of black pepper. They are quick to fix and simple to make—you don't even have to roll out the dough.
—Cheryl Day, Savannah, GA

PREP: 25 min. • **BAKE:** 25 min. • **MAKES:** 1 dozen

- 1½ cups all-purpose flour
- 1½ cups cake flour
- ¼ tsp. sugar
- 2 Tbsp. baking powder
- 1 tsp. fine sea salt
- 1 cup cold unsalted butter, cut into ½-in. cubes
- ½ cup chopped scallions
- 2 cups shredded sharp cheddar cheese
- 1 tsp. freshly ground pepper
- 1½ to 2 cups buttermilk, room temperature
- 1 large egg, room temperature, beaten

1. Position a rack in the middle of the oven and preheat to 375°. Line a baking sheet with parchment.

2. In a large bowl, whisk together flours, sugar, baking powder and salt. Add butter; toss to coat. Cut in butter using a pastry blender, or pinch it with your fingertips, smearing it into the flour. You should have various-sized pieces of butter, ranging from coarse sandy patches to flat shaggy pieces to pea-sized chunks. Stir in the scallions, cheese and pepper.

3. Make a well in the center, pour in 1½ cups buttermilk and gently mix until mixture is crumbly but starting to come together into a shaggy mass. If dough still looks too dry, add up to ½ cup more buttermilk. The dough should be moist and slightly sticky.

4. Turn dough onto itself a few times until it forms a mass. Gently pat down the dough until it resembles a loaf of bread. Dust the top lightly with flour.

5. Using a 3-oz. ice cream scoop, portion dough 1 in. apart onto the prepared baking sheet. Gently flatten biscuits.

6. Lightly brush the tops with beaten egg. Bake, rotating pan halfway through, until biscuits are golden brown, 25-30 minutes.

1 BISCUIT: 351 cal., 23g fat (13g sat. fat), 76mg chol., 591mg sod., 28g carb. (2g sugars, 1g fiber), 9g pro.

TEST KITCHEN TIP

To get tall and flaky biscuits, avoid overworking the dough. Mix it only until it forms a mass. That way, there will still be plenty of air pockets that will add height when baking. Also, be sure to make a clean cut straight down when you are portioning the dough. If you're using a dull scoop, cutter or knife, the edges of the biscuit will seal together and won't rise as tall as it should.

SEEDED WHOLE GRAIN LOAF

SEEDED WHOLE GRAIN LOAF

My husband and I want whole grain bread, but we don't like the spongy store-bought whole wheat breads. I drastically altered a favorite batter bread recipe to create this simple bread-machine dream. The add-ins are just suggestions. Sometimes I use pepitas, sesame seeds or even ¼ cup of a multigrain hot cereal mix.
—Amber Rife, Columbus, OH

PREP: 20 min. • **BAKE:** 4 hours • **MAKES:** 1 loaf (1½ lbs., 16 servings)

- 1⅓ cups warm 2% milk (70° to 80°)
- 3 Tbsp. honey
- 2 Tbsp. canola oil
- 1¼ tsp. salt
- 2⅔ cups whole wheat flour
- 2 Tbsp. old-fashioned oats
- 4 tsp. vital wheat gluten
- 1 Tbsp. millet
- 1 Tbsp. sunflower kernels
- 1 Tbsp. flaxseed
- 1 Tbsp. cracked wheat or additional flaxseed
- 1 pkg. (¼ oz.) active dry yeast

In a bread machine pan, place all the ingredients in the order suggested by manufacturer. Select basic bread setting. Choose crust color and loaf size if available. Bake according to bread machine directions (check dough after 5 minutes of mixing; add 1 to 2 Tbsp. of water or flour if needed).

1 PIECE: 128 cal., 3g fat (1g sat. fat), 2mg chol., 199mg sod., 21g carb. (4g sugars, 3g fiber), 5g pro. **DIABETIC EXCHANGES:** 1 starch, ½ fat.

BANANA OAT MUFFINS

Chopped pecans add pleasant crunch to these hearty muffins with rich banana flavor. They're low in cholesterol, but you'd never know it. My husband and I love them.
—Marjorie Mott, Galatia, IL

TAKES: 30 min. • **MAKES:** 1 dozen

- ¾ cup all-purpose flour
- ¾ cup quick-cooking oats
- 1 tsp. baking powder
- 1 tsp. ground cinnamon
- ½ tsp. baking soda
- ¼ tsp. ground nutmeg
- 2 large egg whites, room temperature
- 1 cup mashed ripe bananas (about 2 medium)
- ½ cup packed brown sugar
- ¼ cup fat-free milk
- ¼ cup canola oil
- ½ cup chopped pecans

1. In a large bowl, combine the first 6 ingredients. In a small bowl, beat the egg whites, bananas, brown sugar, milk and oil. Stir into dry ingredients just until moistened. Stir in pecans.

2. Coat muffin cups with cooking spray; fill two-thirds full with batter. Bake at 400° for 15-20 minutes or until a toothpick comes out clean. Cool for 5 minutes before removing muffins from pan to a wire rack.

1 SERVING: 180 cal., 9g fat (1g sat. fat), 0 chol., 102mg sod., 24g carb. (13g sugars, 2g fiber), 3g pro.

BANANA OAT MUFFINS

BUTTERNUT SQUASH DOUGHNUTS

BUTTERNUT SQUASH DOUGHNUTS

My mother and I used to make several batches of these cake doughnuts at a time. They're not only different, but they're delicious, too!
—Elizabeth Leighton, Lincoln, ME

PREP: 15 min. + chilling • **COOK:** 5 min./batch • **MAKES:** 2 dozen

- 2 large eggs, room temperature
- 1¼ cups sugar
- 1 cup mashed cooked butternut or winter squash of your choice
- ½ cup buttermilk
- 2 Tbsp. butter, softened
- 2 tsp. vanilla extract
- 3½ cups all-purpose flour
- 1½ tsp. baking soda
- 1¼ tsp. ground nutmeg
- 1 tsp. baking powder
- 1 tsp. cream of tartar
- ½ tsp. salt
- ¼ tsp. ground cinnamon
- ¼ tsp. ground ginger
  Oil for deep-fat frying
  Optional: Confectioners' sugar or additional sugar

1. In a bowl, combine the eggs, sugar, squash, buttermilk, butter and vanilla. Combine the dry ingredients; add to squash mixture and mix well. Cover and refrigerate for 2 hours (dough will be very soft).

2. Turn onto a heavily floured surface; roll to ½-in. thickness. Cut with a 2½-in. doughnut cutter. In an electric skillet or deep-fat fryer, heat 1 in. oil to 350°.

3. Fry doughnuts, a few at a time, until golden brown on both sides, 1-2 minutes per side. Drain on paper towels. Dust with sugar if desired.

1 DOUGHNUT: 173 cal., 7g fat (1g sat. fat), 18mg chol., 172mg sod., 26g carb. (11g sugars, 1g fiber), 3g pro.

CINNAMON ROLL COFFEE CAKES

HUCKLEBERRY BEAR CLAWS

Beware: Bear claws may lead to bear hugs! My family can't get enough of these quick, easy pastries made from homegrown huckleberries, especially when the treats are paired with a cup of coffee or tea. Use blueberries if you can't find huckleberries.
—*Nancy Beckman, Helena, MT*

PREP: 40 min. + rising
BAKE: 15 min. + cooling
MAKES: 8 servings

- 6 Tbsp. sugar, divided
- ¼ cup butter, softened
- ¼ cup almond paste
- 1 cup crushed vanilla wafers
- 1 Tbsp. 2% milk
- 1 pkg. (16 oz.) hot roll mix
- 1¼ cups fresh or frozen huckleberries or blueberries
- 1 large egg, beaten
- 2 cups confectioners' sugar
- 2 to 3 Tbsp. water
- 1 Tbsp. lemon juice
  Sliced almonds, optional

1. In a small bowl, beat 4 Tbsp. sugar and the butter and almond paste until crumbly. Gradually add crushed wafers and milk; mix well. Set aside.

2. Prepare hot roll mix batter according to package directions, adding the remaining 2 Tbsp. sugar before mixing batter. On a floured surface, roll dough into a 24x8-in. rectangle. Crumble almond paste mixture to within ½ in. of edges; top with berries. Roll up jelly-roll style, starting with a long side; pinch seam to seal. Cut into 8 pieces.

3. Place 2 in. apart on parchment-lined baking sheets, seam side down. With scissors, cut each piece 4 times along a long side to within ½ in. of edge; curve and separate strips slightly. Cover and let rise in a warm place until almost doubled, about 1 hour.

4. Preheat oven to 400°. Brush rolls with beaten egg. Bake until golden brown, 15-20 minutes. Remove from pans to wire racks to cool completely. For the icing, combine confectioners' sugar, water and lemon juice until smooth; drizzle over rolls. If desired, sprinkle with almonds. Let stand until set.

1 BEAR CLAW: 577 cal., 20g fat (8g sat. fat), 73mg chol., 507mg sod., 92g carb. (56g sugars, 2g fiber), 9g pro.

CINNAMON ROLL COFFEE CAKES

The house would smell so wonderful whenever my mom made these amazing, mouthwatering coffee cakes. Now I bake them for any special gathering. They also make fabulous gifts.
—*Tracey Sorrentino, Commerce, MI*

PREP: 40 min. + rising
BAKE: 20 min. + cooling
MAKES: 4 coffee cakes (12 servings each)

- 2 pkg. (¼ oz. each) active dry yeast
- ⅓ cup warm water (110° to 115°)
- 1 cup warm 2% milk (110° to 115°)
- 1 cup butter, melted
- 2 large eggs, room temperature, beaten
- ½ cup sugar
- 1 tsp. salt
- 5½ to 6¼ cups all-purpose flour
FILLING
- 1 cup butter, softened
- ½ cup packed brown sugar
- 1 Tbsp. ground cinnamon
- 1½ cups chopped pecans
ICING
- 1½ cups confectioners' sugar
- ½ tsp. vanilla extract
- 2 to 3 Tbsp. 2% milk

1. In a large bowl, dissolve yeast in warm water. Add the milk, butter, eggs, sugar, salt and 3 cups flour; beat until smooth.

Stir in enough remaining flour to form a soft dough.

2. Turn onto a lightly floured surface; knead 6-8 minutes or until smooth and elastic. Place in a greased bowl, turning once to grease top. Cover and let rise in a warm place until doubled, about 1 hour.

3. Punch dough down; turn onto a floured surface. Divide into 4 portions. Roll each portion into a 12x8-in. rectangle. In a bowl, cream the softened butter, brown sugar and cinnamon. Spread mixture over each rectangle to within ½ in. of edges. Sprinkle with pecans. Roll up each jelly-roll style, starting with a long side; pinch seams to seal.

4. Place each roll seam side down in a greased 15x10x1-in. baking pan; pinch ends together to form a ring. With scissors, cut from an outside edge two-thirds of the way toward center of ring at 1-in. intervals. Separate strips slightly; twist to allow filling to show, slightly overlapping the previous strip. Cover and let rise in a warm place until doubled, about 30 minutes.

5. Bake at 350° for 20-25 minutes or until golden brown. Remove from pans to wire racks to cool completely. Combine icing ingredients; drizzle over coffee cakes. May be frozen for up to 2 months.

1 PIECE: 184 cal., 11g fat (5g sat. fat), 30mg chol., 133mg sod., 20g carb. (8g sugars, 1g fiber), 2g pro.

**HUCKLEBERRY
BEAR CLAWS**

HALVA & NUTELLA BABKA BUNS

This recipe is the result of many years of tweaking and perfecting. It is a favorite request when visitors come to my farm.
—*Dawn Lamoureux-Crocker, Machiasport, ME*

PREP: 1 hour + rising
BAKE: 15 min.
MAKES: 8 servings

- 3¾ to 4¼ cups all-purpose flour
- ⅓ cup sugar
- ¼ tsp. salt
- 1 Tbsp. active dry yeast
- 6 Tbsp. butter, softened
- ¾ cup warm 2% milk (110° to 115°)
- ½ tsp. vanilla extract
- 2 tsp. grated lemon zest
- 2 large eggs, room temperature
- 1 jar (13 oz.) Nutella
- 6 oz. halva with pistachio, crumbled (about 1 cup)
- ½ cup semisweet chocolate chips
- ½ cup sugar, optional
- ½ water, optional
- 2 Tbsp. butter, optional

1. In a large bowl, combine 1½ cups flour, sugar, salt and yeast. Cut in butter until crumbly. Add warm milk, vanilla, and lemon zest to dry ingredients; beat just until moistened. Add eggs; beat on medium for 2 minutes. Stir in enough remaining flour to form a firm dough. Turn onto a floured surface; knead until smooth and elastic, 5-7 minutes. Place dough in a greased bowl, turning once to grease top. Cover and let rise in a warm place until doubled, about 1 hour.

2. Turn out dough onto a lightly floured surface; divide into 8 pieces. Roll each piece into a 10x5-in. rectangle about ⅛-in. thick. For each, spread Nutella to within ½ in. of edges, sprinkle with 2 Tbsp. halva and 1 Tbsp. chocolate chips. Roll up jelly-roll style, starting with a long side; pinch seam and ends to seal.

3. Using a sharp knife, cut each roll lengthwise in half; carefully turn each half cut side up. Loosely twist strips around each other, keeping cut surfaces facing up; pinch ends together to seal. Repeat for remaining buns. Place cut side up on parchment-lined baking sheets. Cover with kitchen towels; let buns rise in a warm place until almost doubled, about 30 minutes. Preheat oven to 375°.

4. Bake until golden brown, 15-20 minutes. If desired, in a small saucepan, bring the sugar and water to a boil; reduce heat and simmer until sugar is dissolved, 1-2 minutes. Remove from heat and add butter, stirring until melted. Brush over buns. Serve buns warm.

1 BUN: 748 cal., 34g fat (11g sat. fat), 72mg chol., 196mg sod., 102g carb. (52g sugars, 5g fiber), 14g pro.

HALVA & NUTELLA BABKA BUNS

❄ TOMATO-BASIL PULL-APART ROLLS

My nephew helped me create these soft and colorful rolls. He named them wheelies because the spiral shapes reminded him of his toy trucks.
—*Dianna Wara, Washington, IL*

PREP: 30 min. + rising
BAKE: 20 min. • **MAKES:** 1 dozen

- 1 pkg. (¼ oz.) active dry yeast
- 2 Tbsp. sugar
- ¾ cup warm 2% milk (110° to 115°)
- 1 large egg, room temperature
- ¼ cup tomato paste
- 3 Tbsp. olive oil
- 1 tsp. salt
- 2¾ to 3¼ cups bread flour

FILLING

- 1 cup shredded Italian cheese blend
- 2 tsp. dried basil
- ½ tsp. garlic powder

1. Dissolve yeast and sugar in warm milk. In a large bowl, beat egg, tomato paste, oil, salt, yeast mixture and 1 cup flour on medium speed until smooth. Stir in enough remaining flour to form a soft dough (dough will be sticky).

2. Turn onto a floured surface; knead until smooth and elastic, 6-8 minutes. Place in a greased bowl, turning to grease the top. Cover dough; let rise in a warm place until doubled, about 45 minutes.

3. In a bowl, toss filling ingredients. Punch down dough; turn onto a lightly floured surface. Roll into a 16x12-in. rectangle. Sprinkle with filling to within ½ in. of edges. Roll up jelly-roll style, starting with a long side; pinch seam to seal. Cut into 12 slices.

4. Place cut side down in a parchment-lined 10-in. cast-iron skillet. Cover with a kitchen towel; let rise in a warm place until almost doubled, about 45 minutes. Preheat oven to 350°.

5. Bake until golden brown, 20-25 minutes. Remove rolls to a wire rack.

FREEZE OPTION: Securely wrap cooled rolls in foil; place in an airtight container. To use, partially thaw overnight in refrigerator. Reheat rolls, wrapped in foil, in a preheated 300° oven until warm, about 25 minutes.

1 ROLL: 204 cal., 7g fat (2g sat. fat), 24mg chol., 284mg sod., 27g carb. (3g sugars, 1g fiber), 7g pro.

AIR-FRYER
DOUGHNUTS

🕐 🍽 🎉

AIR-FRYER DOUGHNUTS

My sons and I love doughnuts, but in the Florida heat, I rarely want to deep-fry them. I tried making this easy version in my air fryer, and it turned out so well with no mess!

—Christine Hair, Odessa, FL

TAKES: 25 min. • **MAKES:** 8 doughnuts + 8 doughnut holes

- 1 tube (16.3 oz.) large refrigerated buttermilk biscuits (8 count)
- ¾ cup sugar
- 2 tsp. ground cinnamon
- ¼ cup butter, melted
- 1 tsp. vanilla extract

1. Preheat air fryer to 375°. Separate biscuits. Cut out centers using a 1-in. cutter; save centers. In batches, place doughnuts in a single layer in greased air fryer. Cook until golden brown and puffed, about 5 minutes, turning once. In batches, cook doughnut holes until golden brown, 3-4 minutes.

2. Meanwhile, in a shallow dish, combine sugar and cinnamon. In a separate bowl, mix melted butter and vanilla. Brush doughnuts and doughnut holes with butter; toss in sugar mixture. Serve warm.

1 DOUGHNUT AND 1 DOUGHNUT HOLE: 280 cal., 15g fat (8g sat. fat), 23mg chol., 684mg sod., 33g carb. (11g sugars, 1g fiber), 4g pro.

TEST KITCHEN TIP

You can keep the doughnuts in zip-top bags or airtight containers at room temperature for a day or two, but not longer than that. These are best enjoyed fresh, as are many other air-fryer sweets.

BLT MUFFINS

These muffins prove the classic combo of bacon, lettuce and tomato is good for so much more than a sandwich. They're winners at both breakfast and dinner.

—Katie Koziolek, Hartland, MN

PREP: 15 min. • **BAKE:** 20 min. + cooling • **MAKES:** 1 dozen

- 2 cups all-purpose flour
- 1 Tbsp. baking powder
- 1 Tbsp. sugar
- 1 cup 2% milk
- ½ cup mayonnaise
- ¾ cup crumbled cooked bacon (about 12 strips)
- ½ cup chopped seeded plum tomatoes
- 2 Tbsp. minced fresh parsley
  Shredded lettuce, optional

1. In a large bowl, combine the flour, baking powder and sugar. In a small bowl, whisk milk and mayonnaise until smooth. Stir into dry ingredients just until moistened. Fold in the bacon, tomatoes and parsley.

2. Fill greased or paper-lined muffin cups two-thirds full. Bake at 400° for 20-25 minutes or until a toothpick inserted in the center of a muffin comes out clean. Cool for 5 minutes before removing from pan to a wire rack to cool completely. If desired, sprinkle with shredded lettuce.

1 MUFFIN: 185 cal., 10g fat (2g sat. fat), 11mg chol., 385mg sod., 18g carb. (3g sugars, 1g fiber), 6g pro.

BLT MUFFINS

BUCKEYE DOUGHNUT HOLES

BUCKEYE DOUGHNUT HOLES

Ohioans love buckeye nuts so much, they created a quintessential lookalike treat that's in every candy shop and on every dessert spread! I put my own twist on the confection by turning it into a doughnut hole. The fried balls are filled with peanut butter cream and coated in chocolate.
—*Becky Woollands, North Ridgeville, OH*

PREP: 1 hour + rising
COOK: 5 min./batch + standing
MAKES: 5 dozen

- 1 pkg. (¼ oz.) active dry yeast
- 1 cup warm 2% milk (110° to 115°)
- 2 Tbsp. sugar
- 2 Tbsp. shortening
- 1 large egg, room temperature
- ½ tsp. salt
- 3 to 3½ cups all-purpose flour

FILLING
- 4 oz. cream cheese, softened
- ½ cup creamy peanut butter
- 6 Tbsp. confectioners' sugar
  Dash salt
  Oil for deep-fat frying

GANACHE
- 1½ cups semisweet chocolate chips
- ¾ cup heavy whipping cream

1. In a small bowl, dissolve yeast in warm milk. In a large bowl, combine the sugar, shortening, egg, salt, yeast mixture and 2 cups flour; beat on medium speed until smooth. Stir in enough remaining flour to form a soft dough (dough will be sticky).

2. Turn dough onto a floured surface; knead 6-8 minutes or until smooth and elastic. Place in a greased bowl, turning once to grease the top. Cover dough and let rise in a warm place until doubled, about 1 hour.

3. Punch down dough. Turn onto a lightly floured surface; roll to ¾-in. thickness. Cut with a floured 1½-in. biscuit cutter. Place 1 in. apart on greased baking sheets. Cover with kitchen towels; let rise in a warm place until almost doubled, about 50 minutes.

4. Meanwhile, in a large bowl, beat cream cheese, peanut butter, confectioners' sugar and salt until fluffy, 3-5 minutes. Transfer filling to a pastry bag fitted with a small pastry tip; set aside. In an electric skillet or deep fryer, heat oil to 375°. Fry doughnuts, a few at a time, until golden brown, about 1 minute on each side. Drain on paper towels; cool.

5. Cut a small slit with a sharp knife on bottom of each doughnut. Fill each doughnut with peanut butter filling.

6. Place chocolate in a small bowl. In a small saucepan, bring cream just to a boil. Pour over chocolate; let stand 5 minutes. Stir with a whisk until smooth. Dip the doughnuts in ganache, filled side down, leaving tops uncovered. Let stand until set. Refrigerate leftovers.

1 DONUT HOLE: 95 cal., 6g fat (2g sat. fat), 9mg chol., 42mg sod., 10g carb. (4g sugars, 1g fiber), 2g pro.

DID YOU KNOW?

Buckeye sweets are made to look like the inedible nuts of Ohio's state tree, the buckeye. The tree and nut get their name from the nut's resemblance to the eye of a white-tailed deer: shiny and dark on the outside, with a lighter center.

❄ ORANGE CRANBERRY BREAD

The beauty of this festive quick bread is that it makes a delicious post-dinner snack as well as breakfast the next day. I especially like to toast leftover slices and spread them with cream cheese or butter for breakfast.
—*Ron Gardner, Grand Haven, MI*

PREP: 20 min. • **BAKE:** 50 min. + cooling
MAKES: 2 loaves (16 servings each)

- 2¾ cups all-purpose flour
- ⅔ cup sugar
- ⅔ cup packed brown sugar
- 3½ tsp. baking powder
- 1 tsp. salt
- ½ tsp. ground cinnamon
- ¼ tsp. ground nutmeg
- 1 large egg, room temperature
- 1 cup 2% milk
- ½ cup orange juice
- 3 Tbsp. canola oil
- 2 to 3 tsp. grated orange zest
- 2 cups coarsely chopped fresh or frozen cranberries
- 1 large apple, peeled and chopped

1. In a large bowl, combine the flour, sugars, baking powder, salt, cinnamon and nutmeg. Whisk the egg, milk, orange juice, oil and orange zest; stir into dry ingredients just until blended. Fold in the cranberries and apple.

2. Pour into 2 greased 8x4-in. loaf pans. Bake at 350° until a toothpick inserted in the center comes out clean, 50-55 minutes. Cool for 10 minutes before removing from pans to wire racks.

FREEZE OPTION: Securely wrap cooled loaves in foil and freeze. To use, thaw at room temperature.

1 PIECE: 98 cal., 2g fat (0 sat. fat), 8mg chol., 125mg sod., 19g carb. (10g sugars, 1g fiber), 2g pro.

IRISH CHEDDAR & BEER BREAD

I can't think of any meal that doesn't go with this cheesy pull-apart bread. It's amazing alongside eggs and bacon as well as soup.
—*Colleen Delawder, Herndon, VA*

PREP: 35 min. + rising • **BAKE:** 15 min. + cooling • **MAKES:** 2 dozen

- 1 pkg. (¼ oz.) active dry yeast
- 1 cup warm beer or ale, Irish preferred (110° to 115°)
- 4 cups all-purpose flour, divided
- ½ cup sugar
- ½ cup shortening
- 2 tsp. garlic powder
- 1 tsp. kosher salt
- 1 large egg, room temperature
- 6 Tbsp. butter, preferably Irish, melted
- 2 cups shredded white cheddar cheese, preferably Irish

1. In a large bowl, dissolve yeast in warm beer; let mixture sit for 10 minutes. Add 1 cup flour and the sugar, shortening, garlic powder, salt and egg. Beat until smooth. Stir in enough remaining flour to form a firm dough.

2. Turn onto a floured surface; knead until smooth and elastic, 6-8 minutes. Place in a greased bowl, turning once to grease top. Cover and let rise in a warm place until doubled, about 1 hour.

3. Place melted butter in a shallow bowl. Place shredded cheese in another shallow bowl. Punch down dough. Turn onto a lightly floured surface; divide and shape into twenty-four 1½-in. balls. Dip the balls in butter, toss in shredded cheese and place in an aluminum foil- or parchment-lined 13x9-in. baking pan. Sprinkle any remaining cheese over top.

4. Cover with a kitchen towel; let rise in a warm place until almost doubled, about 2 hours. Meanwhile, preheat oven to 350°. Bake until golden brown, 15-20 minutes, covering with foil if necessary.

5. Cool rolls in pan 10 minutes before lifting onto a serving plate. Serve warm.

1 PIECE: 190 cal., 9g fat (4g sat. fat), 21mg chol., 158mg sod., 21g carb. (5g sugars, 1g fiber), 5g pro.

ORANGE CRANBERRY BREAD

PANCAKE & WAFFLE MIX
PAGE 162

Breakfast & Brunch

The rise-and-shine specialties here make a homemade breakfast easier than you might think. Whether you'd like an overnight brunch bake, fluffy waffles or grab-and-go egg muffins, these delightful dishes are sure to tempt your taste buds.

CHECK OUT THESE SPECIALTIES

ARUGULA & MUSHROOM BREAKFAST PIZZA

It's a challenge to be creative with breakfast every morning, and I like to come up with fun foods the kids will love. This is a great recipe for the kids to join in and help make for breakfast. It's also convenient to make ahead and freeze for a weekday.
—*Melissa Pelkey Hass, Waleska, GA*

PREP: 20 min. • **BAKE:** 15 min. • **MAKES:** 6 servings

1 prebaked 12-in. thin whole wheat pizza crust
¾ cup reduced-fat ricotta cheese
1 tsp. garlic powder
1 tsp. paprika, divided
1 cup sliced baby portobello mushrooms
½ cup julienned soft sun-dried tomatoes (not packed in oil)
3 cups fresh arugula or baby spinach
2 Tbsp. balsamic vinegar
2 Tbsp. olive oil
¼ tsp. salt, divided
¼ tsp. pepper, divided
6 large eggs

1. Preheat oven to 450°. Place crust on a pizza pan. Spread with ricotta cheese; sprinkle with garlic powder and ½ tsp. paprika. Top with mushrooms and tomatoes.
2. With clean hands, massage the arugula with vinegar, oil and ⅛ tsp. each salt and pepper until softened; arrange over pizza.
3. Using a spoon, make 6 indentations in arugula; carefully break an egg into each. Sprinkle with the remaining paprika, salt and pepper. Bake until egg whites are completely set and yolks begin to thicken but are not hard, 12-15 minutes.
1 PIECE: 299 cal., 13g fat (4g sat. fat), 194mg chol., 464mg sod., 31g carb. (8g sugars, 5g fiber), 15g pro. **DIABETIC EXCHANGES:** 2 medium-fat meat, 1½ starch, 1 vegetable, 1 fat.

ARUGULA & MUSHROOM BREAKFAST PIZZA

EVERYTHING BREAKFAST SLIDERS

EVERYTHING BREAKFAST SLIDERS

These breakfast sliders combine all your favorite morning foods—like eggs, bacon and bagels—into one tasty package.
—*Rashanda Cobbins, Milwaukee, WI*

PREP: 30 min. • **BAKE:** 15 min. • **MAKES:** 8 servings

8 large eggs
¼ cup 2% milk
2 green onions, thinly sliced
¼ tsp. pepper
8 Tbsp. spreadable chive and onion cream cheese
8 miniature bagels, split
8 slices cheddar cheese, halved
8 slices Canadian bacon
8 cooked bacon strips, halved
GLAZE
2 Tbsp. butter, melted
1½ tsp. maple syrup
⅛ tsp. garlic powder
2 Tbsp. everything seasoning blend

1. Preheat the oven to 375°. Heat a large nonstick skillet over medium heat. In a large bowl, whisk eggs, milk, green onions and pepper until blended; pour into skillet. Cook and stir until eggs are thickened and no liquid egg remains; remove from heat.
2. Spread cream cheese over bagel bottoms; place in a greased 13x9-in. baking dish. Layer each with half a slice of cheese and a slice of Canadian bacon. Spoon scrambled eggs over top. Layer with remaining halved cheese slices, cooked bacon and bagel tops. Stir together butter, maple syrup and garlic powder; brush over bagel tops. Sprinkle with everything seasoning blend.
3. Bake until tops are golden brown and cheese is melted, 12-15 minutes.
1 SLIDER: 415 cal., 26g fat (13g sat. fat), 253mg chol., 1070mg sod., 18g carb. (4g sugars, 1g fiber), 24g pro.

PRESSURE-COOKER FRENCH TOAST

A delicious morning treat, this French toast is made quickly in a pressure cooker, and it's definitely worth waking up for. The pumpkin pie spice and crumbled bacon take it to the next level!

—Joan Hallford, North Richland Hills, TX

PREP: 15 min. + standing
COOK: 20 min. + releasing
MAKES: 6 servings

- 3 large eggs, lightly beaten
- ½ cup half-and-half cream
- ¼ cup packed brown sugar
- 2 tsp. pumpkin pie spice
- 1 tsp. vanilla extract
- 4 cooked bacon strips, crumbled
- 1 loaf (1 lb.) cinnamon-raisin bread, cubed
- ¼ cup chopped pecans, toasted
- 2 Tbsp. confectioners' sugar
  Maple syrup

1. Place trivet insert and ½ cup water in a 6-qt. electric pressure cooker. In a large bowl, whisk eggs, cream, brown sugar, pumpkin pie spice and vanilla until blended. Stir in bacon. Stir in bread; let stand until the bread is softened, about 15 minutes.

2. Transfer to a greased round 2-qt. baking dish. Cover baking dish with foil. Fold an 18x12-in. piece of foil lengthwise into thirds, making a sling. Use the sling to lower the dish onto the trivet. Lock lid; close pressure-release valve. Adjust to pressure-cook on high for 20 minutes. Allow pressure to release naturally for 12 minutes; quick-release any remaining pressure.

3. Using foil sling, carefully remove baking dish. Let stand 10 minutes. Invert French toast onto a serving dish; top with pecans and confectioners' sugar. Serve warm with maple syrup.

1 SERVING: 334 cal., 12g fat (3g sat. fat), 111mg chol., 333mg sod., 47g carb. (19g sugars, 5g fiber), 14g pro.

BAGEL EGG
IN A HOLE WITH
SMASHED AVOCADO

BAGEL EGG IN A HOLE WITH SMASHED AVOCADO

A tasty spin on the classic egg in a hole, this recipe features an egg fried inside a bagel with avocado on top. It's a perfectly quick healthy breakfast or dinner!

—Erin Clarke, Milwaukee, WI

TAKES: 10 min. • **MAKES:** 2 servings

- 1 medium ripe avocado, peeled and cubed
- ¼ tsp. kosher salt
- ⅛ tsp. pepper
- ¼ tsp. crushed red pepper flakes, optional
- 1 whole grain bagel, split
- 1 Tbsp. unsalted butter, softened
- 2 small eggs
  Optional: Minced fresh cilantro, parsley or chives

1. In a small bowl, mash avocado; stir in salt, pepper and, if desired, pepper flakes.

2. Using a paring knife or round cutter, enlarge center hole to at least 1½ in. wide. Spread butter on cut side of bagel. Place bagel, butter sides down, in a skillet over medium heat. Cook until golden brown, 1-2 minutes; remove to plate. Spread avocado mixture over browned sides, building up outside edge slightly.

3. Return bagel to skillet, avocado sides up. Crack egg into center hole. Cook, covered, over medium heat until egg is cooked to desired degree of doneness. Transfer to a serving plate; garnish as desired.

1 BAGEL HALF: 306 cal., 19g fat (6g sat. fat), 108mg chol., 492mg sod., 27g carb. (3g sugars, 8g fiber), 10g pro.

**PRESSURE-COOKER
FRENCH TOAST**

CARAMELIZED BANANA
STEEL-CUT OATS

POT ROAST HASH

I love to cook a Sunday-style pot roast for weeknights. Make it into pot roast hash for any day of the week.
—*Gina Jackson, Ogdensburg, NY*

PREP: 6¼ hours • **COOK:** 15 min.
MAKES: 10 servings

- 1 cup warm water
- 1 Tbsp. beef base
- ½ lb. sliced fresh mushrooms
- 1 large onion, coarsely chopped
- 3 garlic cloves, minced
- 1 boneless beef chuck roast (3 lbs.)
- ½ tsp. pepper
- 1 Tbsp. Worcestershire sauce
- 1 pkg. (28 oz.) frozen potatoes O'Brien

EGGS

- 2 Tbsp. butter
- 10 large eggs
- ½ tsp. salt
- ½ tsp. pepper
  Minced chives

1. In a 5- or 6-qt. slow cooker, whisk water and beef base; add the mushrooms, onion and garlic. Sprinkle roast with pepper; transfer to slow cooker. Drizzle with Worcestershire sauce. Cook, covered, on low 6-8 hours or until meat is tender.
2. Remove roast; cool slightly. Shred the meat with 2 forks. In a large skillet, cook potatoes according to package directions; stir in shredded beef. Using a slotted spoon, add vegetables from slow cooker to skillet; heat through. Discard the cooking juices.
3. For eggs, in another skillet, heat 1 Tbsp. butter over medium-high heat. Break 5 eggs, 1 at a time, into pan. Sprinkle with half of the salt and pepper. Reduce heat to low. Cook until desired doneness, turning after whites are set if desired. Repeat with remaining butter, eggs, salt and pepper. Serve eggs over hash; sprinkle with chives.
FREEZE OPTION: Place shredded pot roast and vegetables in a freezer container; top with cooking juices. Cool and freeze. To use, partially thaw in refrigerator overnight. Heat through in a covered saucepan.
⅔ CUP HASH WITH 1 EGG: 429 cal., 24g fat (8g sat. fat), 281mg chol., 306mg sod., 15g carb. (2g sugars, 2g fiber), 35g pro.

CARAMELIZED BANANA STEEL-CUT OATS

I think the only way to cook steel-cut oats is in a pressure cooker. They come out perfect in a fraction of the time. To jazz things up, I top the oatmeal with sliced bananas, caramelized using my air-fryer attachment. It's such a treat on those cool winter mornings when you're looking for something warm and cozy.
—*Allison Martin, Conway, AR*

PREP: 15 min.
PRESSURE-COOK: 10 min. + releasing
AIR-FRY: 15 min.
MAKES: 3 servings

- 3¼ cups water, divided
- ¾ cup steel-cut oats
- ⅜ tsp. each ground ginger and ground cinnamon, divided
- ⅜ tsp. salt
- ⅜ tsp. vanilla or rum extract
- 1½ tsp. butter
- 1 large banana, sliced
- 3 Tbsp. sugar, divided

1. Place ¾ cup water, ¼ cup oats, ⅛ tsp. each ginger and cinnamon, salt and extract in each of three 1-pint wide-mouth canning jars. Top each with ½ tsp. butter. Center lids on jars; screw on bands until fingertip tight.

2. Place wire rack with handles and remaining 1 cup water in inner pot of large multicooker. Set the jars on rack. Lock lid. Adjust to pressure-cook for 10 minutes.
3. Let pressure release naturally. Remove jars; drain water from inner pot and wipe dry. Unscrew lids from jars; top with sliced bananas. Sprinkle with sugar. Place jars in inner pot on wire rack with handles. Cover with air frying lid. Press air-fry function; select bake. Press timer; set to 15 minutes. Start. Cook until sugar has caramelized.
1 SERVING: 259 cal., 5g fat (2g sat. fat), 5mg chol., 311mg sod., 50g carb. (19g sugars, 5g fiber), 6g pro.

TEST KITCHEN TIPS

- This recipe uses a multicooker. If you don't have one, you can prepare the oats on the stovetop. Simply follow the stovetop directions on the package of steel-cut oats. Divide cooked oats into ramekins, then add bananas. Bake at 325° until bananas are softened and sugar is caramelized.
- To substitute old-fashioned or quick-cooking oats on the stovetop, prepare the oats according to package directions. These types use less water and take less time.

POT ROAST HASH

NECTARINE SMOOTHIES

This nectarine smoothie recipe tastes great on a warm summer day. Enjoy it on your patio or at a picnic!
—*Joni Rodriguez, Silverton, OR*

- -

PREP: 10 min. + freezing
MAKES: 3 servings

- ¾ cup lemon Greek yogurt
- ½ cup orange juice
- 2 Tbsp. lime juice
- 2 Tbsp. honey
- 2 cups crushed ice
- 2 medium nectarines or peaches, peeled, cubed and frozen

Place all ingredients in a blender; cover and process until blended.

1 CUP: 170 cal., 6g fat (4g sat. fat), 15mg chol., 36mg sod., 29g carb. (25g sugars, 2g fiber), 3g pro.

SAVORY TOMATO & OLIVE OATMEAL

Who says oatmeal has to be sweet? I love this recipe because it starts my day in a healthy way. Fresh garlic, tomatoes and basil are bright notes in a breakfast that keeps me satisfied until lunch.
—*Roland McAmis Jr, Greeneville, TN*

- -

TAKES: 20 min. • **MAKES:** 1 serving

- 1 cup reduced-sodium chicken broth
- 1 medium tomato, chopped
- ½ cup quick-cooking oats
- 1 garlic clove, minced
- 3 Greek olives, chopped
- 1 Tbsp. chopped fresh basil
  Optional: Additional chopped fresh basil, grated Parmesan cheese, sunny side up egg and extra virgin olive oil

In a small saucepan, bring broth to a boil over medium-high heat. Stir in tomato, oats and garlic; reduce heat and simmer 2 minutes. Remove from heat; stir in olives and basil. Add toppings as desired.

1½ CUPS: 222 cal., 6g fat (1g sat. fat), 0 chol., 761mg sod., 35g carb. (5g sugars, 5g fiber), 10g pro. **DIABETIC EXCHANGES:** 2 starch, 1 vegetable, 1 fat.

PANCAKE & WAFFLE MIX

This terrific blend provides the ease of a boxed pancake mix with the homemade goodness of fluffy pancakes and waffles.
—*Deb Poitz, Fort Morgan, CO*

- -

TAKES: 10 min.
MAKES: about 7 batches of pancakes or about 4 batches of waffles (11 cups total)

- 8 cups all-purpose flour
- 2 cups buttermilk blend powder
- ½ cup sugar
- 8 tsp. baking powder
- 4 tsp. baking soda
- 2 tsp. salt

ADDITIONAL INGREDIENTS FOR PANCAKES

- 1 large egg, room temperature
- 1 cup water
- 2 Tbsp. vegetable oil

ADDITIONAL INGREDIENTS FOR WAFFLES

- 3 large eggs, separated, room temperature
- 2 cups water
- ¼ cup vegetable oil

1. In a large bowl, combine the first 6 ingredients with a wire whisk. Store in an airtight container in the refrigerator for up to 6 months.

2. To prepare pancakes: In a medium bowl, beat egg, water and oil. Whisk in 1½ cups pancake/waffle mix. Let stand for 5 minutes. Pour batter by ⅓ cupfuls onto a lightly greased hot griddle; turn when bubbles form on top of pancakes. Cook until the second side is golden brown. Makes: about 6 pancakes per batch.

3. To prepare waffles: In a large bowl, beat egg yolks, water and oil. Stir in 2½ cups pancake/waffle mix just until moistened. In a bowl, beat the egg whites until stiff peaks form; fold into the batter. Bake in a preheated waffle iron according to manufacturer's directions until golden brown. Makes: 13 waffles (about 4 in.) per batch.

3 PANCAKES: 170 cal., 6g fat (1g sat. fat), 39mg chol., 349mg sod., 23g carb. (6g sugars, 1g fiber), 5g pro.
2 WAFFLES: 295 cal., 12g fat (2g sat. fat), 91mg chol., 598mg sod., 37g carb. (8g sugars, 1g fiber), 10g pro.

PANCAKE & WAFFLE MIX

SMOKY
VEGAN
BACON

SMOKY VEGAN BACON

This recipe is a must for any vegetarian! You won't believe how similar it is to the real thing.
—Taste of Home *Test Kitchen*

PREP: 15 min. • **COOK:** 5 min./batch • **MAKES:** 12 servings

- 1 large carrot
- 2 Tbsp. maple syrup
- 1 tsp. smoked paprika
- ½ tsp. garlic powder
- ¼ tsp. onion powder
- ⅛ tsp. salt
- ⅛ tsp. liquid smoke
- 2 Tbsp. olive oil

1. With a mandoline or vegetable peeler, cut carrot into long, thin strips. In a shallow bowl, whisk the maple syrup, paprika, garlic powder, onion powder, salt and liquid smoke. Dip carrot slices into syrup mixture, allowing excess to drip off.

2. In a large skillet, heat oil over medium heat. Cook carrot slices in batches until browned, 4-6 minutes, turning once.

1 SLICE: 32 cal., 2g fat (0 sat. fat), 0 chol., 29mg sod., 3g carb. (2g sugars, 0 fiber), 0 pro.

HASH BROWN QUICHE CUPS

Quiche cups are my showstopper potluck dish. Hash browns and Asiago cheese make up the crusts. Eggs, spinach and bacon do the rest.
—Nicole Stone, Gilbertville, IA

TAKES: 30 min. • **MAKES:** 4 servings

- 1 large egg
- ¼ tsp. salt
- ⅛ tsp. pepper
- 2 cups frozen shredded hash brown potatoes, thawed
- ¼ cup shredded Asiago cheese

FILLING

- 3 large eggs
- 1 Tbsp. minced fresh chives
- ⅓ cup shredded Colby-Monterey Jack cheese
- ⅓ cup fresh baby spinach, thinly sliced
- 2 bacon strips, cooked and crumbled

1. Preheat oven to 400°. Grease 8 muffin cups.

2. In a bowl, whisk egg, salt and pepper until blended; stir in the potatoes and Asiago cheese. To form crusts, press about ¼ cup potato mixture onto bottom and up sides of each prepared muffin cup. Bake until light golden brown, 14-17 minutes.

3. For filling, in a small bowl, whisk eggs and chives until blended; stir in cheese and spinach. Spoon into the crusts; top with bacon. Bake for 6-8 minutes or until a knife inserted in the center comes out clean.

FREEZE OPTION: Freeze cooled baked tarts for up to 3 months. To use, reheat tarts on a baking sheet in a preheated 350° oven until heated through, 5-10 minutes.

2 MINI QUICHES: 180 cal., 11g fat (5g sat. fat), 205mg chol., 375mg sod., 8g carb. (1g sugars, 0 fiber), 12g pro. **DIABETIC EXCHANGES:** 2 medium-fat meat, ½ starch.

HASH BROWN
QUICHE CUPS

🍎 MIXED BERRY FRENCH TOAST BAKE

I love this recipe! It's perfect for fuss-free holiday breakfasts or guests because it's scrumptious and so easy to put together the night before.
—*Amy Berry, Poland, ME*

PREP: 20 min. + chilling • **BAKE:** 45 min. • **MAKES:** 8 servings

- 6 large eggs
- 1¾ cups fat-free milk
- 1 tsp. sugar
- 1 tsp. ground cinnamon
- 1 tsp. vanilla extract
- ¼ tsp. salt
- 1 loaf (1 lb.) French bread, cubed
- 1 pkg. (12 oz.) frozen unsweetened mixed berries
- 2 Tbsp. cold butter
- ⅓ cup packed brown sugar
- Optional: Confectioners' sugar and maple syrup

1. Whisk together first 6 ingredients. Place bread cubes in a 13x9-in. or 3-qt. baking dish coated with cooking spray. Pour egg mixture over top. Refrigerate, covered, 8 hours or overnight.
2. Preheat oven to 350°. Remove berries from freezer and French toast from refrigerator and let stand while the oven heats. Bake, covered, 30 minutes.
3. In a small bowl, cut butter into brown sugar until crumbly. Top French toast with berries; sprinkle with brown sugar mixture. Bake, uncovered, until a knife inserted in the center comes out clean, 15-20 minutes. If desired, dust with confectioners' sugar and serve with syrup.
1 SERVING: 310 cal., 8g fat (3g sat. fat), 148mg chol., 517mg sod., 46g carb. (17g sugars, 3g fiber), 13g pro.

MIXED BERRY FRENCH TOAST BAKE

SAUSAGE & GRAVY BISCUIT POCKETS

🔟 ❄ SAUSAGE & GRAVY BISCUIT POCKETS

I love sausage gravy and biscuits, so I thought it'd be a fabulous idea to make them portable for an on-the-go option.
—*Stephanie Matthews, Tempe, AZ*

PREP: 20 min. + cooling • **BAKE:** 15 min. • **MAKES:** 16 servings

- 1 lb. bulk pork sausage
- 2 Tbsp. butter
- ½ cup all-purpose flour
- ½ tsp. salt
- ½ tsp. pepper
- 4 cups 2% milk
- 2 tubes (16.3 oz. each) large refrigerated buttermilk biscuits

1. In a large skillet, cook sausage over medium heat until no longer pink, 3-5 minutes, breaking into crumbles. Add butter; heat until melted. Add flour, salt and pepper; cook and stir until blended. Gradually add milk, stirring constantly. Bring to a boil; cook and stir until thickened, about 3 minutes. Remove from heat; cool to room temperature, about 25 minutes.
2. Preheat oven to 400°. On a lightly floured surface, pat or roll each biscuit into a 6-in. circle. Spoon ½ cup gravy mixture over half of each circle to within ½ in. of edge. Wet edge and fold dough over filling; press edge with a fork to seal.
3. Place on an ungreased baking sheet. Bake until golden brown, 12-14 minutes.
FREEZE OPTION: Cover and freeze unbaked pockets on a waxed paper-lined baking sheet until firm. Transfer to freezer containers; return to freezer. To use, bake pockets on an ungreased baking sheet in a preheated 400° oven until golden brown and heated through, 12-14 minutes. If desired, brush with additional butter.
1 POCKET: 313 cal., 17g fat (6g sat. fat), 28mg chol., 946mg sod., 31g carb. (6g sugars, 1g fiber), 10g pro.

VERMONT BREAKFAST EGG MUFFINS

I tuck all the best foods of Vermont—maple syrup, cheddar cheese, sausage, apples and cranberries—into these cups. They're super portable and make a great addition to your breakfast table or brunch spread.
—*Sharyn LaPointe Hill, Las Cruces, NM*

PREP: 20 min. + standing
BAKE: 20 min.
MAKES: 8 servings

- 16 slices Canadian bacon
- 1½ cups all-purpose flour
- 1½ tsp. baking powder
- 1¼ cups whole milk
- 2 large eggs, lightly beaten
- ¼ cup maple syrup
- 1½ cups shredded extra-sharp white cheddar cheese
- 6 frozen fully cooked pork or turkey breakfast sausage links, thawed and finely chopped
- 1 small Granny Smith apple, finely chopped
- ⅓ cup dried cranberries
  Prepared pesto, optional

1. Preheat oven to 375°. Line each of 16 greased muffin cups with 1 slice Canadian bacon, cutting to fit as needed. Set aside.
2. In a large bowl, whisk flour and baking powder. In another bowl, whisk milk, eggs and maple syrup until blended. Add to flour mixture; stir just until moistened. Fold in the cheese, sausage, apple and cranberries. Let mixture rest 10 minutes. Divide batter among muffin cups, about ¼ cup batter per cup.
3. Bake until golden brown, 20-25 minutes. Cool 5 minutes before removing from pans to wire racks. Serve warm, with pesto sauce if desired.

FREEZE OPTION: Cool baked egg muffins. Place them on waxed paper-lined baking sheets; cover and freeze until firm. Transfer to a freezer container; return to freezer. To use, place in greased muffin pan, cover loosely with foil and reheat in a preheated 350° oven. Or microwave each muffin, uncovered, on high until heated through, 30-60 seconds.
2 MUFFINS: 348 cal., 16g fat (7g sat. fat), 91mg chol., 729mg sod., 35g carb. (15g sugars, 1g fiber), 17g pro

DID YOU KNOW?

Sharp and extra-sharp cheddar cheese have been aged longer than regular cheddar. As cheese ages, it loses moisture and its flavor becomes more pronounced. Using aged cheese in a recipe adds complexity and rich flavor, even to humble dishes like biscuits and mac 'n' cheese. In light cooking, it provides more flavor with less cheese.

VERMONT BREAKFAST EGG MUFFINS

**SAVORY WAFFLES
WITH ASPARAGUS,
GRUYERE & ONION**

SAVORY WAFFLES WITH ASPARAGUS, GRUYERE & ONION

I took one of our family's favorite puff pastry recipes, which uses a similar mix of ingredients, and translated it to savory waffles. It's a change of pace from sweeter fare. Served with a ham steak and fried eggs, it makes a fabulous meal.
—*Leslie Ponce, Miami, FL*

- -

PREP: 35 min. • **BAKE:** 25 min.
MAKES: 6 servings

- 1 **bunch green onions, finely chopped**
- 16 **fresh asparagus spears, trimmed and cut into ¼-in. pieces**
- ¾ **tsp. salt, divided**
- ¼ **tsp. pepper**
- 9 **large eggs, room temperature, divided use**
- 2 **cups all-purpose flour**
- 1 **Tbsp. baking powder**
- ¼ **tsp. cayenne pepper**
- 1½ **cups 2% milk**
- 6 **Tbsp. butter, melted**
- 1 **cup Gruyere cheese, shredded**
- 1 **fully cooked boneless ham steak (12 oz.), cubed**

1. Preheat oven to 350°. Arrange onions and asparagus on a greased 15x10x1-in. baking pan; toss with ¼ tsp. salt and pepper. Roast until lightly browned, 10-12 minutes. Cool slightly; reserve ¼ cup vegetable mixture for topping.
2. Preheat a greased waffle iron. Separate 3 eggs. Whisk the flour, baking powder, cayenne pepper and remaining salt. Add milk, 3 egg yolks and melted butter; mix gently but thoroughly. Stir in remaining onion and asparagus mixture and ¾ cup shredded cheese
3. In another bowl, beat 3 egg whites on high until soft peaks form. Fold into waffle batter. Bake the waffles according to manufacturer's directions until golden brown.
4. Meanwhile, in a large skillet coated with cooking spray, cook ham until heated through; keep warm. In same skillet, fry remaining eggs until yolks are set. To serve, top waffle with ham and 1 egg. Sprinkle with reserved onion and asparagus, and remaining ¼ cup cheese.
1 SERVING: 544 cal., 29g fat (15g sat. fat), 364mg chol., 1493mg sod., 38g carb. (4g sugars, 2g fiber), 33g pro.

CORN CAKES WITH POACHED EGGS & MANGO SALSA

CORN CAKES WITH POACHED EGGS & MANGO SALSA

Don't be intimidated by the poached eggs in this bright can't-miss morning meal.
—*Eva Amuso, Cheshire, MA*

- -

PREP: 40 min. • **COOK:** 5 min./batch
MAKES: 6 servings

- 1 **medium mango, peeled and chopped**
- ½ **cup salsa**
- 2 **Tbsp. minced fresh cilantro**
- 1 **green onion, finely chopped**

CORN CAKES
- 4 **large eggs, room temperature**
- ⅔ **cup all-purpose flour**
- ⅔ **cup cornmeal**
- 4 **tsp. baking powder**
- 1 **tsp. salt**
- ⅛ **tsp. pepper**
- 1 **can (8¼ oz.) cream-style corn**
- ½ **cup 2% milk**
- ½ **cup butter, melted**
- 1 **cup fresh or frozen corn, thawed**
- 4 **green onions, chopped**
- ¼ **tsp. cream of tartar**

POACHED EGGS
- 1 **Tbsp. white vinegar**
- 6 **large eggs**

1. In a small bowl, combine the mango, salsa, cilantro and onion; set aside.
2. Separate 2 eggs. In a large bowl, combine the flour, cornmeal, baking powder, salt and pepper. In another bowl, whisk the remaining eggs, egg yolks, cream-style corn, milk and butter. Stir into dry ingredients just until blended. Fold in corn and onions. In a small bowl, beat egg whites and cream of tartar until stiff peaks form. Fold into batter.
3. Pour batter by ¼ cupfuls onto a greased cast-iron skillet or hot griddle. Cook until golden brown, 2-3 minutes on each side.
4. Meanwhile, place 2-3 in. water in a large skillet with high sides; add vinegar. Bring to a boil; reduce heat and simmer gently. Break cold eggs, 1 at a time, into a custard cup or saucer; holding the cup close to the surface of the water, slip each egg into water.
5. Cook, uncovered, until whites are completely set and yolks are still soft, about 4 minutes. With a slotted spoon, lift eggs out of water. Serve with corn cakes and salsa.
1 SERVING: 455 cal., 25g fat (13g sat. fat), 392mg chol., 1097mg sod., 45g carb. (10g sugars, 4g fiber), 16g pro.

COPYCAT EGG BITES

🖐

COPYCAT EGG BITES

You can substitute Gruyere cheese for the Swiss and ham for the bacon, or add in small-cut veggies to these copycat Starbucks egg bites. I also like to bake these in small Mason jars for fun single-portion presentations. Serve with avocado slices and fresh fruit for a healthy breakfast.
—*Maria Morelli, West Kelowna, BC*

PREP: 10 min. • **BAKE:** 25 min. • **MAKES:** 6 servings

- 6 large eggs
- ¼ cup 4% cottage cheese
- ¼ tsp. salt
- ¼ tsp. pepper
- ½ cup shredded Swiss cheese
- 3 cooked bacon strips, chopped

1. Arrange an oven rack at the lowest rack setting; place a second rack in middle of oven. Place an oven-safe skillet on bottom oven rack; preheat oven and skillet to 300°. Meanwhile, in a small saucepan, bring 2 cups water to a boil.
2. In a blender, puree first 4 ingredients until smooth, about 20 seconds. Line 6 muffin cups with foil liners. Divide the Swiss cheese and bacon among the muffin cups. Pour egg mixture over top.
3. Wearing oven mitts, place muffin tin on top rack. Pull bottom rack out by 6-8 in.; add boiling water to skillet. (Work quickly and carefully, pouring water away from you. Don't worry if some water is left in the saucepan.) Carefully slide bottom rack back into place; quickly close door to trap steam in oven.
4. Bake until eggs puff and are cooked to desired degree of doneness, 25-30 minutes. Serve immediately.
1 EGG BITE: 143 cal., 10g fat (4g sat. fat), 201mg chol., 311mg sod., 1g carb. (1g sugars, 0 fiber), 12g pro.

BREAKFAST IN A PAN

Try this tasty one-pan dish for an easy low-mess breakfast or brunch. This recipe also works well with bacon or sausage instead of ham. Sometimes I saute chopped bell peppers and onions until tender and whisk them in with the eggs for some added flavor and color.
—*Andrea Bolden, Unionville, TN*

PREP: 15 min. • **BAKE:** 25 min. • **MAKES:** 6 servings

- 1 tube (8 oz.) refrigerated crescent rolls
- 2 cups cubed fully cooked ham
- 2 cups frozen shredded hash brown potatoes, thawed
- 5 large eggs
- ½ cup 2% milk
- ½ tsp. pepper
- ⅛ tsp. salt
- 2 cups shredded cheddar cheese

1. Preheat oven to 350°. Unroll crescent dough into a long rectangle; press perforations to seal. Press onto bottom of a greased 13x9-in. baking pan. Top with ham and potatoes.
2. In a large bowl, whisk eggs, milk, pepper and salt until blended; pour over potatoes. Sprinkle with cheese. Bake until set and cheese is melted, 25-30 minutes.
1 PIECE: 434 cal., 26g fat (9g sat. fat), 222mg chol., 1216mg sod., 23g carb. (6g sugars, 0 fiber), 28g pro.

BREAKFAST IN A PAN

FRUITY CROISSANT PUFF

FRUITY CROISSANT PUFF

I got this recipe from a good friend. Sweet, tart, tender and light, it tastes like a Danish.
—*Myra Almer, Tuttle, ND*

PREP: 10 min. + chilling • **BAKE:** 45 min.
MAKES: 6 servings

- 4 large croissants, cut into 1-in. cubes (about 6 cups)
- 1½ cups mixed fresh berries
- 1 pkg. (8 oz.) cream cheese, softened
- 1 cup 2% milk
- ½ cup sugar
- 2 large eggs, room temperature
- 1 tsp. vanilla extract
  Maple syrup, optional

1. Place croissant cubes and berries in a greased 8-in. square baking dish. In a medium bowl, beat cream cheese until smooth. Beat in the milk, sugar, eggs and vanilla until blended; pour over croissants. Refrigerate, covered, overnight.
2. Preheat oven to 350°. Remove the casserole from refrigerator while oven heats. Bake, covered, 30 minutes. Bake, uncovered, until puffed and golden and a knife inserted in the center comes out clean, 15-20 minutes. Let casserole stand 5-10 minutes before serving. If desired, serve with syrup.
1 SERVING: 429 cal., 24g fat (14g sat. fat), 132mg chol., 358mg sod., 44g carb. (27g sugars, 2g fiber), 9g pro.

MAPLE SAUSAGE PATTIES

Maple syrup, sage and thyme give delightful flavor to these homemade sausage patties. They're a definite treat, especially alongside pancakes or French toast.
—*Margaret Eid, Huron, SD*

PREP: 15 min. + chilling • **COOK:** 10 min.
MAKES: 8 servings

- 1 Tbsp. maple syrup
- ½ tsp. salt
- ½ tsp. onion powder
- ½ tsp. rubbed sage
- ½ tsp. dried thyme
- ½ tsp. poultry seasoning
- ½ tsp. ground nutmeg
- ¼ tsp. cayenne pepper
- 1 to 2 tsp. liquid smoke, optional
- 1 lb. ground pork

1. In a large bowl, mix maple syrup, salt, spices and, if desired, liquid smoke. Add pork; mix lightly but thoroughly. Shape into eight 2½-in. patties. Refrigerate, covered, at least 1 hour.
2. In a large skillet coated with cooking spray, cook patties over medium heat until a thermometer reads 160°, 4-6 minutes per side.
1 PATTY: 128 cal., 8g fat (3g sat. fat), 38mg chol., 177mg sod., 2g carb. (2g sugars, 0 fiber), 10g pro.

BREAKFAST BREAD BOWLS

These bread bowls are so elegant, tasty and simple, you'll wonder why you haven't been making them for years. My wife loves when I make these for her in the morning.
—*Patrick Lavin Jr., Birdsboro, PA*

PREP: 20 min. • **BAKE:** 20 min.
MAKES: 4 servings

- ½ cup chopped pancetta
- 4 crusty hard rolls (4 in. wide)
- ½ cup finely chopped fresh mushrooms
- 4 large eggs
- ⅛ tsp. salt
- ⅛ tsp. pepper
- ¼ cup shredded Gruyere or fontina cheese

1. Preheat oven to 350°. In a small skillet, cook pancetta over medium heat until browned, stirring occasionally. Remove with a slotted spoon; drain on paper towels.
2. Meanwhile, cut a thin slice off top of each roll. Hollow out bottom of roll, leaving a ½-in.-thick shell (save removed bread for another use); place shells on an ungreased baking sheet.
3. Add mushrooms and pancetta to bread shells. Carefully break an egg into each; sprinkle the eggs with salt and pepper. Sprinkle with cheese. Bake 18-22 minutes or until egg whites are completely set and yolks begin to thicken but are not hard.
1 BREAKFAST BOWL: 256 cal., 13g fat (5g sat. fat), 206mg chol., 658mg sod., 19g carb. (1g sugars, 1g fiber), 14g pro.

HOW-TO

Make A Bread Bowl

Cut a thin slice off top of roll. Hollow out bottom of roll, leaving a ½-in.-thick shell.

ROASTED VEGETABLE & CHEVRE QUICHE

Roasting the veggies in this rich-yet-bright quiche intensifies their flavors. And the addition of fresh goat cheese lends a wonderful creamy tangy quality.
—*Laura Davis, Chincoteague, VA*

PREP: 45 min. + chilling
BAKE: 25 min. + standing
MAKES: 6 servings

- 1 sheet refrigerated pie crust
- 1 small eggplant, cut into 1-in. pieces
- 1 poblano pepper, cut into 1-in. pieces
- 1 medium tomato, cut into 1-in. pieces
- 2 garlic cloves, minced
- 1 Tbsp. olive oil
- 2 large eggs plus 2 large egg yolks
- ¾ cup half-and-half cream
- 1 tsp. kosher salt
- ½ tsp. pepper
- 1 log (4 oz.) fresh goat cheese, crumbled

1. Unroll pie crust into an ungreased 9-in. tart pan. Refrigerate 30 minutes. Preheat oven to 425°.
2. Line unpricked crust with a double thickness of foil. Fill with pie weights, dried beans or uncooked rice. Bake on a lower oven rack until edge is golden brown, 10-12 minutes. Remove foil and weights; bake until bottom is golden brown, 3-5 minutes longer. Cool on a wire rack.
3. In a large bowl, combine eggplant, pepper, tomato and garlic. Add oil; toss to coat. Transfer to a greased 15x10x1-in. baking pan. Roast 15-20 minutes or until tender, stirring halfway.
4. Reduce oven setting to 375°. Spoon roasted vegetables into crust. In a large bowl, whisk eggs, egg yolks, cream, salt and pepper until blended; pour over top. Sprinkle with goat cheese.
5. Bake on a lower oven rack on a baking sheet until a knife inserted near the center comes out clean, 25-30 minutes. Cover edge with foil if it begins to get too dark. Let stand 10 minutes before cutting.
1 PIECE: 219 cal., 14g fat (7g sat. fat), 83mg chol., 471mg sod., 19g carb. (2g sugars, 0 fiber), 3g pro.

EGG BURRITOS

EGG BURRITOS

Zap one of these frozen burritos in the microwave and you'll stave off hunger all morning. This recipe is my family's favorite combo, but I sometimes use breakfast sausage instead of bacon.
—*Audra Niederman, Aberdeen, SD*

TAKES: 25 min. • **MAKES:** 10 burritos

- 12 bacon strips, chopped
- 12 large eggs
- ½ tsp. salt
- ¼ tsp. pepper
- 10 flour tortillas (8 in.), warmed
- 1½ cups shredded cheddar cheese
- 4 green onions, thinly sliced

1. In a large cast-iron or other heavy skillet, cook bacon until crisp; drain on paper towels. Remove all but 1-2 Tbsp. drippings from pan.
2. Whisk together eggs, salt and pepper. Heat skillet over medium heat; pour in egg mixture. Cook and stir until eggs are thickened and no liquid egg remains; remove from heat.
3. Spoon about ¼ cup egg mixture onto center of each tortilla; sprinkle with the cheese, bacon and green onions. Roll into burritos.
FREEZE OPTION: Cool eggs before making burritos. Individually wrap the burritos in paper towels and foil; freeze in an airtight container. To use, remove foil; place paper towel-wrapped burrito on a microwave-safe plate. Microwave on high until heated through, turning once. Let burrito stand for 15 seconds.
1 BURRITO: 376 cal., 20g fat (8g sat. fat), 251mg chol., 726mg sod., 29g carb. (0 sugars, 2g fiber), 19g pro.

TEST KITCHEN TIP

Breakfast burritos can be a smart choice to start the day because they include a good amount of protein. To make these healthier, use whole wheat tortillas, skip the bacon, reduce the cheese and toss in some sauteed veggies.

FREEZER FRENCH TOAST

I keep a freezer full of these slices and simply pop them into the oven for a homemade breakfast in no time. My family prefers them over frozen store-bought French toast.
—*Diane Perry, Castro Valley, CA*

PREP: 10 min. + freezing • **BAKE:** 20 min. • **MAKES:** 5 servings

- 4 large eggs
- 1 cup 2% milk
- 2 Tbsp. sugar
- 1 tsp. vanilla extract
- ¼ tsp. ground nutmeg
- 10 slices day-old French bread (¾ in. thick)
- 1 to 2 Tbsp. butter, melted
  Optional: Mixed fresh berries and confectioners' sugar

1. In a large bowl, beat eggs, milk, sugar, vanilla and nutmeg. Place bread in a well-greased 13x9-in. baking dish. Pour egg mixture over bread. Let soak for several minutes, turning once to coat. Freeze until firm. Transfer slices to airtight containers; return to freezer.
2. To bake, preheat oven to 450°. Place frozen French toast slices in a single layer on a well-greased baking sheet; dot with butter. Bake for 7 minutes; turn and bake 10-12 minutes longer or until golden brown. If desired, serve with fresh berries and dust with confectioners' sugar.
2 PIECES: 220 cal., 8g fat (4g sat. fat), 159mg chol., 311mg sod., 26g carb. (8g sugars, 1g fiber), 10g pro. **DIABETIC EXCHANGES:** 2 starch, 1 lean meat, ½ fat.
TO MAKE IN AN AIR FRYER: Prepare recipe as directed. Preheat air fryer to 375°. Place frozen French toast slices in a single layer in greased tray in air-fryer basket. Cook 8 minutes; turn and cook until golden brown, 6-7 minutes longer. Top with butter.

SCRAMBLED EGG
HASH BROWN CUPS

SCRAMBLED EGG HASH BROWN CUPS

These tasty breakfast cuties pack all your favorite rise-and-shine ingredients—eggs, hash browns and bacon—into a single-serving cup. Grab one and get mingling!
—*Talon DiMare, Bullhead City, AZ*

PREP: 10 min. • **BAKE:** 35 min. • **MAKES:** 1 dozen

- 1 pkg. (20 oz.) refrigerated Southwest-style shredded hash brown potatoes
- 1¼ cups shredded cheddar-Monterey Jack cheese, divided
- 6 large eggs
- ½ cup 2% milk
- ⅛ tsp. salt
- 1 Tbsp. butter
- 10 thick-sliced bacon strips, cooked and crumbled

1. Preheat oven to 400°. Combine potatoes and ¾ cup cheese. Divide potato mixture among 12 greased muffin cups; press onto bottoms and up sides to form cups. Bake until light golden brown, about 30 minutes.
2. Meanwhile, in a small bowl, whisk the eggs, milk and salt. In a large nonstick skillet, heat butter over medium heat. Pour in egg mixture; cook and stir until eggs are thickened and no liquid egg remains. Stir in bacon. Spoon into cups; sprinkle with remaining ½ cup cheese.
3. Bake until cheese is melted, 3-5 minutes. Cool 5 minutes before removing from pan.
1 HASH BROWN CUP: 180 cal., 10g fat (5g sat. fat), 113mg chol., 487mg sod., 11g carb. (1g sugars, 1g fiber), 10g pro.

FREEZER
FRENCH TOAST

**BANANA OATMEAL COOKIES
PAGE 183**

Cookies, Bars & Candies

Everybody adores wholesome oatmeal cookies, pretty fruit bars and melt-in-your-mouth fudge. Look in these pages to find sweet treats perfect for sharing.

BEST OF THE BEST DISHES

PAN-BANGING CHOCOLATE CHIP COOKIES

These chocolate chip cookies are crunchy on the edges, chewy in the middle.
—*Sarah Kieffer, Columbia Heights, MN*

PREP: 20 min. + freezing
BAKE: 20 min./batch • **MAKES:** 1 dozen

- 2 cups all-purpose flour
- ¾ tsp. salt
- ½ tsp. baking soda
- 1 cup unsalted butter, room temperature
- 1½ cups sugar
- ¼ cup packed brown sugar
- 1 large egg, room temperature
- 2 Tbsp. water
- 1 Tbsp. vanilla extract
- 6 oz. semisweet or bittersweet chocolate, chopped into ½-in. pieces
  Fleur de sel (sea salt), optional

1. Preheat the oven to 350°. Adjust oven rack to the middle position. Line 3 baking sheets with aluminum foil, dull side up, or parchment.

2. In a small bowl, whisk flour, salt and baking soda; set aside.

3. In the bowl of a stand mixer fitted with a paddle attachment, beat butter until creamy, about 1 minute. Add sugars and beat until light and fluffy, 2-3 minutes. Add egg, water and vanilla; mix on low until combined. Add the flour mixture; mix until combined. Stir in chocolate until incorporated.

4. Form dough into ¼-cup (3-oz.) balls. Place 4 balls on a prepared pan. Freeze 15 minutes. Bake until the dough balls have spread flat but are puffed slightly in the center, about 9 minutes. Lift sheet pan up about 4 in. and gently let it drop down against the oven rack, so the edges of the cookies set and the centers fall back. Bake until the cookies puff up again in 2 minutes; repeat lifting and dropping the pan. Repeat a few more times to create ridges around the edge of the cookie. Bake until the cookies have spread out and the edges are golden brown but the centers are much lighter and not fully cooked, 16-18 minutes total. Repeat with the remaining dough. If desired, sprinkle cookies with salt while still warm.

1 COOKIE: 385 cal., 19g fat (12g sat. fat), 52mg chol., 194mg sod., 45g carb. (30g sugars, 1g fiber), 4g pro.

TEST KITCHEN TIPS

- Sprinkling a little sea salt on the cookies at the end of baking makes the chocolate flavor pop!
- Lining the baking sheets with aluminum foil, dull side up, helps create a golden bottom.

PAN-BANGING CHOCOLATE CHIP COOKIES

LAYERED PEANUT
BUTTER BROWNIES

LAYERED PEANUT BUTTER BROWNIES

The combination of chocolate and peanut butter makes these brownies a real crowd-pleaser. They're so good that they won a ribbon at the fair.
—*Margaret McNeil, Germantown, TN*

- -

PREP: 15 min. • **BAKE:** 35 min. • **MAKES:** 2 dozen

- 3 large eggs, room temperature
- 1 cup butter, melted
- 2 tsp. vanilla extract
- 2 cups sugar
- 1¼ cups all-purpose flour
- ¾ cup baking cocoa
- ½ tsp. baking powder
- ¼ tsp. salt
- 1 cup milk chocolate chips

FILLING

- 2 pkg. (8 oz. each) cream cheese, softened
- ½ cup creamy peanut butter
- ¼ cup sugar
- 1 large egg
- 2 Tbsp. 2% milk

1. Preheat oven to 350°. In a large bowl, beat the eggs, butter and vanilla until smooth. Whisk together the dry ingredients; gradually add to egg mixture. Stir in chocolate chips. Set aside 1 cup for topping. Spread remaining batter into a greased 13x9-in. baking pan.

2. For the filling, in a small bowl, beat the cream cheese, peanut butter and sugar until smooth. Beat in egg and milk on low just until combined. Carefully spread over batter. Drop reserved batter by tablespoonfuls over filling. Cut through batter with a knife to swirl.

3. Bake until a toothpick inserted in the center comes out clean, 35-40 minutes (do not overbake). Cool on a wire rack. Refrigerate until serving.

1 BROWNIE: 321 cal., 20g fat (11g sat. fat), 72mg chol., 196mg sod., 32g carb. (24g sugars, 1g fiber), 5g pro.

CANDY CORN COOKIES

Get a head start on these buttery cookies by shaping and chilling the homemade dough ahead of time. When you're ready, just slice and bake the tricolor treats.
—Taste of Home *Test Kitchen*

- -

PREP: 35 min. + chilling • **BAKE:** 10 min./batch • **MAKES:** 5 dozen

- 1½ cups butter, softened
- 1½ cups sugar
- ½ tsp. vanilla extract
- 3 cups all-purpose flour
- 1 tsp. baking soda
- ½ tsp. salt
-    Yellow and orange paste food coloring

1. Cream butter and sugar until light and fluffy, 5-7 minutes. Beat in vanilla. In another bowl, whisk together flour, baking soda and salt; gradually beat into creamed mixture.

2. Divide dough in half. Tint 1 portion yellow. Divide remaining dough into two-thirds and one-third portions. Color the larger portion orange; leave smaller portion plain.

3. Shape each portion of dough into two 8-in. logs. Flatten top and push sides in at a slight angle. Place orange logs on yellow logs; push sides in at a slight angle. Top with plain logs, forming a slightly rounded top. Wrap and refrigerate until firm, about 4 hours.

4. Preheat oven to 350°. Unwrap and cut dough into ¼-in. slices. Place 2 in. apart on ungreased baking sheets.

5. Bake until set, 10-12 minutes. Remove from pans to wire racks to cool.

1 COOKIE: 83 cal., 5g fat (3g sat. fat), 12mg chol., 77mg sod., 10g carb. (5g sugars, 0 fiber), 1g pro.

CANDY
CORN
COOKIES

LEMON SHORTBREAD COOKIES

STRAWBERRY & PEACH LIME CUSTARD BARS

After I baked, my dad would always find his way to the kitchen and ask if he could try what I made. I enjoyed asking him to taste test different creations, like these bars. He was always ready with a compliment. Other fruits can be arranged over the custard, depending on what's in season.
—*Carlin Sierra Tou, Chandler, AZ*

- -

PREP: 20 min. + cooling
BAKE: 20 min. + chilling
MAKES: 2 dozen

- 2 cups graham cracker crumbs
- 1 cup all-purpose flour
- ¾ cup butter, softened
- ½ cup plus 2 Tbsp. sugar, divided
- 5 large egg yolks
- 4 oz. cream cheese, softened
- 1 can (14 oz.) sweetened condensed milk
- ½ cup lime juice
- 2 Tbsp. grated lime zest, divided
- 1 Tbsp. vanilla bean paste
- 2½ cups fresh strawberries, halved
- 1 can (15 oz.) peach halves in light syrup, drained and thinly sliced
- 2 tsp. ground cinnamon

1. Preheat oven to 350°. Line a 13x9-in. baking pan with nonstick foil; set aside. In a large bowl, beat cracker crumbs, flour, butter and ½ cup sugar until combined. Press onto bottom of prepared pan. Bake until lightly browned, 10-15 minutes. Cool on a wire rack.
2. In a large bowl, beat egg yolks and cream cheese until smooth. Beat in milk and lime juice until blended. Stir in 1 Tbsp. lime zest and vanilla paste; pour over the cooled crust. Alternately arrange the strawberries and peaches in closely spaced rows over filling. Combine cinnamon and remaining 2 Tbsp. sugar; sprinkle over fruit.
3. Bake 20-25 minutes or until custard looks set. Cool completely on a wire rack. Cover and refrigerate at least 2 hours or overnight. Sprinkle with remaining 1 Tbsp. lime zest; cut into bars.
1 BAR: 226 cal., 11g fat (6g sat. fat), 64mg chol., 123mg sod., 30g carb. (20g sugars, 1g fiber), 4g pro.

LEMON SHORTBREAD COOKIES

I received this recipe from my cousin, who tried to duplicate cookies she loved from a restaurant. It was in a cookbook she made for the family for Christmas!
—*Lorie Miner, Kamas, UT*

- -

PREP: 25 min.
BAKE: 15 min./batch + cooling
MAKES: 2 dozen

- ½ cup butter, softened
- ⅓ cup sugar
- 4 tsp. grated lemon zest
- 1 tsp. vanilla extract
- 1 cup all-purpose flour
- 2 Tbsp. plus 1½ tsp. cornstarch
- ¼ tsp. ground nutmeg
- ⅛ tsp. salt

DRIZZLE
- ½ cup confectioners' sugar
- 2 to 3 tsp. lemon juice

1. Preheat oven to 350°. In a small bowl, cream butter and sugar until light and fluffy, 5-7 minutes. Beat in lemon zest and vanilla. Combine the flour, cornstarch, nutmeg, and salt; gradually add to creamed mixture and mix well. (Dough will be crumbly.) Shape into a ball.
2. On a lightly floured surface, press dough to ½-in. thickness. Cut with a floured 1-in. fluted cookie cutter; place 1 in. apart on ungreased baking sheets. Prick cookies with a fork. Reroll scraps if desired.
3. Bake until firm, 12-15 minutes. Cool for 2 minutes before carefully removing to wire racks to cool completely.
4. Combine confectioners' sugar and lemon juice; drizzle over cookies. Store in an airtight container.
1 COOKIE: 77 cal., 4g fat (2g sat. fat), 10mg chol., 39mg sod., 10g carb. (5g sugars, 0 fiber), 1g pro.

TEST KITCHEN TIP

Lemon shortbread cookies pair beautifully with coffee, tea or even iced tea. For a little variation, add some chopped, dried lavender buds to your shortbread dough to make lemon-lavender shortbread cookies!

STRAWBERRY & PEACH LIME CUSTARD BARS

GRANDMA'S OATMEAL DATE BARS

While I was growing up, Grandma made this dessert at Christmas. This recipe reminds me of her. And now I fix the bars for my family.
—*Nancy Hawkins, Brookville, IN*

PREP: 30 min. • **BAKE:** 25 min. • **MAKES:** 2 dozen

- 1 lb. pitted dates, quartered
- 1½ cups water
- ½ cup sugar
- 1½ cups all-purpose flour
- 1½ cups old-fashioned oats
- 1 cup packed brown sugar
- 1 tsp. vanilla extract
- ½ tsp. baking soda
- ½ tsp. salt
- ¼ tsp. almond extract
- ¾ cup shortening
  Whipped cream, optional

1. Preheat oven to 350°. In a small saucepan, combine dates, water and sugar. Bring to a boil. Reduce heat; simmer, uncovered, for 7-9 minutes or until thickened and dates are tender, stirring constantly. Remove from heat.

2. In a large bowl, combine flour, oats, brown sugar, vanilla, baking soda, salt and almond extract. Cut in shortening until crumbly. Press half onto bottom of a greased 13x9-in. baking dish. Carefully spread with date mixture.

3. Sprinkle remaining crumb mixture over filling; press down gently. Bake until lightly browned, 25-30 minutes. Cool on a wire rack. Cut into bars. If desired, serve with whipped cream.

1 BAR: 207 cal., 7g fat (2g sat. fat), 0 chol., 79mg sod., 37g carb. (25g sugars, 2g fiber), 2g pro.

GRANDMA'S OATMEAL DATE BARS

AIR-FRYER FUDGY BROWNIES

AIR-FRYER FUDGY BROWNIES

Don't heat up your kitchen! These small-batch air-fryer brownies come together so quickly, and no oven is required. Top with nuts or powdered sugar for a quick homemade treat.
—*Rashanda Cobbins, Milwaukee, WI*

PREP: 10 min. • **BAKE:** 45 min. • **MAKES:** 9 servings

- ⅓ cup butter, cubed
- 1½ cups 60% cacao bittersweet chocolate baking chips, divided
- ¾ cup sugar
- 2 large eggs, room temperature
- 2 Tbsp. water
- 1 tsp. vanilla extract
- ¾ cup all-purpose flour
- ¼ tsp. baking soda
- ¼ tsp. salt

1. Preheat air fryer to 325°. Line a 6-in. square or round cake pan with parchment, letting the ends extend up sides. In a small microwave-safe bowl, melt butter and 1 cup chocolate chips; stir until smooth. Cool slightly. In a small bowl, beat sugar and eggs. Stir in water and vanilla. Combine flour, baking soda and salt; gradually add to chocolate mixture. Fold in remaining ½ cup chocolate chips.

2. Pour into prepared pan. Bake for 40-45 minutes or until a toothpick inserted in center comes out with moist crumbs (do not overbake). Tent with foil as needed to prevent overbrowning. Cool on a wire rack.

3. Lifting with parchment, remove brownies from pan. Cut into squares.

1 BROWNIE: 315 cal., 16g fat (10g sat. fat), 59mg chol., 174mg sod., 43g carb. (32g sugars, 2g fiber), 4g pro.

BANANA ORANGE BARS

I have been making these treats for many years. I don't remember where the recipe came from, but the bars are always a hit.
—*Mary Sturgis, Hingham, MA*

PREP: 15 min. • **BAKE:** 25 min. + cooling
MAKES: 20 servings

- 2 cups mashed ripe bananas (3 to 4 medium)
- 1⅔ cups sugar
- 1 cup canola oil
- 4 large eggs, room temperature
- 2 cups all-purpose flour
- 2 tsp. ground cinnamon
- 1 tsp. baking powder
- 1 tsp. salt
- ½ tsp. baking soda

ORANGE BUTTER FROSTING
- 5 Tbsp. butter, softened
- 4½ cups confectioners' sugar
- 5 Tbsp. orange juice
- ½ tsp. grated orange zest

1. In a large bowl, beat the bananas, sugar, oil and eggs until well blended. In a small bowl, combine the flour, cinnamon, baking powder, salt and baking soda; gradually beat into banana mixture until blended.

2. Pour into a greased 15x10x1-in. baking pan. Bake at 350° for 25-30 minutes or until a toothpick inserted in the center comes out clean. Cool on a wire rack.

3. Cream butter and sugar in a large bowl until light and fluffy, 5-7 minutes. Beat in orange juice and zest until smooth; spread over cake.

1 PIECE: 374 cal., 15g fat (4g sat. fat), 50mg chol., 212mg sod., 59g carb. (46g sugars, 1g fiber), 3g pro.

READER REVIEW

"Wonderful! They looked like the photo and are delicious! I wasn't sure about the banana/orange combination, but the orange flavor in the frosting was light and just enough to complement the banana cake. And, oh, the cake—love the texture, and the cinnamon is perfect."

—LAURAM-J, TASTEOFHOME.COM

CASHEW BAKLAVA

I always wanted to make baklava, but it seemed like so much work. The son of my neighbor's friend showed us both how to make it—it's really easy and so delicious. I like to mix up the nuts in the filling.
—*Lorraine Caland, Shuniah, ON*

PREP: 50 min. • **BAKE:** 20 min. + standing
MAKES: 2 dozen

- 1½ cups salted cashews
- 1½ cups chopped walnuts
- ½ cup sugar
- 1 tsp. ground cardamom
- ½ tsp. ground cinnamon
- ¼ tsp. ground allspice
- ⅔ cup butter, melted
- 16 sheets phyllo dough (14 x9-in.)

SYRUP
- 1⅓ cups sugar
- ⅔ cup water
- ⅔ cup honey
- 3 lemon slices
- 2 whole cloves
- ½ tsp. ground cinnamon

1. Preheat oven to 350°. For filling, in a food processor, combine the cashews, walnuts, sugar, cardamom, cinnamon and allspice. Cover and pulse until nuts are finely chopped. Brush a 13x9-in. baking pan with some of the butter. Unroll phyllo dough; trim to fit into pan.

2. Layer 4 sheets of phyllo dough in prepared pan, brushing each with butter. (Keep remaining dough covered with a damp towel to prevent it from drying out.) Sprinkle with a third of the nut mixture. Repeat layers twice. Top with remaining phyllo dough, brushing each sheet with butter.

3. Using a sharp knife, cut baklava into 6 squares, then cut each square into 4 triangles. Bake until golden brown, 20-25 minutes.

4. Meanwhile, in a large saucepan, combine the syrup ingredients. Bring to a boil. Reduce heat; simmer, uncovered, for 10 minutes, stirring occasionally. Discard lemon slices and cloves. Pour over warm baklava. Cool completely on a wire rack. Cover and let stand overnight.

1 PIECE: 258 cal., 15g fat (4g sat. fat), 13mg chol., 128mg sod., 31g carb. (24g sugars, 1g fiber), 4g pro.

BANANA ORANGE BARS

LEMON ANISE BISCOTTI

With the growing popularity of gourmet coffees, cappuccino and espresso, I'm finding lots of people enjoy these classic Sicilian dipping cookies.
—*Carrie Sherrill, Forestville, WI*

PREP: 25 min.
BAKE: 40 min.
MAKES: 3 dozen

    2   large eggs, room temperature
    1   cup sugar
    ¼   cup canola oil
    ½   tsp. lemon extract
    ¼   tsp. vanilla extract
    2   cups all-purpose flour
    1   tsp. baking powder
    ½   tsp. salt
    4   tsp. grated lemon zest
    2   tsp. aniseed, crushed
OPTIONAL GLAZE:
    2   cups confectioners' sugar
    3   to 4 Tbsp. lemon juice
        Grated lemon zest

1. Preheat oven to 350°. In a small bowl, beat eggs and sugar for 2 minutes or until thickened. Add oil and extracts; mix well. Combine flour, baking powder and salt; beat into egg mixture. Beat in lemon zest and aniseed.

2. Divide dough in half. On a lightly floured surface, shape each portion into a 12x2-in. rectangle. Transfer to a baking sheet lined with parchment. Flatten to ½-in. thickness.

3. Bake until golden and tops begin to crack, 30-35 minutes. Carefully remove to wire racks; cool for 5 minutes.

4. Transfer to a cutting board; cut with a serrated knife into scant ¾-in. slices. Place cut side down on ungreased baking sheets. Bake 5 minutes. Turn and bake until firm and golden brown, 5-7 minutes. Remove to wire racks to cool. If using glaze, whisk confectioners' sugar and lemon juice in a small bowl. Drizzle over biscotti; sprinkle with zest. Store in an airtight container.

1 COOKIE: 65 cal., 2g fat (0 sat. fat), 10mg chol., 50mg sod., 11g carb. (6g sugars, 0 fiber), 1g pro.

5i ❄ PUMPKIN PIE MARSHMALLOWS

Love pumpkin spice lattes? Let these pale orange, fall-flavored marshmallows slowly melt in your favorite hot coffee or cocoa. Pure bliss!
—*Jennifer Rodriguez, West Jordan, UT*

PREP: 30 min.
COOK: 25 min. + standing
MAKES: about 9½ dozen

- ½ cup plus ¾ cup water, divided
- ½ cup pumpkin pie filling
- 4 envelopes unflavored gelatin
- 3 cups sugar
- 1¼ cups light corn syrup
- ¼ tsp. salt
- ½ cup confectioners' sugar
- 1½ tsp. pumpkin pie spice, optional

1. Line a 13x9-in. pan with foil; coat with cooking spray.
2. In a heatproof bowl of a stand mixer, combine ½ cup water and pie filling. Sprinkle gelatin over top to soften.
3. In a large heavy saucepan, combine sugar, corn syrup, salt and remaining water. Bring to a boil, stirring occasionally. Cook, without stirring, over medium heat until a candy thermometer reads 240° (soft-ball stage).
4. Remove from heat; slowly drizzle into gelatin, beating on high speed. Continue beating until very stiff and doubled in volume, about 10 minutes. Spread into prepared pan. Cover and let cool at room temperature 6 hours or overnight.
5. In a small bowl, combine confectioners' sugar and, if desired, pumpkin pie spice. Using foil, lift candy out of pan. Using a lightly buttered knife or kitchen scissors, cut into 1-in. pieces. Roll in confectioners' sugar mixture. Store in an airtight container in a cool, dry place.

TO MAKE AHEAD: Store marshmallows, layered between waxed paper, in airtight containers in the refrigerator up to 1 week.
FREEZE OPTION: Freeze marshmallows in freezer containers for up to 1 month.
1 MARSHMALLOW: 32 cal., 0 fat (0 sat. fat), 0 chol., 9mg sod., 8g carb. (6g sugars, 0 fiber), 0 pro.

CHOCOLATE CHUNK SHORTBREAD

5i CHOCOLATE CHUNK SHORTBREAD

Chocolate is a nice addition to shortbread, as this scrumptious recipe proves. These are great served with a glass of cold milk.
—*Brenda Mumma, Airdrie, AB*

PREP: 20 min. + chilling
BAKE: 20 min./batch + cooling
MAKES: 2 dozen

- ¾ cup (340 grams) butter, softened
- ½ cup (60 grams) confectioners' sugar
- 1 cup (125 grams) all-purpose flour
- ¼ cup (40 grams) cornstarch
- 3 oz. (85 grams) semisweet chocolate, coarsely chopped
  Additional confectioners' sugar

1. Cream butter and sugar in a large bowl until light and fluffy, 5-7 minutes. Combine flour and cornstarch; stir into the creamed mixture. Fold in chocolate.
2. Shape into 1½-in. balls. Place 2 in. apart on ungreased baking sheets. Flatten with a glass dipped in confectioners' sugar. Chill on baking sheets until firm, about 1 hour.
3. Preheat oven to 300°. Bake until edges are lightly browned, 20-25 minutes. Remove to wire racks to cool completely.
1 COOKIE: 105 cal., 7g fat (4g sat. fat), 15mg chol., 46mg sod., 10g carb. (4g sugars, 0 fiber), 1g pro.

5i EASY PEANUT BUTTER FUDGE

My sister shared the recipe for this unbelievably easy candy. I prefer using creamy peanut butter, but the chunky style works just as well.
—*Mary Jane Rummel, Linglestown, PA*

PREP: 15 min. + chilling
MAKES: 2 lbs. (64 pieces)

- 2 tsp. butter, softened
- 2 cups sugar
- ½ cup whole milk
- 1⅓ cups peanut butter
- 1 jar (7 oz.) marshmallow creme

1. Line an 8-in. square pan with foil; grease with butter.
2. In a heavy saucepan, combine sugar and milk; bring to a boil over medium heat, stirring constantly. Boil 3 minutes, stirring constantly. Remove from heat.
3. Stir in peanut butter and marshmallow creme until blended. Immediately spread into prepared pan; cool slightly.
4. Refrigerate until firm. Using foil, lift fudge out of pan. Remove foil; cut into squares. Store between layers of waxed paper in an airtight container.
1 PIECE: 67 cal., 3g fat (1g sat. fat), 0 chol., 28mg sod., 10g carb. (9g sugars, 0 fiber), 1g pro.

CHOCOLATE-DIPPED TRIPLE-GINGER COOKIES

My mother always enjoyed chocolate-covered ginger, so one day she decided to turn her favorite treat into a superbly delightful cookie.
—Bethany Hammond, Vancouver, WA

PREP: 35 min. + chilling
BAKE: 10 min./batch + cooling
MAKES: 8 dozen

- 1 cup shortening
- ½ cup sugar
- ½ cup packed brown sugar
- 1 large egg, room temperature
- 1 cup molasses
- 2 Tbsp. minced crystallized ginger
- 2 tsp. grated fresh gingerroot
- 4⅔ cups all-purpose flour
- 1½ tsp. baking powder
- ¾ tsp. baking soda
- 2 tsp. ground ginger
- ½ tsp. salt
- ½ tsp. ground cinnamon
- ½ tsp. ground nutmeg
- 2 pkg. (10 oz. each) 60% cacao bittersweet chocolate baking chips, melted
- 4 oz. white baking chocolate, melted

1. In a large bowl, cream shortening and sugars until light and fluffy, 5-7 minutes. Beat in egg, then molasses, crystallized ginger and gingerroot. In another bowl, whisk flour, baking powder, baking soda and seasonings; gradually beat into creamed mixture.
2. Divide dough in half. Shape each into a disk; wrap and refrigerate 1 hour or until firm enough to roll.
3. Preheat the oven to 375°. On a lightly floured surface, roll each portion of dough to ⅛-in. thickness. Cut with a floured 2½-in. round or 3-in. gingerbread man cookie cutter. Place 2 in. apart on ungreased baking sheets. Bake until set, 8-10 minutes. Remove from pans to wire racks to cool completely.
4. Dip each cookie halfway into melted dark chocolate, allowing excess to drip off. Place on waxed paper; let stand until set. Drizzle with melted white chocolate; let stand until set.

1 COOKIE: 79 cal., 3g fat (1g sat. fat), 2mg chol., 33mg sod., 12g carb. (7g sugars, 0 fiber), 1g pro.

CHERRY CHEWBILEES

This is a good dish to carry to potlucks and parties. It's a hit at home, too—my husband rates it as one of his favorite desserts.
—Debbi Smith, Crossett, AR

PREP: 25 min. • **BAKE:** 30 min. + chilling
MAKES: 20 servings

- 1¼ cups all-purpose flour
- ½ cup packed brown sugar
- ½ cup butter-flavored shortening
- 1 cup chopped walnuts, divided
- ½ cup sweetened shredded coconut

FILLING

- 2 pkg. (8 oz. each) cream cheese, softened
- ⅔ cup sugar
- 2 large eggs, room temperature
- 2 tsp. vanilla extract
- 2 cans (21 oz. each) cherry pie filling

1. Preheat oven to 350°. Line a 13x9-in. baking pan with foil, letting ends extend up sides; grease foil.
2. Combine flour and brown sugar; cut in shortening until fine crumbs form. Stir in ½ cup nuts and coconut. Set aside ½ cup crumb mixture for the topping. Press remaining mixture into prepared pan. Bake until lightly browned, 12-15 minutes.
3. Meanwhile, for filling, beat cream cheese, sugar, eggs and vanilla until smooth. Spread over hot crust. Bake 15 minutes. Spread pie filling on top. Combine remaining nuts and reserved crumb mixture; sprinkle over cherries. Bake 15 minutes more. Cool completely on a wire rack. Chill. Lifting with foil, remove mixture from pan. Cut into bars.

1 PIECE: 251 cal., 14g fat (5g sat. fat), 34mg chol., 54mg sod., 29g carb. (20g sugars, 1g fiber), 4g pro.

READER REVIEW

"Very easy, ingredients I always have on hand, and delicious! I did add extra cream cheese, sugar and egg (1½ times the original amount) to make the cheesecake layer a little thicker...you can never have too much cream cheese! Very pretty."

—DIANNATREMBLY, TASTEOFHOME.COM

CHOCOLATE-DIPPED TRIPLE-GINGER COOKIES

LEMONY LAYER BARS

BANANA OATMEAL COOKIES

To help interest my kids in cooking, I started with this recipe from my childhood. My mom made these oatmeal banana cookies when I was young. Now my children like them as much as I did, and we quadruple the recipe to serve our large family. You can't eat just one of these goodies packed with chocolate morsels.
—*Jacqueline Wilson, Armstrong Creek, WI*

PREP: 10 min. • **BAKE:** 15 min./batch • **MAKES:** 4 dozen

1½ cups all-purpose flour
1 cup sugar
1 tsp. salt
½ tsp. baking soda
½ tsp. ground cinnamon
¼ tsp. ground nutmeg
¾ cup butter, softened
1 large egg, room temperature
1 cup mashed ripe bananas (about 2)
1¾ cups quick-cooking oats
1 cup semisweet chocolate chips
½ cup chopped walnuts

1. Preheat oven to 375°. In a bowl, combine the first 6 ingredients; beat in butter until mixture resembles coarse crumbs. Add egg, bananas and oats; mix well. Stir in chips and nuts.
2. Drop by tablespoonfuls onto greased baking sheets. Bake until golden brown, 13-15 minutes. Cool on wire racks.
1 COOKIE: 97 cal., 5g fat (3g sat. fat), 12mg chol., 87mg sod., 13g carb. (7g sugars, 1g fiber), 1g pro.

LEMONY LAYER BARS

One of my favorite cakes is a white chocolate cake with coconut lemon filling, dark chocolate frosting and almonds. This version of a seven-layer bar combines all those flavors into an easy-to-eat treat. Using soda cracker crumbs makes the bars a little different. If you prefer a more traditional seven-layer bar, graham cracker crumbs can be used instead.
—*Arlene Erlbach, Morton Grove, IL*

PREP: 20 min. • **BAKE:** 25 min. + cooling • **MAKES:** 2 dozen

2 cups crushed unsalted top saltines
½ cup butter, melted
1 cup white baking chips
1 cup sweetened shredded coconut
1 cup coarsely chopped almonds
1 cup (6 oz.) semisweet chocolate chips
1 can (14 oz.) sweetened condensed milk
¼ cup lemon curd
2 Tbsp. grated lemon zest, divided

1. Preheat the oven to 375°. Line a 13x9-in. baking pan with parchment, letting ends extend up sides. In a large bowl, mix cracker crumbs and butter. Press onto bottom of prepared pan. Sprinkle with white chips, coconut, almonds and chocolate chips.
2. In a small bowl, combine milk, lemon curd and 1 Tbsp. zest. Pour over chips. Sprinkle with remaining 1 Tbsp. zest. Bake until edges are golden brown, 25-30 minutes. Cool completely in pan on a wire rack. Lifting with parchment, remove from pan. Cut into bars. Store in an airtight container.
1 BAR: 245 cal., 14g fat (8g sat. fat), 20mg chol., 98mg sod., 27g carb. (21g sugars, 1g fiber), 4g pro.

BANANA OATMEAL COOKIES

FRENCH SILK PIE
PAGE 189

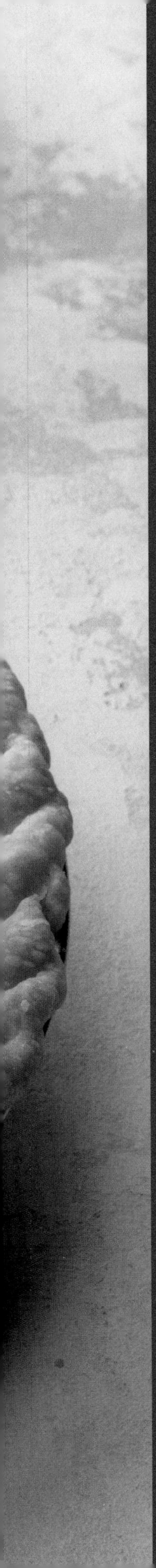

Cakes & Pies

For pretty pink jam cake and playful cupcakes to sun-kissed fruit pies and rich fall-flavored tarts, turn here. The heart-stopping sweets people flip for are tucked inside.

DISHES WE LOVE

UPSIDE-DOWN
STRAWBERRY
SHORTCAKE

UPSIDE-DOWN
STRAWBERRY SHORTCAKE

For a tasty twist, this special shortcake has a berry layer on the bottom. Our family has savored this tempting cake for years.
—*Debra Falkiner, St. Charles, MO*

- -

PREP: 20 min. • **BAKE:** 45 min. • **MAKES:** 15 servings

- 1 cup miniature marshmallows
- 1 pkg. (16 oz.) frozen sweetened sliced strawberries, thawed
- 1 pkg. (3 oz.) strawberry gelatin
- ½ cup shortening
- 1½ cups sugar
- 3 large eggs, room temperature
- 1 tsp. vanilla extract
- 2¼ cups all-purpose flour
- 3 tsp. baking powder
- ½ tsp. salt
- 1 cup 2% milk
  Fresh strawberries and whipped cream

1. Preheat oven 350°. Sprinkle the marshmallows evenly into a greased 13x9-in. baking dish; set aside. In a small bowl, combine strawberries and gelatin powder; set aside.

2. In a large bowl, cream shortening and sugar until light and fluffy, 5-7 minutes. Add eggs, 1 at a time, beating well after each addition. Beat in vanilla. Combine flour, baking powder and salt; add to creamed mixture alternately with milk, beating well after each addition.

3. Pour batter over the marshmallows. Spoon strawberry mixture evenly over batter. Bake until a toothpick inserted in the center comes out clean, 45-50 minutes. Cool 10 minutes before removing from pan to a wire rack to cool completely. Invert onto serving platter (strawberry layer will be on bottom). Garnish with strawberries and whipped cream.

1 PIECE: 288 cal., 8g fat (2g sat. fat), 39mg chol., 214mg sod., 51g carb. (35g sugars, 1g fiber), 4g pro.

SOUTHERN BRULEED PEACH TARTS

This is my creative homage to our beloved southern fresh peach cobbler. It is an upscale presentation with delicious peaches and is very easy to prepare.
—*Mary Louise Lever, Rome, GA*

- -

PREP: 15 min. + standing • **BROIL:** 5 min. • **MAKES:** 12 servings

- 3 medium ripe peaches, peeled and thinly sliced
- 3 Tbsp. peach preserves
- 1 tsp. lemon juice
- ¼ tsp. minced fresh gingerroot
- ¼ tsp. ground cinnamon
- 6 English muffins, split and toasted
- 1 carton (8 oz.) mascarpone cheese
- ⅓ cup packed light brown sugar
  Fresh mint leaves

1. In a large bowl, combine the first 5 ingredients. Let stand for 15 minutes, stirring occasionally. Spread cut sides of English muffins with mascarpone cheese. Drain peaches, reserving liquid. Arrange peaches over muffins; brush with some of the reserved liquid. Place on a foil-lined baking sheet; sprinkle with brown sugar.

2. Broil 3-4 in. from heat for 3-4 minutes or until caramelized and bubbly. Garnish with mint.

NOTE: For an adults-only version, use 1 Tbsp. peach schnapps or Grand Marnier instead of peach preserves.

1 TART: 202 cal., 9g fat (5g sat. fat), 24mg chol., 136mg sod., 27g carb. (13g sugars, 1g fiber), 4g pro.

SOUTHERN BRULEED
PEACH TARTS

**ITALIAN CREAM
CHEESE CAKE**

ITALIAN
CREAM CHEESE CAKE

Buttermilk makes every bite of this
awesome Italian cream cheese cake
moist and flavorful. I rely on this recipe
year-round.
—*Joyce Lutz, Centerview, MO*

- -

PREP: 40 min.
BAKE: 20 min. + cooling
MAKES: 16 servings

- ½ cup butter, softened
- ½ cup shortening
- 2 cups sugar
- 5 large eggs, separated, room temperature
- 1 tsp. vanilla extract
- 2 cups all-purpose flour
- 1 tsp. baking soda
- 1 cup buttermilk
- 1½ cups sweetened shredded coconut
- 1 cup chopped pecans

CREAM CHEESE FROSTING

- 11 oz. cream cheese, softened
- ¾ cup butter, softened
- 6 cups confectioners' sugar
- 1½ tsp. vanilla extract
- ¾ cup chopped pecans

1. Preheat oven to 350°. Grease and flour
three 9-in. round baking pans. In a large
bowl, cream butter, shortening and sugar
until light and fluffy, 5-7 minutes. Beat in
egg yolks and vanilla. Combine flour and
baking soda; add to creamed mixture
alternately with buttermilk. Beat until just
combined. Stir in coconut and pecans.
2. In another bowl, beat egg whites with
clean beaters until stiff but not dry. Fold
a fourth of the egg whites into batter, then
fold in the remaining whites. Pour into
prepared pans.
3. Bake until a toothpick inserted in center
comes out clean, 20-25 minutes. Cool for
10 minutes before removing from pans to
wire racks to cool completely.
4. For frosting, beat cream cheese and
butter until smooth. Beat in confectioners'
sugar and vanilla until fluffy. Stir in the
pecans. Spread the frosting between
layers and over top and sides of cake.
Refrigerate.
1 PIECE: 736 cal., 41g fat (19g sat. fat),
117mg chol., 330mg sod., 90g carb.
(75g sugars, 2g fiber), 7g pro.

HOW-TO

Fold in Egg Whites

After beating egg whites to stiff
peaks, add a fourth of whites to
batter and gently fold in. Add
remaining whites. With a spatula, lift
batter and fold it over the egg whites,
gently incorporating them. Turn the
bowl a bit and continue folding until
few to no white streaks remain.

CLASSIC LEMON
MERINGUE PIE

CLASSIC LEMON MERINGUE PIE

Love lemon meringue pie? This is the
only recipe you'll ever need. The flaky,
tender, made-from-scratch crust is
worth the effort.
—*Lee Bremson, Kansas City, MO*

- -

PREP: 30 min. + standing
BAKE: 25 min. + chilling
MAKES: 8 servings

- 1⅓ cups all-purpose flour
- ½ tsp. salt
- ½ cup shortening
- 1 to 3 Tbsp. cold water

FILLING

- 1¼ cups sugar
- ¼ cup cornstarch
- 3 Tbsp. all-purpose flour
- ¼ tsp. salt
- 1½ cups water
- 3 large egg yolks, lightly beaten
- 2 Tbsp. butter
- 1½ tsp. grated lemon zest
- ⅓ cup lemon juice

MERINGUE

- 4 large egg whites
- ½ cup sugar, divided
- 1 Tbsp. cornstarch
- ½ cup cold water
- ¾ tsp. vanilla extract

1. In a small bowl, combine flour and salt;
cut in shortening until crumbly. Gradually
add 3 Tbsp. cold water, tossing with a fork
until dough forms a ball.

2. Roll out dough to fit a 9-in. pie plate.
Transfer crust to pie plate. Trim to ½ in.
beyond rim of plate; flute edge. Bake at
425° for 12-15 minutes or until lightly
browned.

3. Meanwhile, in a large saucepan,
combine the sugar, cornstarch, flour and
salt. Gradually stir in water until smooth.
Cook and stir over medium-high heat until
thickened and bubbly. Reduce heat; cook
and stir 2 minutes longer.

4. Remove from the heat. Stir a small
amount of hot filling into egg yolks; return
all to the pan, stirring constantly. Bring to
a gentle boil; cook and stir 2 minutes
longer. Remove from the heat. Gently stir

in butter and lemon zest. Gradually stir in
lemon juice just until combined. Pour into
the crust.

5. Place egg whites in a large bowl;
let stand at room temperature for
30 minutes. For meringue, in a saucepan,
combine 2 Tbsp. sugar and cornstarch.
Gradually stir in cold water. Cook and stir
over medium heat until mixture is clear.
Transfer to a bowl; cool.

6. Beat egg whites and vanilla until soft
peaks form. Gradually beat in remaining
sugar, 1 Tbsp. at a time. Beat in cornstarch
mixture on high until stiff peaks form and
sugar is dissolved (meringue will not be
smooth). Spread evenly over hot filling,
sealing edge to crust.

7. Bake pie at 350° for 25 minutes or until
the meringue is golden brown. Cool on a
wire rack for 1 hour. Refrigerate for at
least 3 hours before serving.

1 PIECE: 444 cal., 17g fat (5g sat. fat),
87mg chol., 282mg sod., 68g carb.
(43g sugars, 1g fiber), 5g pro.

FRENCH SILK PIE

(PICTURED ON PAGE 184)

I first prepared French silk pie when I was in high school. Years later, I experimented with the recipe until I was happy with it. Now it's one of my husband's favorites.
—*Lisa Francis, Elba, AL*

PREP: 40 min. • **COOK:** 10 min. + chilling
MAKES: 6 servings

- 1   sheet refrigerated pie crust
- ⅔   cup sugar
- 2   large eggs
- 2   oz. unsweetened chocolate, melted
- 1   tsp. vanilla extract
- ⅓   cup butter, softened
- ⅔   cup heavy whipping cream
- 2   tsp. confectioners' sugar
      Optional: Whipped cream and chocolate curls

1. Cut pie crust in half. Repackage and refrigerate 1 half for another use. On a lightly floured surface, roll out remaining half into an 8-in. circle. Transfer to a 7-in. pie plate; flute edge.

2. Line crust with a double thickness of heavy-duty foil. Bake crust at 450° for 4 minutes. Remove foil; bake until crust is golden brown, about 2 minutes longer. Cool on a wire rack.

3. In a small saucepan, combine sugar and eggs until well blended. Cook over low heat, stirring constantly, until mixture reaches 160° and coats the back of a metal spoon. Remove from the heat. Stir in chocolate and vanilla until smooth. Cool to lukewarm (90°), stirring occasionally.

4. In a small bowl, cream butter until light and fluffy, 3-4 minutes. Add the cooled chocolate mixture; beat on high speed until light and fluffy, about 5 minutes.

5. In another large bowl, beat cream until it begins to thicken. Add confectioners' sugar; beat until stiff peaks form. Fold into chocolate mixture.

6. Pour into crust. Chill at least 6 hours before serving. Garnish with whipped cream and chocolate curls if desired. Refrigerate leftovers.

1 PIECE: 450 cal., 33g fat (19g sat. fat), 139mg chol., 223mg sod., 38g carb. (24g sugars, 1g fiber), 5g pro.

VEGAN VANILLA CUPCAKES

We love using this simple vegan vanilla cupcake recipe as a base to layer on extra flavor. Stir in grated orange zest and chopped pecans, vegan chocolate chips and cinnamon, or your own favorite mix-ins.
—*Taste of Home* Test Kitchen

PREP: 20 min. • **BAKE:** 15 min. + cooling
MAKES: 2 dozen

- 2½   cups all-purpose flour
- 2   tsp. baking powder
- ½   tsp. baking soda
- ¼   tsp. salt
- 1¾   cups refrigerated unsweetened coconut milk
- 1½   cups sugar
- ⅓   cup canola oil
- 2   Tbsp. cider vinegar
- 1   tsp. vanilla extract

FROSTING
- 1   cup dairy-free margarine, softened
- 3   cups confectioners' sugar
- 2   tsp. vanilla extract

1. Preheat oven to 350°. In a large bowl, whisk flour, baking powder, baking soda and salt. In a small bowl, whisk coconut milk, sugar, oil, vinegar and vanilla. Stir into dry ingredients just until moistened.

2. Fill paper-lined muffin cups half full. Bake until a toothpick inserted in the center comes out clean, 15-20 minutes. Cool 10 minutes before removing from pans to wire racks to cool completely.

3. For frosting, in a large bowl, beat margarine until light and fluffy. Beat in confectioners' sugar and vanilla. Frost the cupcakes.

1 CUPCAKE: 255 cal., 11g fat (2g sat. fat), 0 chol., 180mg sod., 38g carb. (27g sugars, 0 fiber), 1g pro.

TEST KITCHEN TIPS

- To make vegan cupcakes, you will need to find substitutes for butter and milk. For this recipe, we used dairy-free margarine for the frosting instead of butter and coconut milk instead of traditional milk, butter or eggs.

- Vegan cupcakes do not need to be refrigerated. You can if you'd like, but you can also store them at room temperature. Both will keep for up to 3 days in an airtight container.

VEGAN VANILLA CUPCAKES

PERFECT PLUM
& PEACH PIE

🍎 PERFECT PLUM & PEACH PIE

I created this recipe for in-season summer fruit. The plums give the pie a splash of color as well as flavor, and the crumb topping is both easy and excellent!
—*Rachel Johnson, Shippensburg, PA*

- -

PREP: 25 min. • **BAKE:** 40 min. + cooling • **MAKES:** 8 servings

   1   sheet refrigerated pie crust
FILLING
   6   medium peaches, peeled and sliced
   6   medium black plums, sliced
   ½   cup all-purpose flour
   ½   cup confectioners' sugar
   ½   tsp. ground cinnamon
   ½   tsp. ground nutmeg
TOPPING
   ¼   cup all-purpose flour
   ¼   cup packed brown sugar
   2   Tbsp. butter, softened
   ¼   tsp. ground cinnamon

1. Preheat oven to 375°. Unroll the crust onto a lightly floured surface; roll into a 12-in. circle. Transfer to a 9-in. deep-dish pie plate; trim and flute edge. Refrigerate while preparing filling.
2. Toss peaches and plums with flour, sugar and spices; transfer to crust. Using a fork, mix topping ingredients until crumbly; sprinkle over fruit.
3. Bake on a lower oven rack until golden brown and bubbly, 40-50 minutes. Cool on a wire rack.
1 PIECE: 311 cal., 10g fat (5g sat. fat), 13mg chol., 125mg sod., 53g carb. (29g sugars, 3g fiber), 4g pro.

PIECAKEN

Why fight over whether cake or pie is better when you can combine the two into one amazing dessert?
—*James Schend, Pleasant Prairie, WI*

- -

PREP: 45 min. + chilling • **BAKE:** 55 min. + cooling
MAKES: 16 servings

   1   pkg. spice cake mix (regular size)
   1   pre-baked pumpkin pie (8 in.)
   1   pkg. chocolate cake mix (regular size)
   1   pre-baked pecan pie (8 in.)
   2   cans (16 oz. each) vanilla frosting
       Optional: Chopped pecans and ground cinnamon

1. Preheat oven to 350°. Line bottoms of 2 greased 9-in. round baking pans with parchment; grease paper. Grease 12 muffin cups.
2. Prepare spice cake mix batter according to package directions. Transfer 1½ cups batter to 1 of the prepared pans. Remove pumpkin pie from pan; place upside down on top of batter. Top with 2½ cups additional batter; tap pan on counter to remove any air bubbles (batter should not completely fill pan). Pour remaining batter into 6 muffin cups.
3. Prepare chocolate cake mix batter according to package directions. Transfer 1½ cups batter to remaining prepared pan. Remove pecan pie from pan; place upside down on top of batter. Top with 2½ cups additional batter; tap pan on counter to remove any air bubbles (batter should not completely fill pan). Pour remaining batter into 6 muffin cups.
4. Bake cupcakes according to package directions, and cake layers until cakes start to pull away from edges of pans and tops are completely set, 50-60 minutes. Cool in pans 1 hour before removing to wire racks; remove paper. Cool completely.
5. If cake layers have rounded tops, trim with a serrated knife to make level. Place 1 cake layer, bottom side up, on a serving plate; spread with 1 cup frosting. Top with remaining cake layer. Frost top and side of cake with remaining frosting. If desired, press chopped pecans onto side of cake and sprinkle ground cinnamon on top of cake. Decorate cupcakes as desired. Refrigerate, covered, at least 1 hour. Refrigerate leftovers.
NOTE: Pies from the freezer section of the grocery store will not work for this recipe; use pre-baked pies from the bakery section.
1 PIECE: 839 cal., 35g fat (9g sat. fat), 98mg chol., 759mg sod., 123g carb. (75g sugars, 2g fiber), 8g pro.

READER REVIEW

"I was floored that this worked! I made it for my brother-in-law's birthday. He loves to bake, and I wanted to make something unconventional. Not only did it come out perfect, it was delicious and my nephew who is usually skeptical of out-of-the-box creations thought it was top-notch. Truly impressive."

—PEAPOD0114, TASTEOFHOME.COM

PIECAKEN

SWEET & PUCKERY CUPCAKES

If you love the pucker of sour candies, then these cupcakes will be right up your alley. The sour dust sprinkled on top of the frosting gives you an instant pucker when you take a bite, but the sweetness soon follows.
—Elizabeth Bramkamp, Gig Harbor, WA

PREP: 30 min. • BAKE: 20 min. + cooling • MAKES: 2 dozen

- 1   pkg. lemon cake mix (regular size)
- ½   cup lemon-lime soda
- ½   cup lemon juice
- 3   large eggs, room temperature
- ¼   cup canola oil
- 1   pkg. (3 oz.) orange or lemon gelatin
- 2   drops lemon oil, optional

FROSTING
- 2   cups butter, softened
- 6   cups confectioners' sugar
- 1   pkg. (3 oz.) orange or lemon gelatin
- 5   to 6 Tbsp. lemon juice
- 1   cup orange colored sugar, optional
- 1   Tbsp. citric acid, optional

1. Preheat oven to 350°. Line 24 muffin cups with paper liners. In a large bowl, combine cake mix, soda, lemon juice, eggs, oil, gelatin and, if desired, lemon oil; beat on low speed 30 seconds. Beat on medium speed 2 minutes. Transfer to prepared pans. Bake for 18-21 minutes or until a toothpick inserted in center comes out clean. Cool in pans 10 minutes before removing to wire racks to cool completely.
2. For frosting, in a large bowl, combine butter, confectioners' sugar, gelatin and lemon juice; beat until smooth. Frost cupcakes. If desired, in a small bowl, stir together sugar and citric acid; dip cupcakes into sugar mix. Store in the refrigerator.
1 CUPCAKE: 384 cal., 19g fat (11g sat. fat), 64mg chol., 293mg sod., 54g carb. (45g sugars, 0 fiber), 2g pro.

PEANUT-CASHEW
MARSHMALLOW PIE

PEANUT-CASHEW MARSHMALLOW PIE

This pie appeals to kids and adults alike! The chocolate crust and caramel topping make it all the more special. I like the nice contrast of the creamy marshmallow filling with the crunchy peanuts. An added bonus is that it can be made ahead of time.
—Lisa Varner, El Paso, TX

PREP: 20 min. + chilling • COOK: 5 min. MAKES: 8 servings

- 4   cups miniature marshmallows
- 1   cup 2% milk
- 1   Tbsp. butter
- 2   tsp. vanilla extract
- 1   cup cold heavy whipping cream
- ½   cup lightly salted dry-roasted peanuts, coarsely chopped
- ½   cup salted cashews, coarsely chopped
- 1   chocolate crumb crust (9 in.)
- ¼   cup hot caramel ice cream topping
- 2   Tbsp. chocolate syrup, optional

1. In a large saucepan, combine marshmallows and milk over medium heat, stirring often, until marshmallows are melted and mixture is smooth. Remove from heat. Transfer mixture to a bowl; stir in butter and vanilla. Place bowl in a pan of ice water. Gently stir until the mixture is cool and begins to thicken, about 5 minutes.
2. In a large bowl, whip heavy cream at high speed until soft peaks form. Gently fold whipped cream into marshmallow mixture. In a small bowl, mix together peanuts and cashews; reserve ¼ cup for topping. Fold remaining nut mixture into marshmallow mixture. Spoon marshmallow mixture into prepared crumb crust. Sprinkle reserved ¼ cup nuts over top. Refrigerate, covered, at least 6 hours or overnight. Drizzle with caramel topping and, if desired, chocolate syrup before serving.
1 PIECE: 441 cal., 26g fat (11g sat. fat), 40mg chol., 259mg sod., 47g carb. (30g sugars, 2g fiber), 7g pro.

SWEET &
PUCKERY
CUPCAKES

STRAWBERRY JAM CAKE

When I need a cake for a special occasion, this is my go-to recipe because everyone is crazy about it. Every year I make it for a cake raffle we have at work for Relay for Life. It has raised a lot of money for a very good cause.

—Tammy Urbina, Warner Robins, GA

- -

PREP: 35 min. • **BAKE:** 25 min. + cooling
MAKES: 12 servings

- 1 cup butter, softened
- 1¾ cups sugar
- 5 large egg whites, room temperature
- 2 cups pureed strawberries
- ½ cup sour cream
- 1 tsp. strawberry extract, optional
- 3 cups cake flour
- 2½ tsp. baking powder
- ¼ tsp. baking soda
- ¼ tsp. salt

FROSTING

- 1 pkg. (8 oz.) cream cheese, softened
- ¼ cup butter, softened
- 6 cups confectioners' sugar
- ¼ cup pureed strawberries
- ½ tsp. strawberry extract, optional
- 1 to 3 drops red food coloring, optional
- ½ cup seedless strawberry jam, divided

Halved or sliced fresh strawberries, optional

1. Preheat oven to 350°. Grease and flour three 9-in. round baking pans.
2. In a large bowl, cream butter and sugar until light and fluffy, 5-7 minutes. Add egg whites, 1 at a time, beating well after each addition. Beat in the strawberries, sour cream and, if desired, extract. Combine the flour, baking powder, baking soda and salt; add to the creamed mixture. Transfer batter to prepared pans.
3. Bake until a toothpick inserted in the center comes out clean, 22-26 minutes. Cool for 10 minutes before removing from pans to wire racks to cool completely.
4. For frosting, in a large bowl, beat cream cheese and butter until fluffy. Add the confectioners' sugar, strawberries and, if desired, the extract and red food coloring; beat until smooth.
5. Place bottom cake layer on a serving plate; top with ¼ cup jam and ½ cup frosting. Repeat layers. Top with the remaining cake layer. Spread remaining frosting over top and side of the cake. Garnish with strawberries if desired.
1 PIECE: 783 cal., 28g fat (17g sat. fat), 72mg chol., 416mg sod., 130g carb. (99g sugars, 1g fiber), 6g pro.

SLOW-COOKER MIXED FRUIT & PISTACHIO CAKE

This cake is so easy to make on a lazy day and a guaranteed-delicious dessert for several days, if you can make it last that long. It's just wonderful for chilly fall days and the holiday season.

—Nancy Heishman, Las Vegas, NV

- -

PREP: 20 min. • **COOK:** 2½ hours + cooling
MAKES: 8 servings

- 1½ cups all-purpose flour
- 1½ tsp. ground cinnamon
- ½ tsp. baking soda
- ½ tsp. baking powder
- ½ tsp. ground allspice
- ¼ tsp. salt
- 1 can (8 oz.) jellied cranberry sauce
- ⅓ cup packed brown sugar
- ⅓ cup buttermilk
- ¼ cup butter, melted
- 2 tsp. grated orange zest
- ½ tsp. orange extract
- 1 large egg, room temperature
- 1 cup mixed dried fruit bits
- 1 cup pistachios
  Sweetened whipped cream, optional

1. In a large bowl, whisk together the first 6 ingredients. In another bowl, combine the next 7 ingredients. Add cranberry mixture to flour mixture; stir until smooth. Add dried fruit and pistachios.
2. Pour batter into a greased 1½-qt. baking dish; place in a 6-qt. slow cooker. Lay a 14x12-in. piece of parchment over top of slow cooker under the lid. Cook, covered, on high until a toothpick inserted in the center comes out clean, about 2½ hours. Remove dish from the slow cooker to a wire rack. Cool 30 minutes before inverting onto a serving platter.
3. Cut into wedges with a serrated knife; if desired, serve with whipped cream.
1 PIECE: 375 cal., 14g fat (5g sat. fat), 39mg chol., 349mg sod., 57g carb. (30g sugars, 4g fiber), 7g pro.

STRAWBERRY JAM CAKE

BANANA-NUT
BUNDT CAKE

BANANA-NUT BUNDT CAKE

Each slice of this luscious cake has a temptingly tropical twist.
—*June Yeates, Bradley, IL*

PREP: 15 min. • **BAKE:** 1 hour + cooling
MAKES: 16 servings

- 3 cups all-purpose flour
- 2 cups sugar
- 1 tsp. baking soda
- 1 tsp. ground cinnamon
- 3 large eggs, room temperature, beaten
- 1 cup canola oil
- 2 cups finely chopped ripe bananas (about 3 medium)
- 1 can (8 oz.) crushed pineapple, undrained
- 1½ tsp. vanilla extract
- ½ cup sweetened shredded coconut
- 1 cup chopped nuts
  Optional: Confectioners' sugar, whipped cream and sliced ripe banana

1. In a large bowl, combine the flour, sugar, baking soda and cinnamon. In another bowl, combine the eggs, oil, bananas, pineapple and vanilla; stir into the dry ingredients just until combined. Fold in coconut and nuts. Pour into a greased 10-in. fluted tube pan.

2. Bake at 350° for 60-70 minutes or until a toothpick inserted in the center comes out clean. Cool for 10 minutes before removing cake from pan to a wire rack to cool completely. If desired, serve with confectioners' sugar, whipped cream and bananas.

1 PIECE: 408 cal., 20g fat (3g sat. fat), 40mg chol., 99mg sod., 53g carb. (32g sugars, 2g fiber), 6g pro.

READER REVIEW

"It turned out great. My first Bundt cake ever. I improvised and made a coffee cinnamon glaze to go over it: 1 cup powdered sugar, 1 tsp. vanilla, 1 tsp. cinnamon, 1 tsp. instant coffee powder, and milk 1 tsp. at a time until the right consistency."

—MAMATURTLEMILLER, TASTEOFHOME.COM

REDMOND PEAR CREME TART

REDMOND PEAR CREME TART

This stunning recipe was inspired by my California hometown and trips to the grocery store with my mom.
—*Sahana Vij, Redmond, CA*

PREP: 20 min. • **BAKE:** 10 min. + chilling
MAKES: 12 servings

- 12 whole graham crackers
- 6 Tbsp. butter, melted
PASTRY CREME FILLING
- ⅓ cup sugar
- ¼ cup cornstarch
  Pinch salt
- 1¾ cups whole milk
- 4 large egg yolks
- 1 Tbsp. butter
- 1½ tsp. vanilla extract
- 4 pears, thinly sliced

1. Preheat the oven to 350°. In a food processor, pulse graham crackers until coarsely crumbled. Transfer to a large bowl; stir in melted butter. Press mixture onto bottom of a 9-in. springform pan or onto bottom and up the side of a 9-in. tart pan. Bake for 8-10 minutes or until crust starts to brown.

2. For filling, in a small bowl, combine sugar, cornstarch and salt. In another bowl, whisk milk and yolks. In a saucepan, melt butter over medium-high heat; stir in sugar mixture and then milk mixture. Cook and stir over medium heat until thickened and bubbly. Reduce heat to low; cook and stir 2 minutes longer. Remove from heat; whisk in vanilla. Let stand in pan for 15 minutes.

3. Spread filling over the crust (filling will be thick). Refrigerate until chilled, about 1 hour. Arrange pear slices around the outside edge, continuing to the center. Serve tart immediately. Refrigerate the leftovers.

1 PIECE: 231 cal., 11g fat (6g sat. fat), 83mg chol., 179mg sod., 31g carb. (17g sugars, 2g fiber), 3g pro.

APPLE RED-HOT SLAB PIE

This dessert is my family's absolute favorite because it holds so many memories for us. Red Hots give the filling a color that makes it an instant hit at parties.
—*Linda Morten, Somerville, TX*

PREP: 45 min. + chilling • **BAKE:** 50 min.
MAKES: 24 servings

- 5 cups all-purpose flour
- 2 Tbsp. sugar
- 2 tsp. salt
- 2 cups cold butter, cubed
- 1 to 1¼ cups ice water

FILLING
- ⅔ cup sugar
- ⅔ cup all-purpose flour
- ½ tsp. salt
- 6 cups thinly sliced peeled Granny Smith apples (about 6 medium)
- 6 cups thinly sliced peeled Gala or Jonathan apples (about 6 medium)
- 1 cup Red Hots
- ¼ cup cold butter
    Vanilla ice cream, optional

1. In a large bowl, mix flour, sugar and salt; cut in butter until crumbly. Gradually add ice water, tossing with a fork until dough holds together when pressed. Divide the dough into 2 portions so that 1 portion is slightly larger than the other. Shape each into a rectangle; cover and refrigerate for 1 hour or overnight.
2. Preheat oven to 375°. For filling, in a large bowl, mix sugar, flour and salt. Add apples and Red Hots; toss to coat.
3. On a lightly floured surface, roll out larger portion of dough into an 18x13-in. rectangle. Transfer to an ungreased 15x10x1-in. baking pan. Press onto the bottom and up the sides of pan. Add filling; dot with butter.
4. Roll out remaining dough; place over filling. Fold bottom crust over edge of top crust; seal and flute or press with a fork to seal. Prick top with a fork.
5. Bake 50-55 minutes or until golden brown and filling is bubbly. Cool on a wire rack. Serve warm. If desired, top with ice cream.

1 PIECE: 349 cal., 18g fat (11g sat. fat), 46mg chol., 383mg sod., 45g carb. (19g sugars, 2g fiber), 3g pro.

FLOURLESS OLIVE OIL CHOCOLATE CAKE

FLOURLESS OLIVE OIL CHOCOLATE CAKE

This flourless chocolate cake is baked with olive oil to create a rich and savory flavor. Top with ice cream, confectioners' sugar or anything sweet to balance out the deep chocolaty flavor.
—*Jenna Barnard, Gilbert, AZ*

PREP: 25 min. • **BAKE:** 25 min. + cooling
MAKES: 8 servings

- 6 large eggs, separated
- 8 oz. bittersweet chocolate, chopped
- ½ cup extra virgin olive oil
- 1 Tbsp. vanilla extract
- 1½ tsp. instant espresso powder
- 1 cup sugar, divided
    Confectioners' sugar
    Optional: Vanilla ice cream, mixed fresh berries and whipped cream

1. Preheat oven to 350°. Coat bottom of a 9-in. springform pan with cooking spray. Top with a sheet of parchment; secure springform ring on top and lock in place. Place egg whites in a clean bowl; let stand while melting chocolate.
2. In top of a double boiler or a metal bowl over simmering water, stir chocolate and oil until smooth. Remove from heat; stir in vanilla and espresso powder. Set aside.

3. Beat egg whites on high speed until soft peaks form. Slowly add ½ cup sugar while beating; beat until stiff peaks. Beat the remaining ½ cup sugar into chocolate mixture. Add the yolks, 1 at a time, until combined. Add a fourth of the egg whites to the chocolate; mix until fully combined. Add the remaining egg whites; gently fold to combine. Transfer batter to prepared pan. Bake 25-30 minutes or until puffed and set. Let cool 10 minutes before serving. Dust with confectioners' sugar; serve with toppings as desired

1 PIECE: 438 cal., 27g fat (9g sat. fat), 140mg chol., 54mg sod., 30g carb. (28g sugars, 1g fiber), 7g pro.

TEST KITCHEN TIP

No springform pan? No problem! This cake can easily be made in a 9-in. round cake pan. Grease the pan, then line the bottom with a round piece of parchment. Grease the parchment, too.

After baking, let the cake cool for 30 minutes. Place a cooling rack on top of the cake, then invert so the rack is on the bottom. Gently lift pan off the cake. Peel away the parchment, then flip the cake onto a serving plate.

PUMPKIN CHOCOLATE TART WITH CINNAMON WHIPPED CREAM

This recipe is a personal favorite. I love the (underappreciated) combination of pumpkin and chocolate. This tart has a chocolate cookie crust, but you can substitute a different cookie for the crust if you'd like. Gingersnaps would be lovely, as would vanilla wafers flavored with cinnamon.

—Jessie Sheehan, Brooklyn, NY

PREP: 40 min. + chilling
BAKE: 30 min. + cooling
MAKES: 12 servings

FOR THE CRUST
- 6 oz. chocolate wafers
- 1 Tbsp. sugar
- 5 Tbsp. unsalted butter, melted

FOR THE FILLING
- 1 cup heavy whipping cream
- 2 large eggs
- 1½ tsp. vanilla extract
- 1¼ cups canned pumpkin
- ⅓ cup packed light brown sugar
- 3 Tbsp. sugar
- ½ tsp. kosher salt
- ½ tsp. ground ginger
- ½ tsp. ground cinnamon
- ¼ tsp. ground nutmeg

FOR THE CHOCOLATE DRIZZLE
- 2 oz. dark baking chocolate, melted

FOR THE CINNAMON WHIPPED CREAM
- 1½ cups heavy whipping cream
- ¼ cup confectioners' sugar
- ½ tsp. vanilla extract
- ¼ tsp. ground cinnamon

1. For the crust, place wafers and sugar in a food processor; process until finely ground. Add melted butter; process until combined. Press crumbs onto the bottom and up side of an ungreased 9-in. tart pan. Freeze for 30 minutes.

2. Preheat oven to 350°. Bake crust until dry, 8-10 minutes, rotating once halfway through baking. Cool on a wire rack.

3. Meanwhile, for the filling, in a large bowl, whisk cream, eggs and vanilla until combined. In a medium saucepan, combine pumpkin, sugars, salt and spices. Cook and stir with a wooden spoon over medium heat until bubbly. Cook and stir mixture 5 minutes longer.

4. Whisk a small amount of hot mixture into egg mixture; return all to pan, whisking constantly. Remove from heat; pour into prepared crust. Place tart pan on a rimmed baking sheet. Bake until center is just set and top appears dull, 30-35 minutes. Cool completely on a wire rack. Refrigerate, covered, at least 4 hours or overnight.

5. Drizzle melted chocolate over tart; let stand until set. For the whipped cream, in a large bowl, beat cream, confectioners' sugar, vanilla and cinnamon until soft peaks form. Serve with tart.

1 PIECE: 370 cal., 27g fat (16g sat. fat), 101mg chol., 191mg sod., 30g carb. (22g sugars, 2g fiber), 4g pro.

PUMPKIN CHOCOLATE TART WITH CINNAMON WHIPPED CREAM

RASPBERRY MATCHA CAKE ROLL

RASPBERRY MATCHA CAKE ROLL

This tender cake roll with whipped cream has a very light texture and is perfect for spring. The raspberries give the whipped cream filling a pretty pale pink color. Strawberries could also be used instead of raspberries.
—*Kaori Shinohara, Paramus, NJ*

PREP: 25 min. + cooling
BAKE: 10 min. + chilling
MAKES: 8 servings

½ cup cake flour
1 Tbsp. matcha (green tea powder)
3 large eggs, separated, room temperature
5 Tbsp. sugar, divided
¼ cup 2% milk
1 Tbsp. avocado or canola oil
½ tsp. vanilla extract
    Confectioners' sugar
FILLING
¾ cup fresh raspberries
2 Tbsp. sugar, divided
⅔ cup heavy whipping cream

1. Preheat oven to 350°. Line bottom of a greased 15x10x1-in. cake pan with parchment. Sift cake flour and matcha powder together twice.
2. In another large bowl, beat egg yolks and 1 Tbsp. sugar until slightly thickened. Beat on high speed until thick and lemon-colored. Beat in milk, oil and vanilla. Fold in flour mixture.
3. Place egg whites in a small bowl. With clean beaters, beat on medium until soft peaks form. Gradually add remaining 4 Tbsp. sugar, 1 Tbsp. at a time, beating on high after each addition until sugar is dissolved. Continue beating until soft glossy peaks form. Fold a fourth of the whites into batter, then fold in the remaining whites. Transfer to prepared pan, spreading evenly.
4. Bake 10-12 minutes or until top springs back when lightly touched. Cool 5 minutes. Invert onto a tea towel dusted with confectioners' sugar. Gently peel off paper. Roll up cake in the towel jelly-roll style, starting with a short side. Cool completely on a wire rack.
5. For filling, in a small bowl, mash raspberries with 1 Tbsp. sugar. Press through a fine-mesh strainer into another bowl; discard seeds. In a large bowl, beat cream until it begins to thicken. Add remaining 1 Tbsp. sugar; beat until stiff peaks form. Gently fold in 2 Tbsp. raspberry puree.
6. Unroll cake; spread filling over cake to within ½ in. of edges. Roll up again, without towel; trim ends. Place on a platter, seam side down. Refrigerate, covered, at least 30 minutes before serving. Serve with remaining raspberry puree. If desired, garnish with additional whipped cream and raspberries.
1 PIECE: 194 cal., 11g fat (6g sat. fat), 93mg chol., 36mg sod., 19g carb. (12g sugars, 0 fiber), 5g pro.

STRAWBERRY PRETZEL CAKE

STRAWBERRY PRETZEL CAKE

This cake has everything: sweet, salty, tangy, creamy and crunchy.
—*Arley Bell, Richmond, VA*

PREP: 1 hour + chilling
BAKE: 25 min. + cooling
MAKES: 16 servings

- 1 pkg. (16 oz.) pretzels
- 1 cup cake flour
- 2 tsp. baking powder
- 1 tsp. baking soda
- ½ tsp. salt
- 4 large eggs, room temperature
- 2 tsp. vanilla extract
- 1½ cups unsalted butter, softened
- 2½ cups sugar
- 1½ cups buttermilk

STRAWBERRY FILLING
- 1½ lbs. fresh strawberries, chopped
- ⅔ cup sugar
- 1½ tsp. vanilla extract

CREAM CHEESE FROSTING
- 2 cups butter, softened
- 1 pkg. (8 oz.) cream cheese, softened
- 2 tsp. vanilla extract
- 6 cups confectioners' sugar
- ½ tsp. salt

1. Preheat oven to 350°. Line bottoms of 3 greased 9-in. round baking pans with parchment; grease paper.
2. In a food processor, process pretzels until finely ground to the consistency of flour. Set aside 3 cups (save remaining for another use). In a large bowl, combine ground pretzels, flour, baking powder, baking soda and salt. In a large bowl, cream butter and sugar until light and fluffy, 5-7 minutes. Add the eggs, 1 at a time, beating well after each addition. Add vanilla; beat to combine. Add the pretzel mixture alternately with the buttermilk, beating after each addition just until combined.
3. Transfer to prepared pans. Bake until a toothpick inserted in center comes out clean, 25-30 minutes, rotating halfway through. Cool 10 minutes before removing to wire racks to cool completely.
4. To prepare filling, in a bowl, combine strawberries, sugar and vanilla. Let stand 20 minutes, stirring occasionally.
5. To prepare frosting, in a large bowl, beat butter, cream cheese and vanilla until blended. Gradually beat in confectioners' sugar and salt until light and fluffy, about 5 minutes.
6. To assemble, drain the strawberries, reserving ½ cup for topping. Place bottom cake layer on a serving plate. Spread with ½ cup frosting; spread half the strawberry mixture to within 1-in. of edge. Repeat layers. Top with the remaining cake layer. Spread a thin layer of frosting over top and sides of cake; chill 15 minutes. Spread remaining frosting over top and sides of cake. Top with reserved strawberries. Refrigerate leftovers.

1 PIECE: 892 cal., 47g fat (29g sat. fat), 169mg chol., 764mg sod., 115g carb. (89g sugars, 2g fiber), 7g pro.

CHOCOLATE-GLAZED CUPCAKES

Because I have a dairy allergy, I'm always on the search for treats I can eat. I prepare these cupcakes with dairy-free chocolate chips and vanilla coconut milk instead of cream.
—*Kirstin Turner, Richlands, NC*

PREP: 25 min. • **BAKE:** 15 min. + cooling
MAKES: 16 cupcakes

- 1½ cups all-purpose flour
- ¾ cup sugar
- ⅓ cup baking cocoa
- 1 tsp. baking soda
- ¾ tsp. salt
- 1 cup water
- ¼ cup unsweetened applesauce
- ¼ cup canola oil
- 1 Tbsp. white vinegar
- 1 tsp. vanilla extract
- ⅔ cup semisweet chocolate chips, optional

GLAZE
- ½ cup semisweet chocolate chips
- ¼ cup half-and-half cream
  Nonpareils, optional

1. Preheat oven to 350°. Line 16 muffin cups with foil liners.
2. In a large bowl, whisk the first 5 ingredients. In another bowl, whisk water, applesauce, oil, vinegar and vanilla until blended. Add to flour mixture; stir just until moistened. If desired, stir in chocolate chips.
3. Fill prepared muffin cups three-fourths full. Bake for 14-16 minutes or until a toothpick inserted in center comes out clean. Cool 5 minutes before removing from pans to wire racks; cool completely.
4. For glaze, in a small saucepan, combine chocolate chips and cream; cook and stir over low heat 3-5 minutes or until smooth. Remove from heat. Cool the mixture at room temperature until glaze is slightly thickened, stirring occasionally, about 30 minutes. Dip tops of cupcakes into glaze. If desired, sprinkle with nonpareils.

1 CUPCAKE: 148 cal., 6g fat (1g sat. fat), 2mg chol., 192mg sod., 23g carb. (13g sugars, 1g fiber), 2g pro.

CHOCOLATE-GLAZED
RASPBERRY ECLAIRS
PAGE 212

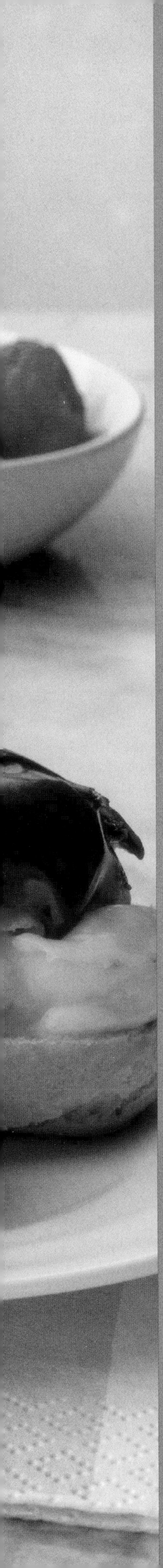

Just Desserts

Rich and decadent or light and refreshing, slow-cooked or no-bake, quick and easy or a pull-out-the-stops extravaganza—this chapter offers up every kind of sweet delight.

BEST OF THE BEST DISHES

TROPICAL COMPOTE DESSERT

FRESH PLUM KUCHEN

I love this stunning cake with apples and pears in autumn, but each year, I secretly can't wait for summer to roll back around so I can pull out the plums. They're the perfect topping for this centerpiece-worthy dessert.
—*Anna Daley, Montague, PE*

PREP: 20 min. • **BAKE:** 40 min. + cooling • **MAKES:** 12 servings

- ¼ cup butter, softened
- ¾ cup sugar
- 2 large eggs, room temperature
- 1 cup all-purpose flour
- 1 tsp. baking powder
- ¼ cup 2% milk
- 1 tsp. grated lemon zest
- 2 cups sliced fresh plums (about 4 medium)
- ½ cup packed brown sugar
- 1 tsp. ground cinnamon
  Confectioners' sugar, optional

1. Preheat oven to 350°. In a small bowl, cream butter and sugar until light and fluffy, 5-7 minutes. Beat in eggs. Combine flour and baking powder; add to the creamed mixture alternately with milk, beating well after each addition. Add lemon zest. Pour into a greased 10-in. springform pan. Arrange plums on top; gently press into batter. Sprinkle with brown sugar and cinnamon.
2. Place pan on a baking sheet. Bake until top is golden and a toothpick inserted in the center comes out clean, 40-50 minutes. Cool for 10 minutes. Run a knife around edge of pan; remove rim. Cool on a wire rack. If desired, dust with confectioners' sugar just before serving.

1 PIECE: 185 cal., 5g fat (3g sat. fat), 46mg chol., 89mg sod., 33g carb. (24g sugars, 1g fiber), 3g pro.

TROPICAL COMPOTE DESSERT

Have the taste of summer throughout the year! To make a more adult version of this recipe, use brandy instead of the extra tropical fruit juice.
—*Taste of Home Test Kitchen*

PREP: 15 min. • **COOK:** 2¼ hours • **MAKES:** 6 servings

- 1 jar (23½ oz.) mixed tropical fruit
- 1 jalapeno pepper, seeded and chopped
- ¼ cup sugar
- 1 Tbsp. chopped crystallized ginger
- ¼ tsp. ground cinnamon
- 1 can (15 oz.) mandarin oranges, drained
- 1 jar (6 oz.) maraschino cherries, drained
- 1 medium firm banana, sliced
- 6 individual round sponge cakes
- 6 Tbsp. sweetened shredded coconut, toasted

1. Drain tropical fruit, reserving ¼ cup liquid. Combine fruit and jalapeno in a 1½-qt. slow cooker. Combine the sugar, ginger, cinnamon and reserved juice; pour over fruit. Cover and cook on low for 2 hours.
2. Stir in the mandarin oranges, cherries and banana; cover and cook 15 minutes longer.
3. Place sponge cakes on dessert plates; top with compote. Sprinkle with coconut.

1 SPONGE CAKE WITH ⅔ CUP COMPOTE AND 1 TBSP. COCONUT : 257 cal., 3g fat (2g sat. fat), 0 chol., 28mg sod., 62g carb., (31g sugars, 3g fiber), 1g pro.

FRESH PLUM KUCHEN

APPLE & PEAR POCKETS

STRAWBERRY SORBET

I first made a raspberry sorbet with an abundance of raspberries I had growing, but this easy recipe is simply amazing with any kind of berry. Strawberry is another of my go-tos.
—*Karen Bailey, Golden, CO*

TAKES: 5 min. + freezing
MAKES: 7 servings

¼ cup plus 1½ tsp. fresh lemon juice
3¾ cups fresh or frozen unsweetened chopped strawberries
2¼ cups confectioners' sugar

Place all the ingredients in a blender or food processor; cover and process until smooth. Transfer to a freezer-safe container; freeze until firm.
NOTE: Homemade sorbet generally lasts for about 2 to 3 months when properly stored in the freezer. Ice crystals may develop after 1 month, so don't wait too long to enjoy it.
½ CUP: 181 cal., 0 fat (0 sat. fat), 0 chol., 2mg sod., 46g carb. (42g sugars, 2g fiber), 1g pro.

TEST KITCHEN TIP

Replace the lemon juice with the juice of a fresh lime or orange for a fun flavor twist.

STRAWBERRY SORBET

APPLE & PEAR POCKETS

We use the sauce from this recipe in our classes to teach students that you can make something delicious and nutritious from local fall tree fruit without added sugar. At home I put the sauce into puff pastry for a truly fabulous yet easy dessert. These taste delicious for about three days if kept in an airtight container.
—*Jan DeBlasi, Berkeley, CA*

PREP: 35 min. • **BAKE:** 20 min.
MAKES: 16 servings

¼ cup unsweetened apple juice
   or water
2 Tbsp. maple syrup
1 vanilla bean or 1 Tbsp. vanilla extract
3 medium apples, peeled and chopped
3 medium pears, peeled and chopped
1 medium lemon, zest and juice
2 pkg. (17.3 oz. each) frozen puff pastry, thawed
1 large egg, beaten
2 Tbsp. coarse sugar, optional
½ tsp. ground cinnamon, optional

1. In a large skillet, bring apple juice and maple syrup to a simmer over medium heat. Split vanilla bean lengthwise. Using the tip of a sharp knife, scrape seeds from the center into skillet; add bean. Cook until liquid has reduced slightly, 1-2 minutes. Add apples and pears; cook and stir until fruit is just tender, 7-9 minutes. Remove from heat; add lemon zest and juice. Cool completely. Remove vanilla bean pods.
2. Preheat oven to 400°. On a lightly floured surface, unroll pastry sheets. Roll each sheet into a 12-in. square; cut each sheet into 4 equal squares. Spoon ¼ cup apple mixture diagonally over half of each square to within ½ in. of edges. Moisten pastry edges with water. Fold 1 corner over filling to the opposite corner, forming a triangle; press edges with a fork to seal.
3. Transfer pockets to greased baking sheets. Brush tops of pastries with beaten egg; prick tops with a fork. If desired, combine coarse sugar and cinnamon; sprinkle over pastries. Bake until golden brown, 18-20 minutes. Remove from pans to wire racks. Serve warm or at room temperature.
FREEZE OPTION: Freeze pastries in freezer containers. To use, reheat on an ungreased baking sheet in a preheated 350° oven until heated through, 5-7 minutes.
1 POCKET: 351 cal., 17g fat (4g sat. fat), 12mg chol., 207mg sod., 46g carb. (9g sugars, 6g fiber), 5g pro.

PRESSURE-COOKER CHOCOLATE CHIP CHEESECAKE

I adapted my favorite cheesecake recipe to work in the pressure cooker. The texture was so incredible, I may never bake it in the oven again! Be sure to use mini chocolate chips—if you use regular-size chips, they will sink to the bottom.
—Michele Kusma, Columbus, OH

- -

PREP: 25 min. + chilling
COOK: 30 min. + releasing
MAKES: 8 servings

- 1 cup graham cracker crumbs
- 1 Tbsp. brown sugar
  Dash salt
- 3 Tbsp. unsalted butter, melted
- 2 pkg. (8 oz. each) cream cheese, softened
- ½ cup sugar
- ½ tsp. vanilla extract
- 2 large eggs, room temperature, lightly beaten
- ½ cup miniature semisweet chocolate chips

1. Place trivet insert and 1 cup water in a 6-qt. electric pressure cooker. Line bottom of greased 6-in. springform pan with parchment. In a small bowl, mix cracker crumbs, brown sugar and salt; stir in butter. Press onto bottom of prepared pan. Freeze while preparing the filling.

2. In a large bowl, beat cream cheese, sugar and vanilla until smooth. Add eggs; beat on low speed just until blended. Fold in chocolate chips. Pour over crust. Cover springform pan with paper towel and foil. Fold an 18x12-in. piece of foil lengthwise into thirds, making a sling. Use sling to lower pan onto trivet.

3. Lock lid; close the pressure-release valve. Adjust to pressure-cook on high for 30 minutes. Allow pressure to release naturally. Using foil sling, carefully remove springform pan. Uncover; cool on a wire rack 10 minutes. Loosen sides from the pan with a knife. Cool for 1 hour longer. Refrigerate overnight, covering when completely cooled.

4. Remove rim from pan. Refrigerate the leftovers.

1 PIECE: 416 cal., 30g fat (17g sat. fat), 115mg chol., 274mg sod., 34g carb. (25g sugars, 1g fiber), 6g pro.

SOUTHERN BANANA PUDDING

This old southern recipe features a comforting custard layered with sliced bananas and vanilla wafers, then it is topped with meringue. I serve it year-round.
—Jan Campbell, Hattiesburg, MS

- -

PREP: 30 min. • **BAKE:** 15 min. + chilling
MAKES: 8 servings

- ¾ cup sugar
- ⅓ cup all-purpose flour
- 2 cups 2% milk
- 2 large egg yolks, lightly beaten
- 1 Tbsp. butter
- 1 tsp. vanilla extract
- 36 vanilla wafers
- 3 medium ripe bananas, cut into ¼-in. slices

MERINGUE
- 2 large egg whites, room temperature
- 1 tsp. vanilla extract
- ⅛ tsp. cream of tartar
- 3 Tbsp. sugar

1. Preheat oven to 350°. In a large saucepan, combine sugar and flour. Stir in milk until smooth. Cook and stir over medium-high heat until thickened and bubbly. Reduce heat; cook and stir 2 minutes longer.

2. Remove from the heat. Stir a small amount of the hot milk mixture into the egg yolks; return all to pan, stirring constantly. Bring to a gentle boil; cook and stir 2 minutes longer. Remove from heat; gently stir in butter and vanilla.

3. In an ungreased 8-in. square baking dish, layer a third of the vanilla wafers, bananas and filling. Repeat layers twice.

4. For meringue, beat egg whites, vanilla and cream of tartar on medium speed until soft peaks form. Gradually beat in sugar, 1 Tbsp. at a time, on high until stiff peaks form. Spread evenly over hot filling, sealing edges to sides of dish. Bake until meringue is golden, 12-15 minutes. Cool on a wire rack 1 hour. Refrigerate for at least 3 hours before serving. Refrigerate any leftovers.

1 SERVING: 293 cal., 7g fat (3g sat. fat), 58mg chol., 121mg sod., 53g carb. (38g sugars, 2g fiber), 5g pro.

PRESSURE-COOKER CHOCOLATE CHIP CHEESECAKE

SOUTHERN
BANANA
PUDDING

MICHIGAN CHERRY JAPANESE-STYLE CHEESECAKE

MICHIGAN CHERRY JAPANESE-STYLE CHEESECAKE

Michigan is known for its amazing cherries, especially the tart ones. They became my muse for this recipe, an international twist on a traditional American cheesecake. I used the distinctive Japanese-style cheesecake, which has an extraordinary light, melt-in-your-mouth texture.
—Laura Kurella, Wellston, MI

PREP: 1 hour + cooling
BAKE: 1 hour 20 min. • MAKES: 12 servings

- 6 Tbsp. butter, cubed
- 4 oz. reduced-fat cream cheese
- ⅔ cup heavy whipping cream
- ¼ cup all-purpose flour
- ¼ cup cornstarch
- 6 large egg yolks, room temperature
- 2 tsp. vanilla extract
- 1½ to 2 tsp. grated lemon zest
- 12 large egg whites, room temperature
- ¾ cup sugar

TOPPING
- ½ cup sugar
- 2 Tbsp. cornstarch
- ¼ tsp. cayenne pepper, optional
- ½ cup water
- 2 cups fresh or frozen pitted tart cherries
- 1 Tbsp. butter
  Confectioners' sugar

1. Preheat oven to 325°. Place a 9-in. springform pan on a double thickness of heavy-duty foil (about 18 in. square). Wrap foil securely around pan. Line bottom and inside of pan with parchment; set aside.
2. In a small saucepan, cook and stir butter and cream cheese over medium heat until melted. Remove from heat; whisk in cream until smooth. Let mixture cool completely.
3. Sift flour and cornstarch together twice; place in a large bowl. In a small bowl, whisk egg yolks, vanilla, lemon zest and the cooled cream cheese mixture until smooth. Add to flour mixture; beat until well blended.
4. In a large bowl with clean beaters, beat egg whites on medium speed until foamy. Gradually add sugar, 1 Tbsp. at a time, beating on high after each addition until sugar is dissolved. Continue beating until soft glossy peaks form. Fold a fourth of the whites into the batter, then fold in remaining whites. Gently transfer batter to the prepared pan. Place springform pan in a larger baking pan; add 1 in. hot water to larger pan.
5. Bake for 25 minutes. Reduce oven setting to 280°. Bake until top is puffed and springs back when lightly touched and the center appears set, 55-65 minutes longer.
6. Meanwhile, for topping, in a small saucepan, mix sugar, cornstarch and, if desired, cayenne. Whisk in water until smooth. Add cherries; cook and stir over medium heat until thickened and bubbly, about 5 minutes. Remove from heat; whisk in butter. Cool completely.
7. Remove springform pan from water bath. Loosen rim from pan with a knife; remove foil. Remove rim from pan; remove paper. Serve cheesecake warm with confectioners' sugar and cherry topping. Refrigerate leftovers.

1 PIECE: 294 cal., 16g fat (9g sat. fat), 132mg chol., 157mg sod., 31g carb. (24g sugars, 1g fiber), 7g pro.

LEMON ICEBOX CAKE

RASPBERRY RICOTTA MUG CAKE

Who wouldn't want to dig in to their own personal cake? Mug cakes are such a fun, casual treat, and you can make as few or as many as you need. The raspberry and ricotta combination makes for a tender crumb that bursts with fresh flavor.
—*Shauna Havey, Roy, UT*

- -

TAKES: 15 min. • **MAKES:** 1 serving

- 4　Tbsp. all-purpose flour
- 3　Tbsp. sugar
- ¾　tsp. baking powder
- ¼　cup whole-milk ricotta cheese
- 3　Tbsp. half-and-half cream, divided
- 1　Tbsp. canola oil
- 1　Tbsp. fresh lemon juice
- 6　fresh raspberries, chopped
- 2　Tbsp. confectioners' sugar
  　Optional: Fresh basil or mint leaves and raspberries

1. In a small bowl, stir together flour, sugar and baking powder. Stir in ricotta, 2 Tbsp. half-and-half, oil and lemon juice until just combined. Top with chopped raspberries; stir to combine. Spoon into a 16-oz. ramekin or microwave-safe mug.
2. Microwave on high until set, 2 to 3 minutes. Stir together the confectioners' sugar and remaining 1 Tbsp. half-and-half; drizzle over warm cake. Garnish if desired. Serve immediately.
1 CAKE: 601 cal., 25g fat (8g sat. fat), 48mg chol., 459mg sod., 84g carb. (58g sugars, 2g fiber), 12g pro.

RASPBERRY RICOTTA MUG CAKE

LEMON ICEBOX CAKE

This easy cake, with subtle lemon flavor and a pleasant crunch from the cookies, makes a stunning centerpiece.
—*Peggy Woodward, Shullsburg, WI*

- -

TAKES: 20 min. + chilling • **MAKES:** 8 servings

- 3　cups heavy whipping cream
- 3　Tbsp. sugar
- 3　Tbsp. grated lemon zest
- 63　Marie biscuits or Maria cookies
  　Lemon slices, optional

1. In a large bowl, beat the cream, sugar and lemon zest on high until stiff peaks form. Cut a small hole in the corner of a pastry bag. Fill with whipped cream.
2. On a serving plate, arrange 7 cookies in a circle, using 1 cookie in the center. Pipe ⅔ cup whipped cream over cookies. Repeat layers 8 times. Refrigerate overnight.
3. If desired, garnish with lemon slices.
1 PIECE: 530 cal., 37g fat (23g sat. fat), 102mg chol., 158mg sod., 44g carb. (17g sugars, 2g fiber), 6g pro.

TEST KITCHEN TIPS

- If you don't have any Maria cookies, you can use graham crackers or Nilla wafers instead.
- Try topping the cake with some fresh berries, such as raspberries or blueberries, or other sliced seasonal fruits.
- To enhance the lemony flavor, add a splash of lemon juice to the whipped cream, or spread a layer of lemon curd over the top of the cake or between the cookie layers.

**SLOW-COOKER
PEACH CRUMBLE**

SLOW-COOKER PEACH CRUMBLE

I look forward to our beach vacation every year, but I don't always relish the time I spend cooking for everybody. This slow cooker dessert (or breakfast!) gives me more time to lie in the sun and enjoy the waves. Melty ice cream is a must.
—Colleen Delawder, Herndon, VA

- -

PREP: 20 min. • **COOK:** 3 hours • **MAKES:** 8 servings

- 1 Tbsp. butter, softened
- 6 large ripe peaches, peeled and sliced (about 6 cups)
- 2 Tbsp. light brown sugar
- 1 Tbsp. lemon juice
- 1 Tbsp. vanilla extract
- 2 Tbsp. coconut rum, optional

TOPPING
- 1 cup all-purpose flour
- ¾ cup packed light brown sugar
- 1½ tsp. baking powder
- 1 tsp. ground cinnamon
- ½ tsp. baking soda
- ⅛ tsp. salt
- 1 cup old-fashioned oats
- 6 Tbsp. cold butter, cubed
  Whipped cream, optional

1. Grease a 6-qt. oval slow cooker with 1 Tbsp. softened butter. Toss peaches with brown sugar, lemon juice, vanilla and, if desired, rum; spread evenly in slow cooker.
2. Whisk together the first 6 topping ingredients; stir in oats. Cut in butter until crumbly; sprinkle over peaches. Cook, covered, on low until peaches are tender, 3-4 hours. If desired, serve with whipped cream.
¾ CUP: 339 cal., 11g fat (7g sat. fat), 27mg chol., 293mg sod., 57g carb. (36g sugars, 4g fiber), 4g pro.

RASPBERRY-WHITE CHOCOLATE LAVA CAKES

There is something so magical about a warm, luscious lava cake. Cutting into it and seeing the warm chocolate come rushing out always brings me joy. I wanted to see if I could do the same thing with white chocolate. Once successful, I added a sprinkling of fresh raspberries.
—Margaret Knoebel, Milwaukee, WI

- -

TAKES: 30 min. • **MAKES:** 5 servings

- ⅔ cup white baking chips
- ½ cup butter, cubed
- 1 cup confectioners' sugar
- 2 large eggs, room temperature
- 2 large egg yolks, room temperature
- 1 tsp. vanilla extract
- 6 Tbsp. all-purpose flour
- 10 fresh raspberries

1. Preheat oven to 425°. In a microwave-safe bowl, melt baking chips and butter for 30 seconds; stir until smooth. Whisk in confectioners' sugar, eggs, egg yolks and vanilla until blended. Fold in flour.
2. Transfer to 5 generously greased 4-oz. ramekins; press 2 raspberries into center of each ramekin. Bake on a baking sheet until a thermometer reads 160° and edges of cakes are set, 14-16 minutes.
3. Remove from oven; let stand 10 minutes. Run a knife around sides of ramekins; invert onto dessert plates. Serve immediately. If desired, garnish with additional raspberries.
1 SERVING: 468 cal., 30g fat (17g sat. fat), 202mg chol., 199mg sod., 46g carb. (37g sugars, 1g fiber), 6g pro.

**RASPBERRY-WHITE
CHOCOLATE LAVA CAKES**

MATCHA CHIA PUDDING

EASY NUTELLA CHEESECAKE

Creamy chocolate-hazelnut spread tops a crust made of crushed Oreo cookies to make this irresistible baked cheesecake.
—*Nick Iverson, Denver, CO*

PREP: 35 min. • **BAKE:** 1¼ hours + chilling
MAKES: 16 servings

  2½ cups lightly crushed Oreo cookies (about 24 cookies)
  ¼ cup sugar
  ¼ cup butter, melted
FILLING
  4 pkg. (8 oz. each) cream cheese, softened
  ½ cup sugar
  2 jars (26½ oz. each) Nutella
  1 cup heavy whipping cream
  1 tsp. salt
  4 large eggs, room temperature, lightly beaten
  ½ cup chopped hazelnuts, toasted

1. Preheat oven to 325°. Pulse cookies and sugar in a food processor until fine crumbs form. Continue processing while gradually adding butter in a steady stream. Press mixture onto bottom of a greased 10x3-in. springform pan. Securely wrap bottom and side of springform in a double thickness of heavy-duty foil (about 18 in. square).
2. For filling, beat cream cheese and sugar until smooth. Beat in Nutella, cream and salt. Add eggs; beat on low speed just until blended. Pour over crust.
3. Bake until a thermometer inserted in the center reads 160°, about 1¼ hours. Cool for 1¼ hours on a wire rack. Refrigerate overnight, covering when completely cooled.
4. Gently loosen rim from pan with a knife; remove rim. Top cheesecake with chopped hazelnuts.
1 PIECE: 900 cal., 62g fat (22g sat. fat), 129mg chol., 478mg sod., 84g carb. (71g sugars, 4g fiber), 12g pro.

TEST KITCHEN TIPS

- A high-sided springform pan is essential for this recipe. It will overflow a pan shorter than 3 in.
- For clean slicing, dip your knife in hot water, then wipe dry. Slice. Repeat as necessary.

MATCHA CHIA PUDDING

This pudding is quick, easy, and super healthy. Combine earthy matcha green tea powder, creamy almond milk and healthy chia seeds for superfood heaven in a little package. Top with tart raspberries and you've got a quick breakfast or perfect midday snack. It is gluten free, vegan, paleo and Whole30-approved!
—*Abra Pappa, New York, NY*

PREP: 10 min. + chilling
MAKES: 4 servings

  2 cups unsweetened almond milk
  3 Tbsp. maple syrup
  2 Tbsp. matcha (green tea powder)
  ½ cup chia seeds
  ½ cup fresh raspberries

In a large bowl whisk together almond milk, maple syrup and matcha. Stir in chia seeds. Let mixture sit for 15 minutes, stir again. Pour into 4 half-pint Mason jars or ramekins. Refrigerate, covered, until thickened, at least 2 hours. Garnish with fresh raspberries.
⅔ CUP: 173 cal., 8g fat (1g sat. fat), 0 chol., 90mg sod., 21g carb. (10g sugars, 9g fiber), 7g pro. **DIABETIC EXCHANGES:** 1½ starch, 1 fat.

STRAWBERRY, BASIL & HONEY PALETAS

This recipe for strawberry paletas is one of my favorites. It's fruity, fragrant, sweet and refreshing—perfect for a warm summer day outdoors.
—*Ericka Sanchez, La Habra, CA*

PREP: 15 min. + freezing
MAKES: 10 servings

  1 lb. chopped fresh strawberries
  ⅓ cup fresh basil leaves
  1½ tsp. fresh lime juice
  ¼ cup raw honey
  3 fresh strawberries

In a blender, puree chopped strawberries, basil and lime juice until smooth. Add the honey and blend to combine. Hull and slice remaining strawberries. Divide among pop molds or cups. Pour pureed mixture into molds, filling almost full. Top molds with holders. If using cups, top with foil and insert sticks through foil. Freeze until firm, at least 4 hours.
1 POP: 42 cal., 0 fat (0 sat. fat), 0 chol., 1mg sod., 11g carb. (9g sugars, 1g fiber), 0 pro. **DIABETIC EXCHANGES:** ½ starch.

**PRESSURE-COOKER
BUTTERNUT RICE PUDDING**

PRESSURE-COOKER BUTTERNUT RICE PUDDING

This tasty rice pudding blends all our favorite flavors of fall into one comforting dessert. The ease of the pressure cooker allows you to limit your dishes and cuts cooking time. If preferred, you can substitute raisins for the dried cranberries.
—Gretchen Monahan, Palmyra, PA

PREP: 35 min. • **COOK:** 15 min. + releasing • **MAKES:** 10 servings

- 3 Tbsp. butter, divided
- ½ cup chopped walnuts
- 2 Tbsp. plus ¾ cup packed brown sugar, divided
- 1 medium butternut squash, halved and seeds removed
- 2¼ cups water, divided
- ⅓ cup dried cranberries
- 1¼ cups uncooked jasmine rice, rinsed
- 4 cups whole milk
- ¼ cup cornstarch
- 1 medium apple, finely chopped
- 1 tsp. vanilla extract
- ½ tsp. ground cinnamon
  Whipped cream, optional

1. Select saute setting on a 6-qt. electric pressure cooker. Adjust for low heat; add 2 Tbsp. butter. When the butter is melted, add walnuts and 2 Tbsp. brown sugar. Cook and stir until nuts are coated, 5-7 minutes. Press cancel. Transfer nuts to a bowl; set aside. Wipe inner pot clean.
2. In the same inner pot, add squash, in batches, cut side down. Select saute setting; adjust for medium heat. Cook for 2 minutes. Press cancel. Return all squash to cooker. Add 1 cup water and cranberries. Lock lid; close pressure-release valve. Adjust to pressure-cook on high for 7 minutes. Allow pressure to release naturally for 10 minutes; quick-release any remaining pressure.
3. Remove squash. Drain cranberries; discard cooking liquid. Place cranberries in a large bowl. When cool enough to handle, remove flesh from squash; discard skins. Place squash in a blender; cover and process until smooth.
4. Wipe inner pot clean. Add rice and remaining 1¼ cups water. Lock lid; close pressure-release valve. Adjust to pressure-cook on high for 4 minutes. Allow pressure to release naturally for 10 minutes; quick-release any remaining pressure. Stir rice into cranberries.
5. In the same inner pot, whisk milk, cornstarch and remaining 1 Tbsp. butter. Select saute setting; adjust for low heat. Simmer until thickened, about 5 minutes. Stir in 1 cup pureed squash (save remaining for another use), apple and remaining ¾ cup brown sugar. Stir in rice mixture, vanilla and cinnamon. Cook and stir until thickened, 5-7 minutes. Press cancel. Pudding will continue to thicken upon standing. Serve warm with candied walnuts and if desired, whipped cream and additional ground cinnamon. Refrigerate leftovers.

¾ CUP: 342 cal., 11g fat (4g sat. fat), 19mg chol., 77mg sod., 56g carb. (29g sugars, 2g fiber), 6g pro.

RICOTTA PEAR DESSERT

Looking to pare down fat and calories? Try this perfect little pear dessert. Apples would be a tasty substitute for this fruity dessert.
—Lee Bremson, Kansas City, MO

TAKES: 15 min. • **MAKES:** 2 servings

- 1 medium ripe pear
- 1 Tbsp. ricotta cheese
- 3 tsp. honey, divided
- 1 Tbsp. chopped walnuts, toasted

1. Core pear from bottom, leaving the stem intact. Cut in half vertically. Slice pear, but not all the way through, leaving slices attached at the stem end.
2. In a small bowl, combine ricotta cheese and 1 tsp. honey. Place pear halves on dessert plates; fan slightly. Spread ricotta mixture over pear slices. Drizzle with the remaining honey; sprinkle with walnuts. Serve immediately.

1 SERVING: 116 cal., 3g fat (1g sat. fat), 3mg chol., 10mg sod., 22g carb. (17g sugars, 2g fiber), 2g pro.

CHERRY DELIGHT DESSERT

This smooth and creamy cheesecake-like treat is light, sweet and pretty, too. Convenience products make it quick and easy to prepare.
—Lanae Powell, McPherson, KS

PREP: 20 min. + chilling • **MAKES:** 6 servings

- ½ cup graham cracker crumbs
- 2 Tbsp. confectioners' sugar
- 2 Tbsp. butter, melted

FILLING

- 4 oz. cream cheese, softened
- ¾ cup confectioners' sugar
- ½ cup whipped topping
- 1 cup cherry pie filling

1. In a bowl, combine the graham cracker crumbs, confectioners' sugar and butter. Press onto the bottom of an 8x4-in. loaf pan coated with cooking spray.
2. In a small bowl, beat cream cheese and confectioners' sugar until smooth; fold in whipped topping. Spread over crust. Spoon pie filling over top. Refrigerate for 1 hour or until chilled.

1 PIECE: 264 cal., 12g fat (8g sat. fat), 31mg chol., 145mg sod., 37g carb. (29g sugars, 0 fiber), 2g pro.

READER REVIEW

"My husband and I love this light and sweet dessert! We may even prefer it to regular cheesecake!"

—SWAGNER, TASTEOFHOME.COM

Make Choux Pastry

Don't let the fancy name fool you! Choux pastry requires no special tools or ingredients—just a keen eye and a wooden spoon.

Once the water, butter, milk sugar and salt are boiling, add in flour and stir constantly until dough comes together in a mass. It will be lumpy at first, then smooth out.

When adding the eggs, beat them in 1 at a time, working fast so they don't scramble.

To pipe perfectly matched eclairs, first draw outlines on underside of the parchment in pencil.

Pierce the side of each eclair as soon as they're finished baking. This releases the steam so that the pastry will be crisp instead of limp.

CHOCOLATE-GLAZED RASPBERRY ECLAIRS

I first made choux pastry in high school for a French class assignment. I loved watching it puff up in the oven. Since then, eclairs have been my favorite pastry to make. They're not as tricky as they seem, and you can make so many amazing flavors. I garnish each eclair either with a single fresh raspberry or with a sprinkling of crushed freeze-dried raspberries.
—*Elisabeth Larsen, Pleasant Grove, UT*

PREP: 1 hour + chilling
BAKE: 25 min. + cooling
MAKES: 1 dozen

- ½ cup sugar
- ¼ cup cornstarch
- 2 cups whole milk
- 4 large egg yolks
- 2 Tbsp. unsalted butter

PASTRY
- ½ cup water
- 6 Tbsp. unsalted butter, cubed
- ¼ cup whole milk
- 2 tsp. sugar
- ¼ tsp. salt
- ¾ cup all-purpose flour
- 3 large eggs, room temperature

GLAZE
- ⅔ cup semisweet chocolate chips
- ½ cup heavy whipping cream
- 1 Tbsp. light corn syrup
- 1 cup fresh raspberries

1. In a small heavy saucepan, mix sugar and cornstarch. Whisk in milk. Cook and stir over medium heat until thickened and bubbly. Reduce heat to low; cook and stir 2 minutes longer. Remove from heat.
2. In a small bowl, whisk a small amount of hot mixture into egg yolks; return all to pan, whisking constantly. Bring to a gentle boil; cook and stir 2 minutes.
3. Immediately transfer to a clean bowl; stir in butter until smooth. Press plastic wrap onto surface; refrigerate until cold.
4. Preheat oven to 425°. For pastry, in a large saucepan, bring water, butter, milk, sugar and salt to a rolling boil. Add flour all at once and beat until blended. Cook over medium heat, stirring vigorously until mixture pulls away from sides of pan and forms a ball. Remove from heat; let stand 5 minutes.
5. Add eggs, 1 at a time, beating well after each addition until smooth. Continue beating until mixture is smooth and shiny.
6. Transfer to a piping bag with a large round tip. Pipe twelve 4½-in. strips about 3 in. apart on parchment-lined baking sheets. Bake for 15 minutes. Reduce oven temperature to 350°; bake until golden brown, 8-10 minutes longer.
7. Pierce the side of each eclair with tip of a sharp knife. Cool on wire racks. Split eclairs open. Pull out and discard soft dough from inside tops and bottoms.
8. For the glaze, in a microwave, melt chocolate chips, cream and corn syrup; stir until smooth. Stir raspberries into chilled pastry filling, mashing berries lightly. Fill eclairs just before serving. Dip tops in chocolate glaze; replace tops. Top with additional fresh raspberries. Let stand until set. Refrigerate leftovers.
FREEZE OPTION: Freeze the unfilled, unglazed eclairs in a freezer container for up to 2 months. Thaw, fill and glaze just before serving.
NOTE: Achieving the right consistency with your choux pastry is the key to successful eclairs, cream puffs and more. To judge if your pastry is the right texture, pull a spatula through your batter when you think it's done. It should drop off the spatula in a nice V shape. If it is too dense, you may need to add 1 more egg.
1 ECLAIR: 295 cal., 18g fat (11g sat. fat), 144mg chol., 96mg sod., 29g carb. (19g sugars, 1g fiber), 6g pro.

TEST KITCHEN TIP

Pressing plastic wrap against the surface of the pastry cream prevents it from forming a rubbery skin while it cools. You can also use parchment paper for this, but plastic is easier to mold to the surface.

**CHOCOLATE-GLAZED
RASPBERRY ECLAIRS**

STRAWBERRIES & CREAM SCONES

I took a leap and veered from my mom's original shortcake recipe. Instead of a short biscuit, I made light sweet-cream scones for the shortcake part. The difference was delightful!
—*Martha Laviolette, South Rockwood, MI*

PREP: 20 min. + freezing • **BAKE:** 15 min.
MAKES: 8 servings

- 2   pints fresh strawberries, sliced
- 1   container (16 oz.) frozen sweetened sliced strawberries, thawed
- 3   cups all-purpose flour
- ⅓   cup sugar
- 1   Tbsp. baking powder
- ¾   tsp. salt
- 2½ cups heavy whipping cream, divided
- 1½ tsp. vanilla extract
- 3   Tbsp. confectioners' sugar
      Grated citrus zest, optional

1. In a large bowl, combine fresh and thawed strawberries. Cover and refrigerate until serving. Line an 8-in. round cake pan with plastic wrap, letting edges hang over sides; set aside.

2. In a large bowl, combine flour, sugar, baking powder and salt. In a small bowl, stir together 1½ cups cream and vanilla. Stir into flour mixture just until moistened. Transfer to prepared pan; pat into an even layer. Cover and freeze 45 minutes or until slightly firm.

3. Preheat oven to 425°. Turn dough onto a lightly floured surface. Cut into 8 wedges. Place wedges on a parchment-lined baking sheet. Brush with 1 Tbsp. whipping cream and, if desired, sprinkle with some additional sugar. Bake until golden brown, 15-18 minutes.

4. Meanwhile, combine the remaining whipping cream and the confectioners' sugar; whip until stiff peaks form. To serve, cut scones in half; top with reserved strawberries and whipped cream. Garnish as desired.

1 SCONE WITH ⅔ CUP STRAWBERRIES AND ¼ CUP WHIPPED CREAM: 549 cal., 28g fat (17g sat. fat), 85mg chol., 425mg sod., 69g carb. (31g sugars, 4g fiber), 8g pro.

TEST KITCHEN TIPS

- To prepare these scones ahead of time, place the shaped, unbaked scones on a baking sheet and freeze them. Once frozen, transfer to an airtight container and keep in the freezer for up to a week. You can bake them without thawing them first—just add another 5-7 minutes of baking time.

- Scones are an ideal base for different mix-ins. Fresh fruit (blueberries or peaches) and dried fruits (raisins, currants or dried cherries, cranberries or apricots) both work well. Miniature chocolate chips or cinnamon chips make a fun twist, too. Try topping your scones with a dusting of cinnamon sugar or make a simple vanilla glaze.

STRAWBERRIES & CREAM SCONES

QUICK BANANAS
FOSTER

ICE CREAM STACK CAKE

Ice cream gets a whole new use in this fun dessert. Vanilla ice cream is used to make the bread, which is then layered with colorful malt-shop flavors. Top it all with fudge sauce and jimmies, and it's like a sliceable sundae! Be sure to use full-fat ice cream.
—*Katherine Kuehlman, Denver, CO*

PREP: 5 min. + freezing • **BAKE:** 30 min. + cooling
MAKES: 1 loaf (6 servings)

- 1 cup vanilla ice cream, softened
- ¾ cup self-rising flour
- 1 Tbsp. sugar
- ½ cup blue moon ice cream, softened
- ½ cup strawberry ice cream, softened
- ¼ cup hot fudge ice cream topping
  Sprinkles, optional

1. Preheat oven to 350°. In a small bowl, combine the ice cream, self-rising flour and sugar. Transfer to a 5¾x3x2-in. loaf pan coated with cooking spray. Bake until a toothpick inserted in the center comes out clean, 30-35 minutes. Cool 10 minutes before removing from pan to a wire rack; cool completely.
2. Line a 5¾x3x2-in. loaf pan with parchment, letting the edges extend up the sides. Cut cake horizontally into thirds. Place the bottom layer into prepared pan. Spread the blue moon ice cream evenly over layer; top with middle cake layer. Spread strawberry ice cream over layer; place the last cake layer on top. Freeze, covered, until firm, 3-4 hours. To serve, remove cake from loaf pan. Spread fudge sauce over top; add sprinkles if desired.
1 PIECE: 197 cal., 6g fat (3g sat. fat), 17mg chol., 246mg sod., 33g carb. (15g sugars, 1g fiber), 4g pro.

QUICK BANANAS FOSTER

Guests are always impressed when I ignite the rum in this delicious classic dessert. Use perfectly ripe bananas for the best results.
—*Mary Lou Wayman, Salt Lake City, UT*

TAKES: 25 min. • **MAKES:** 4 servings

- ⅓ cup butter, cubed
- ¾ cup packed dark brown sugar
- ¼ tsp. ground cinnamon
- 3 medium bananas
- 2 Tbsp. creme de cacao or banana liqueur
- ¼ cup dark rum
- 2 cups vanilla ice cream

1. In a large skillet or flambe pan, melt butter over medium-low heat. Stir in brown sugar and cinnamon until combined. Cut each banana lengthwise and then widthwise into quarters; alternately, cut into ¼-in. slices. Add bananas to the butter mixture; cook, stirring gently, until glazed and slightly softened, 3-5 minutes. Stir in creme de cacao; heat through.
2. In a small saucepan, heat rum over low heat until vapors form on surface. Carefully ignite rum and slowly pour over bananas, coating evenly.
3. Leaving skillet or pan on the cooking surface, gently shake pan back and forth until flames are completely extinguished; serve over ice cream.
1 SERVING: 567 cal., 23g fat (14g sat. fat), 70mg chol., 224mg sod., 80g carb. (72g sugars, 2g fiber), 3g pro

ICE CREAM
STACK CAKE

SIMPLE BBQ BRISKET
PAGE 220

Potluck Pleasers

Cooking for a crowd is a breeze with these delicious and easy recipes. Dig in to irresistible sliders, celebration roasts, gooey caramel rolls and more in this unique chapter.

SWEET & SMOKY PULLED PORK SANDWICHES

These simple sandwiches taste like something you would order from a local barbecue joint. The tender meat basically shreds itself when it's done cooking. It's definitely my favorite pulled pork sandwich of all time.
—*Lauren Adamson, Layton, UT*

PREP: 15 min. • **COOK:** 8 hours
MAKES: 10 servings

- ⅓ cup liquid smoke
- 3 Tbsp. paprika
- 3 tsp. salt
- 3 tsp. pepper
- 1 tsp. garlic powder
- 1 tsp. ground mustard
- 1 boneless pork shoulder butt roast (3 to 4 lbs.)
- 1 bottle (18 oz.) barbecue sauce
- 10 hamburger buns, split

1. In a small bowl, whisk the first 6 ingredients; rub over roast. Place roast in a 5- or 6-qt. slow cooker. Cook, covered, on low until meat is tender, 8-10 hours.
2. Remove roast; cool slightly. Discard cooking juices. Shred pork with 2 forks; return to slow cooker. Stir in barbecue sauce; heat through. Serve on buns.
FREEZE OPTION: Freeze cooled meat mixture in freezer containers. To use, partially thaw in refrigerator overnight. Heat through in a saucepan, stirring occasionally; add water if necessary.
1 SANDWICH: 436 cal., 16g fat (5g sat. fat), 81mg chol., 827mg sod., 44g carb. (20g sugars, 2g fiber), 28g pro.

READER REVIEW

"This is amazing! I can stop searching for the best pulled pork ever now. I'm cooking up 40 pounds of it for our Cub Scouts!"

—LYNGRIFF, TASTEOFHOME.COM

PINA COLADA FRUIT DIP

A taste of the tropics is always welcome and refreshing. This cool and creamy appetizer dip is also terrific to munch on after dinner.
—*Shelly Bevington, Hermiston, OR*

TAKES: 15 min.
MAKES: 10 servings (2½ cups)

- 1 pkg. (8 oz.) cream cheese, softened
- 1 jar (7 oz.) marshmallow creme
- 1 can (8 oz.) crushed pineapple, drained
- ½ cup sweetened shredded coconut
  Assorted fresh fruit or cubed lb. cake

In a small bowl, beat cream cheese and marshmallow creme until fluffy. Fold in pineapple and coconut. Cover and chill until serving. Serve with fruit, pound cake or both.
¼ CUP: 186 cal., 10g fat (6g sat. fat), 25mg chol., 96mg sod., 24g carb. (19g sugars, 0 fiber), 2g pro.

ANTIPASTO SKEWERS

This elegant-looking appetizer is quick and easy to make. It's perfect for dinner parties, cocktail parties and everything in between!
—*Amanda Pederson, West Fargo, ND*

TAKES: 15 min. • **MAKES:** 1 dozen

- 24 grape tomatoes (about 1 pint)
- 1 carton (8 oz.) cherry-size fresh mozzarella cheese
- 12 thin slices hard salami (about ¼ lb.)
- 12 pimiento-stuffed Queen olives
  Italian vinaigrette, optional

On 12 wooden 6-in. skewers, alternately thread tomatoes, mozzarella, folded salami slices and olives. Refrigerate until serving. If desired, drizzle skewers with vinaigrette to serve.
1 SKEWER: 204 cal., 9g fat (4g sat. fat), 24mg chol., 345mg sod., 24g carb. (16g sugars, 7g fiber), 11g pro.

PINA COLADA FRUIT DIP

CHOCOLATE SALTED CARAMEL BARS

I enjoy experimenting with different recipes and combining classic and new flavors. I have been making this shortbread for over 20 years and finally found the perfect pairing! I adore salted caramel and dark chocolate, so I layered these two flavors with my favorite shortbread crust. It's melt-in-your-mouth good, and it is quickly becoming a favorite with my family and friends! For even more gooey goodness, drizzle bottled caramel sauce over the top.
—Lisa Glenn, Sarasota, FL

- -

PREP: 20 min. • **BAKE:** 50 min. + cooling • **MAKES:** 2½ dozen

    2   cups butter, softened
    1½ cups confectioners' sugar
    1   cup sugar
    6   tsp. vanilla extract
    4   cups all-purpose flour
    1   pkg. (14 oz.) caramels
    ⅓   cup heavy whipping cream
    1   tsp. kosher salt
    1   pkg. (12 oz.) dark chocolate chips

1. Preheat oven to 325°. Beat butter, sugars and vanilla until light and fluffy, 5-7 minutes. Gradually beat in flour, mixing well. Press 3 cups of dough onto bottom of a greased 13x9-in. pan. Bake until set, 20-22 minutes.
2. Cool 10 minutes on a wire rack. Meanwhile, in a small saucepan, melt caramels with cream over low heat until smooth. Pour over crust. Sprinkle with salt, then chocolate chips. Drop remaining dough by teaspoonfuls over top. Bake until light golden brown, 30-35 minutes longer. Cool completely on a wire rack.
1 BAR: 334 cal., 18g fat (11g sat. fat), 37mg chol., 199mg sod., 43g carb. (28g sugars, 1g fiber), 3g pro.

PHILLY CHEESESTEAK SLIDERS

This is a wonderful way to use leftover roast beef, but using sliced roast beef from the deli also works.
—Debra Waggoner, Grand Island, NE

- -

PREP: 20 min. + chilling • **BAKE:** 25 min. • **MAKES:** 2 dozen

    2   large green peppers, sliced
    1   large sweet onion, sliced
    1   Tbsp. olive oil
    2   pkg. (12 oz. each) Hawaiian sweet rolls
    1½   lbs. sliced deli roast beef
    12   slices provolone cheese
    ¾   cup butter
    1½   tsp. dried minced onion
    1½   tsp. Worcestershire sauce
    1   tsp. garlic powder

1. In a large skillet, cook the green peppers and onion in oil over medium-high heat until tender, 8-10 minutes. Without separating the rolls, cut each package in half horizontally; arrange bottom halves in a greased 13x9-in. baking pan. Layer with roast beef, pepper mixture and cheese; replace top halves of rolls.
2. In a small saucepan, melt butter, dried onion, Worcestershire sauce and garlic powder. Drizzle over rolls. Cover and refrigerate 8 hours or overnight.
3. Preheat oven to 350°. Remove the sliders from refrigerator 30 minutes before baking. Bake, uncovered, 15 minutes. Cover with foil; bake until cheese is melted, 10 minutes longer.
1 SLIDER: 247 cal., 14g fat (8g sat. fat), 56mg chol., 413mg sod., 18g carb. (7g sugars, 1g fiber), 14g pro.

PHILLY
CHEESESTEAK
SLIDERS

SIMPLE BBQ BRISKET

This brisket cuts like butter—no joke! With just a few ingredients and steps, the recipe is nearly impossible to mess up. The thin, fall-apart-tender slices are delicious on their own but also make everything from tacos to Frito pies taste better.

—*Darla Andrews, Boerne, TX*

PREP: 15 min. • **BAKE:** 6 hours 5 min. • **MAKES:** 20 servings

- 1 whole fresh beef brisket (about 10 lbs.), deckle fat removed
- 1 bottle (21.5 oz.) Asian honey barbecue sauce and marinade
- 1 cup packed brown sugar
- 2 Tbsp. garlic powder
- 2 Tbsp. ground cumin
- 1 Tbsp. salt
- 1 Tbsp. chili powder
- 1 Tbsp. pepper

1. Preheat oven to 300°. Place brisket, fat side up, in a large roasting pan. Pour marinade over brisket. Bake, covered, for 4 hours. Combine remaining ingredients; sprinkle over brisket. Bake, covered, until tender, 2-4 hours longer (a thermometer inserted in brisket should read about 200°).

2. Preheat broiler; uncover brisket. Broil 3-4 in. from heat until fat is bubbly and slightly charred, 4-5 minutes. Cut diagonally across the grain into thin slices. If desired, skim fat from cooking juices and serve with brisket.

FREEZE OPTION: Freeze cooled meat mixture and juices in freezer containers. To use, partially thaw in refrigerator overnight. Heat through in a saucepan, stirring occasionally.

NOTE: For shredded brisket, roast on the longer end of the recommended cook time.

6 OZ. COOKED BEEF: 345 cal., 10g fat (4g sat. fat), 97mg chol., 523mg sod., 14g carb. (12g sugars, 0 fiber), 47g pro.

SIMPLE BBQ BRISKET

OLD-FASHIONED CONEY HOT DOG SAUCE

OLD-FASHIONED CONEY HOT DOG SAUCE

Camping and hot dogs go hand in hand. Roast some franks over the fire, then top them with this irresistible one-pot sauce.

—*Loriann Cargill Bustos, Phoenix, AZ*

PREP: 10 min. • **COOK:** 30 min. • **MAKES:** 2 cups

- 1 lb. lean ground beef (90% lean)
- 1 cup beef stock
- 2 Tbsp. tomato paste
- 1 Tbsp. chili powder
- 1 Tbsp. Worcestershire sauce
- ½ tsp. salt
- ½ tsp. onion powder
- ½ tsp. garlic powder
- ½ tsp. celery salt
- ½ tsp. ground cumin
- ¼ tsp. pepper

Prepare campfire or grill for medium-high heat. In a Dutch oven, cook beef over campfire 8-10 minutes or until no longer pink, breaking into crumbles. Stir in remaining ingredients; bring to a boil. Move Dutch oven to indirect heat. Cook, uncovered, until thickened, 20-25 minutes, stirring occasionally.

FREEZE OPTION: Freeze cooled meat mixture in freezer containers. To use, partially thaw in refrigerator overnight. Heat through in a saucepan, stirring occasionally; add water if necessary.

¼ CUP: 103 cal., 5g fat (2g sat. fat), 35mg chol., 355mg sod., 2g carb. (1g sugars, 1g fiber), 12g pro.

BASIL VEGETABLE STRATA

I've been cooking this strata for years, and my family just can't get enough! Fresh basil gives the healthy brunch dish an added flavor boost.
—*Jean Ecos, Hartland, WI*

PREP: 40 min. + chilling
BAKE: 1 hour + standing
MAKES: 8 servings

- 3 tsp. canola oil, divided
- ¾ lb. sliced fresh mushrooms
- 1 cup finely chopped sweet onion
- 1 large sweet red pepper, cut into strips
- 1 large sweet yellow pepper, thin strips
- 1 medium leek (white portion only), chopped
- ½ tsp. salt
- ½ tsp. pepper
- 10 slices whole wheat bread, cut into 1-in. pieces
- 1½ cups shredded part-skim mozzarella cheese
- ¼ cup grated Parmesan cheese
- 8 large eggs
- 4 large egg whites
- 2½ cups fat-free milk
- ¼ cup chopped fresh basil

1. In a large skillet, heat 1 tsp. oil over medium-high heat. Add mushrooms; cook and stir until tender, 8-10 minutes. Remove from pan.
2. In same pan, heat 1 tsp. oil over medium heat. Add onion; cook and stir until golden brown, 6-8 minutes. Remove from pan and add to the mushrooms.
3. Add remaining oil to pan. Add peppers, leek, salt and pepper; cook and stir until leek is tender, 6-8 minutes. Stir in sauteed mushrooms and onion.
4. In a 13x9-in. baking dish coated with cooking spray, layer half each of the following: bread pieces, vegetable mixture, mozzarella cheese and Parmesan cheese. Repeat layers. In a large bowl, whisk eggs, egg whites and milk until blended; pour over layers. Sprinkle with basil. Refrigerate, covered, overnight.
5. Preheat oven to 350°. Remove strata from refrigerator while oven heats.
6. Bake, covered, 50 minutes. Bake, uncovered, until lightly browned and a knife inserted in the center comes out clean, 10-15 minutes longer. Let stand 10 minutes before serving.

1 PIECE: 322 cal., 13g fat (5g sat. fat), 201mg chol., 620mg sod., 28g carb. (9g sugars, 4g fiber), 24g pro. **DIABETIC EXCHANGES:** 2 medium-fat meat, 1½ starch, 1 vegetable, ½ fat.

HONEY-MAPLE GLAZED HAM

HONEY-MAPLE GLAZED HAM

My graham cracker-crusted ham gets a double coating of a simple honey-maple glaze. The first half melts into the ham while the second half forms a sweet caramelized topping.
—*Alan Sproles, Knoxville, TN*

PREP: 15 min. • **BAKE:** 2 hours
MAKES: 15 servings

- 1 spiral-sliced fully cooked bone-in ham (7 to 9 lbs.)
- ½ cup maple syrup
- ½ cup butter, softened
- ½ cup packed brown sugar
- ½ cup graham cracker crumbs
- ½ cup honey

1. Preheat oven to 325°. Line a roasting pan with heavy-duty foil. Place ham on a rack in prepared pan. Pour maple syrup over ham, separating slices. In a small bowl, beat the remaining ingredients until blended; spread ¾ cup over ham.
2. Bake ham, uncovered, for 1½ hours. Spread remaining butter mixture over ham. Bake until a thermometer reads 140°, basting occasionally with pan drippings, 30-45 minutes longer.

4 OZ. COOKED HAM: 335 cal., 12g fat (6g sat. fat), 109mg chol., 1180mg sod., 27g carb. (24g sugars, 0 fiber), 32g pro.

BASIL VEGETABLE STRATA

PIG OUT!

We're positively squealing over these 10 creative takes on the party app with a cozy wrap.

2

1

4

5

7

8

9

1. HAM & BRIE PASTRIES

Roll 1 sheet frozen puff pastry to a 12-in. square; cut into sixteen 3-in. squares. Place 1 tsp. apricot preserves in center of each square; top with 1 slice ham and 1 cube Brie cheese. Overlap 2 opposite corners of pastry over filling; pinch to seal. Bake on parchment-lined baking sheets at 400° until golden brown, 15-20 minutes.

2. GERMAN PIG IN A BLANKET

Unfold 1 sheet puff pastry; spread ⅓ cup stone-ground mustard to within ½ in. of edges. Layer with ½ cup sauerkraut and 4 chopped cooked bratwurst links. Roll up jelly-roll style. Cut into 16 slices. Place on greased baking sheets. Sprinkle with 1 Tbsp. caraway seeds. Bake at 400° until golden brown, 18-20 minutes.

3. CHORIZO TACOS

In a skillet, heat 2 tsp. canola oil over medium-high heat. Add 1 small chopped onion and 1 chopped seeded poblano pepper; cook and stir until tender, 5-7 minutes. Add 1 lb. fresh chorizo; cook, breaking meat into crumbles, until fully cooked, 12-15 minutes. Drain. Serve on warm mini flour tortillas. Top as desired.

4. BACON PUFF PASTRY TWISTS

Preheat oven to 400°. Unfold 1 sheet puff pastry on a lightly floured surface. Spread with 2 Tbsp. brown sugar; sprinkle with ¼ tsp. ground chipotle pepper. Press the mixture into pastry. Cut into 12 strips. Twist together 1 pastry strip and 1 uncooked bacon strip; place 2 in. apart on greased baking sheets. Bake until pastry is puffed and golden brown, 14-16 minutes.

5. CARROT IN A BLANKET

Cook 24 fresh baby carrots in a small amount of water until crisp tender, 6-8 minutes; drain. Add 1 Tbsp. vegan butter and 2 tsp. liquid smoke; cool. Preheat oven to 325°. Unroll 1 tube refrigerated crescent dough and separate into 8 triangles; cut each triangle lengthwise into 3 thin triangles. Place 1 sprig of parsley on the wide end of each smaller triangle; top with a cooled carrot. Roll up tightly; place, point side down, on a parchment-lined baking sheet. Top with a pinch of sea salt. Bake until golden brown and heated through, 14-16 minutes.

6. SPAM IN A BLANKET

Preheat oven to 325°. Cut 1 can reduced-sodium Spam lengthwise into 24 pieces. Cut two 8-oz. cans unsweetened pineapple rings into thirds. Unroll 1 tube refrigerated crescent dough and separate into 8 triangles; cut each triangle lengthwise into 3 thin triangles. Place 1 Spam piece on the wide end of each smaller triangle; top with a pineapple piece. Roll up tightly; place, point side down, on a parchment-lined baking sheet. Brush with 1 Tbsp. teriyaki sauce and sprinkle with sesame seeds. Bake until golden brown on the bottom and heated through, 14-16 minutes.

7. PORK PHYLLO CUPS

Preheat oven to 325°. Place 1 pkg. frozen miniature phyllo tart shells on an ungreased baking sheet. Divide 1 cup finely diced cooked pork among shells; top with ¼ cup crumbled feta cheese and 2 Tbsp. tapenade. Bake until heated through, 8-10 minutes. Garnish with rosemary if desired.

8. ASPARAGUS-PROSCIUTTO WRAPS

Mix 3 Tbsp. softened butter, 1 Tbsp. Dash Onion & Herb Seasoning Blend and ¼ tsp. garlic salt. Unfold 1 pkg. thawed puff pastry sheets onto a lightly floured surface. Spread with 1½ Tbsp. butter mixture and sprinkle with ½ cup feta. Top with some sliced prosciutto, pressing lightly to adhere. Cut each sheet into 12 strips. Wrap each strip around an asparagus spear; place on parchment-lined baking sheets. Bake at 425° 15 minutes or until golden brown.

9. PORK TAQUITOS

Saute 1 chopped onion in oil until tender. Add 1 tsp. garlic, 2 tsp. cumin, 1 tsp. each oregano and chili powder, and ¼ tsp. cayenne; cook 1 minute. Add 2 cups shredded pork, 1 cup Mexican cheese blend, ¼ cup each cilantro and salsa verde, and 1 Tbsp. lime juice. Cook until cheese is melted. Place 2 Tbsp. filling over lower third of each of twelve 6-in. corn tortillas. Roll up tightly; secure with toothpicks. Bake at 400° on a greased baking sheet for 8 minutes.

10. BREAKFAST PIG IN A BLANKET

Preheat oven to 325°. Cut 4 hard-boiled eggs into 6 wedges each. Unroll 1 tube crescent dough and separate into 8 triangles; cut each triangle lengthwise into 3 thin triangles. Place 1 piece uncooked breakfast sausage, cut in half widthwise, on the wide end of each smaller triangle; top with egg wedge and a cherry tomato half. Roll up tightly; place, point side down, on a parchment-lined baking sheet. Brush with beaten egg; sprinkle with poppy seeds. Bake until golden brown and heated through, 14-16 minutes.

**CARAMEL
PECAN ROLLS**

CARAMEL PECAN ROLLS

Soft and sweet, these rolls will get a lip-smacking smile from everyone. They rise nice and high, hold their shape and have a gooey, scrumptious caramel sauce.
—*Carolyn Buschkamp, Emmetsburg, IA*

PREP: 40 min. + rising • **BAKE:** 20 min. • **MAKES:** 2 dozen

- 2 cups 2% milk
- ½ cup water
- ½ cup sugar
- ½ cup butter
- ⅓ cup cornmeal
- 2 tsp. salt
- 7 to 7½ cups all-purpose flour
- 2 pkg. (¼ oz. each) active dry yeast
- 2 large eggs, room temperature

TOPPING
- 2 cups packed brown sugar
- ½ cup butter
- ½ cup 2% milk
- ½ to 1 cup chopped pecans

FILLING
- ¼ cup butter, softened
- ½ cup sugar
- 2 tsp. ground cinnamon

1. In a saucepan, combine the first 6 ingredients; bring to a boil, stirring frequently. Set aside to cool to 120°-130°. In a bowl, combine 2 cups flour and yeast. Add cooled cornmeal mixture; beat on low until smooth. Add eggs and 1 cup of flour; mix for 1 minute. Stir in enough remaining flour to form a soft dough.

2. Turn the dough onto a floured board; knead until smooth and elastic, 6-8 minutes. Place in a greased bowl, turning once to grease top. Cover and let rise in a warm place until doubled, about 1 hour.

3. Combine the first 3 topping ingredients in a saucepan; bring to a boil, stirring occasionally. Pour into 2 greased 13x9-in. baking pans. Sprinkle with pecans; set aside.

4. Punch dough down; divide in half. Roll each into a 12x15-in. rectangle; spread with butter. Combine sugar and cinnamon; sprinkle over butter. Roll up dough from one long side; pinch seams and turn ends under. Cut each roll into 12 slices. Place 12 slices, cut side down, in each baking pan. Cover and let rise in a warm place until nearly doubled, about 30 minutes.

5. Bake at 375° for 20-25 minutes or until golden brown. Let cool 1 minute; invert onto a serving platter.

1 ROLL: 365 cal., 13g fat (7g sat. fat), 47mg chol., 319mg sod., 57g carb. (28g sugars, 2g fiber), 6g pro.

READER REVIEW

"I've made this several times. The rolls are sweet and moist. I now use 50% more of both the topping and filling, as that's my preference. By far my favorite sweet roll recipe!"

—KIRBYMCCREARY, TASTEOFHOME.COM

MOUNTAIN HAM SUPREME

MOUNTAIN HAM SUPREME

Little kids think it's really neat how the sandwiches look like mountains in the pan. Very tasty, too.
—*Keri Cotton, Eagan, MN*

PREP: 20 min. + chilling • **BAKE:** 45 min. • **MAKES:** 12 servings

- 12 slices bread
- 1 lb. ground fully cooked ham
- 2 cups shredded cheddar cheese
- ½ cup mayonnaise
- 1 tsp. ground mustard
- 6 large eggs
- 2¼ cups 2% milk
- ¼ tsp. salt
- ¼ tsp. pepper

1. Toast bread. Mix ham, cheese, mayonnaise and ground mustard. Spread ham mixture over 6 slices of bread; top with remaining slices to make 6 sandwiches. Cut sandwiches in half diagonally.

2. In a greased 13x9-in. baking dish, arrange sandwich triangles cut side down, with points facing up, pressing together as needed to fit in 2 rows. Whisk the eggs, milk, salt and pepper until well blended. Pour over sandwich triangles. Refrigerate, covered, overnight.

3. Remove casserole from refrigerator 30 minutes before baking. Preheat oven to 300°. Bake, uncovered, until a knife inserted in center comes out clean, 45-50 minutes.

1 SERVING: 366 cal., 24g fat (9g sat. fat), 137mg chol., 903mg sod., 17g carb. (4g sugars, 1g fiber), 19g pro.

PIZZA SLIDERS

Our love for Italian food and pizza gave me the idea for these irresistible pizza sliders. These would be delicious as a lunch, light dinner or party appetizer. Who could turn down pizza in a slider?

—*Joan Hallford, North Richland Hills, TX*

- -

PREP: 20 min. • **COOK:** 15 min.
MAKES: 1 dozen

1	medium green pepper, chopped
1	cup sliced fresh mushrooms
1	Tbsp. canola oil
1½	cups pizza or marinara sauce
1	pkg. (12 oz.) Hawaiian sweet rolls
1	cup sliced pepperoni
⅔	cup chopped ripe olives
1½	cups shredded mozzarella cheese
2	Tbsp. grated Parmesan cheese
2	Tbsp. Italian salad dressing

1. Preheat oven to 375°. In a large skillet, cook green pepper and mushrooms in oil over medium-high heat 6-8 minutes or until tender. Pour in pizza sauce and stir to combine. Set aside.

2. Without separating rolls, cut package in half horizontally; arrange bottom halves on a greased baking sheet. Spread with pizza sauce mixture and layer with the pepperoni, olives and mozzarella; replace top halves of rolls. Brush dressing over rolls and sprinkle with Parmesan.

3. Bake, uncovered, 12-15 minutes or until rolls are heated through and mozzarella is melted. Cover with foil if top browns too quickly. Remove and let stand 5 minutes before slicing.

1 SLIDER: 227 cal., 12g fat (5g sat. fat), 34mg chol., 486mg sod., 21g carb. (8g sugars, 2g fiber), 10g pro.

SPAGHETTI SQUASH WITH MEAT SAUCE

Neither my mother nor I had tried spaghetti squash before, so when we cooked this recipe together, all we could do was grin and say wow! It's fun to separate the noodle-like strands from the squash shell, but the eating is the best part!

—*Lina Vainauskas, Shaw Air Force Base, SC*

- -

PREP: 10 min. • **COOK:** 25 min.
MAKES: 6 servings

1	medium spaghetti squash (about 8 in. long)
1	cup water
1	lb. lean ground beef (90% lean)
1	large onion, chopped
1	medium green pepper, chopped
1	tsp. garlic powder
2	tsp. dried basil
1½	tsp. dried oregano
1	tsp. salt
½	tsp. pepper
¼	to ½ tsp. chili powder
1	can (28 oz.) tomato puree
1	cup grated Parmesan cheese, divided

1. Preheat oven to 375°. Slice squash lengthwise and scoop out seeds. Place squash, cut side down, in a baking dish. Add water and cover tightly with foil. Bake 20-30 minutes or until easily pierced with a fork.

2. Meanwhile, in a cast-iron or other heavy large skillet, cook beef over medium heat, crumbling meat, until no longer pink; drain. Add onion, green pepper, herbs and seasonings; cook and stir until onion is tender, 5-7 minutes. Stir in tomato puree. Cover and cook over low heat, stirring occasionally.

3. Scoop out squash, separating the strands with a fork. Just before serving, stir ½ cup Parmesan cheese into meat sauce. Serve sauce over spaghetti squash with remaining ½ cup Parmesan cheese.

1 SERVING: 351 cal., 12g fat (5g sat. fat), 59mg chol., 763mg sod., 36g carb. (4g sugars, 8g fiber), 23g pro. **DIABETIC EXCHANGES:** 3 lean meat, 2 starch.

PIZZA SLIDERS

SPAGHETTI SQUASH
WITH MEAT SAUCE

S'MORES CRISPY BARS

My aunt always brought s'mores-style bars to our family's summer cottage. Plain or frosted, they're perfect for eating on the run.
—*Elizabeth King, Duluth, MN*

PREP: 15 min. + cooling • **MAKES:** 2 dozen

- ¼ cup butter, cubed
- 1 pkg. (10 oz.) miniature marshmallows
- 6 cups Rice Krispies
- 1½ cups crushed graham crackers
- 1 cup milk chocolate chips

FROSTING

- ¾ cup butter, softened
- 1 cup confectioners' sugar
- 1 jar (7 oz.) marshmallow creme

TOPPING

- ¼ cup crushed graham crackers
- 2 milk chocolate candy bars (1.55 oz. each)

1. In a 6-qt. stockpot, melt butter over medium heat. Add marshmallows; cook and stir until melted. Remove from heat. Stir in cereal and crushed crackers. Fold in chocolate chips. Press mixture into a greased 13x9-in. baking pan. Cool to room temperature.

2. For frosting, in a small bowl, beat butter and confectioners' sugar until smooth. Beat in marshmallow creme on low speed just until blended. Spread over bars. Sprinkle crushed crackers over frosting. Cut into bars. Break each candy bar into 12 pieces; place a piece on each bar.

1 BAR: 270 cal., 12g fat (7g sat. fat), 23mg chol., 158mg sod., 40g carb. (26g sugars, 1g fiber), 2g pro.

CARAMELIZED HAM & SWISS BUNS

My next-door neighbor shared this recipe with me, and I simply cannot improve it! You can make it ahead and cook it quickly when company arrives. The flavor combination is so delicious.
—*Iris Weihemuller, Baxter, MN*

PREP: 25 min. + chilling • **BAKE:** 30 min. • **MAKES:** 1 dozen

- 1 pkg. (12 oz.) Hawaiian sweet rolls
- ½ cup horseradish sauce
- ¾ lb. sliced deli ham
- 6 slices Swiss cheese, halved
- ½ cup butter, cubed
- 2 Tbsp. finely chopped onion
- 2 Tbsp. brown sugar
- 1 Tbsp. spicy brown mustard
- 2 tsp. poppy seeds
- 1½ tsp. Worcestershire sauce
- ¼ tsp. garlic powder

1. Without separating rolls, cut rolls in half horizontally; arrange bottom halves of rolls in a greased 9x9-in. baking pan. Spread cut side of roll bottoms with horseradish sauce. Layer with ham and cheese; replace tops.

2. In a small skillet, heat butter over medium-high heat. Add onion; cook and stir until tender, 1-2 minutes. Stir in remaining ingredients. Pour over rolls. Refrigerate, covered, several hours or overnight.

3. Preheat oven to 350°. Remove rolls from refrigerator for 30 minutes before baking. Bake, covered, 25 minutes. Bake, uncovered, until golden brown, 5-10 minutes longer.

1 SANDWICH: 315 cal., 17g fat (9g sat. fat), 61mg chol., 555mg sod., 29g carb. (13g sugars, 2g fiber), 13g pro.

BEEF BIRRIA TACOS

BEEF BIRRIA TACOS

Birria tacos have gained traction all over social media. If you haven't seen them yet, they're juicy tacos loaded with a brothy red sauce and tender shredded meat. What a treat!
—*Ericka Sanchez, La Habra, CA*

- -

PREP: 45 min. + marinating
COOK: 2 hours • **MAKES:** 10 servings

- 8 dried guajillo chiles, stems removed
- 2 dried pasilla chiles, stems removed
- 4 cups hot water
- 1 medium white onion, halved and divided
- 1 roma tomato, quartered
- 4 garlic cloves
- 1½ tsp. chicken bouillon granules
- 8 whole peppercorns
- 1 tsp. dried thyme
- 1 tsp. dried Mexican oregano
- ½ tsp. cumin seeds
- 1 boneless beef chuck roast (3 lbs.), quartered
- 1 tsp. salt
- ½ tsp. pepper
- 3 bay leaves
- 20 corn tortillas (6 in.)
  Shredded Oaxaca cheese or other melting cheese, optional
  Optional toppings: Chopped onion, chopped cilantro, sliced radishes and lime wedges

1. In a large bowl, combine chiles and hot water; let stand 30 minutes. In a blender, puree 1 onion half, the tomato, garlic, bouillon, peppercorns, thyme, oregano, cumin and soaked chiles with soaking liquid until smooth. Strain mixture through a fine sieve.
2. Place beef in a Dutch oven; sprinkle with salt and pepper. Add bay leaves and remaining onion half. Add strained sauce and 2 cups cold water; stir to combine. Refrigerate, covered, 2 hours or up to 24 hours.
3. Place Dutch oven over medium heat. Bring mixture to a boil; reduce heat and simmer, covered, until beef is tender and starting to fall apart, 1½-2 hours. Remove meat and set aside; remove onion pieces and bay leaves and discard. Continue to simmer liquid, uncovered, until reduced by half, about 30 minutes. Shred meat with 2 forks; return to pan.
4. To serve, dip a tortilla into the meat mixture, thoroughly coating with sauce. Place the tortilla onto a griddle, comal or cast-iron skillet over medium heat. Sprinkle with cheese if desired; cook until cheese melts. Top with beef; fold tortilla over to form a taco. Serve with toppings as desired.

2 TACOS: 370 cal., 16g fat (5g sat. fat), 89mg chol., 447mg sod., 27g carb. (1g sugars, 5g fiber), 31g pro.

GREEN BEAN-CHERRY TOMATO SALAD

My grandmother made a cold green bean salad with potatoes for every family barbecue. Now I bring my own version of the recipe to parties. With added color and taste from the cherry tomatoes, this favorite is even better.
—*Angela Lemoine, Howell, NJ*

- -

PREP: 25 min. • **COOK:** 10 min.
MAKES: 12 servings

- 1½ lbs. fresh green beans, trimmed
- 1 pint cherry tomatoes, halved
- 1 small red onion, halved and thinly sliced
- 3 Tbsp. red wine vinegar
- 1½ tsp. sugar
- ¾ tsp. dried oregano
- ¾ tsp. salt
- ¼ tsp. garlic powder
- ¼ tsp. pepper
- ¼ cup olive oil

1. In a 6-qt. stockpot, bring 6 cups water to a boil. Add green beans in batches; cook, uncovered, 2-3 minutes or just until crisp-tender. Remove beans and immediately drop into ice water. Drain and pat dry.
2. Transfer beans to a large bowl. Add tomatoes and onion; toss to combine. In a small bowl, whisk vinegar, sugar, oregano, salt, garlic powder and pepper. Gradually whisk in oil until blended. Pour over bean mixture; toss to coat.

1 SERVING: 65 cal., 5g fat (1g sat. fat), 0 chol., 153mg sod., 6g carb. (2g sugars, 2g fiber), 1g pro. **DIABETIC EXCHANGES:** 1 vegetable, 1 fat.

GREEN BEAN-CHERRY TOMATO SALAD

SUMMER ORZO
PAGE 243

JUICY CHERRY PIE
PAGE 244

THREE-BEAN
BAKED BEANS
PAGE 245

WATERMELON CUPS
PAGE 245

YUMMY CORN
CHIP SALAD
PAGE 244

CRISPY FRIED
CHICKEN
PAGE 243

Holiday & Seasonal Celebrations

Every season brings special occasions to celebrate. Look here for the festive menu ideas that will make your gatherings sparkle the whole year through.

CHECK OUT THESE SPECIALTIES

Take-It-Easy
EASTER

Five quick-prep and make-ahead recipes
let you celebrate with a special
Sunday spread—without missing
a minute of the egg hunt.

**BIBB LETTUCE WITH
ROASTED RED ONIONS**

**FIVE SPICE PLUM
BAKED HAM**

**POTATOES
LYONNAISE**

VERTICAL
CARROT CAKE

CHEESY BAKED
ASPARAGUS

FIVE SPICE PLUM BAKED HAM

Baked ham is one of my favorite dishes, and this recipe adds something a little bit different to that classic dish. The plum goes really well with the ham and the Asian spices!

—*Elisabeth Larsen, Pleasant Grove, UT*

PREP: 15 min. • **COOK:** 2 hours
MAKES: 20 servings

- 1   fully cooked bone-in ham (7 to 9 lbs.)
- 2   cups plum jam
- ¼   cup reduced-sodium soy sauce
- 4   Tbsp. packed brown sugar
- 3   Tbsp. orange juice
- 2   garlic cloves, minced
- 1   tsp. ground ginger
- 1   tsp. Chinese five-spice powder

1. Preheat oven to 325°. Place ham on a rack in a shallow roasting pan. Using a sharp knife, score the surface of the ham with ¼-in.-deep cuts in a diamond pattern.
2. In a large saucepan, stir together the remaining ingredients. Bring mixture to a boil and simmer until sugar is dissolved, 1-2 minutes. Reserve half the mixture; keep warm. Pour remaining half over the ham. Bake, uncovered, until a thermometer reads 140°, 2-2½ hours. Baste occasionally with pan drippings. Cover loosely with foil if ham browns too quickly. Serve with remaining sauce mixture.

4 OZ. HAM: 227 cal., 4g fat (1g sat. fat), 70mg chol., 958mg sod., 25g carb. (23g sugars, 0 fiber), 24g pro.

FIVE SPICE PLUM BAKED HAM

Carve A Ham

Here's the best way to get every tasty bit of sweet-smoky meat off the bone.

Place ham, precut side down, on a large cutting board. Pierce fork into the top corner of the meat and carve along the bone with a sharp knife to remove the boneless section.

Slice the boneless section vertically. Set the slices on a serving plate, tenting with foil to keep warm.

With the remaining bone-in portion, insert fork into the meat directly next to the bone. Make horizontal cuts until you reach the bone.

Finally, slice bone-in portion vertically along the bone. This cuts off the horizontal slices, which fall neatly onto the board. Transfer them to the serving plate and serve.

CHEESY BAKED ASPARAGUS

POTATOES LYONNAISE

Potatoes lyonnaise is a classic side dish I learned to make in culinary school. I keep switching up the herbs to give it a different flavor. It is very simple to make and couldn't be more comforting. It's fantastic for casual dinners, but also elegant enough for the holidays.

—*James Schend, Pleasant Prairie, WI*

PREP: 10 min. • **COOK:** 25 min. • **MAKES:** 6 servings

- 4   medium russet potatoes (about 1½ lbs.), peeled and thinly sliced
- 1   tsp. salt
- 6   Tbsp. butter, divided
- 1   small onion, halved and thinly sliced
- 1   tsp. minced fresh rosemary
- ½   tsp. pepper

1. In a large saucepan or Dutch oven, combine potatoes, salt and enough cold water to cover by 1 in. Bring to a boil; reduce heat and simmer until potatoes are slightly cooked but still al dente, 3-4 minutes. Drain.

2. Meanwhile, in a large skillet, melt 3 Tbsp. butter over medium heat. Add onion; cook, stirring frequently, until golden brown, 10-12 minutes. Remove onion; set aside. In same skillet, melt remaining 3 Tbsp. butter. Add the potatoes; cook, stirring occasionally, until potatoes are golden brown, 8-10 minutes. Add onion, rosemary and pepper; toss to combine. Cook until heated through.

⅔ CUP: 190 cal., 12g fat (7g sat. fat), 31mg chol., 134mg sod., 21g carb. (2g sugars, 2g fiber), 2g pro.

CHEESY BAKED ASPARAGUS

This is an ideal fresh asparagus recipe with a rich, creamy sauce and cashews. It's a favorite vegetable dish that is easy to prepare.

—*Jerry Gulley, Pleasant Prairie, WI*

PREP: 20 min. • **BAKE:** 25 min. • **MAKES:** 10 servings

- 3   lbs. fresh asparagus, trimmed
- 1   cup heavy whipping cream
- ½   tsp. kosher salt
- ½   tsp. pepper
- 1½ cups shredded mozzarella cheese
- 1   cup chopped cashews
- 1   cup grated Parmesan cheese

Preheat oven to 400°. Arrange asparagus in a greased 13x9-in. baking dish; add cream, salt and pepper. Top with mozzarella, cashews and Parmesan cheese. Bake until asparagus is tender and cheese is melted and golden brown, 25-30 minutes. Transfer dish to wire cooling rack; let stand 5 minutes before serving.

1 SERVING: 261 cal., 21g fat (10g sat. fat), 47mg chol., 447mg sod., 10g carb. (3g sugars, 2g fiber), 11g pro.

TEST KITCHEN TIPS

- If you're unsure how much of the end to trim off, let the stalk tell you. Gently bend the asparagus—you'll be able to feel where it wants to break. Snap off the stalk end as far down as you easily can. To work in bulk, use a chef's knife to slice off about an inch of the tough, white-colored ends.

- Store this prepared asparagus dish in an airtight container in the refrigerator for up to 3 days.

POTATOES LYONNAISE

VERTICAL CARROT CAKE

This vertical spin on a cherished classic is packed with spices and sure to impress. The browned butter cream cheese frosting truly takes the cake over the top!
—*Mark Neufang, Milwaukee, WI*

- -

PREP: 1½ hours + chilling
BAKE: 20 min. + cooling
MAKES: 16 servings

CARROT CAKE

- ½ cup plus 1 Tbsp. all-purpose flour
- ½ tsp. ground ginger
- ½ tsp. ground cinnamon
- ¼ tsp. ground nutmeg
- ¼ tsp. salt
- ⅛ tsp. ground cloves
- 1 cup pecan halves, toasted
- ½ lb. carrots, peeled and finely grated
- 1 Tbsp. minced fresh gingerroot
- ½ tsp. grated orange zest
- 8 large eggs, separated, room temperature
- ⅔ cup plus 2 Tbsp. sugar, divided

BROWNED BUTTER CREAM CHEESE FROSTING

- 1½ cups unsalted butter, cubed and divided
- 4 large egg whites
- 1 cup sugar
  Dash salt
- 1 tsp. vanilla extract
- 2 pkg. (8 oz. each) cream cheese, softened

VERTICAL CARROT CAKE

1. Preheat oven to 350°. Line 2 greased 15x10x1-in. baking pans with parchment; grease paper. Set aside. Sift flour, ground ginger, cinnamon, nutmeg, salt and cloves together twice. Place pecans in a food processor; pulse until finely ground. Transfer to a bowl; toss with carrots, fresh ginger and zest.

2. In a large bowl, beat egg yolks until slightly thickened. Gradually add ⅔ cup sugar, beating on high speed until thick and lemon-colored. Fold in flour mixture, then carrot mixture.

3. Place egg whites in another large bowl. With clean beaters, beat egg whites on medium until soft peaks form. Gradually add remaining sugar, 1 Tbsp. at a time, beating on high after each addition until sugar is dissolved. Continue beating until stiff glossy peaks form. Fold a fourth of the whites into batter, then fold in the remaining whites. Transfer to prepared pans, spreading evenly.

4. Bake until golden brown and tops spring back when lightly touched, 18-22 minutes. Cool 5 minutes. Invert cakes onto tea towels dusted with confectioners' sugar. Gently peel off paper; trim ends. Roll up cakes in towels jelly-roll style, starting with a short side. Cool completely on a wire rack.

5. For the frosting, place 1 cup butter in a small heavy saucepan; melt over medium heat. Heat until golden brown, 5-7 minutes, stirring constantly. Remove from heat. Cool until thick and creamy, but not hard, stirring occasionally.

6. Meanwhile, in a heatproof bowl of stand mixer, whisk egg whites, 1 cup sugar and salt until blended. Place over simmering water in a large saucepan over medium heat. Whisking constantly, heat mixture 8-10 minutes or until a thermometer reads 160°. Remove from heat. With whisk attachment of stand mixer, beat on high speed until cooled to 90°, about 7 minutes. Using the paddle attachment, gradually beat in remaining ½ cup butter, a few tablespoons at a time, on medium speed

until smooth. Beat in vanilla and cooled browned butter until smooth; transfer to another bowl. Add the cream cheese to mixer bowl; beat until smooth. Gradually add buttercream back to the bowl; beat until combined.

7. Unroll cakes; cut each into two 15x5-in. strips. Spread 1 cup frosting on each strip to within ½ in. of edges. Refrigerate until frosting is firm, at least 20 minutes.

8. To assemble cake, tightly roll up 1 strip jelly-roll style, starting with a short side, lifting slightly as you roll. Carefully align seam of roll with short side of another strip. Continue to roll, jelly-roll style, adding remaining strips; seal seam. Carefully stand rolled cake on its end on a serving platter. Spread remaining frosting over top and sides of cake. Refrigerate at least 2 hours or overnight. Let stand at room temperature 15 minutes before slicing.

1 PIECE: 445 cal., 34g fat (18g sat. fat), 167mg chol., 193mg sod., 30g carb. (25g sugars, 1g fiber), 7g pro.

HOW-TO

Make A Vertical Carrot Cake

This masterpiece is sure to garner oohs and ahhs —but it's easier to pull off than you might think.

With a small offset spatula, spread 1 scant cup frosting to edges of each cake strip. Chill the prepared strips for 15-20 minutes to firm up the frosting.

Carefully roll up first cake strip, starting with a short end. If the cake cracks a bit, no worries! There will be less cracking as the roll gets larger, and the interior cracks will be hidden.

Position the first cake roll at a short end of the next cake strip. Roll the 2 together. Repeat with the remaining 2 cake strips, making 1 large roll. Carefully stand roll on 1 of its ends on a serving plate.

Spread the remaining frosting over the cake in a thin layer. Use slightly more frosting where the seams of the roll meet to ensure it stays in place.

BIBB LETTUCE WITH ROASTED RED ONIONS

Forget boring tossed salads! This side will have your guests asking for the recipe. Top with bacon, or substitute feta for the Gorgonzola for a change of taste.
—*Josh Carter, Birmingham, AL*

- -

PREP: 25 min. • **BAKE:** 20 min.
MAKES: 8 servings

- 2 medium red onions, cut into ¼-in. wedges
- 1 Tbsp. olive oil
- ⅛ tsp. salt
- ⅛ tsp. pepper
- 1⅓ cups balsamic vinegar
- 6 Tbsp. orange juice
- 4 heads Boston or Bibb lettuce, halved lengthwise
- ½ cup crumbled Gorgonzola cheese
  Toasted chopped walnuts, optional

1. Preheat oven to 400°. Place onions on a foil-lined baking sheet. Drizzle with oil. Sprinkle with salt and pepper; toss to coat. Roast until tender, 20-25 minutes, stirring occasionally.

2. In a small saucepan, combine vinegar and juice. Bring to a boil; cook until reduced by half, 8-10 minutes.

3. Top lettuce halves with roasted onions. Drizzle with sauce and top with cheese. Sprinkle with additional black pepper and, if desired, chopped walnuts.

1 SERVING: 101 cal., 4g fat (2g sat. fat), 6mg chol., 135mg sod., 15g carb. (13g sugars, 1g fiber), 2g pro. **DIABETIC EXCHANGES:** 2 vegetable, 1 fat.

TEST KITCHEN TIP

Not a fan of Gorgonzola? Use feta or shaved Parmesan instead. Try pecans instead of walnuts, or add sliced pears for more crunch. The possibilities are up to you!

BIBB LETTUCE WITH ROASTED RED ONIONS

OFF TO THE RACES

You can bet on a good time at this Kentucky Derby blowout. Pastel embellishments, homemade mint juleps and a themed game make for thoroughbred fun.

PECAN TARTS

MINT JULEP

BENEDICTINE SPREAD

KENTUCKY HOT BROWN SLIDERS

BENEDICTINE SPREAD

PECAN TARTS

Guests will be running for seconds of these sweet morsels at your Run for the Roses party. The flaky crust and rich center make for a mouthwatering treat.
—*Jean Rhodes, Tignall, GA*

PREP: 20 min. + chilling • **BAKE:** 25 min. + cooling
MAKES: about 20

- 3 oz. cream cheese, softened
- ½ cup butter, softened
- 1 cup all-purpose flour
- ¼ tsp. salt

FILLING
- 1 large egg
- ¾ cup packed dark brown sugar
- 1 Tbsp. butter, melted
- 1 tsp. vanilla extract
- ⅔ cup chopped pecans

1. Preheat oven to 325°. In a small bowl, beat the cream cheese and butter until fluffy; blend in flour and salt. Refrigerate for 1 hour. Shape into 1-in. balls; press onto the bottom and up the sides of greased mini-muffin cups.
2. For filling, in a small bowl, beat the egg. Add brown sugar, butter and vanilla; mix well. Stir in pecans. Spoon into tart shells.
3. Bake until lightly browned and set, 25-30 minutes. Cool for 15 minutes before carefully removing from pans.
1 TART: 145 cal., 10g fat (4g sat. fat), 29mg chol., 101mg sod., 14g carb. (8g sugars, 1g fiber), 2g pro.

BENEDICTINE SPREAD

This version of a traditional Kentucky cucumber spread comes from our Test Kitchen. Serve it as an appetizer dip or sandwich filling.
—*Taste of Home Test Kitchen*

TAKES: 15 min. • **MAKES:** 1¾ cups

- 1 pkg. (8 oz.) cream cheese, softened
- 1 Tbsp. mayonnaise
- ¼ tsp. salt
- ⅛ tsp. white pepper
- ⅛ tsp. dill weed
- 1 drop green food coloring, optional
- ¾ cup finely chopped peeled cucumber, patted dry
- ¼ cup finely chopped onion
  Optional: Snack rye bread, pita bread wedges and assorted fresh vegetables

In a small bowl, combine cream cheese, mayonnaise, salt, white pepper, dill and, if desired, food coloring; beat until smooth. Stir in cucumber and onion. Cover and refrigerate until serving. Serve with snack rye bread, pita bread wedges or vegetables as desired.
2 TBSP.: 65 cal., 6g fat (3g sat. fat), 16mg chol., 98mg sod., 1g carb. (1g sugars, 0 fiber), 1g pro.

READER REVIEW

"Excellent with baby carrot dippers as well as crackers. This spread would be delicious on grilled salmon, too. Even better the next day!"
—DEBGLASS11, TASTEOFHOME.COM

PECAN TARTS

5i
MINT JULEP

(SHOWN ON PAGE 238)

It'll be hats off to you if you serve this classic cocktail at your Kentucky Derby soiree. The subtly sweet sipper made with bourbon and fresh mint is an absolute must-have.
—Taste of Home *Test Kitchen*

PREP: 30 min. + chilling
MAKES: 10 servings (2½ cups syrup)

MINT SYRUP
- 2 cups sugar
- 2 cups water
- 2 cups loosely packed chopped fresh mint

EACH SERVING
- ½ to ¾ cup crushed ice
- ½ to 1 oz. bourbon
  Mint sprig

1. For syrup, combine sugar, water and chopped mint in a large saucepan. Bring to a boil over medium heat; cook until sugar is dissolved, stirring occasionally. Remove from the heat; cool to room temperature.
2. Line a mesh strainer with a double layer of cheesecloth or a coffee filter. Strain syrup; discard mint. Cover and refrigerate syrup for at least 2 hours or until chilled.
3. For each serving, place ice in a metal julep cup or rocks glass. Pour 2-4 Tbsp. mint syrup and bourbon into the glass; stir until mixture is well chilled. Garnish with mint sprig.
⅓ CUP: 197 cal., 0 fat (0 sat. fat), 0 chol., 6mg sod., 42g carb. (39g sugars, 1g fiber), 1g pro.

HOW-TO

Luck of the Draw

Have guests pick from a fedora or bowler hat a numbered piece of paper randomly assigned to a racehorse. Whoever selects the winning horse's number wins a prize at the party's end.

KENTUCKY HOT BROWN SLIDERS

I transformed the Hot Brown sandwich, traditionally open-faced, into a party-ready slider. This easy-to-eat finger food was originally meant for a Kentucky Derby get-together, but it's so tasty, I now serve it anytime. Just cover and refrigerate the assembled sandwiches so you can pop them in the oven when company arrives.
—*Blair Lonergan, Rochelle, VA*

PREP: 20 min. • **BAKE:** 30 min.
MAKES: 12 servings

- 1 pkg. (12 oz.) Hawaiian sweet rolls
- 3 Tbsp. mayonnaise
- 12 slices deli turkey, folded into quarters
- 12 slices cooked bacon strips, halved widthwise
- 1 jar (4 oz.) diced pimientos, drained, or 2 plum tomatoes, cut into 12 slices
- 6 slices Gruyere cheese, halved
- ¼ cup grated Parmesan cheese
- ½ cup butter, cubed
- 2 Tbsp. finely chopped onion
- 2 Tbsp. brown sugar
- 1½ tsp. Worcestershire sauce
- ¼ tsp. garlic powder

1. Preheat the oven to 350°. Without separating rolls, cut the package of rolls in half horizontally; arrange bottom halves in a greased 11x7-in. baking pan. Spread mayonnaise evenly across the bottom halves. Top each with the turkey, bacon, pimientos, Gruyere and Parmesan cheese. Replace top halves of rolls.
2. In a small skillet, melt butter over medium heat. Add onion; cook and stir until tender, 1-2 minutes. Whisk in brown sugar, Worcestershire sauce and garlic powder. Cook and stir until sugar is dissolved; drizzle over sandwiches.
3. Cover and bake for 25 minutes. Uncover; bake until golden brown, 5-10 minutes longer.
1 SLIDER: 327 cal., 21g fat (10g sat. fat), 67mg chol., 652mg sod., 20g carb. (9g sugars, 1g fiber), 16g pro.

KENTUCKY HOT BROWN SLIDERS

SUMMER
ORZO

THREE-BEAN
BAKED BEANS

JUICY CHERRY PIE

WATERMELON
CUPS

CRISPY FRIED
CHICKEN

YUMMY CORN
CHIP SALAD

Family Affair

We've got food for all your folks! These
six picnic-perfect recipes are sure to satisfy
every uncle, cousin and kiddo at the reunion—
oh, and earn their compliments, too.

CRISPY FRIED CHICKEN

This fried chicken can be served hot or pulled out of the fridge the next day as leftovers. Either way, folks love it.
—*Jeanne Schnitzler, Lima, MT*

PREP: 15 min. • **COOK:** 15 min./batch
MAKES: 12 servings

- 4 cups all-purpose flour, divided
- 2 Tbsp. garlic salt
- 1 Tbsp. paprika
- 3 tsp. pepper, divided
- 2½ tsp. poultry seasoning
- 2 large eggs
- 1½ cups water
- 1 tsp. salt
- 2 broiler/fryer chickens (3½ to 4 lbs. each), cut up
  Oil for deep-fat frying

1. In a large shallow dish, combine 2⅔ cups flour, garlic salt, paprika, 2½ tsp. pepper and poultry seasoning. In another shallow dish, beat eggs and 1½ cups water; add salt and the remaining 1⅓ cups flour and ½ tsp. pepper. Dip the chicken in egg mixture, then place in the flour mixture, a few pieces at a time. Turn to coat.
2. In a deep-fat fryer, heat oil to 375°. Fry chicken, several pieces at a time, until chicken is golden brown and juices run clear, 7-8 minutes on each side. Drain on paper towels.

5 OZ. COOKED CHICKEN: 543 cal., 33g fat (7g sat. fat), 137mg chol., 798mg sod., 17g carb. (0 sugars, 1g fiber), 41g pro.

TEST KITCHEN TIPS

- Soaking the chicken in buttermilk before frying will give you moist and juicy results. The acid in the buttermilk helps break down the protein, creating tender meat.
- Neutral oils with a high smoke point, such as canola, vegetable and peanut oil, are ideal for frying chicken.
- A thrifty alternative to purchased garlic salt is to mix up your own. Just combine 1 tsp. garlic powder with 3 tsp. of table salt or other fine-grained salt. The ratio works the same for onion salt, too.

SUMMER ORZO

SUMMER ORZO

I'm always looking for fun ways to use the fresh veggies that come in my Community Supported Agriculture box, and this salad is one of my favorite creations. I like to improvise with whatever I have on hand; feel free to do the same here!
—*Shayna Marmar, Philadelphia, PA*

PREP: 30 min. + chilling
MAKES: 16 servings

- 1 pkg. (16 oz.) orzo pasta
- ¼ cup water
- 1½ cups fresh or frozen corn
- 24 cherry tomatoes, halved
- 2 cups crumbled feta cheese
- 1 medium cucumber, seeded and chopped
- 1 small red onion, finely chopped
- ¼ cup minced fresh mint
- 2 Tbsp. capers, drained and chopped, optional
- ½ cup olive oil
- ¼ cup lemon juice
- 1 Tbsp. grated lemon zest
- 1½ tsp. salt
- 1 tsp. pepper
- 1 cup sliced almonds, toasted

1. Cook orzo according to package directions for al dente. Drain orzo; rinse with cold water and drain well. Transfer to a large bowl.
2. In a large nonstick skillet, heat ¼ cup water over medium heat. Add corn; cook and stir until crisp-tender, 3-4 minutes. Add to orzo; stir in tomatoes, feta cheese, cucumber, onion, mint and, if desired, capers. In a small bowl, whisk oil, lemon juice, lemon zest, salt and pepper until blended. Pour over orzo mixture; toss to coat. Refrigerate 30 minutes.
3. Just before serving, stir in almonds.

¾ CUP: 291 cal., 15g fat (4g sat. fat), 15mg chol., 501mg sod., 28g carb. (3g sugars, 3g fiber), 11g pro.

YUMMY CORN CHIP SALAD

YUMMY CORN CHIP SALAD

Corn chips give a special crunch and an unexpected flavor to this potluck favorite. Bacon adds a hint of smokiness, while the cranberries bring a touch of sweetness. It's the perfect picnic companion!
—*Nora Friesen, Aberdeen, MS*

TAKES: 25 min. • **MAKES:** 12 servings

- ¾ cup canola oil
- ¼ cup cider vinegar
- ¼ cup mayonnaise
- 2 Tbsp. yellow mustard
- ½ tsp. salt
- ¾ cup sugar
- ½ small onion
- ¾ tsp. poppy seeds

SALAD
- 2 bunches leaf lettuce, chopped (about 20 cups)
- 1 pkg. (9¼ oz.) corn chips
- 8 bacon strips, cooked and crumbled
- 1 cup shredded part-skim mozzarella cheese
- 1 cup dried cranberries

1. For dressing, place first 7 ingredients in a blender. Cover; process until smooth. Stir in poppy seeds.

2. Place salad ingredients in a large bowl; toss with dressing. Serve immediately.

1⅓ CUPS: 436 cal., 30g fat (4g sat. fat), 12mg chol., 456mg sod., 38g carb. (24g sugars, 2g fiber), 7g pro.

JUICY CHERRY PIE

Cherry season is in the heart of summer. For this pie, choose fresh tart cherries that are bright in color, shiny and plump. They also should feel relatively firm when pressed lightly.
—*Karen Berner, New Canaan, CT*

PREP: 35 min. + chilling
BAKE: 55 min. + cooling
MAKES: 8 servings

- 2½ cups all-purpose flour
- ½ tsp. salt
- ⅔ cup cold unsalted butter, cubed
- ⅓ cup shortening
- 6 to 10 Tbsp. ice water

FILLING
- 5 cups fresh tart cherries, pitted
- 2 tsp. lemon juice
- ¼ tsp. almond extract
- 1 cup sugar
- ⅓ cup all-purpose flour
- 1 tsp. ground cinnamon

SUGAR TOPPING
- 1 Tbsp. 2% milk
- 1 tsp. sugar

1. In a large bowl, mix flour and salt; cut in butter and shortening until crumbly. Gradually add ice water, tossing with a fork until dough holds together when pressed. Divide dough in half. Shape each into a disk; wrap. Refrigerate 1 hour or overnight.

2. Preheat oven to 375°. For filling, place the cherries in a large bowl; drizzle with lemon juice and almond extract. In a small bowl, mix the sugar, flour and cinnamon. Sprinkle over the cherries and toss gently to coat.

3. On a lightly floured surface, roll 1 dough portion into a ⅛-in.-thick circle; transfer to a 9-in. pie plate. Trim crust even with rim. Add filling.

4. Roll remaining dough into a ⅛-in.-thick circle; cut out stars or other shapes using cookie cutters. Place the top crust over filling. Trim, seal and flute edge. If desired, decorate top with cutouts.

5. Bake 40 minutes. For topping, brush top of pie with milk; sprinkle with sugar. Bake until crust is golden brown and filling is bubbly, 15-20 minutes longer. Cool on a wire rack.

1 PIECE: 521 cal., 24g fat (12g sat. fat), 41mg chol., 155mg sod., 72g carb. (34g sugars, 3g fiber), 6g pro.

JUICY CHERRY PIE

THREE-BEAN BAKED BEANS

WATERMELON CUPS

This lovely appetizer is almost too pretty to eat! Sweet watermelon cubes hold a refreshing topping that showcases cucumber, red onion and fresh herbs.
—Taste of Home *Test Kitchen*

- -

TAKES: 25 min. • **MAKES:** 16 appetizers

- 16   seedless watermelon cubes (1 in.)
- ⅓   cup finely chopped cucumber
- 5   tsp. finely chopped red onion
- 2   tsp. minced fresh mint
- 2   tsp. minced fresh cilantro
- ½   to 1 tsp. lime juice

1. Using a small melon baller or measuring spoon, scoop out the center of each watermelon cube, leaving a ¼-in. shell (save centers for another use).
2. In a small bowl, combine the remaining ingredients; spoon into watermelon cubes.
1 PIECE: 7 cal., 0 fat (0 sat. fat), 0 chol., 1mg sod., 2g carb. (2g sugars, 0 fiber), 0 pro.

READER REVIEW

"What a refreshing little treat! We're not fans of cilantro, so I substituted parsley, as one of the other reviews mentioned. Easy to make and fun to eat!"

—SGRONHOLZ TASTEOFHOME.COM

THREE-BEAN BAKED BEANS

I got this recipe from my aunt and made a couple of changes to suit our tastes. With ground beef and bacon mixed in, these satisfying beans are a big hit at backyard barbecues and church picnics. I'm always asked to bring my special beans.
—*Julie Currington, Gahanna, OH*

- -

PREP: 20 min. • **BAKE:** 1 hour
MAKES: 12 servings

- ½   lb. ground beef
- 5   bacon strips, diced
- ½   cup chopped onion
- ⅓   cup packed brown sugar
- ¼   cup sugar
- ¼   cup ketchup
- ¼   cup barbecue sauce
- 2   Tbsp. molasses
- 2   Tbsp. prepared mustard
- ½   tsp. chili powder
- ½   tsp. salt
- 2   cans (15 oz. each) pork and beans, undrained
- 1   can (16 oz.) butter beans, rinsed and drained
- 1   can (16 oz.) kidney beans, rinsed and drained

1. Preheat oven to 350°. In a large skillet, cook and crumble beef with bacon and onion over medium heat until beef is no longer pink; drain.
2. Stir in sugars, ketchup, barbecue sauce, molasses, mustard, chili powder and salt until blended. Stir in the beans. Transfer to a greased 2½-qt. baking dish. Bake, covered, until bean mixture reach desired thickness, about 1 hour.
FREEZE OPTION: Freeze cooled bean mixture in freezer containers. To use, partially thaw in refrigerator overnight. Heat through in a saucepan, stirring occasionally; add water if necessary.
¾ CUP: 269 cal., 8g fat (2g sat. fat), 19mg chol., 708mg sod., 42g carb. (21g sugars, 7g fiber), 13g pro.

WATERMELON CUPS

GOOD WITCH
BAD WITCH

**Which are you? Pick your poison, then party on!
This pink and green spread with yummy goodies
will cast a spell on even your witchiest pals.**

WHICH WITCH?
Differing balloon arches
and a Wicked Witch of
the East-inspired striped
table runner easily
and adorably separate
your table into two
distinct sides.

GOOD WITCH
CAKE

TURKEY, GOUDA &
APPLE TEA SANDWICHES

MYSTICAL MIX
Green and pink stir-ins, such as M&M's, take neutral-colored snack mixes up a notch.

CONFETTI
SNACK MIX

BAD WITCH
CAKE

DUELING DECOR
Play up each side's theme by opting for dark and spooky table decor on one side and pink and shimmery on the other.

CHERRY LEMON-
LIME PUNCH

BAD WITCH CAKE

GOOD WITCH CAKE

2. Pour into prepared pans. Bake until a toothpick inserted in center comes out clean, 40-45 minutes. Cool 10 minutes before removing from pans to wire racks to cool.

3. For frosting, beat butter until smooth. Beat in the confectioners' sugar, vanilla, salt and enough milk to reach the desired consistency. Remove 1½ cups frosting; tint with pink or black food coloring. Tint remaining frosting dark pink or green with food coloring.

4. If the cake layers have rounded tops, trim with a serrated knife to level. Place 1 cake layer on a serving plate; spread with ⅔ cup dark pink or green frosting. Repeat layers. Top with remaining layer. Frost top and sides of cake.

5. For gold stars, place melted yellow candy coating in piping bag fitted with a small round tip; pipe star shapes onto waxed paper. Or, for black hats, pipe melted black candy coating into witch hat shapes on waxed paper. Let stand until set. Top cake with desired sprinkles. Place light pink or black frosting in piping bag fitted with large star tip; pipe onto top of cake. Just before serving, gently stand 1 star or witch hat on top of cake. Adhere remaining decorations and pearls to sides.

1 PIECE: 882 cal., 35g fat (22g sat. fat), 114mg chol., 504mg sod., 135g carb. (115g sugars, 1g fiber), 6g pro.

CONFETTI SNACK MIX
(SHOWN ON PAGE 247)

I've made this party mix for many years, and I usually double the recipe. It makes a delightful gift, and everyone always asks for the recipe.
—*Jane Bray, Temple Terrace, FL*

- -

TAKES: 10 min. • **MAKES:** 7 cups

4 cups Golden Grahams
1 cup dry-roasted peanuts
1 cup dried banana chips
1 cup raisins
1 cup milk chocolate M&M's

In a large bowl, combine all ingredients. Store in an airtight container.

¼ CUP: 125 cal., 6g fat (3g sat. fat), 1mg chol., 98mg sod., 18g carb. (12g sugars, 1g fiber), 2g pro.

GOOD WITCH/ BAD WITCH CAKE

If you're looking for an extra-special dessert to serve for Halloween, these magical cakes will delight every witch at your Emerald City celebration.
—Taste of Home *Test Kitchen*

- -

PREP: 1¼ hours • **BAKE:** 40 min. + cooling
MAKES: 16 servings

¾ cup butter, softened
2½ cups packed brown sugar
4 large eggs, room temperature
6 oz. semisweet chocolate, melted and cooled
3 tsp. vanilla extract
3 cups all-purpose flour
3 tsp. baking soda
1 tsp. salt
1½ cups sour cream
1½ cups water

FROSTING
1¼ cups butter, softened
10 cups confectioners' sugar
3 tsp. vanilla extract
¼ tsp. salt
½ to ⅔ cup 2% milk
   Pink gel food coloring or black and green gel food coloring
4 oz. yellow or black candy coating disks, melted
   Pink sprinkles, pink sanding sugar and pink pearls, or black sprinkles, black sanding sugar and black pearls

1. Preheat oven to 350°. Line 3 greased 8-in. round baking pans with parchment; grease paper. Cream butter and brown sugar until light and fluffy, 5-7 minutes. Add eggs, 1 at a time, beating well after each addition. Beat in melted chocolate and vanilla. Combine the flour, baking soda and salt; add to creamed mixture alternately with sour cream, beating well after each addition. Gradually beat in water.

SPRITZ COOKIES

Here's a sure standout on your treat tray. The cheery cookies get their bright-pink color from cranberry-flavored gelatin.
—*Kristen Rahn, Burnsville, MN*

- -

PREP: 30 min.
BAKE: 10 min./batch + cooling
MAKES: 5 dozen

- ½ cup butter, softened
- ½ cup butter-flavored shortening
- ½ cup sugar
- ¼ cup cranberry gelatin powder (about 4 oz.)
- 1 large egg, room temperature
- 1 tsp. vanilla extract
- 2 cups all-purpose flour
- ½ tsp. baking powder
- ¼ tsp. salt
  Colored coarse sugar, optional

1. Preheat oven to 375°. In a large bowl, cream butter, shortening, sugar and gelatin until light and fluffy, 5-7 minutes. Beat in egg and vanilla. Combine the flour, baking powder and salt; gradually add to creamed mixture and mix well.
2. Using a cookie press fitted with the disk of your choice, press dough 2 in. apart onto ungreased baking sheets. If desired, sprinkle with coarse sugar.
3. Bake cookies 6-8 minutes or until set (do not brown). Remove to wire racks to cool completely.
1 COOKIE: 58 cal., 3g fat (1g sat. fat), 8mg chol., 27mg sod., 6g carb. (3g sugars, 0 fiber), 1g pro.

CHERRY LEMON-LIME PUNCH

SPRITZ COOKIES

CHERRY LEMON-LIME PUNCH

To keep the punch cold while adding extra color, I like to make an ice ring out of cherry soda pop. The flavor always brings folks back for more.
—*Carol Van Sickle, Versailles, KY*

- -

TAKES: 15 min. • **MAKES:** 22 servings (5½ qt.)

- 8 cups cold water
- 1 can (12 oz.) frozen lemonade concentrate, thawed plus ¾ cup thawed lemonade concentrate
- 2 liters ginger ale, chilled
- 1 liter cherry lemon-lime soda, chilled
  Optional: Maraschino cherries and lemon wedges

In a large punch bowl, combine water and lemonade concentrate. Stir in ginger ale and lemon-lime soda. If desired, garnish with maraschino cherries and lemon wedges. Serve immediately.
1 CUP: 102 cal., 0 fat (0 sat. fat), 0 chol., 13mg sod., 26g carb. (24g sugars, 0 fiber), 0 pro.

TEST KITCHEN TIP

Ladle prepared punch into cups, then add your pick of strawberries and raspberries or blackberries and green grapes. Crush fruit gently so your drink matches your coven's color!

TURKEY, GOUDA & APPLE TEA SANDWICHES

These fun mini sandwiches are a tasty addition to any fall function. The cranberry mayo lends a unique flavor twist, and the apples add a nice crunch. These sammies will be the life of the party!
—*Taste of Home Test Kitchen*

- -

TAKES: 25 min. • **MAKES:** 4 dozen

- ⅔ cup reduced-fat mayonnaise
- 2 Tbsp. whole-berry cranberry sauce
- 24 very thin slices wheat or white bread, crusts removed
- 12 slices deli turkey
- 2 medium apples, thinly sliced
- 12 thin slices smoked Gouda cheese
- 4 cups fresh baby spinach

1. Place mayonnaise and cranberry sauce in a small food processor. Cover and process until blended. Spread over each bread slice.
2. Layer the turkey, apples, cheese and spinach over each of 12 bread slices; top with remaining bread. Cut each sandwich into quarters.
TO MAKE AHEAD: Cranberry spread can be prepared a day in advance; cover and store in the refrigerator.
1 TEA SANDWICH: 59 cal., 3g fat (2g sat. fat), 8mg chol., 150mg sod., 5g carb. (1g sugars, 0 fiber), 3g pro.

BUTTERY
ROLLS

MASHED RED
POTATOES

SEASONED
ROAST TURKEY

THANK GOODNESS!

It's the feast you've been looking forward to all year!
Come to the table with a near-and-dear classic or a twist on tradition.
Either way, there's so much deliciousness to share.

SIMPLE ROAST
BRUSSELS SPROUTS

SWEET
CANDIED
CARROTS

MAPLE-HONEY
CRANBERRY SAUCE

CRANBERRY
APPLE SLAB PIE

PARMESAN KALE CASSEROLE

I tried coming up with a creative way to use kale, and the result was a cheesy casserole. When my husband sampled it, he absolutely loved it. Bits of summer sausage add heartiness.
—*Diana Johnson, Auburn, WA*

PREP: 10 min. • **BAKE:** 25 min.
MAKES: 6 servings

1½ cups heavy whipping cream
½ cup finely chopped summer sausage
3 garlic cloves, minced
2 pkg. (16 oz. each) frozen cut kale, thawed and squeezed dry (about 3 cups total)
¾ cup panko bread crumbs
¾ cup grated Parmesan cheese

1. Preheat oven to 350°. In a large skillet, combine cream, sausage and garlic; bring to a boil. Reduce heat; simmer, uncovered, 3-5 minutes or until slightly thickened. Stir in kale. Add the bread crumbs and cheese; toss to combine.
2. Transfer to a greased 8-in. square baking dish. Bake 25-30 minutes or until edges are golden brown.
¾ CUP: 361 cal., 35g fat (17g sat. fat), 85mg chol., 412mg sod., 17g carb. (4g sugars, 3g fiber), 12g pro.

PARMESAN KALE CASSEROLE

MAKE-AHEAD TURKEY GRAVY

MAKE-AHEAD TURKEY GRAVY

As far as my family is concerned, I can never have enough homemade gravy on hand for Thanksgiving dinner! The base for this flavorful gravy is prepared with turkey wings and can be prepared in advance.
—*Linda Fitzsimmons, Fort Edward, NY*

PREP: 2¼ hours • **COOK:** 10 min.
MAKES: 4¼ cups

2 turkey wings (1½ to 2 lbs.)
2 medium onions, quartered
2 cartons (32 oz. each) reduced-sodium chicken broth, divided
2 medium carrots, cut into 2-in. pieces
2 celery ribs with leaves, cut into 2-in. pieces
4 fresh thyme sprigs
½ cup plus 2 Tbsp. all-purpose flour
1 Tbsp. butter
¼ tsp. pepper

1. Place turkey wings and onions in a greased 13x9-in. baking pan. Bake, uncovered, at 400° for 1¼ hours, turning them once.
2. Transfer wings and onions to a Dutch oven. While 13x9-in. pan is still warm, carefully add 2 cups broth. Using a spatula, gently scrape any brown bits off bottom of pan; pour into Dutch oven with wings. Add 4 cups broth, carrots, celery and thyme to Dutch oven. Bring to a boil. Reduce heat; simmer, uncovered, about 45 minutes.
3. Strain; discard wings and vegetables. (Can be made ahead to this point and stored in the refrigerator for up to 2 days.) Skim fat from cooking liquid. Add enough remaining broth to measure 3½ cups; set aside.
4. In a large saucepan, whisk flour and remaining broth until smooth. Gradually stir in cooking liquid. Bring to a boil; cook and stir for until thickened, about 2 minutes. Stir in butter and pepper.
NOTE: Chilling liquid after straining helps to solidify any fats on the surface, which makes skimming off the fat and removing it very easy!
3 TBSP.: 61 cal., 2g fat (1g sat. fat), 12mg chol., 234mg sod., 5g carb. (1g sugars, 1g fiber), 5g pro.

MAPLE-HONEY CRANBERRY SAUCE

This recipe is simple, quick and a family favorite. I'll often make a double batch for us to use on meats, spread on toast or even garnish desserts.
—*Rebecca Israel, Mansfield, PA*

TAKES: 25 min. • **MAKES:** 2 cups

- 2 cups fresh or frozen cranberries
- ½ cup maple syrup
- ½ cup honey
- 1 Tbsp. grated orange zest
  Additional orange zest, optional

In a large saucepan, combine the cranberries, syrup, honey and orange zest. Cook over medium heat until the berries pop, about 15 minutes. Cover and store in the refrigerator. If desired, top with additional orange zest before serving.

2 TBSP.: 64 cal., 0 fat (0 sat. fat), 0 chol., 2mg sod., 17g carb. (15g sugars, 1g fiber), 0 pro.

SPICED AMARETTO CRANBERRY SAUCE: Add ¼ cup amaretto and 1 tsp. apple pie spice to the cranberry mixture. Proceed as directed. Top with toasted sliced almonds.

TEST KITCHEN TIPS

- You can serve this sauce any way you like it, though most home cooks serve it at room temperature or chilled. Either way, it's excellent paired with these Thanksgiving sides.
- Store the cranberry sauce in an airtight container in the refrigerator. With its high sugar content, it can last up to 10 days when stored properly.
- Use it for a fall brunch by spreading it over French toast or waffles, with dessert, or on a savory piece of toast. Cranberries have many health benefits, so use any excuse to add them to your plate.

MASHED RED POTATOES

PESTO MASHED RED POTATOES

MASHED RED POTATOES

These simple-yet-satisfying chunky mashed potatoes are rich enough to stand on their own—but a big pat of butter on top sure never hurts.
—*Taste of Home Test Kitchen*

TAKES: 30 min. • **MAKES:** 12 servings

- 4½ lbs. red potatoes, cut into 1-in. pieces
- 6 Tbsp. butter, cubed
- 1½ tsp. salt
- ¾ tsp. pepper
- 1 to 1⅓ cups heavy whipping cream, warmed

1. Place the potatoes in a large saucepan or Dutch oven and cover with water. Bring to a boil. Reduce heat; cover and cook for 10-15 minutes or until tender. Drain.

2. In a large bowl, mash potatoes with butter, salt, pepper and enough cream to achieve desired consistency.

¾ CUP: 242 cal., 13g fat (8g sat. fat), 38mg chol., 356mg sod., 28g carb. (2g sugars, 3g fiber), 4g pro.

PESTO MASHED RED POTATOES: Prepare recipe as directed. Just before serving, swirl ⅓ cup prepared pesto into potatoes and drizzle potatoes with extra virgin olive oil.

SPICED AMARETTO CRANBERRY SAUCE

MAPLE-HONEY CRANBERRY SAUCE

SEASONED
ROAST TURKEY

SMOKY GRILLED
TURKEY DRUMSTICKS

SEASONED ROAST TURKEY

A stunning Thanksgiving bird doesn't need any fuss. Rubbing the skin with melted butter keeps it moist and tender.
—*Nancy Reichert, Thomasville, GA*

- -

PREP: 15 min. • **BAKE:** 2¾ hours + standing
MAKES: 15 servings

- ¼ cup butter, melted
- 2 tsp. salt
- 2 tsp. garlic powder
- 2 tsp. seasoned salt
- 1½ tsp. paprika
- 1 tsp. ground ginger
- ¾ tsp. pepper
- ½ tsp. dried basil
- ¼ tsp. cayenne pepper
- 1 turkey (13 to 15 lbs.)

1. Preheat oven to 325°. In a small bowl, combine the first 9 ingredients. Place turkey, breast side up, on a rack in a roasting pan; pat dry. Brush with butter mixture.
2. Bake, uncovered, 2¾-3¼ hours or until a thermometer inserted in thickest part of thigh reads 170°-175°. (Cover loosely with foil if turkey browns too quickly.) Cover and let stand 20 minutes before carving.

4 OZ. COOKED TURKEY: 488 cal., 24g fat (8g sat. fat), 221mg chol., 698mg sod., 1g carb. (0 sugars, 0 fiber), 63g pro.
SMOKY GRILLED TURKEY DRUMSTICKS: Substitute 6 turkey drumsticks (1½ lbs. each) for the whole turkey. Add 3 cups soaked applewood chips to grill. Place drumsticks on greased grill rack. Grill, covered, over indirect medium heat, 40-45 minutes or until a thermometer reads 175°. Turn the drumsticks occasionally throughout cooking.

BUTTERY ROLLS

These lovely golden dinner rolls are tender, fluffy and delicious when eaten warm from the oven.
—*Debbie Leonard, Roseburg, OR*

- -

PREP: 30 min. + rising • **BAKE:** 15 min.
MAKES: 2 dozen

- 4 to 4⅓ cups bread flour
- 2¼ tsp. active dry yeast
- 1½ tsp. salt
- 1 cup warm milk (70° to 80°)
- ½ cup butter, softened
- ¼ cup sugar
- 2 large eggs, lightly beaten, room temperature

1. In a large bowl, combine 3 cups flour, yeast and salt. In a small saucepan, heat the milk, butter and sugar to 120°-130°. Add to dry ingredients; beat on medium speed 2 minutes. Add the eggs; beat to combine. Stir in enough remaining flour to form a soft dough (dough will be sticky).
2. Turn dough onto a lightly floured surface; knead until smooth and elastic, 6-8 minutes. Place in a greased bowl; turn once to grease the top. Cover and let rise in a warm place until doubled, about 1 hour.
3. Punch down dough. Turn onto a lightly floured surface. Divide into 24 portions; shape into balls. Place in a greased 13x9-in. baking pan. Cover and let rise in a warm place until almost doubled, about 1 hour. Bake at 375° for 15-18 minutes or until golden brown.

1 ROLL: 138 cal., 5g fat (3g sat. fat), 27mg chol., 189mg sod., 19g carb. (3g sugars, 1g fiber), 4g pro.
PARMESAN-HERB ROLLS: Add 2 tsp. Italian seasoning and 1 tsp. granulated garlic to the flour mixture. Proceed as directed. Just prior to baking, brush rolls with 1 Tbsp. olive oil and sprinkle with 1 Tbsp. grated Parmesan cheese and 1 tsp. Italian seasoning. Bake as directed.

PARMESAN-HERB ROLLS

BUTTERY ROLLS

SWEET CANDIED
CARROTS

SPICED CARROTS
WITH PISTACHIOS

SWEET CANDIED CARROTS

These tender, vibrant carrots have a buttery glaze and a mild sweetness. This is a simple dish, but it sure makes carrots seem special.
—*P. Lauren Fay-Neri, Syracuse, NY*

- -

TAKES: 30 min. • **MAKES:** 8 servings

- 2 lbs. carrots, sliced
- ¼ cup butter
- ¼ cup packed brown sugar
- ¼ tsp. salt
- ⅛ tsp. white pepper
   Minced fresh parsley, optional

1. Place carrots in a large saucepan; add 1 in. water. Bring to a boil. Reduce heat; cover and simmer for 8-10 minutes or until crisp-tender. Drain and set aside.
2. In the same pan, combine the butter, brown sugar, salt and pepper; cook and stir until butter is melted. Return carrots to the pan; cook and stir over medium heat for 5 minutes or until glazed. If desired, sprinkle with parsley.
½ CUP: 125 cal., 6g fat (4g sat. fat), 15mg chol., 174mg sod., 18g carb. (14g sugars, 3g fiber), 1g pro.
SPICED CARROTS WITH PISTACHIOS: Prepare carrots as directed, stirring ½ cup golden raisins, ⅓ cup toasted pistachios and 1 tsp. apple pie spice into the brown sugar mixture.

SIMPLE ROAST BRUSSELS SPROUTS

Oven temps vary, so keep an eye on these Brussels sprouts to make sure they get crisp but don't burn. Feel free to toss in some fresh herbs for variety.
—*Karen Keefe, Phoenix, AZ*

- -

PREP: 10 min. • **COOK:** 20 min. • **MAKES:** 6 servings

- 2 lbs. Brussels sprouts, halved
- 6 bacon strips, chopped
- 2 Tbsp. olive oil
- ½ tsp. kosher salt
- ½ tsp. pepper
- 2 Tbsp. balsamic glaze

Preheat oven to 450°. In a large bowl, toss Brussels sprouts, bacon, olive oil, salt and pepper. Transfer to a 15x10x1-in. baking sheet. Roast, stirring halfway through cooking, until sprouts are tender and lightly browned, 20-25 minutes. Drizzle with balsamic glaze; serve warm.
¾ CUP: 227 cal., 16g fat (4g sat. fat), 18mg chol., 381mg sod., 16g carb. (5g sugars, 5g fiber), 8g pro.
ITALIAN-INSPIRED BRUSSELS SPROUTS: While the Brussels sprouts are roasting, saute ½ cup finely diced pancetta until crisp. Toss cooked sprouts with the pancetta, 1 tsp. fresh thyme leaves, a drizzle of balsamic vinegar and some freshly grated Parmesan cheese.

READER REVIEW

"I made these Brussels sprouts over the summer and they are delicious, so I'm making them tomorrow as a side dish for Christmas dinner. The bacon flavors the Brussels sprouts very nicely."

— KRISTINECHAYES576, TASTEOFHOME.COM

SIMPLE ROAST
BRUSSELS SPROUTS

ITALIAN-INSPIRED
BRUSSELS SPROUTS

CRANBERRY APPLE SLAB PIE

My husband loves pie, so I made one with apples, raspberries and cranberries. It's so good, I bend the rules and let the grandkids have it for breakfast.

—Brenda R. Smith, Curran, MI

PREP: 45 min. +chilling • **BAKE:** 45 min. + cooling
MAKES: 24 servings

Dough for 2 double-crust pies
2¼ cups sugar
⅓ cup all-purpose flour
7 medium tart apples, peeled and sliced (about 8 cups)
3 cups fresh or frozen cranberries
2 tsp. grated orange zest
1½ tsp. ground nutmeg
1½ tsp. ground cinnamon
6 cups frozen or fresh raspberries
Optional: Egg wash, additional sugar or coarse sugar, and whipped cream

1. Divide dough into 2 portions so that 1 is slightly larger than the other; wrap and refrigerate 1 hour or overnight.

2. Roll out larger portion of dough between 2 pieces of waxed paper into a 18x13-in. rectangle. Remove top sheet of waxed paper; place a 15x10x1-in. baking pan upside down over crust. Lifting with waxed paper, carefully invert crust into pan. Remove waxed paper; press crust onto bottom and up sides of pan. Allow to chill while preparing filling.

3. In a Dutch oven, mix sugar and flour; stir in apples, cranberries, orange zest and spices. Bring to a boil over medium-high heat. Reduce heat; simmer, uncovered, 10-12 minutes or until apples are tender and juices are thickened, stirring occasionally. Remove from heat; stir in raspberries. Set aside to cool completely.

4. Preheat oven to 375°. Add filling to prepared crust.

5. On a well-floured surface, roll the remaining dough into a ⅛-in.-thick rectangle; cut into 1½-in.-wide strips. Arrange strips over filling, sealing ends to bottom crust. If desired, brush crust with egg wash; sprinkle with additional sugar or coarse sugar.

6. Bake on lowest oven rack 45-50 minutes or until the crust is golden brown and filling is bubbly. Cool on a wire rack. If desired, serve with whipped cream.

1 PIECE: 352 cal., 16g fat (10g sat. fat), 40mg chol., 207mg sod., 51g carb. (25g sugars, 4g fiber), 4g pro.

DOUGH FOR 2 DOUBLE-CRUST PIES: Combine 2½ cups all-purpose flour, 3 Tbsp. sugar and ½ tsp. salt; cut in ½ cup cold butter and ½ cup cold shortening until crumbly. Beat 1 egg yolk with ¼ cup ice water; gradually add to flour mixture, tossing with a fork until dough holds together when pressed, adding more water as necessary. Repeat to make a second batch of dough. Combine doughs and shape into 2 disks, 1 slightly larger than the other; wrap and refrigerate 1 hour.

DECORATE WITH FALL-THEMED CUTOUT SHAPES: Change up the pie's top crust and decorate with fall-themed cutout shapes. Instead of cutting strips after rolling out the second portion of dough, use floured 1-in. cookie cutters to make festive shapes. Sprinkle the shapes with granulated sugar for glisten and crunch. Arrange the shapes on top of the pie before baking.

CRANBERRY APPLE SLAB PIE

SLAB PIE DECORATED WITH FALL CUTOUTS

A FEAST
of FISHES

Start your classic Christmas Eve menu with fresh-caught recipes inspired by the Feast of the Seven Fishes.

CRAB AU GRATIN

BOURBON MAPLE SALMON

ROASTED PARMESAN POTATO WEDGES

CRAB AU GRATIN

When the holidays roll around, I love to serve this warm, comforting appetizer. It has a rich taste and is easy to whip up with convenient canned crab.
—*Suzanne Zick, Maiden, NC*

PREP: 20 min. • **BAKE:** 10 min.
MAKES: about 2 cups

- 2 Tbsp. plus 1 tsp. butter, divided
- 3 Tbsp. all-purpose flour
- ½ tsp. salt
- ⅛ tsp. paprika
- ½ cup half-and-half cream
- ½ cup whole milk
- ¼ cup white wine or chicken broth
- 1 can (6 oz.) crabmeat, drained, flaked and cartilage removed or ⅔ cup chopped imitation crabmeat
- 1 can (4 oz.) mushroom stems and pieces, drained and chopped
- 1½ tsp. minced chives
- ½ cup shredded cheddar cheese
- 1 Tbsp. dry bread crumbs
  Assorted crackers and fresh vegetables

1. In a large saucepan, melt 2 Tbsp. butter. Stir in the flour, salt and paprika until smooth. Gradually add the cream, milk and wine. Bring to a boil; cook and stir for 1-2 minutes or until thickened. Stir in the crab, mushrooms and chives; heat through. Stir in cheese just until melted.
2. Transfer to a greased shallow 1-qt. baking dish. Melt remaining butter; toss with bread crumbs. Sprinkle over crab mixture. Bake, uncovered, at 400° for 10-15 minutes or until bubbly. Let stand for 5 minutes. Serve with crackers and vegetables. If desired, sprinkle with additional minced chives.
2 TBSP.: 64 cal., 4g fat (2g sat. fat), 22mg chol., 185mg sod., 2g carb. (1g sugars, 0 fiber), 4g pro.

TEST KITCHEN TIPS

- Some of the best melting cheeses include fontina, Gouda, provolone, mozzarella and Gruyere. Substitute any of these in equal amounts for the cheddar in this recipe.
- Crackers are always a natural choice for crabmeat au gratin, but also try celery sticks, broccoli, pita chips or slices of sourdough or French bread.

ROASTED PARMESAN POTATO WEDGES

ROASTED PARMESAN POTATO WEDGES

These potatoes have an irresistible cheese and herb coating.
—*Linda Rock, Stratford, WI*

PREP: 10 min. • **BAKE:** 45 min.
MAKES: 6 servings

- 4 russet potatoes (about 2 lbs.)
- 2 tsp. canola oil
- ½ cup grated Parmesan cheese
- 1 tsp. dried basil
- 1 tsp. seasoned salt
- ¼ tsp. onion powder
- ¼ tsp. garlic powder
- ¼ tsp. pepper

1. Preheat oven to 350°. Cut each potato lengthwise in half. Cut each half into 3 wedges. In a large bowl, sprinkle potatoes with oil; toss to coat. Combine the remaining ingredients. Add to the potatoes; toss to coat.
2. Arrange potatoes in a single layer on a 15x10x1-in. baking pan coated with cooking spray. Sprinkle with any remaining coating. Bake until golden brown and tender, 45-55 minutes.
4 WEDGES: 179 cal., 4g fat (1g sat. fat), 5mg chol., 387mg sod., 31g carb., 3g fiber), 6g pro. **DIABETIC EXCHANGES:** 2 starch, ½ fat.

BOURBON MAPLE SALMON

This flavorful salmon feels fancy for a holiday but is so simple to make!
—*Diane Higgins, Tampa, FL*

PREP: 10 min. + standing • **COOK:** 10 min.
MAKES: 4 servings

- 4 salmon fillets (6 oz. each)
- ¼ cup packed brown sugar
- ¼ cup maple syrup
- 3 Tbsp. bourbon
- 2 Tbsp. olive oil
- ¼ cup chopped walnuts
- 4 green onions, chopped
- 4 bacon strips, cooked and crumbled

Place salmon in a shallow dish. Combine brown sugar, maple syrup and bourbon; pour over salmon. Let stand 15 minutes. In a large skillet, heat oil over medium heat. Add salmon; cook until fish just begins to flake easily with a fork, 4-6 minutes on each side. Remove and keep warm. Add walnuts, green onions and bacon to skillet; heat through. Serve with salmon.
1 SERVING: 475 cal., 30g fat (6g sat. fat), 94mg chol., 237mg sod., 16g carb. (13g sugars, 1g fiber), 33g pro.

MERRY & BRIGHT BRUNCH

Oh, hooray, it's Christmas Day! Kick off the celebration with a jolly spread of rise-and-shine eats.

PROSCIUTTO, APPLE & CHEESE STRATA

MINI CHERRY MUFFINS

FENNEL ORANGE SALAD

FENNEL ORANGE SALAD

You'll need just a few ingredients to fix this fresh-tasting salad. The combination of crisp fennel and juicy oranges is delightful. To reduce last-minutes prep, make it the day before you plan to serve it.
—*Nina Hall, Spokane, WA*

TAKES: 30 min. • MAKES: 4 servings

- 1   fennel bulb with fronds (about ¾ lb.)
- 4   medium oranges, peeled and sliced
- ⅓ cup orange juice
- 4   tsp. olive oil
- 1   Tbsp. grated orange zest
- ¼ tsp. salt
- ⅛ tsp. pepper
      Pomegranate seeds, optional

1. Finely chop enough fennel fronds to measure ¼ cup; set aside. Cut fennel bulb in half lengthwise; remove and discard the tough outer layer, fennel core and any green stalks. Cut widthwise into thin slices and measure 3 cups; place in a large bowl. Add orange slices.
2. In a jar with a tight-fitting lid, combine the orange juice, oil, orange zest, salt and pepper; shake well. Pour over fennel and oranges; toss gently. Sprinkle with reserved fronds and, if desired, pomegranate seeds.

1 CUP: 143 cal., 5g fat (1g sat. fat), 0 chol., 193mg sod., 25g carb. (0 sugars, 6g fiber), 3g pro. **DIABETIC EXCHANGES:** 1 fruit , 1 vegetable, 1 fat.

MINI CHERRY MUFFINS

These pretty mini muffins are perfect for Christmas morning. Make them the night before and keep them on the counter in an airtight container.
—Taste of Home *Test Kitchen*

TAKES: 30 min. • MAKES: about 2 dozen

- ¾ cup butter, softened
- ¾ cup sugar
- 1   large egg, room temperature
- ½ cup plain yogurt
- ½ tsp. almond extract
- 1   cup all-purpose flour
- ¼ tsp. baking soda
- ¼ tsp. salt
- ½ cup red candied cherries, chopped

1. In a small bowl, cream butter and sugar. Beat in egg, yogurt and extract. Combine the flour, baking soda and salt; stir into creamed mixture just until moistened. Fold in cherries.
2. Fill greased or paper-lined miniature muffin cups two-thirds full. Bake at 350° for 15-17 minutes or until a toothpick comes out clean. Cool for 5 minutes before removing from pans to wire racks.

1 MUFFIN: 111 cal., 6g fat (4g sat. fat), 24mg chol., 92mg sod., 13g carb. (9g sugars, 0 fiber), 1g pro.

PROSCIUTTO, APPLE & CHEESE STRATA

PROSCIUTTO, APPLE & CHEESE STRATA

This is one of my favorite things to make for holidays and special celebrations! It's a wonderful, sweet and savory dish that incorporates elements of the cuisine I grew up enjoying. Plus, you can prepare it the night before and just throw it in the oven in the morning.
—*Danielle Pfanstiehl, Andover, CT*

PREP: 20 min. + chilling • BAKE: 50 min. + standing
MAKES: 6 servings

- 6   large eggs
- 1¼ cups 2% milk
- ½ tsp. ground cinnamon
- ¼ tsp. salt
- ¼ tsp. pepper
- 7   cups day-old cubed bread (1-in. cubes)
- ½ lb. sliced prosciutto, cut into 2-in. strips
- 2   medium Pink Lady apples, peeled and thinly sliced
- 1   pkg. (10 oz.) frozen chopped spinach, thawed and squeezed dry
- 1   cup chopped Brie cheese
- 1   cup shredded white cheddar cheese, divided

1. In a large bowl, whisk eggs, milk, cinnamon, salt and pepper until blended. Stir in bread, prosciutto, apples, spinach, Brie and ½ cup cheddar cheese. Transfer to a greased 13x9-in. baking dish; sprinkle with remaining ½ cup cheddar cheese. Refrigerate, covered, overnight.
2. Preheat oven to 350°. Remove strata from refrigerator while oven heats. Bake, covered, 30 minutes. Uncover and bake until a knife inserted near the center comes out clean, 20-25 minutes longer. Let stand 10 minutes before serving.

1 SERVING: 478 cal., 25g fat (12g sat. fat), 266mg chol., 1430mg sod., 31g carb. (10g sugars, 3g fiber), 33g pro.

Special
SOUTHERN
DINNER

Y'all come and sit a spell for this down-home holiday menu made the southern way.

CANDIED SWEET POTATOES

CORNBREAD DRESSING

**APPLE-GLAZED
HOLIDAY HAM**

APPLE-GLAZED HOLIDAY HAM

Each Christmas I'm asked to prepare this entree. I'm happy to oblige because it is easy to assemble, bakes for a few hours unattended and is simply delicious.
—Emory Doty, Jasper, GA

- -

PREP: 10 min. • **BAKE:** 2½ hours • **MAKES:** 15 servings

- 1　spiral-sliced fully cooked bone-in ham (7 to 9 lbs.)
- ½　cup packed brown sugar
- ½　cup unsweetened applesauce
- ½　cup unsweetened apple juice
- ¼　cup maple syrup
- ¼　cup molasses
- 1　Tbsp. Dijon mustard
　　Dash ground ginger
　　Dash ground cinnamon

1. Place ham on a rack in a shallow roasting pan. Bake, uncovered, at 325° for 2 hours.
2. In a small saucepan, combine remaining ingredients. Cook and stir over medium heat until heated through. Brush ham with some glaze; bake 30-60 minutes longer or until a thermometer reads 140°, brushing occasionally with remaining glaze.
4 OZ. HAM: 242 cal., 6g fat (2g sat. fat), 93mg chol., 1138mg sod., 17g carb. (15g sugars, 0 fiber), 31g pro.

TEST KITCHEN TIP

A fully cooked ham can be stored for up to 1 week in the refrigerator. To further extend its shelf life, freeze ham in covered airtight containers or heavy-duty freezer bags.

APPLE-GLAZED HOLIDAY HAM

CANDIED SWEET POTATOES

5i

CANDIED SWEET POTATOES

My town is known as the yam capital of the United States. This is a simple recipe that goes well with baked ham or roasted turkey.
—Essie Nealey, Tabor City, NC

- -

PREP: 40 min. + cooling • **BAKE:** 15 min. • **MAKES:** 10 servings

- 3　lbs. sweet potatoes
- ½　cup packed brown sugar
- 1　tsp. ground cinnamon
- ¼　cup butter, cubed
- ¼　cup corn syrup
　　Optional: Chopped walnuts and minced fresh thyme

1. Place sweet potatoes in a Dutch oven and cover with water. Cover and bring to a boil; boil gently 30-45 minutes or until potatoes can be easily pierced with the tip of a sharp knife.
2. While potatoes cool, preheat oven to 375°. When cool enough to handle, peel the potatoes and cut into wedges. Place in an ungreased 11x7-in. baking dish. Sprinkle with brown sugar and cinnamon. Dot with butter; drizzle with corn syrup.
3. Bake, uncovered, 15-20 minutes or until bubbly, basting with sauce occasionally.
1 SERVING: 248 cal., 5g fat (3g sat. fat), 12mg chol., 59mg sod., 51g carb. (31g sugars, 4g fiber), 2g pro.

CORNBREAD DRESSING

There's nothing quite like cornbread dressing at Thanksgiving.
—*Drew Weeks, Edisto Island, SC*

PREP: 20 min. + cooling • **BAKE:** 45 minutes
MAKES: 13 servings

- 1 cup all-purpose flour
- 1 cup cornmeal
- 2 Tbsp. sugar
- 1 Tbsp. baking powder
- ½ tsp. salt
- 1 large egg, room temperature, lightly beaten
- ⅔ cup water
- ⅓ cup fat-free milk
- 2 Tbsp. canola oil

DRESSING

- 10 slices bread, toasted and cubed
- 3 cups chopped celery
- 1⅓ cups chopped onion
- 1 tsp. canola oil
- 3 tsp. reduced-sodium chicken bouillon granules or 1½ vegetable bouillon cubes
- ¼ cup boiling water
- 1 can (14½ oz.) reduced-sodium chicken broth or vegetable broth
- 2 large eggs, lightly beaten
- 2 tsp. dried parsley flakes
- 1½ tsp. rubbed sage
- 1 tsp. each poultry seasoning, dried basil and rosemary, crushed
- ½ tsp. each salt and dried thyme

1. Preheat oven to 375°. For cornbread, in a bowl, combine flour, cornmeal, sugar, baking powder and salt. In a small bowl, whisk egg, water, milk and oil. Stir into flour mixture just until blended. Transfer to a greased 8-in. square baking pan. Bake until a toothpick inserted in the center comes out clean, 15-20 minutes. Cool in pan on a wire rack. Crumble into a large bowl. Reduce oven temperature to 350°.

2. For stuffing, stir the bread cubes into cornbread crumbs. In a nonstick skillet, cook chopped celery and onion in oil until tender, about 6 minutes. Stir into cornbread mixture.

3. In a small bowl, dissolve bouillon in water. In a large bowl, combine the broth, eggs, seasonings and bouillon mixture. Pour over cornbread mixture; toss to coat evenly.

4. Transfer to a greased 13x9-in. baking dish. Cover and bake for 20 minutes. Uncover; continue baking until lightly browned, 25-30 minutes longer.

¾ CUP: 197 cal., 4g fat (1g sat. fat), 14mg chol., 592mg sod., 33g carb. (5g sugars, 2g fiber), 6g pro.
DIABETIC EXCHANGES: 2 starch.

PRALINE PEACH COBBLER

Cobbler is a delicious dessert for picnics and potluck dinners. It can be served cold or warm and is especially good topped with a generous scoop of vanilla ice cream.
—*Maithel Martin, Kansas City, MO*

PREP: 30 min. • **BAKE:** 25 min.
MAKES: 12 servings

- 1½ cups plus 2 tsp. sugar, divided
- 2 Tbsp. cornstarch
- 1 tsp. ground cinnamon
- 1 cup water
- 8 cups sliced peeled peaches
- 2 cups self-rising flour
- ½ cup shortening
- ½ cup buttermilk
- 3 Tbsp. butter, melted
- ¼ cup packed brown sugar
- 1 cup chopped pecans

1. In a large saucepan, mix 1½ cups sugar, cornstarch and cinnamon. Stir in water until smooth. Add peaches. Bring to a boil over medium heat; cook and stir for 2 minutes or until thickened. Pour into a lightly greased 13x9-in. baking dish; set aside.

2. In a bowl, combine flour and remaining sugar; cut in shortening until mixture resembles coarse crumbs. Add buttermilk and stir just until moistened. If needed, add additional buttermilk, 1 Tbsp. at a time, until dough clings together. Turn onto a floured surface; knead gently 6-8 times. Roll into a 12x8-in. rectangle.

3. Combine butter, brown sugar and pecans; spread over the dough to within ½ in. of edges. Starting with long side, roll up jelly-roll style. Cut into twelve 1-in. pieces. Place on top of the peach mixture. Bake, uncovered, at 400° for 25-30 minutes or until golden brown.

NOTE: If self-rising flour is not available, substitute 2 cups all-purpose flour, 1 Tbsp. baking powder and 1 tsp. salt.

1 PIECE: 409 cal., 18g fat (4g sat. fat), 8mg chol., 282mg sod., 61g carb. (40g sugars, 4g fiber), 4g pro

CORNBREAD DRESSING

All Aboard!

DIY hot cocoa choc-cuterie includes all the fixin's necessary for a sweet, seasonal sipping party.

HOMEMADE MARSHMALLOWS

Chocolate-Covered Oreos

Microwave **1 pkg. white baking chips** and **1 Tbsp. shortening** until melted. Dip 1 side of **Oreos** in melted mixture; drizzle with remaining mixture. Sprinkle with **rose gold nonpareils**. Freeze until set.

CHOCOLATE-DIPPED BEVERAGE SPOONS

HOT CHOCOLATE BOMBS

Hot Cocoa Fillers

Your sweet board doesn't have to be loaded with all homemade goodies. There are plenty of store-bought items to incorporate!

Buttermints

Candy-coated pretzels

Caramel candies & caramel bits

Chocolate & white baking chips

Chocolate Kisses

Liqueurs

Peppermint sticks & stirrers

Pirouette cookies & biscotti

Whipped cream

HOLIDAY HOT CHOCOLATE MIX

HOLIDAY HOT CHOCOLATE MIX

HOMEMADE MARSHMALLOWS

(SHOWN ON PAGE 266)

Homemade marshmallows are fun to eat on a stick or to stir into your favorite hot chocolate. Their melt-in-your-mouth texture appeals to the young and the young at heart.

—*Jennifer Andrzejewski, Carmel Valley, CA*

PREP: 55 min. + standing
MAKES: 15 marshmallows

- ½ cup cold water
- 3 envelopes unflavored gelatin
- 2 cups sugar
- 1 cup light corn syrup
- ½ cup water
- ¼ tsp. salt
- 1 tsp. almond extract
- ½ cup confectioners' sugar, divided
   Lollipop sticks

1. In a large bowl, combine cold water and gelatin; set aside.

2. Meanwhile, in a large heavy saucepan over medium heat, combine the sugar, corn syrup, water and salt. Bring to a boil, stirring occasionally. Cover and cook for 2 minutes to dissolve sugar crystals; uncover and cook on medium-high heat, without stirring, until a candy thermometer reads 240° (soft-ball stage).

3. Remove from the heat and gradually add to gelatin. Beat on medium speed for 14 minutes. Add extract; beat 1 minute longer. Meanwhile, sprinkle 2 Tbsp. confectioners' sugar into a greased 13x9-in. pan.

4. With greased hands, spread the marshmallow mixture into prepared pan. Top with 2 Tbsp. confectioners' sugar. Cover and cool at room temperature for 6 hours or overnight.

5. Cut 15 snowflakes with a greased 2½-in. snowflake-shaped cookie cutter; toss in remaining confectioners' sugar. If desired, gently press lollipop stick into each snowflake. Store in an airtight container in a cool, dry place.

1 MARSHMALLOW: 82 cal., 0 fat (0 sat. fat), 0 chol., 24mg sod., 21g carb. (16g sugars, 0 fiber), 1g pro.

HOLIDAY HOT CHOCOLATE MIX

This is the recipe I make for holiday gifts. I put it in decorative jars and tie pretty ribbons around the jars for a festive gift.

—*Debbie Klejeski, Sturgeon Lake, MN*

TAKES: 10 min. • **MAKES:** 3 qt. mix

- 1 pkg. (25.6 oz.) nonfat dry milk powder, about 10 cups
- 1 jar (6 oz.) nondairy coffee creamer, about 1¾ cups
- 3¾ cups instant chocolate drink mix (Nesquik)
- ½ cup confectioners' sugar

Place all ingredients in a very large bowl or kettle. Stir until well blended. Store in an airtight container or pack into small gift containers. To serve, add ¼ cup chocolate mix to ⅔ cup hot water.

¼ CUP MIX: 316 cal., 2g fat (1g sat. fat), 8mg chol., 305mg sod., 57g carb. (53g sugars, 2g fiber), 17g pro.

TEST KITCHEN TIP

Tuck a jar of the hot chocolate mix into a basket with homemade marshmallows, candy-cane stirrers, hazelnut liqueur, chocolate-dipped spoons, or even a cute pair of cozy socks.

CHOCOLATE-DIPPED BEVERAGE SPOONS

(PICTURED ON PAGE 266)

These make cute gifts during the holidays. To set the chocolate quickly, simply chill the dipped spoons in the freezer.

—*Marcy Boswell, Menifee, CA*

PREP: 45 min. + chilling • **MAKES:** 2 dozen

- 1 cup milk chocolate chips
- 3½ tsp. shortening, divided
- 1 cup white baking chips
- 24 metal, wooden or plastic spoons
   Optional: Coarse sugar or chocolate sprinkles

In a microwave-safe bowl, melt milk chocolate chips with 2 tsp. shortening; stir until smooth. Repeat with white baking chips and remaining shortening. Dip spoons into either mixture, tapping handles on bowl edges to remove excess. Place on a waxed paper-lined baking sheet. Pipe or drizzle milk chocolate over white-dipped spoons and white mixture over milk chocolate-dipped spoons. Use a toothpick or skewer to swirl chocolate. If desired, decorate with coarse sugar or sprinkles. Chill for 5 minutes or until set. Use as stirring spoons for coffee or cocoa.

1 SPOON: 81 cal., 5g fat (3g sat. fat), 3mg chol., 12mg sod., 8g carb. (8g sugars, 0 fiber), 1g pro.

51

HOT CHOCOLATE BOMBS

These hot chocolate-filled spheres are all the rage! Make them ahead of time as a holiday gift or to have on hand when you have a hot chocolate craving.
—*Rashanda Cobbins, Milwaukee, WI*

- -

PREP: 45 min. + chilling + decorating
MAKES: 6 chocolate bombs

- 22 oz. semisweet chocolate, such as Baker's Chocolate, finely chopped
- ½ cup baking cocoa
- ½ cup nonfat dry milk powder
- ¼ cup confectioners' sugar
- 6 Tbsp. vanilla marshmallow bits (not miniature marshmallows)
  Optional: Sprinkles, colored sanding sugar and melted candy melts

1. Place chocolate in a microwave-safe bowl. Microwave, uncovered, on high for 1 minute; stir. Microwave, stirring every 30 seconds, until chocolate is melted and smooth, 1-2 minutes longer. Chocolate should not exceed 90°.
2. Add 1 Tbsp. melted chocolate into a silicone sphere-shaped mold (2½-in. diameter). Brush the melted chocolate evenly inside molds, all the way to edges, rewarming melted chocolate as needed. Refrigerate molds until chocolate is set,

3-5 minutes. Brush a thin second layer of chocolate in molds. Refrigerate until set, 8-10 minutes. Place remaining melted chocolate into a piping bag fitted with a small round decorating tip; set aside.
3. Remove the chocolate hemispheres from molds. In a medium bowl, whisk together baking cocoa, milk powder and confectioners' sugar. Place 3 Tbsp. cocoa mixture into each of 6 of the chocolate hemispheres. Top each with 1 Tbsp. marshmallow bits.
4. Pipe a small amount of melted chocolate on edges of the 6 filled hemispheres; carefully adhere empty halves to filled halves, pressing lightly to seal, using additional melted chocolate if necessary. If desired, decorate with optional ingredients. Refrigerate until set. Store in a tightly sealed container.
TO PREPARE HOT CHOCOLATE: Place hot chocolate bomb in a mug; add 1 cup warm milk and stir to dissolve.

1 CHOCOLATE BOMB: 619 cal., 34g fat (20g sat. fat), 1mg chol., 31mg sod., 36g carb. (29g sugars, 4g fiber), 10g pro.
SALTED CARAMEL HOT CHOCOLATE BOMBS: Fill spheres with hot cocoa mix, 1 Tbsp. caramel chips and a pinch of flake sea salt. Drizzle outside with melted dark chocolate and melted caramel chips and sprinkle with flake sea salt.

PEPPERMINT HOT CHOCOLATE BOMBS: Fill spheres with hot cocoa mix, 1 Tbsp. white baking chips and 1 Tbsp. finely crushed peppermint candies. Drizzle outside with melted white chocolate tinted pink and red and top with additional crushed peppermint candies.

HOW-TO

Make Hot Chocolate Bombs

Using a food-safe paintbrush, coat molds evenly with the melted chocolate; chill.

Fill half of the chocolate hemispheres with the hot cocoa mixture.

On the filled hemispheres, pipe a small amount of melted chocolate on edges.

Carefully adhere the empty halves on top, pressing lightly to seal. Use more melted chocolate if needed.

HOT CHOCOLATE BOMBS

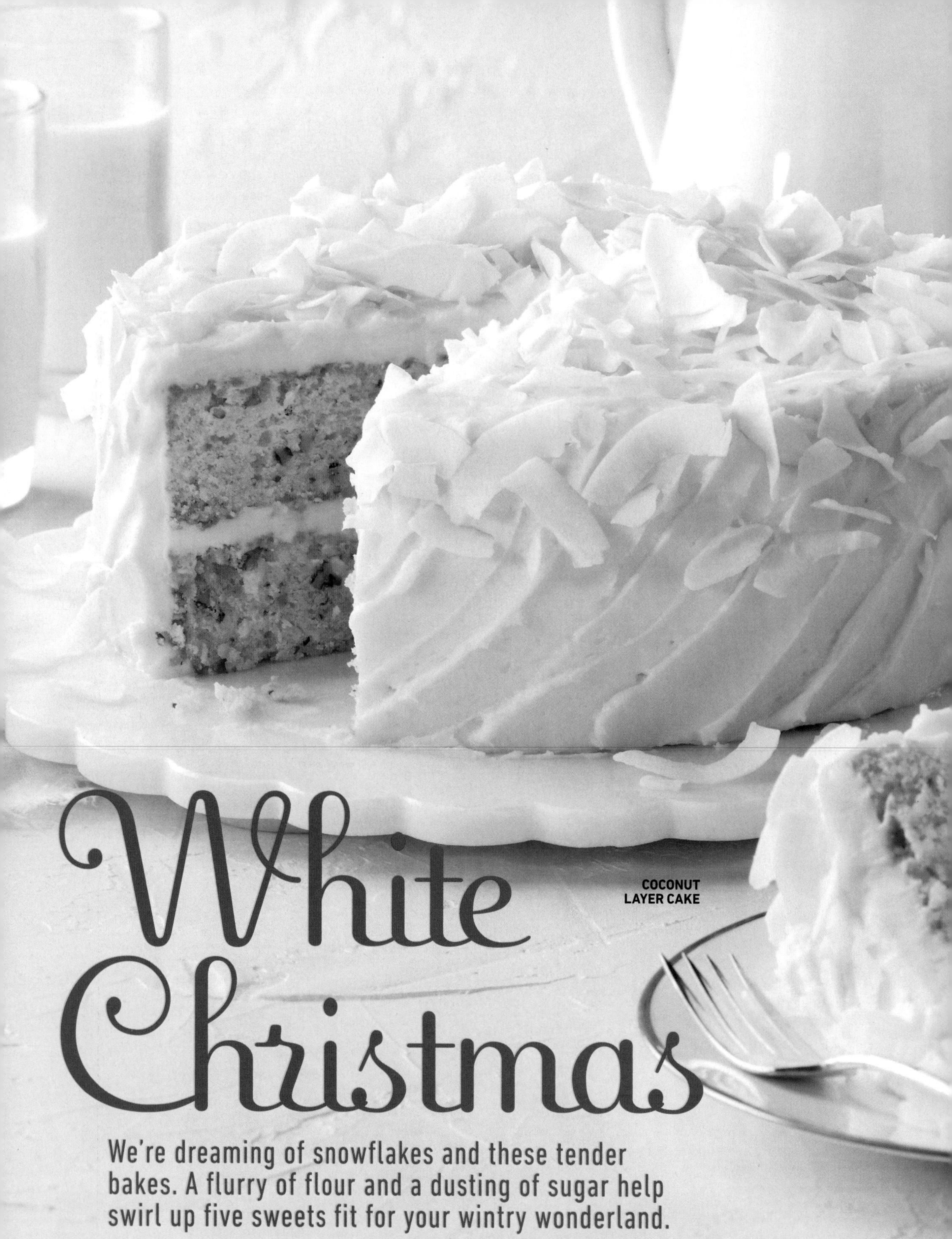

COCONUT
LAYER CAKE

White Christmas

We're dreaming of snowflakes and these tender bakes. A flurry of flour and a dusting of sugar help swirl up five sweets fit for your wintry wonderland.

COCONUT LAYER CAKE

You can make this delectable coconut cake without the pecans if you prefer.
—*Marilyn Dick, Centralia, MO*

PREP: 30 min. • **BAKE:** 40 min. + cooling
MAKES: 16 servings

- 5 large eggs, separated
- ½ cup butter, softened
- ½ cup shortening
- 2 cups sugar
- 1 tsp. vanilla extract
- 2 cups all-purpose flour
- ½ tsp. baking soda
- 1 cup buttermilk
- 2 cups sweetened shredded coconut
- ½ cup chopped pecans

FROSTING
- 1 pkg. (8 oz.) cream cheese, softened
- ¼ cup butter, softened
- 4 cups confectioners' sugar
- 1 tsp. vanilla extract
- ¼ cup sweetened shredded coconut, toasted
  Pecan halves, optional

1. Place egg whites in a large bowl; let stand at room temperature 30 minutes. Preheat oven to 325°. Meanwhile, line bottoms of 2 greased 9-in. round baking pans with parchment; grease paper.
2. Cream butter, shortening, sugar and vanilla until light and fluffy, 5-7 minutes. Add egg yolks, 1 at a time, beating well after each addition. In another bowl, whisk together the flour and baking soda; beat into creamed mixture alternately with buttermilk. Stir in shredded coconut and chopped pecans.
3. With clean beaters, beat egg whites on medium speed until stiff peaks form; fold gently into batter. Transfer batter to prepared pans.
4. Bake until a toothpick inserted in center comes out clean, 40-45 minutes. Cool cakes for 10 minutes before removing from pans to wire racks; remove paper. Cool completely.
5. For frosting, beat cream cheese, butter, confectioners' sugar and vanilla until smooth and creamy. Spread between layers and over top and sides of cake. Top with coconut and pecan halves if desired. Store in refrigerator.
1 PIECE: 571 cal., 28g fat (15g sat. fat), 96mg chol., 239mg sod., 75g carb. (62g sugars, 1g fiber), 6g pro.

HAWAIIAN WEDDING CAKE COOKIES

HAWAIIAN WEDDING CAKE COOKIES

Macadamia nuts and pineapple help give these sweet treats their tropical name.
—*Darlene Brenden, Salem, OR*

PREP: 20 min. • **COOK:** 15 min. + cooling
MAKES: 1½ dozen

- ½ cup butter, softened
- ¼ cup confectioners' sugar
- ½ tsp. vanilla extract
- 1 cup all-purpose flour
- ½ cup finely chopped macadamia nuts, toasted
- 2 Tbsp. finely chopped candied pineapple
  Additional confectioners' sugar

1. In a small bowl, cream the butter, confectioners' sugar and vanilla until light and fluffy, 5-7 minutes. Gradually add flour and mix well. Stir in the nuts and pineapple. Shape into 1-in. balls. Place 2 in. apart on ungreased baking sheets.
2. Bake at 350° for 14-16 minutes or until lightly browned. Remove to wire racks to cool completely. Roll cooled cookies in additional confectioners' sugar.
1 COOKIE: 108 cal., 8g fat (4g sat. fat), 14mg chol., 57mg sod., 8g carb. (2g sugars, 1g fiber), 1g pro.

READER REVIEW

"My mother-in-law always made these at Christmas, so it was time to bring them back! They are light and so tasty!"

—RENA55, TASTEOFHOME.COM

PEPPERMINT BARK TRIFLE

PEPPERMINT BARK TRIFLE

We're always looking for showstopping desserts, especially during the holidays. This one is impressive, but it couldn't be easier. No one will ever notice it's made with a store-bought cake.
—*James Schend, Pleasant Prairie, WI*

PREP: 20 min. + chilling
MAKES: 12 servings

- 2 pkg. (8 oz. each) cream cheese, softened
- ½ cup sugar
- 3 Tbsp. 2% milk
- 1 tsp. peppermint extract
- 3 cups heavy whipping cream, whipped
- 1 prepared angel food cake (8 to 10 oz.), cut into 1-in. cubes
- 3 Tbsp. crushed peppermint candies
- 1½ lbs. Swirled Peppermint Bark (recipe on p. 275)

1. In a bowl, beat cream cheese, sugar, milk and extract until smooth. Fold in whipped cream; set aside.
2. Place a third of the cake in a 3- or 4-qt. trifle dish or serving bowl. Top with a third of each of the cream cheese mixture, crushed peppermint and peppermint bark. Repeat layers twice; garnish with additional bark. Cover and refrigerate at least 4 hours.
1 CUP: 426 cal., 35g fat (22g sat. fat), 106mg chol., 279mg sod., 25g carb. (13g sugars, 0 fiber), 5g pro.

⑤ⅰ
SWISS MERINGUE SHELLS
Folks will think you fussed when you bring out these sweet, cloud-like cups topped with fresh berries.
—*Linda Braun, Park Ridge, IL*

PREP: 15 min. + standing
BAKE: 1 hour + cooling
MAKES: 8 servings

- 3 large egg whites
- ½ tsp. vanilla extract
- ¼ tsp. cream of tartar
- ¾ cup sugar
    Whipped cream, optional
    Berries of your choice
    Confectioners' sugar, optional

1. Place egg whites in a small bowl; let stand at room temperature for 30 minutes. Add vanilla and cream of tartar; beat on medium speed until soft peaks form. Gradually beat in sugar, 1 Tbsp. at a time, on high until stiff glossy peaks form and sugar is dissolved.
2. Drop 8 mounds onto parchment-lined baking sheet. Shape into 3-in. cups with the back of a spoon. Bake at 225° until set and dry, 1 to 1½ hours. Turn oven off; leave meringues in oven for 1 hour.

3. Cool on wire racks. Store in an airtight container. If desired, fill shells with whipped cream. Top with berries. Top with confectioners' sugar as desired.
1 SERVING: 80 cal., 0 fat (0 sat. fat), 0 chol., 21mg sod., 19g carb. (18g sugars, 0 fiber), 1g pro.
STRAWBERRY MERINGUE CUPS: In a chilled large bowl, beat 2 cups heavy whipping cream until it begins to thicken. Add ¾ cup confectioners' sugar; beat until stiff peaks form. Just before serving, spoon into meringue shells. Top with 1 pint sliced fresh strawberries.
MOCHA MERINGUE CUPS: In a heavy saucepan, melt 2 cups milk chocolate chips with 1 cup heavy whipping cream and 1 tsp. instant coffee granules; stir until smooth. Remove from the heat; stir in 1 tsp. vanilla. Transfer to a small mixing bowl; refrigerate until chilled. Beat on high speed until stiff peaks form. Pipe or spoon into meringue cups.

TEST KITCHEN TIP

The meringue mixture should be glossy, slightly thickened and stable enough to create stiff peaks when you lift the beaters from the mixture.

SWISS MERINGUE SHELLS

PEPPERMINT SUGAR COOKIES

PEPPERMINT SUGAR COOKIES

These peppermint sugar cookies take my taste buds right to winter. The crisp, distinct taste of peppermint reminds me of peppermint bark that I hurry straight to the store and buy, each and every holiday season. I am adding the cornstarch because it helps keep the cookies stable and tender which, really gives them a melt in your mouth bite. Don't overbake these—let's keep them soft.
—*Emily Hutchinson, Arlington, WA*

PREP: 30 min. + chilling • **BAKE:** 10 min./batch + cooling
MAKES: 2 dozen

- 1   cup unsalted butter, softened
- ½   tsp. salt
- 1   cup sugar
- ½   cup confectioners' sugar
- 1   large egg, room temperature
- 1   tsp. vanilla extract
- ½   tsp. peppermint extract
- 2¾ cups all-purpose flour
- ½   tsp. baking powder
- ¼   cup cornstarch

1. In the bowl of a stand mixer, beat the butter and salt for 30 seconds. Add sugars; beat 1 minute. Add egg and extracts and mix to combine.
2. Combine dry ingredients; add to butter mixture. Mix just until dough forms. Cover and chill at least 15 minutes.
3. Preheat oven to 375°. On a lightly floured surface, roll out dough to ¼-in. thickness. Cut with a floured 3-in. cookie cutter. Place 2 in. apart on parchment-lined baking sheets. Bake until cookies puff up and are a dull matte on top but not browned, 6-8 minutes. Let stand 1 minute before removing to wire racks to cool completely.
1 COOKIE: 171 cal., 8g fat (5g sat. fat), 28mg chol., 64mg sod., 23g carb. (11g sugars, 0 fiber), 2g pro.

WHITE CHOCOLATE TRUFFLES

This is the perfect holiday gift candy. It is so easy to make and will look so pretty in a gift box.
—*Gloria Nolan, Peoria, PA*

PREP: 20 min. + chilling • **MAKES:** 5 dozen

- 8   Tbsp. butter, cubed
- 2   Tbsp. heavy whipping cream
- 18   oz. white candy coating, coarsely chopped
- ¼   cup confectioners' sugar
       Coarse or confectioners' sugar

1. In top of a double boiler or a metal bowl over barely simmering water, melt butter into cream; remove from heat. Gradually add candy coating, stirring continuously with rubber spatula until candy coating begins to melt. Return to heat; stir constantly until mixture is smooth. Stir in confectioners' sugar. (If the mixture separates, beat with a mixer for 30 seconds.) Pour into an 8-in. square pan. Chill for 20 minutes or until slightly hardened.
2. Using a melon baller or spoon, scoop out and shape into 1-in. balls. Roll in coarse sugar. Store truffles in an airtight container in the refrigerator.
NOTE: White confectionery coating is found in the baking section of most grocery stores. It is sometime labeled almond bark or candy coating and is often sold in bulk packages of 1-1½ pounds.
1 TRUFFLE: 62 cal., 4g fat (3g sat. fat), 5mg chol., 12mg sod., 7g carb. (6g sugars, 0 fiber), 0 pro.

WHITE CHOCOLATE TRUFFLES

All Bark

Stumped by stocking stuffers, hostess gifts and cookie platters? Make your mark with whimsical chocolate bark festive enough to be straight from St. Nick.

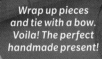

Wrap up pieces and tie with a bow. Voila! The perfect handmade present!

START BY LINING A 15x10x1-IN. PAN WITH PARCHMENT; SET ASIDE. IN A DOUBLE BOILER OR METAL BOWL OVER HOT WATER, MELT 10-12 OZ. CHOPPED CHOCOLATE UNTIL TWO-THIRDS MELTED. REMOVE FROM HEAT; STIR UNTIL SMOOTH.

1. Buddy Bark
Stir 6 Tbsp. crushed uncooked ramen noodles, ¼ cup mini marshmallows, 3 Tbsp. M&M's and 1 Tbsp. sprinkles into melted milk chocolate. Spread into pan; top with additional mix-ins.

2. Malted Milk Bark
Stir ¼ cup malted milk powder into melted dark chocolate. Fold in ¾ cup chopped malted milk balls. Spread into pan; top with additional chopped malted milk balls.

3. Cookies & Cream Bark
Stir ¾ cup crushed Oreo cookies into melted white chocolate. Spread into pan; top with crushed Oreos.

4. Strawberry Pretzel Bark
Stir 1 cup crumbled pretzels into melted ruby chocolate. Spread into pan; top with one 1.2-oz. pkg. freeze-dried strawberries and additional crumbled pretzels.

5. Swirled Peppermint Chocolate Bark
Stir ½ tsp. peppermint oil into melted white chocolate. Spread into pan. Melt ¼ cup dark chocolate in another bowl. Drizzle over white layer; cut through with a knife to swirl. Sprinkle with 2 Tbsp. crushed peppermint candies.

6. Tropical Bark
Stir ¼ cup each chopped macadamia nuts, shredded coconut and candied ginger into melted white chocolate. Spread into pan; top with additional nuts, coconut and ginger.

7. Peanut Powerhouse Bark
Stir ¼ cup each Reese's Pieces, mini peanut butter cups and salted peanuts into melted dark chocolate. Spread into pan; top with additional mix-ins.

8. Chocolate Bacon Bark
Stir 9 cooked and crumbled bacon strips into melted dark chocolate. Spread into pan; top with additional chopped bacon.

9. Spicy Mole Bark
Stir ⅓ cup crumbled tortilla chips, ¼ cup golden raisins, 2 Tbsp. salted pumpkin seeds, 1 Tbsp. sesame seeds, 1 tsp. each cinnamon and ground ancho chile, and ⅛ tsp. pepper flakes into melted milk chocolate. Spread into pan; top with additional tortilla chips, raisins, and pumpkin and sesame seeds.

10. Matcha Crunch Bark
Stir 2 Tbsp. matcha powder and ¼ tsp. culinary lemon oil into melted white chocolate; fold in 1 cup crumbled rice crackers. Spread into pan.

AFTER SPREADING MIXTURE INTO PAN AND TOPPING, REFRIGERATE UNTIL FIRM, 15-20 MINUTES. BREAK OR CUT INTO PIECES. STORE IN AN AIRTIGHT CONTAINER.

General Index

✓ Indicates an Eat Smart recipe

Pina Colada Fruit Dip, 218
Pumpkin Pie Marshmallows, 181
S'mores Crispy Bars, 228

MATCHA
✓Matcha Chia Pudding, 209
Matcha Crunch Bark, 275
Raspberry Matcha Cake Roll, 198

MEAT LOAVES & MEATBALLS
Mexican Meat Loaf, 76
Pressure-Cooker Cherry Bourbon
    Ham Balls, 13
Shortcut Meatball & Tortellini
Minestrone Soup, 46
Southern-Style Meat Loaf, 89

MUSHROOMS
✓30-Minute Coq au Vin, 56
Asparagus Galette with Goat Cheese, 15
✓Basil Vegetable Strata, 221
Crab au Gratin, 259
Easy Ground Beef Stroganoff, 58
Hamburger Steaks with Mushroom
    Gravy, 54
✓Mushroom & Brown Rice Hash
    with Poached Eggs, 67
Parmesan Pork Tenderloin, 76
Pressure-Cooker Thai Sweet Chili
Pork Bowls, 85

NECTARINES
✓Berry Nectarine Salad, 30
Grilled Nectarines with Burrata &
    Honey, 29
✓Nectarine Smoothies, 162

NOODLES
Buddy Bark, 275
DIY Ramen Soup, 105
Easy Ground Beef Stroganoff, 58
✓Light-But-Hearty Tuna Casserole, 93
Slow-Cooked Thai Drunken
    Noodles, 109

NUTELLA
Easy Nutella Cheesecake, 209
Halva & Nutella Babka Buns, 152

NUTS (also see Peanuts & Peanut Butter)
Air-Fryer Pecan Chicken Sliders, 38
Bacon-Almond Green Beans, 126
Banana-Nut Bundt Cake, 195
Banana Nut Pancakes, 102
Best Ever Veggie Burger, 50
Caramel Pecan Rolls, 225
Cashew Baklava, 179
Cheesy Baked Asparagus, 235

Dad's Creamed Peas & Pearl Onions, 125
Gorgonzola Pear Salad, 25
Guava Jam Baked Brie en Croute
    with Pistachios, 10
Hawaiian Wedding Cake Cookies, 271
Italian Cream Cheese Cake, 187
Lemony Chicken Salad, 34
One-Pot Creamy Tomato Pasta, 72
Parsnip, Pear & Pecan Salad, 28
Peanut-Cashew Marshmallow Pie, 192
Pecan Tarts, 240
Praline Peach Cobbler, 265
Slow-Cooker Mixed Fruit &
    Pistachio Cake, 193
Spiced Carrots with Pistachios, 256
Sweet & Savory Pineapple
    Cheese Ball, 11
✓Toasted Pecan Vinaigrette, 30
Tropical Bark, 275

OATS
Banana Oat Muffins, 149
Banana Oatmeal Cookies, 183
Best Ever Veggie Burger, 50
Blueberry Oatmeal Pancakes, 101
Caramelized Banana Steel-Cut Oats, 160
Golden Oat Pancakes, 97
Grandma's Oatmeal Date Bars, 178
✓Savory Tomato & Olive Oatmeal, 162
Slow-Cooker Peach Crumble, 208

OLIVES
Antipasto Skewers, 218
Chopped Greek Salad in a Jar, 107
Fiesta Ravioli, 113
Pizza Sliders, 226
✓Savory Tomato & Olive Oatmeal, 162
Smoked Salmon Dip, 9

ONIONS
✓Bibb Lettuce with Roasted
    Red Onions, 237
Creamy Celery Root & Pearl Onions, 137
Cucumber Onion Dip, 9
Dad's Creamed Peas & Pearl Onions, 125
Parmesan Pork Tenderloin, 76
Scallion & Cheddar Cathead
    Biscuits, 148
Smoked Salmon Dip, 9
So-Easy Sticky Chicken Wings, 8
Sweet Zucchini Relish, 140
✓Tomato Bounty Salsa, 113

ORANGES & ORANGE JUICE
Banana Orange Bars, 179
Banh Mi Baby Back Ribs, 87
✓Fennel Orange Salad, 261
Ginger Orange Squash, 126

PARSNIPS
Parsnip Latkes with Lox &
    Horseradish Creme, 21
Parsnip, Pear & Pecan Salad, 28

PASTA (also see Noodles)
Bacon Alfredo Pasta in a Jar, 106
Baked Feta Pasta, 90
Basil Cheese Butterfly Pasta, 138
Caprese Pasta Salad, 35
Copycat Pasta Da Vinci, 84
Creamy Beef Lasagna, 90
Fiesta Ravioli, 113
✓Italian Sausage Veggie Skillet, 66
Lemon Parmesan Orzo, 141
One-Pot Black Bean Enchilada Pasta, 65
One-Pot Creamy Tomato Pasta, 72
✓One-Pot Sausage & Basil Pasta, 54
Pork & Cheesy Macaroni Sliders, 20
Quick & Easy Skillet Lasagna, 65
Shortcut Meatball & Tortellini
    Minestrone Soup, 46
Spinach & Squash Pierogi Casserole, 81
✓Summer Orzo, 243

PEACHES
A Creole's Peach Jam, 137
✓Grilled Peach Couscous Salad, 34
Peach Caprese Salad, 29
✓Perfect Plum & Peach Pie, 190
Praline Peach Cobbler, 265
Slow-Cooker Peach Crumble, 208
Southern Bruleed Peach Tarts, 186
Strawberry & Peach Lime
    Custard Bars, 176

PEANUTS & PEANUT BUTTER
Buckeye Doughnut Holes, 154
Easy Peanut Butter Fudge, 181
Honey Peanut Apple Dip, 9
Layered Peanut Butter Brownies, 175
Peanut Butter Fruit Dip, 9
Peanut-Cashew Marshmallow Pie, 192
Peanut Powerhouse Bark, 275
✓Peanut Turkey Satay, 57

PEARS
Apple & Pear Pockets, 203
Gorgonzola Pear Salad, 25
Parsnip, Pear & Pecan Salad, 28
Redmond Pear Creme Tart, 195
Ricotta Pear Dessert, 211

PEAS
Dad's Creamed Peas & Pearl Onions, 125
Ham & Swiss Salad in a Jar, 107

Alphabetical Index

✓ Indicates an Eat Smart recipe